D1503749

MICROSOFT® OFFICE 2007

QuickSteps

CAROLE MATTHEWS
MARTY MATTHEWS

New York Chicago San Francisco
Lisbon London Madrid Mexico City
Milan New Delhi San Juan
Seoul Singapore Sydney Toronto

The McGraw·Hill Companies

Cataloging-in-Publication Data is on file with the Library of Congress

McGraw-Hill books are available at special quantity discounts to use as premiums and sales promotions, or for use in corporate training programs. To contact a special sales representative, please visit the Contact Us page at www.mhprofessional.com.

Information has been obtained by McGraw-Hill from sources believed to be reliable. However, because of the possibility of human or mechanical error by our sources, McGraw-Hill, or others, McGraw-Hill does not guarantee the accuracy, adequacy, or completeness of any information and is not responsible for any errors or omissions or the results obtained from the use of such information.

MICROSOFT® OFFICE 2007 QUICKSTEPS

1234567890   CCI CCI   0198

ISBN   978-0-07-159985-6
MHID   0-07-159985-1

SPONSORING EDITOR / Roger Stewart

EDITORIAL SUPERVISOR / Janet Walden

PROJECT MANAGER / Vasundhara Sawhney (International Typesetting and Composition)

SERIES CREATORS AND EDITORS / Marty and Carole Matthews

ACQUISITIONS COORDINATOR / Carly Stapleton

COPY EDITOR / Claire Splan

PROOFREADER / Madhu Prasher

INDEXER / Claire Splan

PRODUCTION SUPERVISOR / George Anderson

COMPOSITION / International Typesetting and Composition

ILLUSTRATION / International Typesetting and Composition

ART DIRECTOR, COVER / Jeff Weeks

COVER DESIGN / Pattie Lee

SERIES DESIGN / Bailey Cunningham

To Susan Sherman and Dan Paulson, wonderful friends
who are always a joy to be with.

About the Authors

Carole and Marty Matthews have been programmers, system analysts, managers, executives, and entrepreneurs in the software business for many years. For the last 25 years they have authored, co-authored, or managed the writing and production of over 90 books, which have sold approximately a million and a half copies. They live on an island in Puget Sound in Washington State.

Contents at a Glance

11

12

13

14

Acknowledgments

We are, as always, indebted to the editing, layout, proofreading, indexing, and project management expertise of a number of people, only some of whom we know. We thank all of them and in particular acknowledge:

- **Roger Stewart**, editorial director and sponsoring editor of this book and the QuickSteps series

- **Janet Walden**, editorial supervisor

- **George Anderson**, production supervisor

- **Vasundhara Sawhney**, project manager

- **Carly Stapleton**, acquisitions coordinator

- **Claire Splan**, copy editor and indexer

- **Madhu Prasher**, proofreader

- **International Typesetting and Composition**, layout and production

Introduction

QuickSteps books are recipe books for computer users. They answer the question "How do I..." by providing a quick set of steps to accomplish the most common tasks with a particular operating system or application.

The sets of steps are the central focus of the book. QuickSteps sidebars show how to quickly perform many small functions or tasks that support the primary functions. QuickFacts sidebars supply information that you need to know about a subject. Notes, Tips, and Cautions augment the steps; they are presented in a separate column so as not to interrupt the flow of the steps. The introductions are minimal rather than narrative, and numerous illustrations and figures, many with callouts, support the steps.

Microsoft Office 2007 QuickSteps describes in one book the most commonly used features of Microsoft Office Word 2007, Microsoft Office Excel 2007, Microsoft Office PowerPoint 2007, and Microsoft Office Outlook 2007. Should you find that there is some advanced feature of one of these applications that you need more information about, please see one of these other McGraw-Hill QuickSteps books:

- *Microsoft Office Word 2007 QuickSteps*
- *Microsoft Office Excel 2007 QuickSteps*
- *Microsoft Office PowerPoint 2007 QuickSteps*
- *Microsoft Office Outlook 2007 QuickSteps*
- *Microsoft Office Access 2007 QuickSteps*

Conventions Used in This Book

Microsoft Office 2007 QuickSteps uses several conventions designed to make the book easier for you to follow:

- A ⦿ in the How To list in each chapter references a QuickSteps sidebar in the chapter, and a ⊘ references a QuickFacts sidebar.

- **Bold type** is used for words or objects on the screen that you are to do something with—for example, "click **Start** and click **Computer**."

- *Italic type* is used for a word or phrase that is being defined or otherwise deserves special emphasis.

- Underlined type is used for text that you are to type from the keyboard.

- SMALL CAPITAL LETTERS are used for keys on the keyboard, such as ENTER and SHIFT.

- When you are expected to enter a command, you are told to press the key(s). If you are to enter text or numbers, you are told to type them.

How to...

Chapter 1
Stepping into Office

Microsoft Office is the most widely used of all office suite offerings. Most personal computers (PCs) have some version of Office installed, and most people with PCs probably have Office available to them as well as some experience in its use. The upgrade of Office 2003 to Office 2007 is a significant event, resulting in a totally new user interface. As you may know, Office is both very simple to use and highly sophisticated, offering many features that commonly go unused. Office delivers a high degree of functionality even when only a small percentage of its capabilities are used. The purpose of this book is to acquaint you with how to use the upgrade to Office 2007 within four primary Office programs: Word, Excel, PowerPoint, and Outlook. You will learn not only how to access the newly placed common everyday features, but also many of those additional features that can enhance your experience of using Office.

In this chapter you will familiarize yourself with Office; see how to start and leave programs; use Office's new 2008 windows, panes, ribbon, toolbars, and menus; learn how to get help; and find out how to customize your new Office.

Start and Leave an Office Program

Starting an Office program depends on how it was installed and what has happened to it since its installation. In this section you'll see a surefire way to start Office programs and some alternatives. You'll also see how to leave an Office program.

Figure 1-1: The foolproof way to start an Office program such as Microsoft Word is via the Start menu.

Use the Start Menu to Start Office

If no other icons for or shortcuts to the Office program you want to start are available on your desktop, you can always start an Office program using the Start menu:

1. Start your computer if it is not already running, and log on to Windows if necessary.

2. Click **Start**. The Start menu opens.

3. Click **All Programs**, click **Microsoft Office**, and click the Office program name, such as **Microsoft Office Word 2007**, as shown in Figure 1-1.

Start an Office Program in Different Ways

In addition to using All Programs on the Start menu, a program can be started in several other ways.

USE THE START MENU ITSELF

The icons of the program you use most often are displayed on the left side of the Start menu. If you frequently use Word, for instance, its icon will appear there. To use this technique:

1. Click **Start**. The Start menu opens.

2. Click the icon for the Office program, such as **Microsoft Word**, on the left of the Start menu.

PIN THE OFFICE PROGRAM TO THE TOP OF START

If you think you may use a certain program more frequently, you can keep it at the top of the Start menu by "pinning" it there:

1. Click **Start** to open the Start menu.

2. Right-click (click the right mouse button) the icon for the Office program, such as the Word icon, and click **Pin To Start Menu**.

CREATE A DESKTOP SHORTCUT

An easy way to start an Office program is to create a shortcut icon on the desktop and use it to start the program.

1. Click **Start**, click **All Programs**, and click **Microsoft Office**.

2. Right-click the program name, such as **Microsoft Office Word 2007**, click **Send To**, and click **Desktop (Create Shortcut)**.

LEAVING AN OFFICE PROGRAM

To leave a program when you are done using it:

• In Word, Excel, or PowerPoint, click the **Office** button in the upper-left corner of the Office program window, and click **Close**.

–Or–

• In any Office Program, click the **Close** icon on the right of the title bar. ☒

USE THE QUICK LAUNCH TOOLBAR

The Quick Launch toolbar is a small area on the taskbar next to the Start button. You can put an Office program icon on the Quick Launch toolbar and use it to start your program. If your Quick Launch toolbar is not visible, open it and put an Office program icon, such as Word, there.

1. Right-click a blank area of the taskbar, click **Toolbars**, and click **Quick Launch**. The Quick Launch toolbar is displayed.

2. Click **Start**, click **All Programs**, click **Microsoft Office**, and drag the Office program, such as **Microsoft Office Word 2007** to where you want it on the Quick Launch toolbar. An i-beam icon will help you place it.

3. Then, click the icon on the Quick Launch toolbar to start the Office program.

Explore an Office Program

Office 2007 uses a wide assortment of windows, ribbon tabs, toolbars, menus, and special features to accomplish its functions. Much of this book explores how to find and use all of those items. In this section you'll see and learn to use the most common features of the default window, including the parts of the window, the tabs on the ribbon, and the task pane. (We are using Word for our examples, although most of the Office programs are very similar except for Outlook, which varies in significant ways, as you'll see in Chapter 11. Specific differences in similar programs will be pointed out in the individual program chapters.)

Explore an Office Program Window

The Office 2007 window has many features to aid you in creating and editing documents. An example view (this one showing Word) is presented to you when you first start a program and is shown in Figure 1-2. You can see the primary parts of the ribbon in Figure 1-3. Although we are using Word as our example,

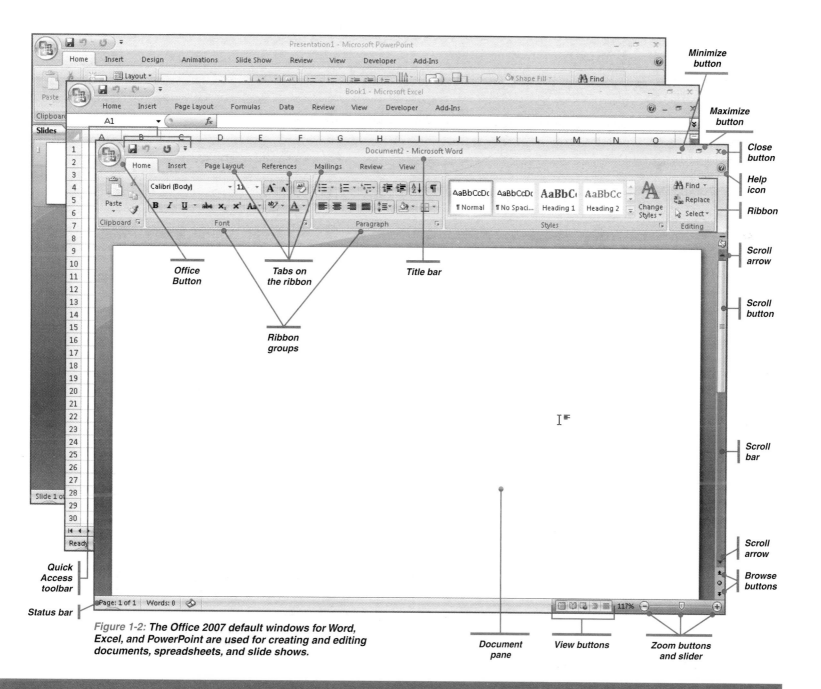

Minimize button

Maximize button

Close button

Help icon

Ribbon

Scroll arrow

Scroll button

Scroll bar

Scroll arrow

Browse buttons

Office Button

Tabs on the ribbon

Title bar

Ribbon groups

Quick Access toolbar

Status bar

Document pane

View buttons

Zoom buttons and slider

Figure 1-2: *The Office 2007 default windows for Word, Excel, and PowerPoint are used for creating and editing documents, spreadsheets, and slide shows.*

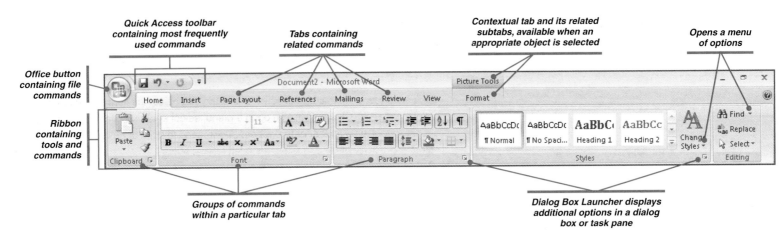

Office button containing file commands

Quick Access toolbar containing most frequently used commands

Tabs containing related commands

Contextual tab and its related subtabs, available when an appropriate object is selected

Opens a menu of options

Ribbon containing tools and commands

Groups of commands within a particular tab

Dialog Box Launcher displays additional options in a dialog box or task pane

Figure 1-3: Organized into tabs and then groups, the commands and tools on the ribbon allow you to create, edit, and otherwise work with documents.

the principal features of the window, including the various ribbon tabs, are described further in this chapter and specific differences are explained in other chapters of this book.

Use the Mouse

A *mouse* is any pointing device—including trackballs, pointing sticks, and graphic tablets—with two or more buttons. This book assumes a two-button mouse. Moving the mouse moves the pointer on the screen. You *select* an object on the screen by moving the pointer so that it is on top of the object and then pressing the left button on the mouse.

You may control the mouse with either your left or right hand; therefore, the buttons may be switched. (See *Windows Vista QuickSteps* (McGraw-Hill, 2007), for instructions on how to switch the buttons.) This book assumes the right hand controls the mouse and the left mouse button is "*the* mouse button." The right button is always called the "right mouse button." If you switch the buttons, you must change your interpretation of these phrases.

UNDERSTANDING THE RIBBON

(Continued)

components, such as tables, links, and charts to your slide (or spreadsheet or document). Each Office program has a default set of tabs with additional *contextual* tabs that appear as the context of your work changes. For instance, when you select a picture, a Format tab containing shapes and drawing tools that you can use with the particular object appears beneath the defining tools tab (such as the Picture Tools tab); when the object is unselected, the Format tab disappears. The ribbon contains labeled buttons you can click to use a given command or tool. Depending on the tool, you are then presented with additional options in the form of a list of commands, a dialog box or task pane, or galleries of choices that reflect what you'll see in your work. Groups that contain several more tools than can be displayed in the ribbon include a *Dialog Box Launcher* icon that takes you directly to these other choices. The ribbon also takes advantage of new Office 2007 features, including a live preview of many potential changes (for example, you can select text and see it change color as you point to various colors in the Font Color gallery). See the accompanying sections and figures for more information on the ribbon and other elements of the Office windows.

TIP

To gain working space in the document pane, you can minimize the size of the ribbon. To do this, double-click the active tab name. Click it again to restore the size of the ribbon. You can also press **CTRL-F1** to toggle the size of the ribbon.

Five actions can be accomplished with the mouse:

- **Point** at an *object* on the screen (a button, an icon, a menu or one of its options, or a border) to highlight it. To *point* means to move the mouse so that the tip of the pointer is on top of the object.

- **Click** an object on the screen to *select* it, making that object the item that your next actions will affect. Clicking will also open a menu, select a menu option, or activate a button or "tool" on a toolbar or the ribbon. *Click* means to point at an object you want to select and quickly press and release the left mouse button.

- **Double-click** an object to open or activate it. *Double-click* means to point at an object you want to select, then press and release the left mouse button twice in rapid succession.

- **Right-click** an object to open a context menu containing commands used to manipulate that object. *Right-click* means to point at an object you want to select, then quickly press and release the right mouse button. For example, right-clicking selected text opens this context menu shown here.

- **Drag** an object to move it on the screen to where you want it moved within the document. *Drag* means to point at an object you want to move and then press and hold the left mouse button while moving the mouse. The object is dragged as you move the mouse. When the object is where you want it, release the mouse button.

Use Tabs and Menus

Tabs are displayed at the top of the ribbon or a dialog box. Menus are displayed when you click a down arrow on a button on the ribbon, a dialog box, or a toolbar. Here are some of the ways to use tabs and menus:

- To open a tab or menu with the mouse, click the tab or menu.

- To open a tab or menu with the keyboard, press **ALT** and the underlined letter in the tab or menu name. For example, press **ALT-F** to open the Office Button menu.

USING THE MINI TOOLBAR

When you select or highlight text a mini text toolbar is displayed that allows you to perform some direct text function, such as making text bold or centering a paragraph. This toolbar contains a subset of the tools contained in the Fonts and Paragraph groups of the Home tab.

DISPLAY THE TEXT TOOLBAR

1. Select text by clicking it or dragging over the text.

2. Then place the pointer over the text and a vague image of the mini toolbar is displayed. Place your pointer over it to clarify the image.

–Or–

You can also right-click the selected text and click on the mini toolbar to remove the context menu.

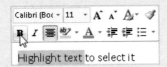

USE A TEXT TOOL

Click the button or icon on the mini toolbar that represents the tool.

HIDE THE MINI TOOLBAR

You can hide the mini toolbar by changing the default.

1. Click the **Office** button and click the program name options button, such as **Word Options**.

2. Click the **Popular** option.

3. Click **Show Mini Toolbar On Selection** to remove the checkmark.

4. Click **OK** to finalize the choice.

(The identifying keys are displayed when you press **ALT** by itself.)

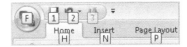

- To select a tab or menu command, click the tab or menu to open it, and then click the option.

- A number of menu options have a right-pointing arrow on their right to indicate that a submenu is associated with that option. To open the submenu, move the mouse pointer to the menu option with a submenu (it will have a right-pointing arrow). The submenu will open. Move the mouse pointer to the submenu, and click the desired option.

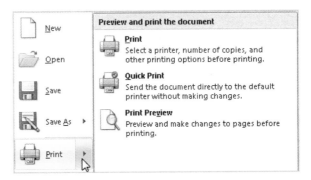

Use Various Views

Each of the Office programs presents documents in several views, allowing you to choose which view facilitates the task you are doing. To access a view, click the **View** tab and then click a Document Views group button. Here are the various views for Word, Excel, and PowerPoint:

Word Document Views group

- **Word** displays five possible views:
  - **Print Layout** displays the text as it looks on a printed page.
  - **Full Screen Reading** replaces the ribbon with a Full Screen toolbar. Click **View Options** to select options for displaying and using this screen view, such as whether to allow typing, track changes, display one or two pages, enlarge text, show comments, and so on. Click **Close** to return to the normal view.

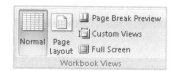

Excel Workbook Views

- **Web Layout** shows how the text will look as a web page.
- **Outline** displays the text in outline form with a contextual Outlining tab on the ribbon. You can use this view to promote and demote levels of text and rearrange levels, as shown in the Outline Tools group. With the Show Document button, you can toggle commands to extend your ability to create, insert, link, merge, split, and lock the document. Click **Close Outline View** to return to normal view.
- **Draft** displays the text of the document in draft status for quick and easy editing. Headings and footings may not be visible.

- **Excel** displays five possible views:
  - **Normal** displays the normal spreadsheet view with numbered rows and lettered columns.
  - **Page Layout** displays the spreadsheet as it will be printed.
  - **Page Break Preview** displays where the spreadsheet has page breaks and will allow you to change them.
  - **Custom Views** allows you to select a custom view or add the current view to the list of Custom Views.
  - **Full Screen** eliminates the menus and status bar to display only spreadsheet.
- **PowerPoint** contains seven possible views:

PowerPoint Presentation Views

  - **Normal** displays the larger slide pane with the Slides and Outline pane on the left.
  - **Slide Sorter** view displays thumbnails of slides in the slides pane.
  - **Notes Page** displays a "split" page showing the slide and any notes that have been entered for that slide.
  - **Slide Show** activates the slide show.
  - **Slide Master** displays the formatting for the overall slide show.
  - **Handout Master** displays the master for any handouts that can be printed to accompany the slide show.
  - **Notes Master** displays the notes master defining the look of the notes.

Personalize and Customize Office 2007 Programs

You can personalize your Office program, or make it your own, by changing the personal defaults for such options as the tools available on the Quick Access toolbar or your User Name and initials. You can customize your Office program by customizing the general defaults on editing, proofing, display, and other options. Many of these options will be discussed in the appropriate chapters. Here we will look at the Quick Access toolbar, display, and other popular options.

Work with the Quick Access Toolbar

The Quick Access toolbar that is normally at the top left of the Word, Excel, and PowerPoint windows can become a "best friend" if you modify it so that it fits your own way of working.

ADD TO THE QUICK ACCESS TOOLBAR

The Quick Access toolbar contains the commands most commonly used. The default tools are Save, Undo, and Redo. You can add additional commands to it that you personally prefer:

1. Click the **Office** button and click the applicable Options button, such as **Word Options**.

2. Click the **Customize** option and, if in Word, you will see the dialog box shown in Figure 1-4.

3. Open the drop-down list box on the left and select the type of command you want from the listed options.

4. In the left-most list box, find and click the command you want to add to the toolbar, and then click **Add** to move its name to the right list box. Repeat this for all the commands you want in the toolbar.

5. Click **OK** when you are finished.

NOTE

You can add a command to the Quick Access toolbar from the ribbon by right-clicking the button and choosing **Add To Quick Access Toolbar**.

TIP

In Word, to change keyboard shortcuts for a specific command, click **Customize** opposite Keyboard Shortcuts in the Customize option of the Word Options dialog box. Under **Categories** select the command source you want, and then click the appropriate **Commands**. Under Current Keys, you'll see the shortcut key currently in use. Change or add the shortcut key by pressing it while the insertion point is in the **Press New Shortcut Key** text box. Click **Close** when you're through.

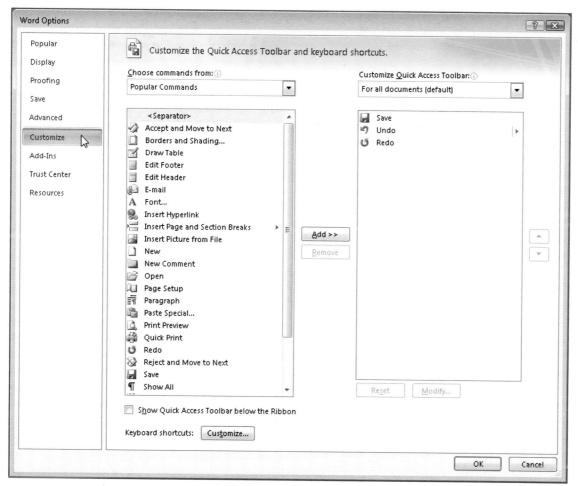

Figure 1-4: *You can customize the Quick Access toolbar by adding and removing commands for easy and quick access using the Options, such as these for Word.*

MOVE THE QUICK ACCESS TOOLBAR

To move the Quick Access toolbar beneath the ribbon, right-click the Quick Access toolbar and click **Show Quick Access Toolbar Below The Ribbon**.

Show or Hide ScreenTips

When you hold your pointer over a command or tool, a screen tip is displayed. The tip may be just the name of the tool or command, or it may be enhanced with a small description. You can hide the tips, or cause them to be enhanced or not:

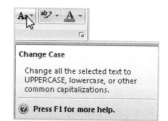

1. Click the **Office** button in Word, Excel, or PowerPoint and click the Options button, such as **Word Options**.

2. Click the **Popular** option.

3. Open the **ScreenTip Style** drop-down list and choose the option you want.

4. Click **OK** to finalize the choice.

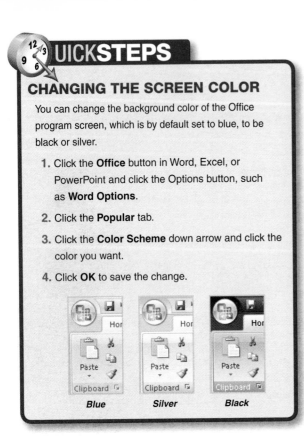

QUICKSTEPS

CHANGING THE SCREEN COLOR

You can change the background color of the Office program screen, which is by default set to blue, to be black or silver.

1. Click the **Office** button in Word, Excel, or PowerPoint and click the Options button, such as **Word Options**.

2. Click the **Popular** tab.

3. Click the **Color Scheme** down arrow and click the color you want.

4. Click **OK** to save the change.

Blue   **Silver**   **Black**

Add Identifying Information

You can add identifying information to a document to make it easier to organize and find information during searches, especially in a shared environment. In Word, Excel, and PowerPoint (Outlook doesn't have this capability):

1. Click the **Office** button, click **Prepare** on the left, and click **Properties** in the right pane. A Document Properties panel containing standard identifiers displays under the ribbon, as shown for Word in Figure 1-5.

2. Type identifying information, such as Title, Subject, and Keywords (words or phrases that are associated with the document).

3. To view more information about the document, click the **Document Properties down arrow** in the panel's title bar, and click **Advanced Properties**. Review each tab in the Properties dialog box to see the information available and make any changes or additions. Close the Properties dialog box when finished.

4. When finished with the Document Properties panel, click the "X" at the right end of the panel's title bar to close it.

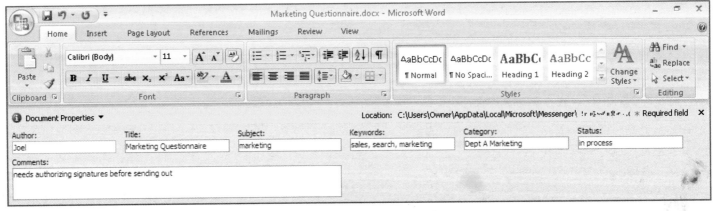

Figure 1-5: A Document Properties panel displays beneath the ribbon, allowing you to more easily locate a document using search tools if you add identifying data.

QUICKSTEPS

SETTING PREFERENCES

Setting preferences allows you to adapt your Office program to your needs and inclinations. The Word, Excel, or PowerPoint Options dialog box provides access to these settings.

Click the **Office** button, and then click the Options button, such as **Word Options**.

SELECT DISPLAY ELEMENTS TO SHOW (WORD ONLY)

Click the **Display** option, as shown in Figure 1-6:

- Click the **Page Display Options** that you want to display.
- Click the formatting marks you want to see—**Show All Formatting Marks** is a good choice.
- Click the **Printing Options** you want.

SET GENERAL POPULAR OPTIONS

1. Click the **Popular** options (see Figure 1-7 for Word's popular options. The options will differ from program to program):

   - Review and select (checkmark) the options that are correct for your situation. Earlier in this chapter, you saw how to disable the mini toolbar, show and hide screen tips, and change the color scheme of the Word window. If you are unsure about other options, keep the default and see how well those settings work for you.

   - Type the **User Name** you want displayed in documents revised using Track Changes.

Continued . . .

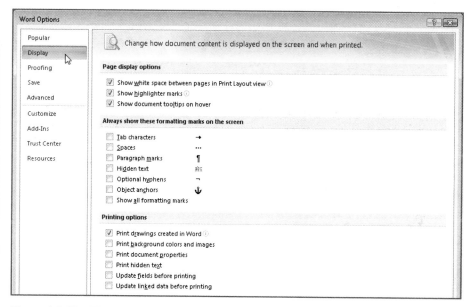

Figure 1-6: *The Display options in the Word Options dialog box provides page display, formatting, and printing preferences.*

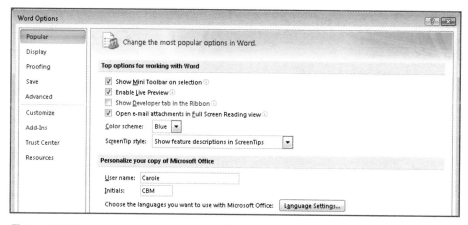

Figure 1-7: *Many basic preferences used in Word are set in the Popular Options dialog box.*

QUICKSTEPS

SETTING PREFERENCES *(Continued)*

- Type **Initials** associated with the User Name that will be displayed in comments you insert into a document.

- Click Language Settings to select the languages you'll be using in Office.

2. When you have set the Popular and Display Options as you want, click each of the other options, review the settings, and make the changes you want. These are discussed further in the applicable chapters.

3. When you have finished selecting your preferences, click **OK** to close the Office program Options dialog box.

NOTE

If you are not connected to the Internet, a limited version of Help is also available offline.

Get Help

Help can be accessed from online Microsoft servers. A different kind of help that includes the Thesaurus and Research features is also available.

Open Help

The Office Help system is maintained online at Microsoft. It is easily accessed.

Click the **Help** icon 🔘 and, as an example, the Word Help window will open, shown in Figure 1-8.

- Find the topic you want and click it.

–Or–

- Type words in the Search text box and click **Search**.

Figure 1-8: When you click the Help icon you will see the Office program Help dialog box where you can click the topic you want or search for more specific words.

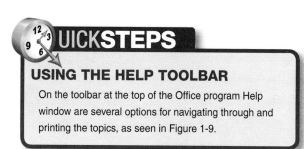

USING THE HELP TOOLBAR

On the toolbar at the top of the Office program Help window are several options for navigating through and printing the topics, as seen in Figure 1-9.

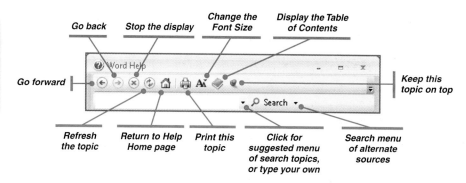

Go back · Stop the display · Change the Font Size · Display the Table of Contents

Go forward · Keep this topic on top

Refresh the topic · Return to Help Home page · Print this topic · Click for suggested menu of search topics, or type your own · Search menu of alternate sources

Figure 1-9: The Help toolbar helps you navigate through the topics and then print them out.

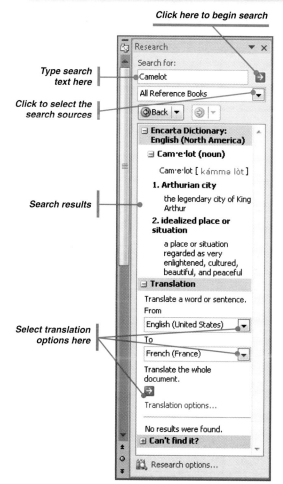

Click here to begin search

Type search text here

Click to select the search sources

Search results

Select translation options here

Figure 1-10: In the Research pane, you can search a dictionary, a thesaurus, an encyclopedia, and several other sources.

Do Research

You can do research on the Internet using Office's Research command. This displays a Research task pane that allows you to enter your search criteria and specify references to search.

1. Click the **Review** tab and in the Proofing group, click **Research**. You may be asked for the language you are using. Click it and the Research task pane will appear on the right of the Slide pane, as shown in the example in Figure 1-10.

2. Type your search criteria in the Search For text box.

3. To change the default reference (All Reference Books), click its down arrow to open the drop-down list and click a reference to be searched.

4. Click the arrow to the right of the search box to start the search. The results will be displayed in the task pane.

5. Click **Close** to close the task pane.

Use the Thesaurus

You can find synonyms for words with the Thesaurus feature.

1. To use the Thesaurus, first select the text you want to use for the search.

2. Then click the **Review** tab and in the Proofing group, click **Thesaurus**. The Research task pane will appear with the most likely synonyms listed.

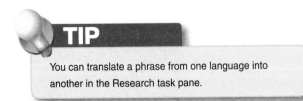
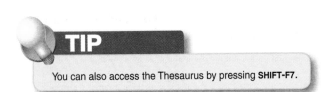

a. Click a listed word to search for its synonyms.

b. Click the word down arrow to insert, copy, or look up the word.

3. Click Close to remove the task pane.

Translate a Document

To translate a whole document from one language to another:

1. Click the **Review** tab and in the Proofing group, click **Translate**. The Search task pane will appear with the Translation as its source reference.

2. Click the **From** and **To** down arrows and click the appropriate languages.

3. Click the green arrow to begin the translation. A Translate Whole Document message will appear that informs you that your document will be sent over the Internet to a special service, WorldLingo, to be translated.

4. Click **Yes** to start the translation. Your translated document will appear in a browser window; an example is shown in Figure 1-11.

Figure 1-11: **You can translate a document using WorldLingo as the translator.**

ACCESSING MICROSOFT RESOURCES

Microsoft maintains online a resource center that you can easily access. This resource window allows you to communicate with Microsoft about Office and specific program subjects. In Word, Excel, and PowerPoint:

1. Click the **Office** button and click the Options button, such as **Word Options**.

2. Click the Resources option. Here are your choices, as shown in Figure 1-12:

   - Click **Get Updates** to find out if updates are available for Microsoft Office. (See the next section, "Update Your Office Program.")

   - Click **Run Microsoft Office Diagnostics** to run a diagnostic program if Microsoft Office seems to be operating incorrectly. The program will automatically capture data and send it to Microsoft to be diagnosed.

   - Click **Contact Us** to send a message to Microsoft experts. You may be seeking advice for a problem or making suggestions for improvements to the product.

   - Click **Activate Microsoft Office** if you cannot access all features within the Office program. If you have already activated Office, a message will be displayed telling you so.

   - Click **Go To Microsoft Office Online** to access new product information, tips for using products, downloads (for product updates, free demos, and third-party downloads), clip art, templates, and so on.

Continued . . .

Update Your Office Program

Microsoft periodically releases updates for Office programs (these are almost always problem fixes and not enhancements). You can check on available updates, download them, and install them from your Office program. In Word, Excel, and PowerPoint:

1. Click the **Office** button and click the Options button, such as **Word Options**. This will open the Options dialog box. Click **Resources**.

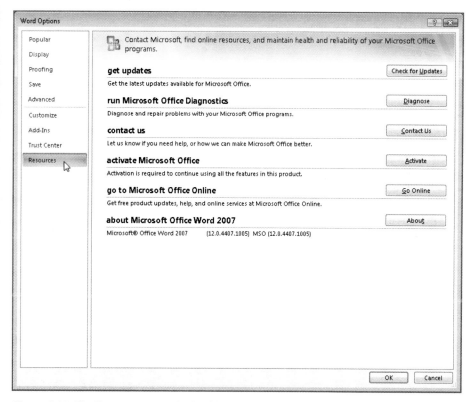

Figure 1-12: The Resources page in the Office program Options dialog box facilitates communication with Microsoft.

ACCESSING MICROSOFT
RESOURCES *(Continued)*

- Click **About Microsoft Office** *programname* **2007** to open the About Microsoft Office dialog box, which gives the version, licensing information, and so on.

2. On the Resources option page, next to Get Updates, click the **Check For Updates** button. The Internet browser opens and connects to the Microsoft Online web site, as shown in Figure 1-13.

3. Click **Check For Updates**. Your system will be checked for any necessary updates, and you will be given the opportunity to download and install them if you choose. When you have downloaded the updates you want, close your web browser.

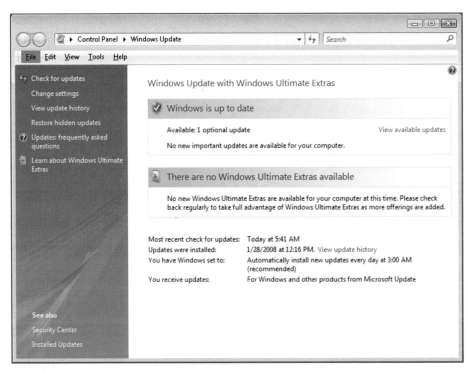

Figure 1-13: ***One of the primary reasons to check for and download Office and Windows updates is to get needed security patches.***

How to...

Chapter 2
Working with Documents

Microsoft Office Word 2007 allows you to create and edit *documents*, such as letters, reports, invoices, plays, and books. The book you are reading now was written in Word. Documents are printed on one or more pages and are probably bound by anything from a paper clip to stitch binding. In the computer, a document is called a *file*, an object that has been given a name and is stored on a disk drive. For example, the name given to the file for this chapter is Chap02.doc. "Chap02" is the filename and ".doc" is the file extension. Most files produced by previous editions of Word used the .doc extension. Documents saved with Word 2007 by default are saved with the .docx extension.

In this chapter you'll see how to create new documents and edit existing ones. This includes ways to enter, change, and delete text, as well as to find, select, copy, and move text.

Create a New Document

In the days before computers, creating a new document was termed "starting with a clean sheet of paper." Today, it is "starting with a blank screen"— actually, a blank area within a window on the screen, as shown in Figure 2-1. Your ribbon options may vary depending on the size of your window: minimized windows display abbreviated options, such as Editing in Figure 2-1.

You can create a new document in two ways: using the default or "normal" document or using a unique template on which to base the document.

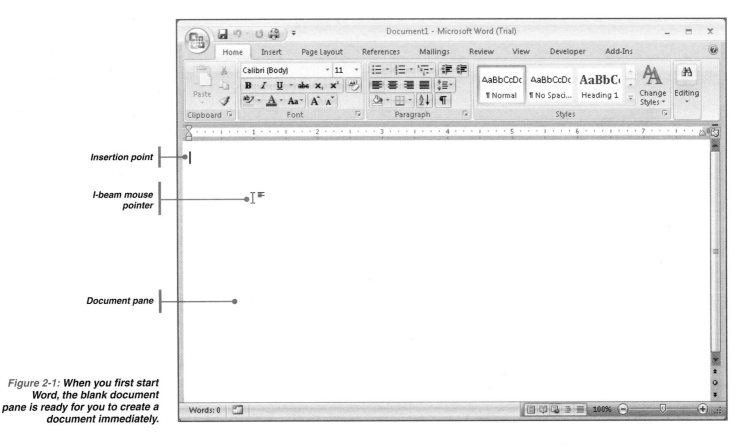

Insertion point

I-beam mouse pointer

Document pane

Figure 2-1: When you first start Word, the blank document pane is ready for you to create a document immediately.

NOTE

The remainder of this chapter assumes that Word has been started and is open on your screen.

NOTE

You can also create and use your own templates, as described in Chapter 4.

Start a New Document

Simply starting Word opens up a blank document pane into which you can start typing a new document immediately. The blinking bar in the upper-left of the document pane, called the *insertion point*, indicates where the text you type will appear.

To start Word, use one of the ways described at the beginning of Chapter 1.

Use a Unique Template

A template is a special kind of document that is used as the basis for other documents you create. The template is said to be "attached" to the document, and every Word document must have a template attached to it. The template acts as the framework around which you create your document. The document that is opened automatically when you start Word 2007 uses a default template (referred to as "the Normal template") called Normal.dotm (previous versions used Normal.dot) that contains standard formatting settings. Other templates can contain boilerplate text, formatting for the types of document they create, and even automating procedures. Word is installed on your computer with a number of templates that you can use, and you can access other templates through Office Online.

USING A TEMPLATE ON YOUR COMPUTER

With Word open on your computer:

1. Click the **Office button**, and then click **New**. The New Document dialog box will open, as shown in Figure 2-2.

2. In the Templates pane you have these options:

   a. **Blank and Recent**   For a new blank template and templates you have used recently.

   b. **Installed Templates**   For templates stored on your computer.

   c. **My Templates**   For custom templates you have created.

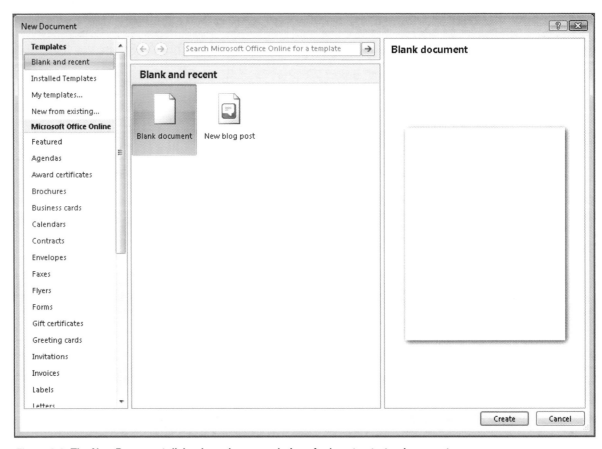

Figure 2-2: *The New Document dialog box gives you choices for how to start a document.*

    d. New From Existing   For templates you can copy from existing documents.

    e. Microsoft Office Online   For template categories that can be obtained from Microsoft's online resources.

3. Click **Installed Templates**. Click the template you want and then on the bottom of the right pane next to Create New, click **Document**, as shown in Figure 2-3.

4. Click **Create**. A document with the selected template opens.

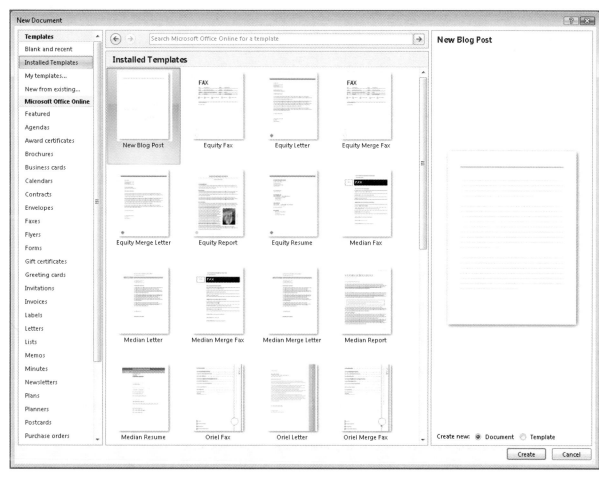

Figure 2-3: Word installs a number of templates on your computer automatically.

USING AN OFFICE ONLINE TEMPLATE

With Word open on your computer:

1. Click the **Office button**, and then click **New**. The New Document dialog box will open.

2. In the Templates pane beneath **Microsoft Office Online** is a list of categories of templates. Click the category you want to see, and you'll see the possibilities for that category, as seen in Figure 2-4.

3. Find the template you want and click **Download** in the right pane. A new document is opened with the template in Word.

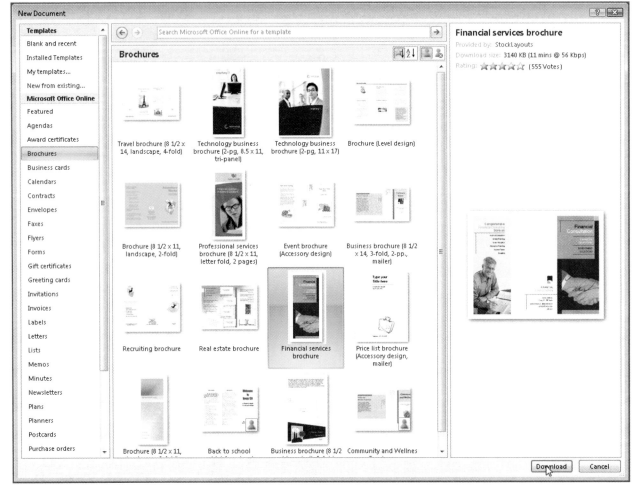

Figure 2-4: Microsoft offers many templates online for Word and its other products.

Open an Existing Document

After creating and saving a document, you may want to come back and work on it later. You may also want to open and work on a Word or other document created by someone else. To do this, you must first locate the document and then open it in Word. You can locate the document either directly from Word or search for it in either Word or Windows.

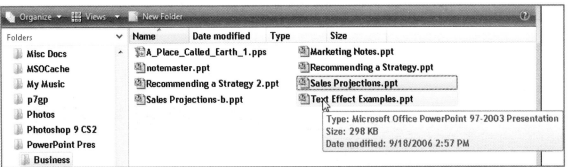

Figure 2-5: *When you hold the mouse pointer over a document name, you get additional information about the document.*

Locate an Existing Document

With Word open on your screen:

1. Click the **Office button**, and click **Open**. The Open dialog box will appear.

2. Double-click the folder or sequence of folders you need to open in order to find the document.

3. When you have found the document you want to open (see Figure 2-5), double-click it. It will appear in Word, ready for you to begin your work.

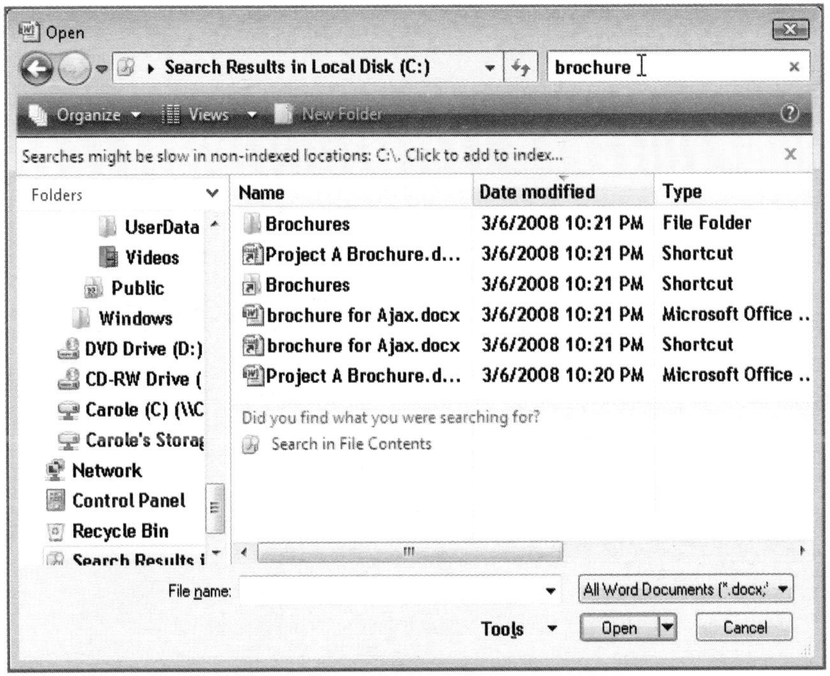

Search for an Existing Document

If you have a hard time finding a document using the direct approach just described, you can search for it either in Word or in Windows.

SEARCH FOR A DOCUMENT IN WORD

A document search performed in Word looks for a piece of text that is contained in the document or some property of the document such as the name of the author, the creation date, or the name of the file. The Basic search is for text in the document.

1. Click the **Office button** and click **Open**. The Open dialog box is displayed. Display the folder or drive that you want to search.

2. In the Search text field on the top of the dialog box, begin to enter the text you want to search for (see Figure 2-6). As you type the search will begin. The results will be listed in the right pane of the dialog box, beneath the search text.

3. Double-click the file you want or select it and click **Open** to open it in Word.

Figure 2-6: *As you type the text you want to search for, the search automatically begins and the results are listed beneath the search text.*

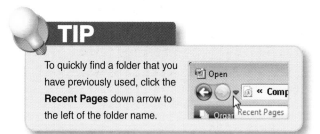

USE SEARCH AND SORT

To sort the files within the search results file, you can use the column headings. You can sort files by some special property, such as name, date, folder type, author, or tag.

1. Open the Open dialog box (see the preceding set of steps), locate the folder containing the file you want, and type your search text. The search results will be listed below as you type.

2. Point to a column heading by which you want to sort the results and click the down arrow.

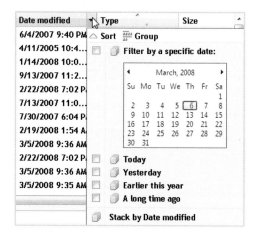

3. Click the **Sort** option and the files will be resorted.

USE ADVANCED FILTERS IN WINDOWS

Windows Explorer allows you to modify searches with filters for files, including Word documents. In Windows Vista:

1. Click **Start** to open the Start menu, and then click **Computer** on the right panel.

2. Click **Organize** | **Layout** | **Search Pane**. A Show Only search bar will be displayed below the folder name.

3. Click **Document** in the search bar to restrict the search to document files.

4. Click the **Advanced Search** down arrow on the right end of the search bar. The Advanced Search pane will open as seen in Figure 2-7. (Clicking Advanced Search again will close it.)

Figure 2-7: *Using Windows Vista, you can use advanced filters to narrow your search for a specific file or files.*

5. You have these filter options:

   - **Date**   To filter by date modified or created, click the down arrow and then click the option you want. Click the next down arrow to the right to choose whether the date is equal to or before or after a date entered in the calendar select box to the right.

   - **Size**   To filter by file size, click the down arrow to the right to choose whether the size is equal to or larger or smaller than the file size entered in the text box to the right.

   - **Name**   To filter for file name, type the file name in the Name text box.

   - **Tags**   To filter for tags, type the tag in the Tag text box.

   - **Authors**   To filter by author name, type the author in the Authors text box.

6. Click the Include Non-indexed, Hidden, And System Files checkbox to show these types of files in the search.

7. Click Search.

Import a Document

If you have a word processing document created in a program other than Word, you can most likely open it and edit it in Word.

1. Click the **Office button**, and click **Open**. The Open dialog box will appear.

2. Find the folder or sequence of folders you need to open in order to find the document.

3. On the bottom of the dialog box, click the down arrow on the drop-down list box to the right of File Name to display the list of files that you can directly open in Word, as shown next (see Table 2-1 for a complete list).

FILE TYPE	EXTENSION
Plain text files	.txt
Rich Text Format file	.rtf
Web page files	.htm, .html, .mht, .mhtml
Windows Write	.wri
Word Macro-Enabled Templates	.docm
Word 97 to 2003 files	.doc
Word 97 to 2003 template files	.dot
Word 2007 document files (macro enabled)	.docx (.docm)
Word 2007 template files	.dotx
WordPerfect 5.*x* and 6.*x* files	.doc, .wpd
Works 6.0 to 9.0 files	.wps
XML files	.xml

*Table 2-1: **File Types That Word Can Open Directly***

4. Click the file type you want to open. The Open dialog box will list only files of that type.

5. Double-click the file that you want to open. Depending on the file, you may get one of several messages.

Write a Document

Whether you create a new document or open an existing one, you will likely want to enter and edit text. Editing, in this case, includes adding and deleting text as well as selecting, moving, and copying it.

Enter Text

To enter text in a document that you have newly created or opened, simply start typing. The characters you type will appear in the document pane at the insertion point and in the order that you type them.

QUICKSTEPS

ENTERING SPECIAL CHARACTERS

Entering a character that is on the keyboard takes only a keystroke, but many other characters and symbols exist beyond those that appear on the keyboard. For example: ©, £, Ã, Ω, Љ, and •. You can enter these characters using either the Symbol dialog box or a sequence of keys.

SELECT SPECIAL CHARACTERS FROM THE SYMBOL DIALOG BOX

1. Move the insertion point to where you want to insert the special character(s).

Continued . . .

QUICKSTEPS

ENTERING SPECIAL CHARACTERS

(Continued)

2. Click the **Insert** tab, and then click **Symbol** in the Symbols group. A Symbol menu will open containing the symbols you most commonly use. If the symbol you want is on the list, click it and the symbol is inserted in the document.

3. If the symbol you want is not on the menu, click **More Symbols**. The Symbol dialog box will open.

   - Click the **Symbols** tab for characters within font styles.

   - Click the **Special Characters** tab for common standard characters, as shown in Figure 2-8.

4. Click the character you want, click **Insert** and then click **Close**. You should see the special character or symbol where the insertion point was.

ENTER SPECIAL CHARACTERS FROM THE KEYBOARD

You can use keyboard shortcut keys to enter symbols and special characters. The numeric part of the shortcut must be entered on the numeric keypad.

1. Move the insertion point to where you want to insert the special characters.

2. Press **NUM LOCK** to put the numeric keypad into numeric mode.

Continued . . .

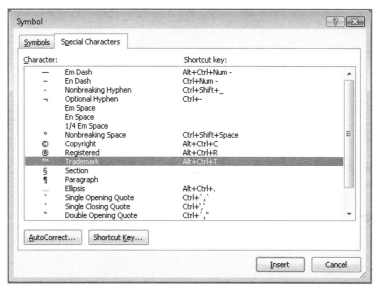

*Figure 2-8: **The Symbol dialog box contains special characters as well as several complete alphabets and symbol sets.***

Determine Where Text Will Appear

The *insertion point*, the blinking vertical bar shown earlier in Figure 2-1, determines where text that you type will appear. In a new document, the insertion point is obviously in the upper-left corner of the document pane. It is also placed there by default when you open an existing document. You can move the insertion point within or to the end of existing text using either the keyboard or the mouse.

MOVE THE INSERTION POINT WITH THE KEYBOARD

When Word is open and active, the insertion point moves every time you press a character or directional key on the keyboard (unless a menu or dialog box is open or the task pane is active). The directional keys include **TAB**, **BACKSPACE**, and **ENTER** as well as the four arrow keys, and **HOME**, **END**, **PAGE UP**, and **PAGE DOWN**.

QUICKSTEPS

ENTERING SPECIAL CHARACTERS
(Continued)

3. Press and hold **ALT** while pressing all four digits (including the leading zero) on the numeric keypad.

4. Release **ALT**. The special character will appear where the insertion point was.

The shortcut keys for some of the more common special characters are shown in Table 2-2.

CHARACTER	NAME	SHORTCUT KEYS
•	Bullet	ALT-0149
©	Copyright	ALT-CTRL-C
™	Trademark	ALT-CTRL-T
®	Registered	ALT-CTRL-R
¢	Cent	CTRL-/ , C
£	Pound	ALT-0163
€	Euro	ALT-CTRL-E
–	En dash	CTRL-NUM-
—	Em dash	ALT-CTRL-NUM-

*Table 2-2: **Shortcut Keys for Common Characters***

NOTE

In Table 2-2, the "," means to release the previous keys and then press the following key(s). For example, for a ¢, press and hold **CTRL** while pressing **/**, then release **CTRL** and the **/**, and press **C**. In addition, "NUM" means to press the following key on the numeric keypad. So, "NUM-" means to press "-" in the top-right of the numeric keypad.

NOTE

When you click a common symbol or special character in the Symbol dialog box, you'll see the shortcut keys for the character.

MOVE THE INSERTION POINT WITH THE MOUSE

When the mouse pointer is in the document pane, it appears as an I-beam, as you saw in Figure 2-1. The reason for the I-beam is that it fits between characters on the screen. You can move the insertion point by moving the I-beam mouse pointer to where you want the insertion point and clicking.

Insertion|Point

Insert vs. Overtype Text

When you press a letter or a number key with Word in its default mode (as it is when you first start it), the insertion point and any existing text to the right of the insertion point is pushed to the right and down on a page. This is also true when you press the **TAB** or **ENTER** keys. This is called *insert* mode: new text pushes existing text to the right.

In previous versions of Word if you press the **INSERT** (or **INS**) key, Word is switched to *overtype* mode, and the OVR indicator is enabled in the status bar. In Word 2007 this capability is turned off by default and the **INSERT** (or **INS**) key does nothing. The reason is that more often than not the **INSERT** (or **INS**) key gets pressed by mistake and you find out about this after you have typed over a lot of text you didn't want to type over. To turn on this capability, click the **Office button | Word Options | Advanced**, and under Editing Options click **Use The Insert Key To Control Overtype Mode**.

In overtype mode, any character key you press types over (replaces) the existing character to the right of the insertion point. Overtype mode does not affect the **ENTER** key, which continues to push existing characters to the right of the insertion point down. The **TAB** key does replace characters to the right, *unless* it is pressed at the beginning of the line, in which case it is treated as an indent and pushes the rest of the line to the right.

1

3

4

5

6

7

8

9

10

TIP

You can insert multiple special characters in sequence by selecting one after the other in the Symbol dialog box.

TIP

The AutoCorrect feature, which is discussed in Chapter 4, also provides a quick way of entering commonly used special characters such as Copyright, Trademark, Registered, and en and em dashes.

CAUTION

In Word 2007 there is no "OVR" in the status bar to indicate that you are in overtype mode, which replaces existing text with what you are typing.

NOTE

In both insert and overtype modes, the directional keys move the insertion point without regard to which mode is enabled.

NOTE

Section breaks are used to define columns within a page and to define different types of pages, as you might have with differently formatted left and right pages. The use of section breaks, columns, and different types of pages are described in Chapter 4.

Insert Line or Page Breaks

In Word, as in all word processing programs, simply keep typing and the text will automatically wrap around to the next line. Only when you want to break a line before it would otherwise end must you manually intervene. There are four instances where manual line breaks are required:

- **At the End of a Paragraph**   To start a new paragraph, press **ENTER**.
- **At the End of a Short Line Within a Paragraph**   To start a new line, press **SHIFT-ENTER**.
- **At the End of a Page**   To force the start of a new page, press **CTRL-ENTER**.
- **At the End of a Section**   To start a new section, press **CTRL-SHIFT-ENTER**.

You can also enter a page break using the mouse:

With the insertion point where you want the break, click the **Insert** tab and click **Page Break** in the Pages group. A page break will be inserted in the text.

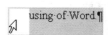

Select Text

In order to copy, move, or delete text, you first need to select it. *Selecting text* means to identify it as a separate block from the remaining text in a document. You can select any amount of text, from a single character up to an entire document. As text is selected, it is highlighted with a colored background, as you can see in Figure 2-9. You can select text with both the mouse and the keyboard.

SELECT TEXT WITH THE MOUSE

You can select varying amounts of text with the mouse.

- **Select a single word** by double-clicking that word.
- **Select a single line** by clicking on the far left of the line when the I-beam mouse pointer becomes an arrow (this area on the left where the mouse pointer becomes an arrow is called the *selection bar*).

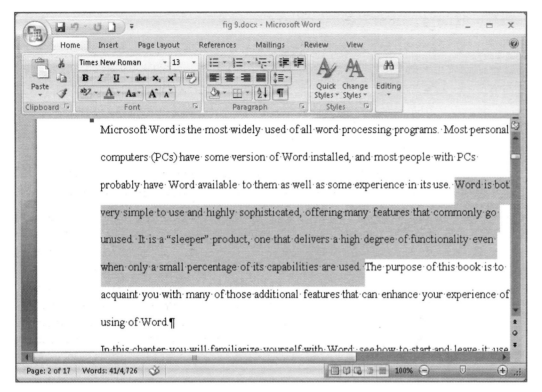

*Figure 2-9: **You will always know what you are moving, copying, or deleting because it is highlighted on the screen.***

- **Select a single sentence** by pressing and holding **CTRL** while clicking in the sentence.
- **Select a single paragraph** by double-clicking in the selection bar opposite the paragraph.
- **Select an entire document** by pressing and holding **CTRL-SHIFT** while clicking in the selection bar anywhere in the document. (The selection bar is on the far-left edge of the document.)
- **Select one or more characters** in a word, or select two or more words by clicking:
  1. Click to place the insertion point to the left of the first character.
  2. Press and hold **SHIFT** while clicking to the right of the last character. The selected range of text will be highlighted.

- **Select one or more characters** in a word or select two or more words by dragging:
  1. Move the mouse pointer to the left of the first character.
  2. Press and hold the mouse button while dragging the mouse pointer to the right of the last character. The selected text will be highlighted.

SELECT TEXT WITH THE KEYBOARD

Use the arrow keys to move the insertion point to the left of the first character you want to select.

- Press and hold **SHIFT** while using the arrow keys to move the insertion point to the right of the last character you want to select.
- To select a line, place the pointer at the beginning of a line. Press and hold **SHIFT** and press **END**.
- To select the entire document from the keyboard, press **CTRL-A**.

Copy and Move Text

Copying and moving text is very similar. Think of copying text as moving it and leaving a copy behind. Both copying and moving are done in two steps:

1. Selected text is copied or cut from its current location to the Clipboard.

2. The contents of the Clipboard are pasted to a new location identified by the insertion point.

USE THE CLIPBOARD

The *Clipboard* is a location in the computer's memory that is used to store information temporarily. There are actually two Clipboards that can be used:

- The **Windows Clipboard** can store one object, either text or a picture, and pass that object within or among Windows programs. Once an object is cut or copied to the Windows Clipboard, it stays there until another object is cut or copied to the Clipboard or until the computer is turned off. The Windows Clipboard is used by default.

- The **Office Clipboard** can store up to 24 objects, both text and pictures, and pass those objects within or among Office programs. Once the Office Clipboard is enabled, all objects that are cut or copied are kept on the Office Clipboard until the 25th object is cut or copied, which will replace the first object. All objects on the Office Clipboard are lost from the Clipboard when the computer is turned off.

CUT TEXT

When you *cut text*, you place it on the Clipboard and delete it from its current location. When the Clipboard contents are pasted to the new location, the text has been *moved* and no longer exists in its original location. To cut and place text on the Clipboard, select it and then:

- Press **CTRL-X**.

  –Or–

- Click the **Home** tab, and then click Cut in the Clipboard group.

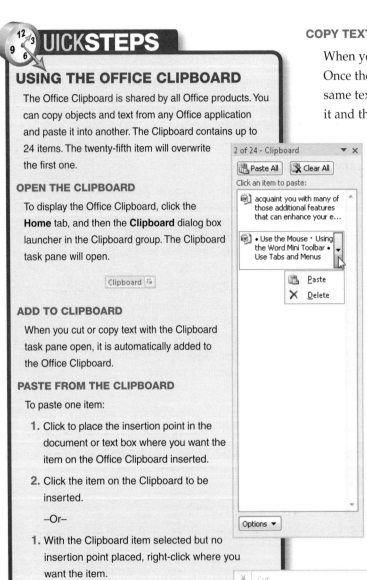

QUICKSTEPS

USING THE OFFICE CLIPBOARD

The Office Clipboard is shared by all Office products. You can copy objects and text from any Office application and paste it into another. The Clipboard contains up to 24 items. The twenty-fifth item will overwrite the first one.

OPEN THE CLIPBOARD

To display the Office Clipboard, click the **Home** tab, and then the **Clipboard** dialog box launcher in the Clipboard group. The Clipboard task pane will open.

ADD TO CLIPBOARD

When you cut or copy text with the Clipboard task pane open, it is automatically added to the Office Clipboard.

PASTE FROM THE CLIPBOARD

To paste one item:

1. Click to place the insertion point in the document or text box where you want the item on the Office Clipboard inserted.

2. Click the item on the Clipboard to be inserted.

   –Or–

1. With the Clipboard item selected but no insertion point placed, right-click where you want the item.

2. Select **Paste** from the context menu.

Continued . . .

COPY TEXT

When you *copy* text to the Clipboard, you also leave it in its original location. Once the Clipboard contents are pasted to the new location, you have the same text in two places in the document. To copy text to the Clipboard, select it and then:

- Press **CTRL-C**.

  –Or–

- Click the **Home** tab, and then click **Copy** in the Clipboard group.

PASTE TEXT

To complete a copy or a move you must *paste* the text from the Clipboard onto either the same or another document where the insertion point is located. A copy of the text stays on the Clipboard and can be pasted again. To paste the contents of the Clipboard:

- Press **CTRL-V**

  –Or–

- Click the **Home** tab, and then click **Paste** (in the upper Clipboard area) in the Clipboard group.

USE THE PASTE OPTIONS SMART TAG

The Paste Options smart tag appears when you paste text. It asks you if you want to Keep Source Formatting (the original formatting of the text), Match Destination Formatting (change the formatting to that of the surrounding text), or Keep Text Only (remove all formatting from the text). Set Default Paste displays the Word Options dialog box so that you can set defaults for pasting text during a cut or copy action. The Paste Options smart tag is most valuable when you can see the paste operation has resulted in formatting you don't want.

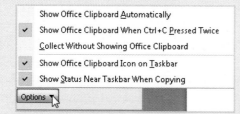
UNDO A MOVE OR PASTE

You can undo a move or paste by:

- Pressing **CTRL-Z**

  –Or–

- Clicking **Undo** in the Quick Access toolbar

REDO AN UNDO

You can redo many undos by:

- Pressing **CTRL-Y**

  –Or–

- Clicking **Redo** in the Quick Access toolbar

Delete Text

Deleting text removes it from its current location *without* putting it in the Clipboard. To delete a selected piece of text:

- Press **DELETE**, or **DEL**.

- On the Home tab, click **Cut** in the Clipboard group.

Edit a Document

After entering all the text into a document, most people want to edit it and, possibly, revise it at a later date. You'll want to be able to move around the document, quickly moving from location to location.

Move Around in a Document

Word provides a number of ways to move around a document using the mouse and the keyboard.

MOVE WITH THE MOUSE

You can easily move the insertion point by clicking in your text anywhere on the screen, but how do you move to some place you cannot see? You have to

USING THE OFFICE CLIPBOARD

(Continued)

- **Collect Without Showing Office Clipboard** copies items to the Clipboard without displaying it.

- **Show Office Clipboard Icon On Taskbar** displays the icon 📋 on the right of the Windows taskbar when the Clipboard is being used.

- **Show Status Near Taskbar When Copying** displays a message about the items being added to the Clipboard as copies are made.

NOTE

To close the Office Clipboard and revert to the Windows Clipboard, click the close icon, or click **Close** at the top of the task pane (you may need to click the down arrow to the left of the close icon). The items you placed on the Office Clipboard while it was open will stay there until you shut down Word, but only the last item you cut or copied after closing the Office Clipboard down will be displayed.

TIP

Place your pointer over the Clipboard icon in the taskbar to see how many items are currently on it.

---

change what you are looking at, and Word provides two sets of tools to use with the mouse to do just that: the scroll bars and the browse buttons, as shown in Figure 2-10.

USE THE SCROLL BARS

There are two scroll bars, one for moving vertically within the document, and one for moving horizontally. These are only displayed when your text is too wide or too long to be completely displayed on the screen. Each scroll bar contains four controls for getting you where you want to go. Using the vertical scroll bar, you may:

- **Move upward by one line** by clicking the upward pointing scroll arrow.

- **Move upward or downward** by dragging the scroll button in the corresponding direction.

- **Move by one screen's height** by clicking in the scroll bar above the scroll button to move towards the beginning of the document, or by clicking below the scroll bar to move towards the end of the document.

- **Move downward by one line** by clicking the downward pointing scroll arrow.

The horizontal scroll bar has similar controls, only these are used for moving in a horizontal plane.

USE THE BROWSE BUTTONS

The browse buttons allow you to specify the type of object by which you want to browse through the document. The most obvious browse object, and the default, is a page. With that as the object, you can browse through a document going forward or back a page at a time.

Clicking the center **Select Browse Object** opens a menu of objects from which to select. By selecting one of these objects—such as a page, a heading, a comment, or an edit—you can move through the document going from one chosen object to the next. Often overlooked, this feature can be very handy. Place the pointer over the options to find out what the picture or icon represents.

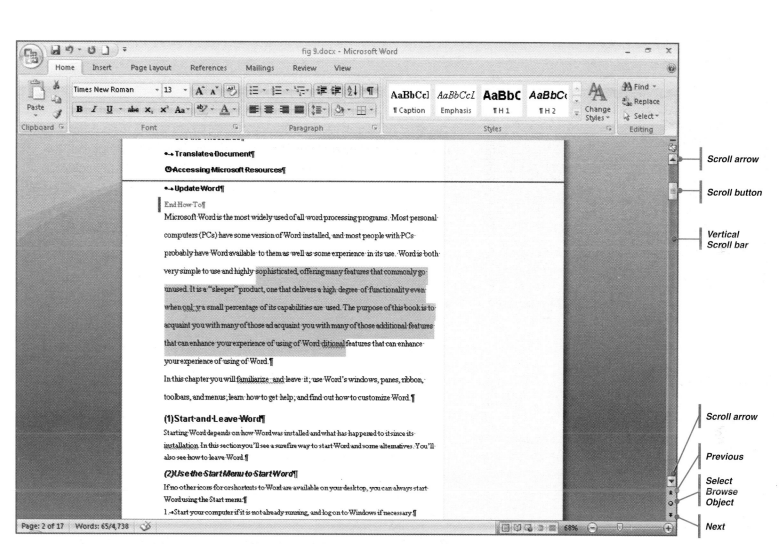

Figure 2-10: *The scroll bars and browse buttons allow you to move easily to different locations within your document.*

MOVE WITH THE KEYBOARD

These keyboard commands, used for moving around your document, also move the insertion point:

- **One character left or right** using the LEFT or RIGHT ARROW
- **One line up or down** using the UP or DOWN ARROW
- **One word left or right** using CTRL-LEFT ARROW or CTRL-RIGHT ARROW

TIP

You can generally undo the last several operations by repeatedly issuing one of the Undo commands.

NOTE

Under certain circumstances, especially while formatting, the Redo option becomes Repeat.

NOTE

You can recover deleted text using Undo in the same way you can reverse a cut or a paste.

NOTE

You select a picture by clicking it. Once selected, a picture can be copied, moved, and deleted from a document in the same way as text, using either the Windows or Office Clipboards.

- **One paragraph up or down** using CTRL-UP ARROW or CTRL-DOWN ARROW
- **To the beginning or end of a line** using HOME or END
- **To the beginning or end of a document** using CTRL-HOME or CTRL-END
- **One screen up or down** using PAGE UP or PAGE DOWN
- **To the previous or next instance of the current browse object** using CTRL-PAGE UP or CTRL-PAGE DOWN
- **To the top or bottom of the window** using CTRL-ALT-PAGE UP or CTRL-ALT-PAGE DOWN

GO TO A PARTICULAR LOCATION

The Go To command opens the dialog box, shown in Figure 2-11, that allows you to go immediately to the location of some object, such as a page, a footnote, or a table. You can open the dialog box by:

- Pressing the **F5** function key
- Pressing **CTRL-G**
- Clicking the **Home** tab, clicking **Find** in the Editing group, and clicking the **Go To** tab.
- Clicking **Select Browse Object** beneath the vertical scroll bar, and then clicking **Go To**.
- Double-clicking the left end of the status bar in the *Page x of y* area.

After opening the dialog box, select the object you want to go to from the list on the left, and then enter the number or name of the object in the text box on the right. For example, select **Page** on the left and enter <u>5</u> on the right to go to page 5.

Find and Replace Text

Often, you'll want to find something that you know is in the document, but you are not sure where, or even how many times, that item occurs. This is especially true when you want to locate names or words that are sprinkled throughout a document. For example, if you had repeatedly referred to a table on page 4 and, for some reason or another, the table had moved to page 5, you would need to search for all occurrences of "page 4" and change them to "page 5." In this example, you not only want to *find* "page 4," but you also want to *replace* it with "page 5."

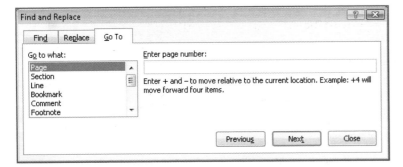

Figure 2-11: The Go To command allows you to go to a particular page as well as to other particular items within a document.

Word allows you to do a simple search for a word or phrase as well as to conduct an advanced search for parts of words, particular capitalization, and words that sound alike.

FIND TEXT—SIMPLE CASE

In the simple case where you just want to search for a word or phrase:

1. Click the **Home** tab and click **Find** in the Editing group. The Find And Replace dialog box will open.
2. Enter the word or phrase you want to search for in the Find What text box.
3. Click **Find Next**. The first occurrence in the document below the current insertion point will be highlighted, as you can see in Figure 2-12.
4. To find additional occurrences continue to click **Find Next** or press **SHIFT-F4**. When you are done (you will be told when the entire document has been searched), click Close.

FIND TEXT—ADVANCED CASE

By clicking **More** in the Find And Replace dialog box, you will find that Word provides a number of features to make your search more sophisticated (see Figure 2-13). These include specifying the direction of the search as well as the following:

- **Match Case**   Only specific capitalization of a word or phrase.
- **Find Whole Words Only**   Only whole words, so when searching for "equip" you don't get "equipment."

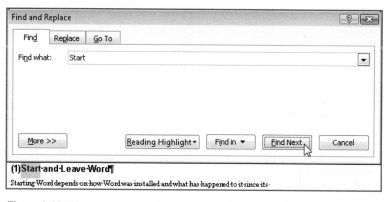

Figure 2-12: *When you search for a word or phrase, the Find command can highlight individual occurrences or all occurrences at once.*

- **Use Wildcards**   Words or phrases that contain a set of characters by using wildcards to represent the unknown part of the word or phrase (see the "Using Wildcards" QuickSteps).
- **Sounds Like**   Words that sound alike but are spelled differently (homonyms).
- **Find All Word Forms**   A word in all its forms—noun, adjective, verb, or adverb (for example, ski, skier, and skiing).
- **Match Prefix or Match Suffix**   Words containing a common prefix or suffix.
- **Ignore Punctuation Characters**   Words without regard for any punctuation. This is especially needed when a word might be followed by a comma or period.

If you want your search to find just the word "ton" and not words like "Washington" or "tonic," you can either put a space at both the beginning and end of the word in Find What (" ton "), or click **More** in the Find And Replace dialog box and then click **Find Whole Words Only**. The latter is the preferred way to do this because putting a space after the word would not find the word followed by a comma or a period.

If you find that the Find and Replace dialog box is getting in the way after finding the first occurrence of a word or phrase, you can close the dialog box and use **SHIFT-F4** to find the remaining occurrences. Also, once you have used Find, you can close the Find and Replace dialog box and use the Find Next or Previous Browse buttons at the bottom of the vertical scroll bar to browse by Find, or you can press **CTRL-PAGE DOWN** or **CTRL-PAGE UP** to move quickly from one instance of the search term to the next.

Instead of repeatedly clicking **Find Next** to highlight each occurrence of an item, in the Find and Replace dialog box, you can click **Reading Highlight | Highlight All | Find In | Main Document | Find Next**. This will highlight all occurrences of what you are searching for and allow you to observe them, but as soon as you click anywhere in the document, the highlights will all go away. If you press **SHIFT-F4, CTRL-PAGE UP, CTRL-PAGE DOWN**, or one of the browse buttons, you will select the next occurrence, but all occurrences will remain highlighted.

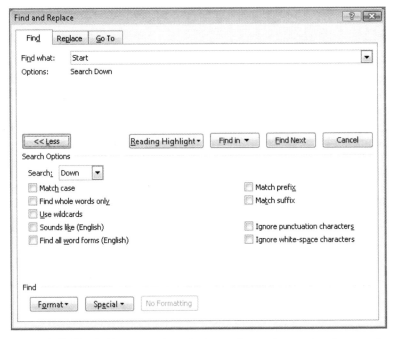

Figure 2-13: *Word offers a number of advanced ways to search a document.*

- **Ignore White-Space Characters**   Characters such as spaces, tabs, and indents.

- **Format**   Specific types of formatting, such as for fonts, paragraphs, etc.

- **Special**   Specific special characters, such as paragraph marks, em dashes (—), or nonbreaking spaces (can't be the first or last character in a line).

REPLACE TEXT

Often, when searching for a word or phrase, you want to replace it with something else. Word lets you use all the features of Find and then replace what is found.

1. Click the **Home** tab and click **Replace** in the Editing group. The Find And Replace dialog box will open.

2. Enter the word or phrase you want to search for in the Find What text box.

Figure 2-14: *You can replace text either on a one-by-one basis or universally.*

3. Enter the word or phrase you want to replace the found item(s) in the Replace With text box, as you can see in Figure 2-14.

4. Click **Find Next**. The first occurrence in the document below the current insertion point will be highlighted.

5. You have these options:

   - Click **Replace** if you want to replace this instance with the text you entered. Word replaces this instance and automatically finds the next instance.

   - Click **Find Next** if you don't want to replace the text that was found and find the next occurrence.

   - Click **Replace All**, if you want to replace all occurrences of the word you found.

6. When you are done, click Close.

Complete and Save a Document

When you have completed a document or feel that you have done enough to warrant saving it and putting it aside for a while, you should go though a completion procedure that includes checking the spelling and grammar, determining where to save the document, and then actually saving it.

Check Spelling and Grammar

By default, Word checks spelling and grammar as you type the document, so it might be that these functions have already been performed. You can tell if Word is checking the spelling and grammar by noticing if Word automatically places a wavy red line under words it thinks are misspelled and if a wavy green line appears beneath words and phrases whose grammar is questioned. You can turn off automatic spell and grammar checking. You can also have these features run using an array of options. You can also ask Word to perform a spell and/or grammar check whenever you want—most importantly, when you are completing a document. when only a small percentage

QUICKFACTS

USING WILDCARDS

Wildcards are characters that are used to represent one or more characters in a word or phrase when searching for items with similar or unknown parts. You must select the **Use Wildcards** checkbox, and then type the wildcard characters along with the known characters in the Find What text box. For example, typing **page ?** will find both "page 4" and "page 5." The "?" stands for any single character.

Find what:	page ?
Options:	Search Down, Use Wildcards

Table 2-3 shows the characters Word has defined as wildcard characters when used in the Find command to replace one or more characters.

NOTE

When searching with wildcards, both Find Whole Words Only and Match Case are turned on automatically and cannot be turned off; however, the checkboxes for these features are cleared but dim.

CHARACTER	USED TO REPLACE	EXAMPLE	WILL FIND	WON'T FIND
?	A single character	Page ?	Page 4 or Page 5	Page1
*	Any number of characters	Page *	Page 4 and Page 5	Pages1-5 (no space)
<	The beginning of a word	<(corp)	Corporate	Incorporate
>	The end of a word	(ton)>	Washington	Toner
\	A wildcard character	What\?	What?	What is
[cc]	One of a list of characters	B[io]b	Bib or Bob	Babe
[c-c]	One in a range of characters	[l-t]ook	look or took	Book
[!c-c]	Any character except one in the range	[!k-n]ook	book or took	Look
{n}	n copies of the previous character	Lo{2}	Loo or Look	Lot
{n,}	n or more copies of the previous character	Lo{1,}	Lot or Look	Late
{n,m}	n to m copies of the previous character	150{1,3}	150 to 1500	15
@	Any number of copies of the previous character	150@	15, 150, or 1500	1400

Table 2-3: Wildcard Characters Used in Find

CONTROL SPELL AND GRAMMAR CHECKING

Word provides a number of settings that allow you to control how spelling and grammar checking is performed.

1. Click the **Office button**, click **Word Options**, and click the **Proofing** option on the left. The dialog box shown in Figure 2-15 will be displayed.

2. If you wish to turn off automatic spell checking, uncheck **Check Spelling As You Type**.

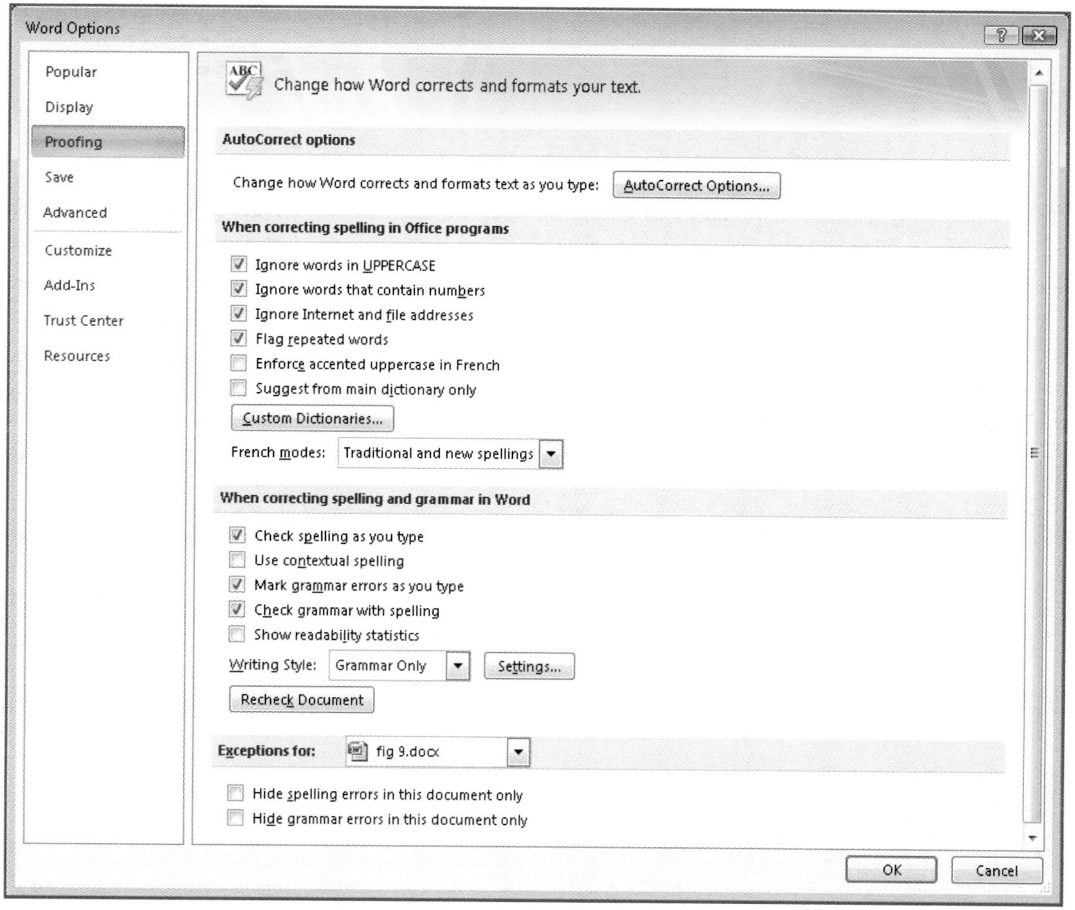

Word Options

ABC ✓ Change how Word corrects and formats your text.

- Popular
- Display
- **Proofing**
- Save
- Advanced
- Customize
- Add-Ins
- Trust Center
- Resources

AutoCorrect options

Change how Word corrects and formats text as you type: [AutoCorrect Options...]

When correcting spelling in Office programs

☑ Ignore words in UPPERCASE
☑ Ignore words that contain numbers
☑ Ignore Internet and file addresses
☑ Flag repeated words
☐ Enforce accented uppercase in French
☐ Suggest from main dictionary only

[Custom Dictionaries...]

French modes: [Traditional and new spellings ▼]

When correcting spelling and grammar in Word

☑ Check spelling as you type
☐ Use contextual spelling
☑ Mark grammar errors as you type
☑ Check grammar with spelling
☐ Show readability statistics

Writing Style: [Grammar Only ▼] [Settings...]

[Recheck Document]

Exceptions for: 📄 fig 9.docx [▼]

☐ Hide spelling errors in this document only
☐ Hide grammar errors in this document only

[OK] [Cancel]

*Figure 2-15: **By default, Word checks spelling and grammar as you type, but you can disable those utilities in the Tools Options dialog box.***

3. If you wish to turn off the automatic grammar checking, uncheck **Mark Grammar Errors As You Type**.

4. Click **Settings** under Grammar to set the rules by which the grammar checking is done.

5. Click **OK** twice to close both the Grammar Settings and Options dialog boxes.

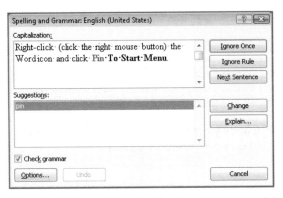

Figure 2-16: *The spelling checker is a gift to those of us who are "spelling challenged"!*

NOTE

In the Spelling Grammar English dialog box, you may not see Ignore All, Change All, or Autocorrect at first, as seen in Figure 2-16. Instead you may see Ignore Rule, which allows you to ignore the rule that was seemingly violated by the reported error. You may also see Explain, which allows you to see further explanation of why the word or phrase was flagged as an error. When a rule is not the cause of the flagged error, the Ignore All, Change All, and Autocorrect will be displayed.

INITIATE SPELL AND GRAMMAR CHECKING

To manually initiate spell and grammar checking:

1. Click the **Review** tab and click **Spelling and Grammar** in the Proofing group. The Spelling and Grammar dialog box will open and begin checking. When a word is found that Word believes might not be correct, the dialog box will display both the perceived error and one or more suggestions for its correction (see Figure 2-16).

2. You have these options for flagged spellings:

   - If you wish not to correct the perceived error, click **Ignore Once** for this one instance, or click **Ignore All** for all instances. (See the Note this page for an explanation of why you may not see Ignore All when the dialog box first displays.)

   - Click **Change** for this one instance, or click **Change All** for all instances if you wish to replace the perceived error with the highlighted suggestion. If one of the other suggestions is a better choice, click it before clicking Change or Change All.

   - Click **Add To Dictionary** if you want Word to add your spelling of the word to the dictionary to be used for future documents. If you want Word to automatically correct this misspelling with the selected correction every time you type the incorrect word, click **AutoCorrect**. (See Chapter 4 for more on AutoCorrect.)

   - Click **Options** to display the Word Options Proofing dialog box where you can reset many of the spelling and grammar checking rules.

   - Click **Undo** to reverse the last action.

3. When Word has completed checking the spelling and grammar, you'll see a message to that effect. Click **OK**.

Save a Document for the First Time

The first time you save a document, you have to specify where you want to save—that is, the disk drive and the folder or subfolder in which you want it saved. Since this is your first time saving the file, the Save As dialog box will open so that you can specify the location and enter a file name.

1. Click the **Office button**, and click **Save As**.

2. Click the icon on the left for the major area (for example, Favorite Links or Folders) in which the file is to be saved.

SAVING A DOCUMENT

After you have initially saved a document and specified its location, you can quickly save it whenever you wish.

SAVE A DOCUMENT

To save a file:

- Click the **Office button** and click **Save**.

  –Or–

- Click the **Save** icon in the Quick Access Toolbar.

  –Or–

- Press **CTRL-S**.

SAVE A COPY OF YOUR DOCUMENT

When you save a document under a different name, you create a copy of it.

1. Click the **Office button**, and click **Save As**.

2. In the Save As dialog box, enter the new name in the File Name text box. Then, open the **Save In** list box and identify the path to the folder you want.

3. Click **Save**.

SAVE A DOCUMENT AS A TEMPLATE

To save a newly created document as a template from which to create new documents:

1. Click the **Office button** and point to **Save As**. From the pop-up menu, click **Word Template**. In the **Save As Type** drop-down list box, verify that it is the type for a **Word Template (*.dotx)**.

2. Enter a name (without an extension) for your template in the File Name text box.

3. Click **Save**.

3. If you want to store your new document in a folder that already exists in the major area, double-click that folder to open it.

4. If you want to store your new document in a new folder, click the **New Folder** icon in the toolbar, type the name of the new folder, and click **OK**. The new folder will open. (You can create yet another new folder within that folder using the same steps.)

5. When you have the folder(s) open in which you want to store the document, enter the name of the document, as shown in Figure 2-17, and then click **Save**.

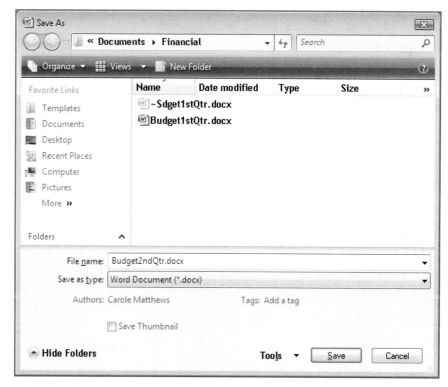

Figure 2-17: When saving a file, you don't have to enter a file extension. The ".docx" extension will be supplied by Word automatically.

TIP

As good as Word's automatic saving is, it is a great idea to manually save your document frequently (like a couple of times an hour). Doing this can save you from the frustration of working several hours on a document only to lose it.

NOTE

When you first open Word, the save interval is set to a default of 10 minutes.

TIP

AutoRecover is a reserve parachute that you don't want to test unless you must. AutoRecover gives you the impression that you have lost your work. In fact, if you follow the instructions and choose to recover the AutoRecover document, you may not lose anything—at most, you might lose only the very last thing that you did.

Save a Document Automatically

It is important to save a document periodically as you work. Having Word save it automatically will reduce the chance of losing data in case of a power failure or other interruption.

1. Click the **Office button**, click **Word Options,** and click the **Save** option on the left.

2. Beneath Save Documents, click **Save AutoRecover Info Every** to place a checkmark next to it.

3. In the Minutes box, use the arrows to select or enter a time for how often Word is to save your document.

4. Click **OK** to close the dialog box.

Chapter 3
Formatting a Document

Plain, unformatted text conveys information, but not nearly as effectively as well-formatted text, as you can see by the two examples in Figure 3-1. Word provides numerous ways to format your text. Most fall under the categories of text formatting, paragraph formatting, and page formatting, which are discussed in the following sections of this chapter. Additional formatting that can be applied at the document level is discussed in Chapter 4.

This chapter discusses the direct, or manual, application of formatting. Much of the character and paragraph formatting discussed in this chapter is commonly applied using styles that combine a number of different individual formatting steps, saving significant time over direct formatting. (Styles are discussed in Chapter 4.) Direct formatting is usually applied only to a small amount of text that needs formatting different from its style.

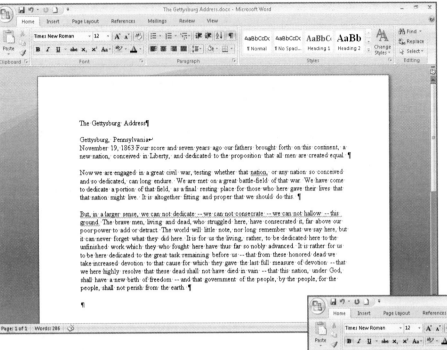

Figure 3-1: Formatting makes text both more readable and more pleasing to the eye.

Format Text

Text formatting covers the formatting that you can apply to individual characters and includes selection of fonts, font size, color, character spacing, and capitalization.

Apply Character Formatting

Character formatting can be applied using keyboard shortcuts, the Home tab on the ribbon, and a Formatting dialog box. Of these, clicking the **Home** tab and clicking the **Font dialog launcher** to open the Font dialog box (see Figure 3-2) provides a comprehensive selection of character formatting

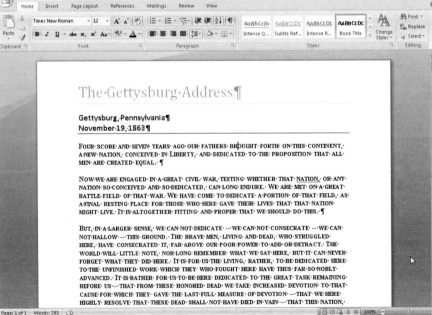

Font dialog box

Font | **Character Spacing**

Font: Times New Roman

Font style:	Size:
Bold	12
Regular	8
Italic	9
Bold	10
Bold Italic	11
	12

Tahoma
Teletext 43
Teletext 83
Tempus Sans ITC
Times New Roman

Font color: Automatic
Underline style: (none)
Underline color: Automatic

Effects

- ☐ Strikethrough
- ☐ Double strikethrough
- ☐ Superscript
- ☐ Subscript
- ☐ Shadow
- ☐ Outline
- ☐ Emboss
- ☐ Engrave
- ☑ Small caps
- ☐ All caps
- ☐ Hidden

Preview

BROUGHT

This is a TrueType font. This font will be used on both printer and screen.

Default... | OK | Cancel

Figure 3-2: The Font dialog box provides the most complete set of character formatting controls.

and spacing alternatives. In the sections that immediately follow, the Font dialog box can be used to accomplish the task being discussed. Keyboard shortcuts and the Font and Paragraph groups on the Home tab (see Figure 3-3) often provide a quicker way to accomplish the same task, and keyboard shortcuts (summarized in Table 3-1) allow you to keep your hands on the keyboard.

MINI-FORMATTING TOOLBAR

In Word 2007, when you right-click on text, you get both a context menu and a mini-formatting toolbar. When you select text and place your pointer on the selection the mini-formatting toolbar also appears. This toolbar has several of the buttons available in the Home tab's Font and Paragraph groups. In the next sections when we point out that you can use the Home tab Font group to accomplish a function, it is likely that you can do the same function with the mini-formatting toolbar by selecting text or right-clicking on it. However, to reduce repetition, using the mini-formatting toolbar will not be stressed further in this chapter.

SELECT A FONT

A *font* is a set of characters that share a particular design, which is called a *typeface*. When you install Windows, and again when you install Office, a number of fonts are automatically installed on your computer. You can see the

NOTE

Prior to applying formatting, you must select the text to be formatted. Chapter 2 contains an extensive section on selecting text.

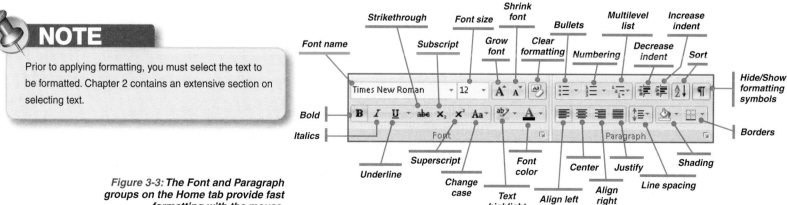

Figure 3-3: The Font and Paragraph groups on the Home tab provide fast formatting with the mouse.

APPLY FORMATTING	SHORTCUT KEYS	APPLY FORMATTING	SHORTCUT KEYS
Align left	CTRL-L	Indent paragraph	CTRL-M
Align right	CTRL-R	Italic	CTRL-I
All caps	CTRL-SHIFT-A	Justify paragraph	CTRL-J
Bold	CTRL-B	Line space—single	CTRL-1
Bulleted list	CTRL-SHIFT-L	Line space—1.5	CTRL-5
Center	CTRL-E	Line space—double	CTRL-2
Change case	SHIFT-F3	Normal style	CTRL-SHIFT-N
Copy format	CTRL-SHIFT-C	Paste format	CTRL-SHIFT-V
Decrease font size	CTRL-SHIFT-<	Reset character formatting	CTRL-SPACEBAR
Increase font size	CTRL-SHIFT->	Reset paragraph formatting	CTRL-Q
Decrease font size one point	CTRL-[	Small caps	CTRL-SHIFT-K
Increase font size one point	CTRL-]	Subscript	CTRL-=
Open font dialog box	CTRL-D	Superscript	CTRL-SHIFT-=
Font name	CTRL-SHIFT-F	Symbol font	CTRL-SHIFT-Q
Hang paragraph	CTRL-T	Un-hang paragraph	CTRL-SHIFT-T
Heading level 1	ALT-CTRL-1	Un-indent paragraph	CTRL-SHIFT-M
Heading level 2	ALT-CTRL-2	Underline continuous	CTRL-U
Heading level 3	ALT-CTRL-3	Underline double	CTRL-SHIFT-D
Hidden character	CTRL-SHIFT-H	Underline word	CTRL-SHIFT-W

*Table 3-1: **Formatting Shortcut Keys***

fonts on your computer by clicking the down arrow next to the font name in the Home tab Font group and then scrolling the list (your most recently used fonts are at the top, followed by all fonts listed alphabetically). You can also see the list of fonts in the Font dialog box, where you can select a font in the Font list and see what it looks like in the Preview window at the bottom of the dialog box.

TIP

You can also open the Font dialog box by right-clicking the selected text you want to format and then clicking **Font** or by clicking the **Font dialog launcher** in the Font group.

NOTE

Several types of fonts are included in the default set that is installed with Windows and Office. Alphabetic fonts come in two varieties: serif fonts, such as **Times New Roman** or **Century Schoolbook**, with the little ends or *serifs* on the ends of each of the character's lines, and *sans serif* ("without serifs") fonts, such as **Arial** and **Century Gothic**, without the ends. Sans serif fonts are generally used for headings and lists, while serif fonts are generally used for body text. Finally, there are symbol fonts, such as Wingdings and Webdings, with many special characters, such as smiling faces ("smilies"), arrows, and pointing fingers.

TIP

At the top of the Font Size list box you can type in half point sizes, such as 10.5, as well as sizes that are not on the list, such as 15.

By default, the Calibri font is used for body text in all new documents using the default Normal template. To change this font:

1. Select the text to be formatted (see Chapter 2).
2. Click the **Home** tab and click the **Font** down arrow in the Font group. Scroll the list until you see the font you want, and then click that font.

APPLY BOLD OR ITALIC STYLE

Fonts come in four styles: regular (or "Roman"), bold, italic, and bold-italic. The default is, of course, regular, yet fonts such as Arial Black and Eras Bold appear bold. To make fonts bold, italic, or bold-italic:

1. Select the text to be formatted (see Chapter 2).
2. Press **CTRL-B** to make it bold, and/or press **CTRL-I** to make it italic.

   –Or–

   Click the **Bold** icon in the Font group, and/or click the **Italic** icon.

B *I*

CHANGE FONT SIZE

Font size is measured in *points*, which is the height of a character, not its width. For most fonts, the width varies with the character, the letter "i" taking less room than "w." (The Courier New font is an exception, with all characters having the same width.) There are 72 points in an inch. The default font size is 11 points for body text, with standard headings varying from 11 to 14 points. For smaller print 8-point type is common, and below 6 point is unreadable. To change the font size of your text:

1. Select the text to be formatted (see Chapter 2).
2. In the Home tab, click the **Font Size** down arrow in the Font group, scroll the list until you see the font size you want, and then click that font.

   –Or–

   Press **CTRL-SHIFT-<** to decrease the font size, or press **CTRL-SHIFT->** to increase the font size.

12
8
9
10
11
12
14
16
18
20
22

UNDERLINE TEXT

Several forms of underlining can be applied:

1. Select the text to be formatted (see Chapter 2).

2. Click the **Underline** down arrow in the Home tab Font group and click the type of underline you want.

    –Or–

    Press **CTRL-U** to apply a continuous underline under the entire selection.

    –Or–

    Press **CTRL-SHIFT-W** to apply an underline under each word in the selection.

    –Or–

    Press **CTRL-SHIFT-D** to apply a double underline under the entire selection.

USE FONT COLOR

To change the color of text:

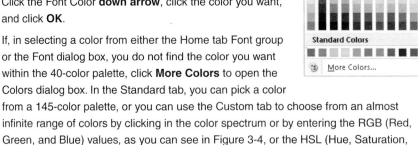

1. Select the text to be formatted (see Chapter 2).

2. Click the **Home** tab, and click **Font Color** in the Font group to apply the current selected color.

    –Or–

    Click the **Font dialog launcher** for the Font dialog box. Click the Font Color **down arrow**, click the color you want, and click **OK**.

3. If, in selecting a color from either the Home tab Font group or the Font dialog box, you do not find the color you want within the 40-color palette, click **More Colors** to open the Colors dialog box. In the Standard tab, you can pick a color from a 145-color palette, or you can use the Custom tab to choose from an almost infinite range of colors by clicking in the color spectrum or by entering the RGB (Red, Green, and Blue) values, as you can see in Figure 3-4, or the HSL (Hue, Saturation, and Luminescent) values.

TIP

The Underline Style drop-down list in the Font dialog box, as with the Underline button in the ribbon, contains underline choices beyond those the other methods provide—dotted, wavy, and so on.

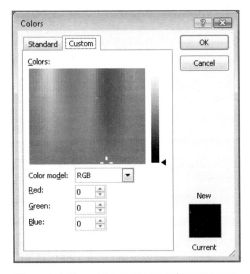

Figure 3-4: **You can create any color you want in the Custom tab of the Colors dialog box.**

RESET TEXT

Figure 3-5 shows some of the formatting that has been discussed. All of those can be reset to the Plain Text, or the default formatting. To reset text to default settings:

1. Select the text to be formatted (see Chapter 2).

2. Click **Clear Formatting** in the Home tab Font group.

-Or-

Press **CTRL-SPACEBAR**. (This will not reset a Font Size change if it is the only difference with the default.)

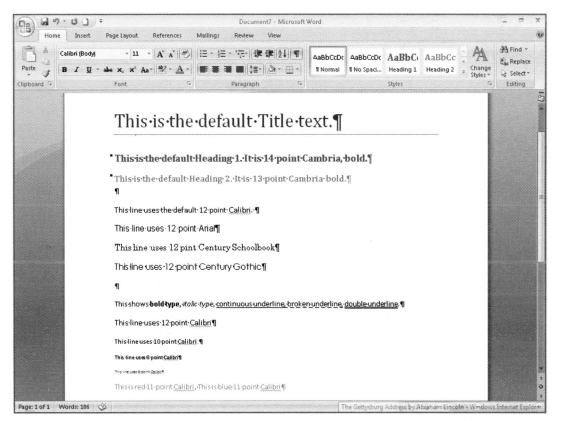

Figure 3-5: Character formatting must be applied judiciously or it will detract from the appearance of a document.

USING THE FONT DIALOG BOX

Although you can apply many effects, such as superscript, emboss, and small caps, using the Fonts group in the Home tab, you have an alternative way to make these changes. Here is how you can use the Font dialog box, shown in Figure 3-6, to change text effects.

1. Select the text you want to change the formatting for.

2. Click the **Home** tab and click the **Font Dialog Launcher** in the Font group to open the Font dialog box. If it isn't already selected, click the **Font** tab.

3. In the Effects area, click the options that you think you want to apply (some are mutually exclusive, such as Superscript and Subscript).

4. Check the results in the Preview area. When you are satisfied, click **OK**.

NOTE

Character spacing, especially kerning, is predominantly used when you are creating something like a brochure, flyer, or newspaper ad in which you want to achieve a typeset look.

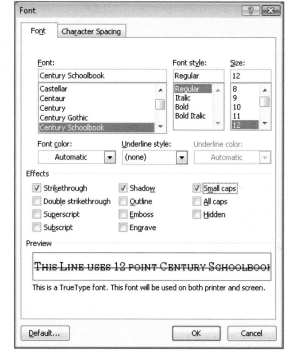

Figure 3-6: The Font dialog box is an alternative way to add text effects, such as strikethrough, shadow, and small caps.

Set Character Spacing

Character spacing in this case is the amount of space between characters on a single line. Word gives you the chance to increase and decrease character spacing as well as scale the size of selected text, raise and lower vertically the position of text on the line, and determine when to apply kerning (how the space for certain characters such as "A" and "V" can overlap) in the Character Spacing tab of the Font dialog box. To apply character spacing:

1. Select the text to be formatted.

2. Click the **Home** tab, click the **Font Dialog Launcher** to open the Font dialog box, and click the **Character Spacing** tab. You have these options:

   • **Scale**   To select the percentage scale factor that you want to apply. (This is not recommended. It is better to change the font size so as not to distort the font.)

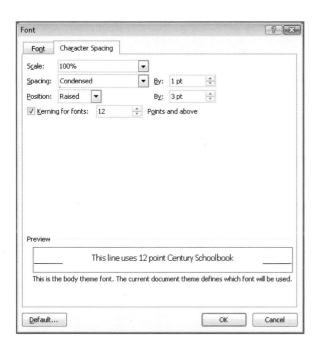

Figure 3-7: *The spacing of text can have as much to do with its appearance as the choice of font.*

- **Spacing**   To select the change in spacing (Expanded or Condensed) that you want and the amount of that change.

- **Position**   To select the change in position (Raised or Lowered) that you want and the amount of that change.

- **Kerning For Fonts**   To determine if you want to apply kerning rules and the point size at which you want to do that.

3. Check the results in the Preview area, an example of which is shown in Figure 3-7. When you are satisfied, click **OK**.

Change Capitalization

You can, of course, capitalize a character you are typing by pressing and holding **SHIFT** while you type. You can also press **CAPS LOCK** to have every letter that you type be capitalized, and then press **CAPS LOCK** again to turn off capitalization. You can also change the capitalization of existing text:

1. Select the text whose capitalization you want to change.

2. In the Home tab, in the Font group, click **Change Case**. Select one of these options:

- Click **Sentence Case** to capitalize the first character of every selected sentence.

- Click **Lowercase** to display all selected words in lowercase.

- Click **UPPERCASE** to display all selected words in all caps. All characters of every selected word will be capitalized.

- Click **Capitalize Each Word** to put a leading cap on each selected word.

- Click **tOGGLE cASE** to change all lowercase words into uppercase and uppercase words into lowercase.

Create a Drop Cap

A *drop cap* is an enlarged capital letter at the beginning of a paragraph that extends down over two or more lines of text. To create a drop cap:

1. Select the character or word that you want to be formatted as a drop cap.

2. Click the **Insert** tab, and click **Drop Cap** in the Text group. A context menu will open. You have these choices:

- Click **Dropped** to have the first lettered dropped within the paragraph text.
- Click **In Margin** to set the capital letter off in the margin.
- Click **Drop Cap Options** to see further options. You can change the font, specify how many lines will be dropped (3 is the default), and specify how far from the text the dropped cap will be placed. Click OK to close the Drop Cap dialog box.

The paragraph will be reformatted around the enlarged capital letter. To the right are the two options of putting the dropped cap in the paragraph or in the margin.

NOTE

To remove a drop cap, select the character or word, click **Drop Cap** in the Insert tab Text group, and click **None** from the context menu.

Format a Paragraph

Paragraph formatting, which you can apply to any paragraph, is used to manage alignment, indentation, line spacing, bullets or numbering, and borders. In Word, a paragraph consists of a paragraph mark (created by pressing **ENTER**) and any text or objects that appear between that paragraph mark and the previous paragraph mark. A paragraph can be empty, or it can contain anything from a single character to as many characters as you care to enter.

Set Paragraph Alignment

Four types of paragraph alignment are available in Word (see Figure 3-8): left aligned, centered, right aligned, and justified. Left aligned, right aligned, and centered are self-explanatory. Justified means that the text in a paragraph is spread out between the left and right page margins. Word does this by adding space between words, except for the last line of a paragraph. To apply paragraph alignment:

1. Click in the paragraph you want to align. (You don't need to select the entire paragraph.)

TIP

You can also open the Paragraph dialog box by right-clicking the paragraph you want to format and clicking **Paragraph**.

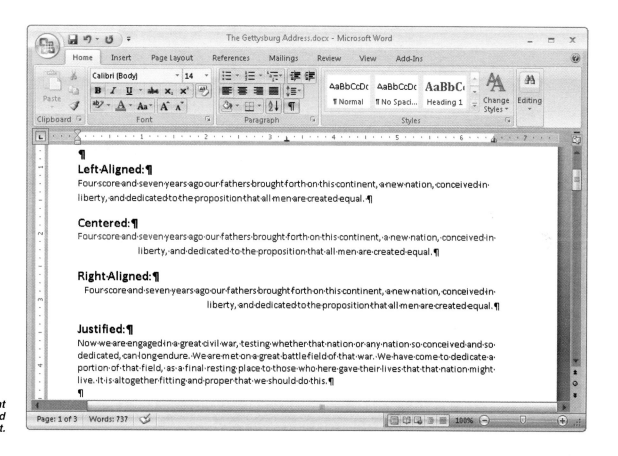

Figure 3-8: Paragraph alignment provides both eye appeal and separation of text.

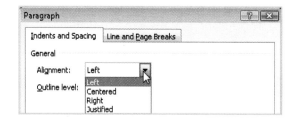

2. For left alignment, press **CTRL-L**; for right alignment, press **CTRL-R**; for centered, press **CTRL-E**; and for justified, press **CTRL-J**.

–Or–

In the Home tab Paragraph group, click the **Align Left**, **Center**, **Align Right**, or **Justify** buttons respectively, depending on which you want to do.

–Or–

In the Home tab Paragraph group, click the **Paragraph Dialog Launcher** to open the Paragraph dialog box. In the Indents And Spacing tab, click the **down arrow** opposite Alignment, click the type of alignment you want, and click **OK**.

Indent a Paragraph

Indenting a paragraph in Word means to:

- Move either the left or right edge (or both) of the paragraph inward towards the center
- Move the left side of the first line of a paragraph inward toward the center
- Move the left side of the first line of a paragraph leftward, away from the center, for a *hanging indent*

See Figure 3-9.

CHANGE THE LEFT INDENT

To move the left edge of an entire paragraph to the right:

1. Click in the paragraph to select it.

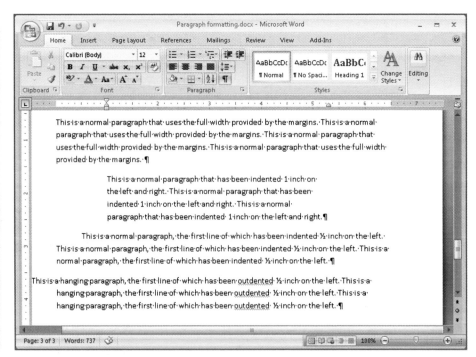

Figure 3-9: Indenting allows you to separate a block of text visually.

---

2. In the Home tab Paragraph group, click **Increase Indent** one or more times to indent the left edge 1/2-inch each time.

–Or–

Press **CTRL-M** one or more times to indent the left edge 1/2-inch each time.

–Or–

In the Page Layout tab Paragraph group, click the **Left Indent** spinner.

–Or–

Open the Paragraph dialog box. In the Home tab Paragraph group, click the **Paragraph Dialog Launcher.** In the Indents And Spacing tab under Indentation opposite Left, click the spinner's increase arrow (up) until you get the amount of indentation you want, and then click **OK**.

REMOVE A LEFT INDENT

To move the left edge of an entire paragraph back to the left:

1. Click in the paragraph to select it.

2. In the Home tab, click **Decrease Indent** in the Paragraph group one or more times to un-indent the left edge 1/2-inch each time.

–Or–

Press **CTRL-SHIFT-M** one or more times to un-indent the left edge 1/2-inch each time.

–Or–

In the Home tab Paragraph group click **Paragraph Dialog Launcher** to open the Paragraph dialog box. In the Indents And Spacing tab, under Indentation opposite Left, click the decrease arrow (down) until you get the amount of indentation you want, and then click **OK**.

CHANGE THE RIGHT INDENT

To move the right edge of an entire paragraph to the left:

1. Click in the paragraph to select it.

2. In the Page Layout tab Paragraph group, click the **Right Indent** spinner.

–Or-

Open the Paragraph dialog box. In the Home tab Paragraph group, click the **Paragraph Dialog Launcher**. In the Indents And Spacing tab under Indentation opposite Right, click the increase arrow (up) until you get the amount of indentation you want, and then click **OK**.

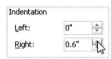

INDENT THE FIRST LINE

To move the right edge of an entire paragraph to the left:

1. Click in the paragraph to select it.

2. Open the Paragraph dialog box. In the Home tab Paragraph group, click the **Paragraph Dialog Launcher**. In the Indents And Spacing tab under Indentation, click the **Special** down arrow and click **First Line**. Click the **By** spinner to set the amount of indentation you want, and then click **OK**.

MAKE A HANGING INDENT

To indent all of a paragraph except the first line:

1. Click in the paragraph to select it.

2. Press **CTRL-T** one or more times to indent the left edge of all but the first line 1/2-inch each time.

   –Or–

   Open the Paragraph dialog box. In the Home tab Paragraph group, click the **Paragraph Dialog Launcher**. In the Indents And Spacing tab, under Indentation, click the **Special** down arrow, and select **Hanging**. Enter the amount of the indent, and click **OK**.

REMOVE A HANGING INDENT

To un-indent all but the first line of a paragraph:

1. Click in the paragraph to select it.

2. Press **CTRL-SHIFT-T** one or more times to un-indent the left edge of all but the first line 1/2-inch each time.

   –Or–

TIP

You can reset to the default all paragraph formatting, including indents and hanging indents, by pressing **CTRL-Q**.

QUICKSTEPS

USING THE RULER FOR INDENTS

You can use the horizontal ruler for setting tabs and indents.

DISPLAY THE RULER

To display the ruler:

1. Click the **View** tab.

2. In the Show/Hide group, click **Ruler**. A vertical and horizontal ruler will be displayed on the top and left side of the document window.

   –Or–

   Click **View Rulers** at the top of the vertical scroll bar.

SET PARAGRAPH LEFT INDENT

To move the whole paragraph to the left:

1. Click or select the paragraph to be indented.

2. Drag the **Left Indent box** where you want the paragraph moved.

SET RIGHT SIDE INDENT

To move the right side of the paragraph to the left:

1. Click or select the paragraph to be indented.

2. Drag the **Right Indent tab** on the right of the ruler to the left where you want the paragraph moved.

Continued ...

Open the Paragraph dialog box. In the Home tab Paragraph group, click the **Paragraph Dialog Launcher**. In the Indents And Spacing tab, under Indentation, click the **Special** down arrow, and select **None**. Click **OK**.

Determine Line and Paragraph Spacing

The vertical spacing of text is determined by the amount of space between lines, the amount of space added before and after a paragraph, and where you break lines and pages.

SET LINE SPACING

The amount of space between lines is most often set in terms of the line height, with *single-spacing* being one times the current line height, *double-spacing* being twice the current line height, and so on. You can also specify line spacing in points, as you do the size of type. Single-spacing is just under 14 points for 12-point type. To set line spacing for an entire paragraph:

1. Click in the paragraph you want to set the line spacing for.

2. In the Home tab Paragraph group, click the **Line Spacing** down arrow, and then click the line spacing, in terms of lines, that you want to use.

–Or–

Press **CTRL-1** for single-spacing, press **CTRL-5** for one and one-half line spacing, and press **CTRL-2** for double-spacing.

–Or–

USING THE RULER FOR INDENTS

(Continued)

SET FIRST LINE INDENT OR HANGING INDENT

To set the first line to be either indented to the right or left of the rest of the paragraph, or to create a hanging indent:

1. Click or select the paragraph to be indented.

   • To indent the first line, drag the top marker, the First Line Indent on the left of the ruler, to the right or left of where you want the first line moved.

   Hanging Indent ┃━━┫ ┃━ **First Line Indent**

   • To create a hanging indent, drag the lower marker, the Hanging Indent on the left of the ruler, to the right where you want the paragraph, except for the first line, to be moved.

NOTE

To specify a particular amount of space between lines other than a number of lines, in the Paragraph dialog box select **Exactly** for the Line Spacing and then enter or select the number of points to use between lines. With 12-point type, single spacing is about 14 points, one and one-half line spacing (1.5) is about 21 points, and so on. With 11-point type, single spacing is about 12 points.

CAUTION

If you reduce the line spacing below the size of the type (below 12 points for 12 point type, for example) the lines will begin to overlap and become hard to read.

In the Home tab Paragraph group, click the **Paragraph Dialog Launcher** to open the Paragraph dialog box. In the Indents And Spacing tab under Spacing, click the **Line Spacing** down arrow and from the menu select the line spacing you want to use, as shown in Figure 3-10. Click **OK**.

ADD SPACE BETWEEN PARAGRAPHS

In addition to specifying space between lines, you can add extra space at the beginning and end of paragraphs. Many people simply add an extra blank line between paragraphs, but it does not always look that good. If you are using single spacing, leaving a blank line will leave an extra 14 points (with 12-point type) between paragraphs. Common paragraph spacing is to leave 3 points before the paragraph and 6 points afterward, so if you have two

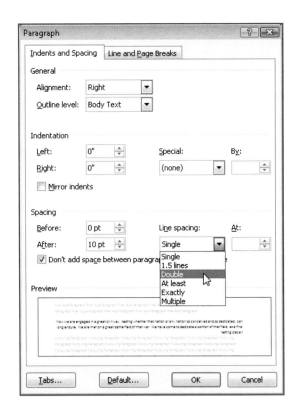

*Figure 3-10: **Line spacing is another way you can improve readability of a document.***

of these paragraphs one after the other you would have a total of 9 points, in comparison to the 14 points from an extra blank line. To add extra space between paragraphs:

1. Click in the paragraph you want to add space to.

2. In the Page Layout tab Paragraph group, click the **Spacing** spinners to set the spacing for before and after paragraphs.

–Or–

In the Home tab Paragraph group, click the **Paragraph Dialog Launcher** to open the Paragraph dialog box. In the Indents And Spacing tab under Spacing, click the **Before** Spinner or enter a number in points ("pt") for the space you want to add before the paragraph. If desired, do the same thing for the space after the paragraph. When you are ready, click **OK**.

SET LINE AND PAGE BREAKS

The vertical spacing of a document is also affected by how lines and pages are broken and how much of a paragraph you force to stay together or be with text either before or after it.

You can break a line and start a new one in two ways, depending on whether you want to create a new paragraph:

- **Create a new paragraph** by moving the insertion point to where you want to break the line and pressing **ENTER**.

- **Stay in the same paragraph** by moving the insertion point to where you want to break the line and pressing **SHIFT-ENTER**.

- **Break a page** and start a new one by pressing **CTRL-ENTER**.

  –Or–

  Click the **Insert** tab and click **Page Break** in the Pages group.

  –Or–

  Click the **Page Layout** tab and click **Breaks** in the Page Setup group. Click **Page** from the menu.

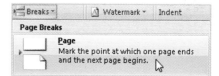

HANDLE SPLIT PAGES

When a paragraph is split over two pages, you have several ways to control how much of the paragraph is placed on which page.

1. Click in the paragraph you want to change.

2. Click the **Home** tab, click the **Paragraph Dialog Launcher**, and click the **Line And Page Breaks** tab.

3. Click the following options that are correct for your situation, and then click **OK**.

   - **Widow/Orphan Control**   Adjusts the pagination to keep at least two lines on one or both pages. For example, if you have three lines, without Widow/Orphan Control one line is on the first page and two on the second. When you turn on this control, all three lines will be placed on the second page. Widow/Orphan Control is on by default.

   - **Keep With Next**   Forces the entire paragraph to stay on the same page with the next paragraph. Keep With Next is used with paragraph headings, which you want to keep with the paragraph.

   - **Keep Lines Together**   Forces all lines of a paragraph to be on the same page. Keep Lines Together can be used for a paragraph title where you want all of it on one page.

   - **Page Break Before**   Forces a page break before the start of the paragraph. Page Break Before is used with major section headings or titles, which you want to start on a new page.

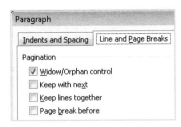

Use Numbered and Bulleted Lists

Word provides the means to automatically number or add bullets to paragraphs and then format the paragraphs as hanging indents so the numbers or bullets stick out to the left (see Figure 3-11).

CREATE A NUMBERED LIST USING AUTOCORRECT

You can create a numbered list as you type. Word will automatically format it according to your text. Word's numbered lists are particularly handy because

---

This is an example of a numbered list—in this case, numbered steps:

1. Select the text to be numbered.
2. Click the **Home** tab.
3. On the Paragraph group, click the **Numbering** button.

This is an example of a bulleted list which is used often to display:

- Items not related sequentially
- Alternative ways to do or perceive things
- Items or ideas grouped in some way

Figure 3-11: Bullets and numbering help organize thoughts into lists.

you can add or delete paragraphs in the middle of the list and have the list automatically renumber itself. To start a numbered list:

1. Press **ENTER** to start a new paragraph.

2. Type 1, either press the **SPACEBAR** twice or press **TAB**, and then type the rest of what you want in the first item of the numbered list.

3. Press **ENTER**. The number "2" automatically appears, and both the first and the new line are formatted as hanging indents. Also, the AutoCorrect lightning icon appears as you type the first line.

```
ℬ    1    this is the first line
     2    this is the second line
```

4. After typing the second item in your list, press **ENTER** once again. The number "3" automatically appears. Type the item and press **ENTER** to keep numbering the list.

5. When you are done, press **ENTER** twice. The numbering will stop and the hanging indent will be removed.

If you click on the AutoCorrect icon, you may choose to undo the automatic numbering that has already been applied, stop the automatic creation of numbered lists, and control the use of AutoCorrect (see Chapter 4 for more on AutoCorrect).

CREATE A NUMBERED OR BULLETED LIST BEFORE YOU TYPE TEXT

You can also create a numbered or bulleted list before you start typing the text they will contain:

1. Press **ENTER** to start a new paragraph.

2. In the Home tab Paragraph group, click **Numbering** to begin a numbered list, or click **Bullets** to start a bulleted list.

```
ℬ ▾ 1    this is the first line
    Undo Automatic Numbering
    Stop Automatically Creating Numbered Lists
    Control AutoFormat Options...
```

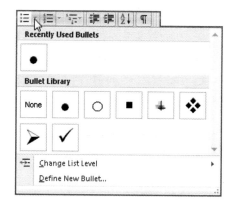

Figure 3-12: Clicking the Bullets down arrow displays a list of choices for formatting bullets. A similar menu is displayed when you click the Numbering down arrow.

3. Type the first item and press **ENTER** to start the second numbered or bulleted item with the same style as the first item. When you are done with the list, press **ENTER** twice to stop the automatic list.

–Or–

Click **Numbering** or click **Bullets** in the Home tab Paragraph group to stop the list.

CUSTOMIZE BULLETS AND NUMBERS

You saw in Figure 3-12 that Word offered seven different types of bullets. Similarly, Word offers eight different styles for numbering paragraphs. For those to whom eight choices is not enough, there is a Define New option for both bullets and numbering that includes the ability to select from hundreds of pictures and import others to use as bullets. To use custom bullets or numbering:

1. Click the **Home** tab and click the **Bullets** or **Numbering** down arrow to open the Bullets or the Numbering context menu.

2. For either Bullets or Numbering, you have these choices:

● For bullets, click **Define New Bullet** and the Define New Bullet dialog box opens (see Figure 3-13). Click **Font** and then select the font and other attributes in the dialog box for the character that you want to use, or, alternatively, click **Symbol** to select a symbol, or click **Picture** to choose from a number of picture bullets that are included in Office's clip art (Figure 3-14). To use your own picture, click **Import** and select that picture. Click **OK** to close the Picture dialog box, select both the bullet and text position, click **OK** again, and use the new bullet.

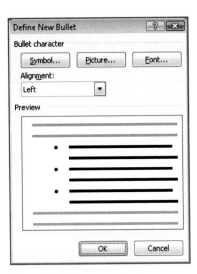

Figure 3-13: You can select any character in any font to use as a bullet.

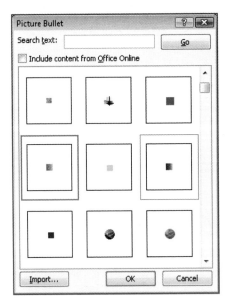

Figure 3-14: Word provides a number of pictures that can be used as bullets.

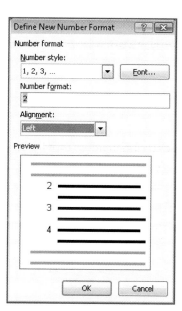

Figure 3-15: Numbered paragraphs can use numbers, letters, or even uppercase or lowercase Roman numerals.

TIP

You can switch a numbered list to a bulleted one or vice versa by selecting the list and clicking the other icon in the Home tab Paragraph group.

• For numbering, click **Define New Number Format** and the dialog box opens (see Figure 3-15). Click the **Number Style** down arrow to choose the style (numbers, capital letters, lowercase letter, Roman numerals, and so on), click **Font** to choose the numbers formatted with a particular font, and click **OK** to close the Font dialog box. Press **TAB** to select the number in the **Number Format** text box and type a sample of the number you want (delete the period for a number without the period). Click the **Alignment** down arrow to choose between Right alignment, Left, or Centered. Click **OK** to apply the customized numbering.

REMOVE NUMBERING AND BULLETING

To remove the numbering or bulleting formatting (both the numbers or bullets and the hanging indent):

1. Select the paragraphs from which you want to remove the numbering or bulleting.

2. In the Home tab Paragraph group, click **Numbering** or **Bullets**, as appropriate.

Add Borders and Shading

Borders and shading allow you to separate and call attention to text. You can place a border on any or all of the four sides of selected text, paragraphs, and pages; and you can add many varieties of shading to the space occupied by selected text, paragraphs, and pages—with or without a border around them (see Figure 3-16). You can create horizontal lines as you type, and you can add other borders from both the Formatting toolbar and the Borders and Shading dialog box.

Figure 3-16: Borders and shading can be applied to text, blank paragraphs, phrases, characters, and words.

The Gettysburg Address

Gettysburg, Pennsylvania
November 19, 1863

Four score and seven years ago our fathers brought forth on this continent, a new nation, conceived in liberty, and dedicated to the proposition that all men are created equal.

Now we are engaged in a great civil war, testing whether that nation or any nation so conceived and so dedicated, can long endure. We are met on a great battlefield of that war. We have come to dedicate a portion of that field, as a final resting place for those who here gave their lives that that nation might live. It is altogether fitting and proper that we should do this.

CREATE HORIZONTAL LINES AS YOU TYPE

Horizontal lines can be added as their own paragraph as you type:

1. Press **ENTER** to create a new paragraph.

2. Type --- (three hyphens) and press **ENTER**. A single, light horizontal line will be created between the left and right margin.

   –Or–

   Type === (three equal signs) and press **ENTER**. A double horizontal line will be created between the left and right margin.

   –Or–

   Type ___ (three underscores) and press **ENTER**. A single, heavy horizontal line will be created between the left and right margin.

Hyphens
Underscores
Equal signs

ADD BORDERS AND SHADING TO TEXT

Borders and shading can be added to any amount of text, from a character to pages:

1. Select the text for which you want to have a border or shading.

2. In the Home tab, click the **Borders** down arrow in the Paragraph group, and then select the type of border you want to apply. If you have selected less than a paragraph you can only select a four-sided box (you actually can select less, but you will get a full box).

   –Or–

   In the Home tab, click **Borders** in the Paragraph group, and click **Borders And Shading** on the context menu. The Borders and Shading dialog box will open as shown in Figure 3-17.

   - To add text or paragraph borders, click the **Borders** tab, click the type of box (Custom for less than four sides), the line style, color, and width you want. If you want less than four sides and are working with paragraphs, click the sides you want in the Preview area.

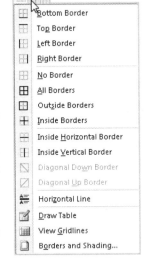

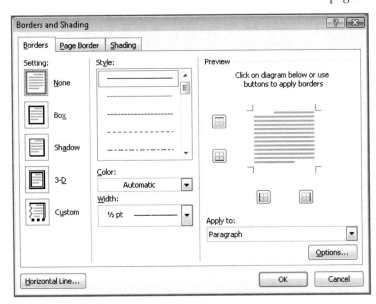

Figure 3-17: Borders can be created with many different types and widths of lines.

- Click **Options** to set the distance the border is away from the text.

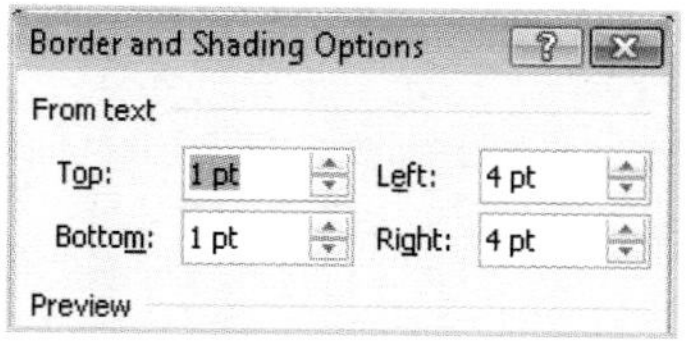

Border and Shading Options

From text

Top:	1 pt	Left:	4 pt
Bottom:	1 pt	Right:	4 pt

Preview

- To add page borders, click the **Page Border** tab, click the type of box (Custom for less than four sides), the line style, color, width you want, and any art you want to use for the border. If you want less than four sides, click the sides you want in the Preview area. Click **Options** to set the distance the border is away from either the edge of the page or the text. (Figure 3-16 contains a page border.)

- To add shading, click the **Shading** tab, click the color of shading, or fill, you want. If desired, select a pattern (this is independent of the fill), and choose whether to apply it to the entire page, paragraph, or just to the selected text.

- To add a graphic horizontal line, click **Horizontal Line** on the bottom of the dialog box, click the line you want, and click OK.

When you are done with the Borders and Shading dialog box, click **OK**.

QUICKSTEPS

TURNING ON FORMATTING MARKS

To make formatting and what is causing the spacing in a document easier to see, you can display some of the formatting marks. In the Home tab Paragraph group, click the **Show/Hide Formatting Marks** ¶ to show all of the formatting marks—paragraph marks ¶ , tabs, and spaces, among other characters—as you can see in Figure 3-18.

You can fine-tune exactly which formatting marks to display by clicking the **Office button**, clicking **Word Options**, and clicking the **Display** option. Under Always Show These Formatting Marks On The Screen, you can choose which marks to display.

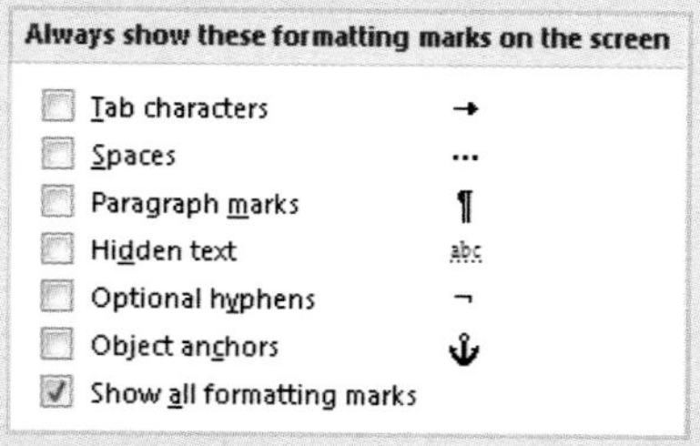

Always show these formatting marks on the screen

☐	Tab characters	→
☐	Spaces	...
☐	Paragraph marks	¶
☐	Hidden text	abc
☐	Optional hyphens	¬
☐	Object anchors	⚓
☑	Show all formatting marks	

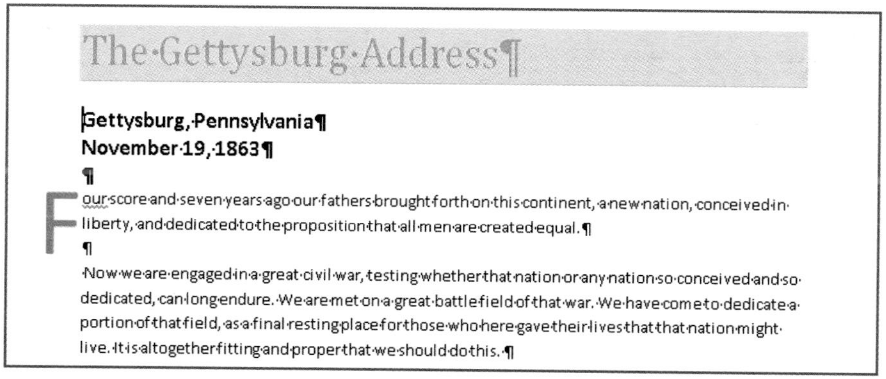

The·Gettysburg·Address¶

Gettysburg,·Pennsylvania¶
November·19,·1863¶
¶
Four·score·and·seven·years·ago·our·fathers·brought·forth·on·this·continent,·a·new·nation,·conceived·in·liberty,·and·dedicated·to·the·proposition·that·all·men·are·created·equal.¶
¶
·Now·we·are·engaged·in·a·great·civil·war,·testing·whether·that·nation·or·any·nation·so·conceived·and·so·dedicated,·can·long·endure.·We·are·met·on·a·great·battlefield·of·that·war.·We·have·come·to·dedicate·a·portion·of·that·field,·as·a·final·resting·place·for·those·who·here·gave·their·lives·that·that·nation·might·live.·It·is·altogether·fitting·and·proper·that·we·should·do·this.·¶

Figure 3-18: Turning on formatting marks helps you see what is making your document look the way it does.

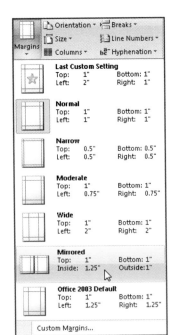

QUICKSTEPS

COPYING FORMATTING

Often, you'll want a word, phrase, or paragraph formatted like an existing word, phrase, or paragraph. Word allows you to copy just the formatting.

USE THE FORMAT PAINTER

1. Drag across the word, phrase, or paragraph whose formatting you want to copy. In the case of a paragraph, make sure you have included the paragraph mark (see the "Turning on Formatting Marks" QuickSteps).

2. In the Home tab Clipboard group, click the **Format Painter**.

3. With the special point (brush and I-beam), drag across the word, phrase, or paragraph (including the paragraph mark) you want formatted.

> Now·we·are·engaged

COPY FORMATS WITH THE KEYBOARD

1. Select the word, phrase, or paragraph whose formatting you want to copy.

2. Press **CTRL-SHIFT-C** to copy the format.

3. Select the word, phrase, or paragraph (including the paragraph mark) you want formatted.

4. Press **CTRL-SHIFT-V** to paste the format.

COPY FORMATTING TO SEVERAL PLACES

If you want to copy formatting to several separate pieces of text or paragraphs:

1. Drag across the text with formatting to be copied.

2. In the Home tab Clipboard group, double-click the **Format Painter**.

3. Drag across each piece of text or paragraph that you want to format.

4. When you are done, click the **Format Painter** again, or press **ESC**.

Format a Page

Page formatting has to do with overall formatting items, such as margins, orientation, size, and vertical alignment of a page. You can set options for page formatting either from the Page Layout tab or in a dialog box.

Set Margins

Margins are the space between the edge of the paper and the text. To set margins:

1. Open the document whose margins you want to set. If you want the margins to apply only to a selected part of a document, select that part now.

2. Click the **Page Layout** tab, and click **Margins** in the Page Setup group. A menu will open, as shown in Figure 3-19. If you have set custom margins previously, they will be displayed in the menu.

3. Click the option you want.

Figure 3-19: You can select from a group of "canned" margins, according to the needs of your document, or create a custom margin.

Use a Dialog Box to Format a Page

You can do much of the page formatting using the Page Layout dialog box.

1. In the Page Layout tab, click the **Page Setup Dialog Launcher**. The Page Setup dialog box is displayed, as shown in Figure 3-20.

2. Click the **Margins** tab. You have these options:

   - Under Margins, click the spinners or manually enter the desired distance in inches between the particular edge of the paper and the start or end of text.

   - Under Orientation, click either **Portrait** or **Landscape**, depending on which you want.

   - Under Pages, click the **Multiple Page** down arrow and select an option: Click **Mirror Margins** when the inside gutter is larger to handle binding, **2 Pages Per Sheet** when a normal sheet of paper is divided into two pages, and **Book Fold** when you are putting together a section of a book ("a signature") with four, eight, or more pages in the signature.

   - If you want these changes to apply only to the selected part of a document, click **This Point Forward** under Preview Apply To.

3. When you are done setting margins, click **OK**.

Use Mirror Margins

Mirror margins allow you to have a larger "inside" margin, which would be the right margin on the left page and the left margin on the right page, or

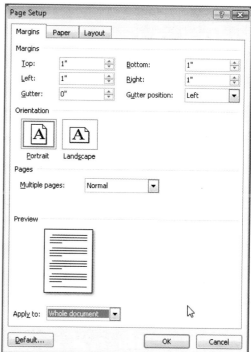

Figure 3-20: *Many page formatting tasks can be done on the Page Setup dialog box.*

any other combination of margins that are mirrored between the left and right pages. To create mirror margins:

1. Open the document whose margins you want mirrored.

2. Click the **Page Layout** tab and click **Margins** in the Page Setup group.

3. Click the **Multiple Pages** down arrow and click **Mirrored**, as shown earlier in Figure 3-19. When you do that the left and right margins change to inside and outside.

Determine Page Orientation

Page orientation specifies whether a page is taller than it is wide, called "portrait," or wider than it is tall, called "landscape." For 8½-inch by 11-inch letter size paper, if the 11-inch side is vertical (the left and right edges), which is the standard way of reading a letter, then it is portrait. If the 11-inch side is horizontal (the top and bottom edges), then it is landscape. Portrait is the default orientation in Word. To change it:

1. Open the document whose orientation you want to set. If you want the orientation to apply only to a selected part of a document, select that part now.

2. In the Page Layout tab, click **Orientation** in the Page Setup group.

3. On the menu click the option you want.

Specify Paper Size

Specifying the paper size gives you the starting perimeter of the area within which you can set margins and enter text or pictures.

1. In the Page Layout tab, click the **Size** down arrow in the Page Setup group. A menu will open, shown in Figure 3-21.

2. Click the size of paper you want.

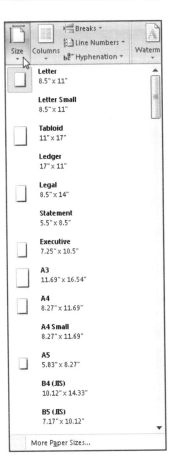

Figure 3-21: Choose the paper size from a selection of popular sizes in the Page Layout tab.

When you turned on the formatting marks (see "Turning on Formatting Marks," earlier in this chapter), you might have felt a bit disappointed that they didn't tell you more. You can direct Word to track inconsistencies in your formatting as you type.

1. Click the **Office button** and click **Word Options**.

2. Click **Advanced** on the left pane.

3. Under Editing Options, click both **Keep Track of Formatting**, and **Mark Formatting Inconsistencies**.

☑ Keep track of formatting
☐ Mark formatting inconsistencies

Set Vertical Alignment

Just as you saw how you can right align, center, left align, and justify text between margins under "Set Paragraph Alignment," you can also specify vertical alignment, so text is aligned at the top, bottom, or center of the page, or justified between the top and bottom.

1. In the Page Layout tab, click the **Page Setup Dialog Launcher**. The Page Setup dialog box will open.

2. In the Layout tab, under Page, click the **Vertical Alignment** down arrow, and click the vertical alignment that you want to use.

3. Click **OK** when you are done.

Chapter 4
Customizing a Document

Microsoft Word 2007 provides a number of tools that combine text creation, layout, and formatting features that you can use to customize your documents. Two of the most common tools used at a broad level are styles and templates. Word also provides several other features, such as AutoFormat and AutoText, which help make document creation and formatting easier.

This chapter discusses creating documents through the use of styles and templates; formatting your documents using tabs, headers and footers, and outlines; and inserting front and end matter, such as tables of contents and indexes. The chapter also discusses Word's writing aids, such as AutoText, hyphenation, an equation builder, and the thesaurus.

UNDERSTANDING THEMES, STYLES, AND TEMPLATES

Word 2007 has changed the way you apply formatting to documents. You can now quickly and easily make your documents look professional and consistent by using canned themes, styles, and templates. A *theme* changes the background, layout, color, fonts, and effects used in a document. Themes can be similar throughout most of the Office suite, so if you choose a theme in Word, you likely will be able to apply that theme to Excel or PowerPoint documents as well. Every document has a theme.

A *style* applies a specific set of formatting characteristics to individual characters or to entire paragraphs within the theme. For example, you can apply styles to headings, titles, lists, and other text components. Consequently, styles determine how the overall design comes together in its look and feel. Styles are beneficial to document creation, because they provide a consistent look and feel to all text selected for formatting. Every theme has a certain set of styles assigned to it. You can change styles within a theme and change themes within a document.

A *template* contains a theme, with its unique style of formatting, and is used to set up a document for the first time. You open a template file, save it as a document file, and then enter your own contents into it. In this way, you can standardize the look of all documents that are based on a given template.

Figure 4-1: The Quick Styles gallery shows you canned options for formatting headings, text, and paragraphs.

Use Styles

Word 2007 provides a gallery of Quick Styles that provides you with sets of canned formatting choices, such as font, boldface, and color that you can apply to headings, titles, text, and lists. You use Quick Styles by identifying what kind of formatting a selected segment of text needs, such as for a header or title. Then you select the style of formatting you want to apply to the document. You can easily apply Quick Styles, change them, and create new ones.

Identify Text with a Style

To identify a segment of text within your document with a consistent style, such as for a heading, you apply a Quick Style from the gallery.

1. Select the text to be formatted, for example, a title or heading.
2. Click the **Home** tab, and click the **Styles More** down arrow in the Styles group. The Quick Styles gallery is displayed, as shown in Figure 4-1.
3. Point at the thumbnails to see the effects of each style on your text, and then click the thumbnail of the style you want to apply.

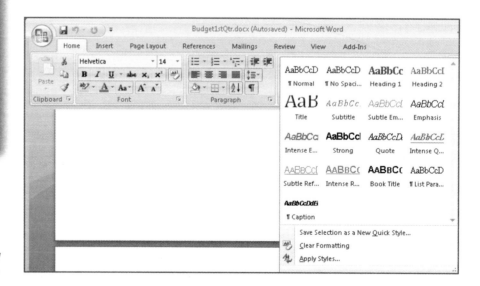

If you do not find the style you want in the Quick Styles gallery for a segment of text, press **CTRL-SHIFT-S** to display the Apply Styles dialog box. Click the **Style Name** down arrow to find the style you want.

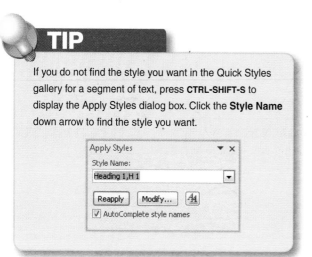

Apply Style Sets to a Document

Before you begin entering text, or after you have identified the components in your document, you can apply a consistent set of color, styles, and fonts to your document using the Change Styles function.

1. Open the document that you want to contain a style set. It can be either a blank document or one that has already had the components identified, such as title, headings, and lists.

2. Click the **Home** tab, click **Change Styles** in the Styles group, and click **Style Set**. A menu is displayed.

3. Click the style you want. The document will be changed. However, if you have components that are not identified with the Quick Styles, such as headings, they will not receive the formatting properly.

Save a New Quick Style

To create a new Quick Style option that will appear in the Quick Styles gallery:

1. Format the text using the mini-formatting toolbar or the commands in the Home tab Font group.

2. Right-click the selected text, click **Styles**, and click **Save Selection As A New Quick Style**. The Create New Style From Formatting dialog box appears.

3. Type the name you want for the style, and click **OK**. It will appear in the Quick Styles gallery.

Modify a Style

1. In the Home tab Styles group, click either **Quick Styles** or the **Styles More** down arrow. (If the window is narrow enough, the set of styles becomes a button, and you click the button in place of the down arrow.) The Quick Styles gallery is displayed.

2. Right-click the style to be changed, and click **Modify** on the context menu. The Modify Style dialog box appears, as shown in Figure 4-2.

   –Or–

   Click **Apply Styles** from the bottom of the gallery. The Apply Styles dialog box appears. Click the **Style Name** down arrow, and click the name of the style you wish to change. Click **Modify**, and the Modify Style dialog box appears.

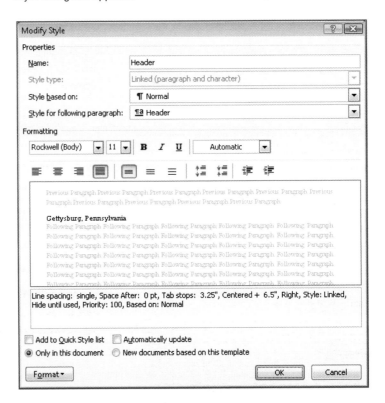

Figure 4-2: You can change a style by modifying it in the Modify Style dialog box.

TIP

To use a modified style in the New Styles gallery, click the **Add To Quick Style List** check box in the Modify Style dialog box. The modified style is added to the gallery of styles in the Styles group.

CAUTION

You should not click the Automatically Update check box when using the Normal style. Automatic Update can very easily change a style that you may not want to change.

UICKSTEPS

DELETING A STYLE

You might choose to delete a style that you created for a one-time-use document and don't ever plan to use again. You can delete a style from the gallery or from the document being used.

DELETE/RESTORE A STYLE FROM THE GALLERY

To delete a style just from the gallery:

1. In the Home tab Styles group, click **Quick Styles** or the **Styles More** down arrow to display the Quick Styles gallery.

2. Right-click the style you want to delete, and click **Remove From Quick Styles Gallery**.

The style will be removed from the Quick Styles gallery. However, this does not mean that the style is gone; it is still in the list of styles.

Continued . . .

3. Change any formatting options you want.

4. To display more options, click **Format** in the lower-left area, and then click the attribute—for example, **Font** or **Numbering**—that you want to modify. Click **OK**.

5. Repeat step 4 for any additional attributes you want to change, clicking **OK** each time you are finished.

6. Type a new name for the style, if desired, unless you want to change existing formatted text.

7. Click **OK** to close the Modify Styles dialog box.

Automatically Update a Style

Sometimes, you may make changes to a style and want to have those changes automatically updated within a document.

1. Follow the steps in the previous section, "Modify a Style," to display the Modify Style dialog box.

2. After making the changes you want, click the **Automatically Update** check box. Word will automatically redefine the style you selected whenever you apply manual formatting.

Use Themes

One way that you can make a document look professional is by using themes. Themes combine coordinated colors, fonts (for body text and headings), and design effects (such as special effect uses for lines and fill effects) to produce a unique look. You can use the same themes with PowerPoint and Excel as well, thereby standardizing a look. All documents have themes; one is assigned to a new document by default.

ASSIGN A THEME TO YOUR DOCUMENT

To apply a theme to a document:

1. Click the **Page Layout** tab. Click **Themes** in the Themes group to display a gallery of themes, as seen in Figure 4-3.

2. Click the theme you want, and it will be applied to the current document.

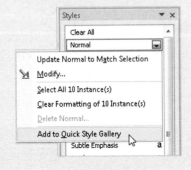

QUICKSTEPS

DELETING A STYLE (Continued)

To restore the style to the gallery:

1. In the Home tab Styles group, click the **Styles Dialog Box Launcher**. The Styles task pane is displayed.

2. Right-click the style that you want to restore, and click **Add To Quick Style Gallery**.

DELETE A STYLE FROM A DOCUMENT

To completely delete a style from a document:

1. In the Home tab Styles group, click the **Styles Dialog Box Launcher**. The Styles task pane is displayed.

2. Right-click the style to be deleted, and click **Delete** *stylename* from the context menu. A dialog box appears.

3. Click **Yes** to confirm that you want to delete the style.

Some styles cannot be deleted; the command to delete them will be unavailable or grayed out, such as with the Normal or Heading style. If you delete a style from the document, any text formatted with that style will be reformatted with the Normal style.

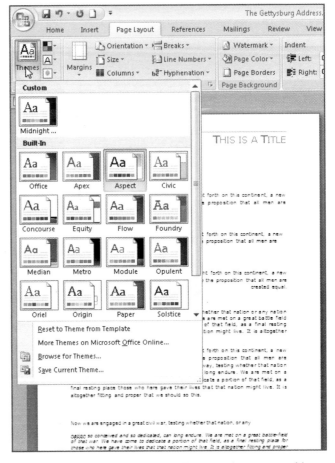

Figure 4-3: Use themes to standardize your documents with other Office products, such as PowerPoint and Excel.

Change a Theme

Themes can be changed to fit your own document requirements. You can then change a theme by altering the fonts, color, and design effects.

CHANGE THE COLOR OF A THEME

Each theme consists of a set of four colors for text and background, six colors for accents, and two colors for hyperlinks. You can change any single color element

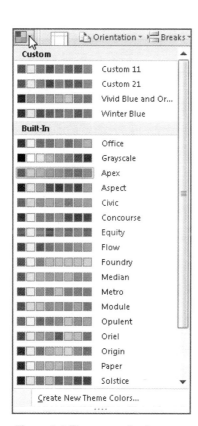

Figure 4-4: *The menu of color combinations offers alternatives for your theme colors.*

or all of them. When you change the colors, the font styles and design elements remain the same.

1. With your document open, click the **Page Layout** tab.
2. Click **Theme Colors**. The menu of color combinations will be displayed, as seen in Figure 4-4. Any revised or custom themes that you have created are listed at the top.
3. Point at the rows of color combinations to see which ones appeal to you. You'll see the color change reflected in your open document.
4. When you find the color combination you want, click it.

CHANGE THEME FONTS

Each theme includes two fonts: the *body* font is used for general text entry, and a *heading* font is used for headings. The default fonts used in Word for a new, plain document are Calibri for body text and Cambria for headings. After you have assigned a theme to a document, the fonts may be different, and they can be changed.

1. In the Page Layout tab Themes group, click **Theme Fonts**. The drop-down list displays various theme fonts. The current theme font combination is highlighted in its place in the list.
2. Point to each font combination to see how the fonts will appear in your document.
3. Click the font name combination you decide upon. When you click a font name combination, the fonts will replace both the body and heading fonts in your document on one or selected pages.

CREATE A NEW THEME FONT SET

You may also decide that you want a unique set of fonts for your document. You can create a custom font set that is available in the list of fonts for your current and future documents.

1. In the Page Layout tab Themes group, click **Theme Fonts**.
2. Click **Create New Theme Fonts** at the bottom of the drop-down list.
3. In the Create New Theme Fonts dialog box (see Figure 4-5), click either or both the **Heading Font** and **Body Font** down arrows to select a new font combination. View the new combination in the Sample area.

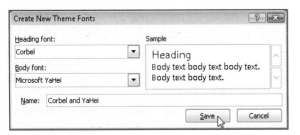

Figure 4-5: You can choose a heading or body font from the fonts available in your Office program.

4. Type a new name for the font combination you've selected, and click **Save**. Custom fonts are available for selection at the top of the Theme Fonts drop-down list.

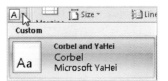

CHANGE THEMED GRAPHIC EFFECTS

Shapes, illustrations, pictures, and charts include graphic effects that are controlled by themes. Themed graphics are modulated in terms of their lines (borders), fills, and effects (such as shadowed, raised, and shaded). For example, some themes simply change an inserted rectangle's fill color, while other themes affect the color, the weight of the border, and whether it has a 3-D appearance.

1. In the Page Layout tab Themes group, click **Theme Effects**. The drop-down list displays a gallery of effects combinations. The current effects combination is highlighted.

2. Point to each combination to see how the effects will appear in your document, assuming you have a graphic or chart inserted on the document page (see Chapter 14 for information on inserting charts and graphics).

3. Click the effects combination you want.

Create a Custom Theme

You can create a new theme, save it, and use it in your documents. You select a group of text, background, accent, and hyperlink colors, and then give them a collective name.

1. In the Page Layout tab Themes group, click **Theme Colors**.

2. At the bottom of the menu of colors, click the **Create New Theme Colors** link. The Create New Theme Colors dialog box appears, as shown in Figure 4-6.

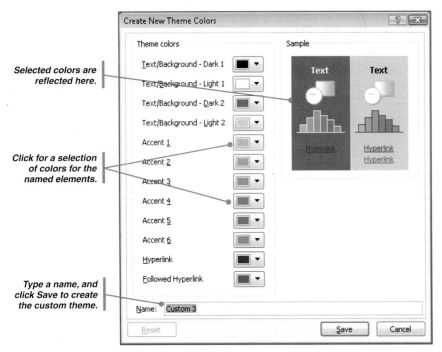

Selected colors are reflected here.

Click for a selection of colors for the named elements.

Type a name, and click Save to create the custom theme.

Figure 4-6: The Create New Theme Colors dialog box allows you to create a new theme to use with multiple documents.

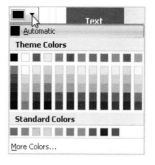

TIP

To restore the original colors in the Sample area in the Create New Theme Colors dialog box and start over, click **Reset**.

NOTE

You may find that you want to change something in a custom theme after you've been using it for awhile. To edit a custom theme, click the **Theme Colors** button in the Page Layout tab Themes group, and right-click the custom theme you want to edit. From the context menu, click **Edit**. The Edit Theme Colors dialog box, similar to that shown in Figure 4-6, will appear.

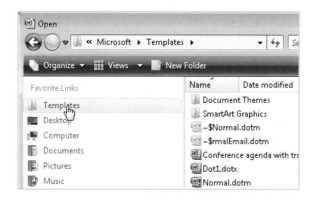

3. To select a color for one of the color groups, click the text/ background/accent/ hyperlink group, and click the color you want to test. It will be displayed in the Sample area.

4. Go through each set of colors that you want to change.

5. When you find a group of colors that you like, type a name in the **Name** text box, and click **Save**.

Use Templates

A *template* is a collection of styles, associated formatting and design features, and colors used to determine the overall appearance of a document, A Word 2007 template file has an extension of .dotx. Templates are always attached to documents, as you saw in Chapter 2.

Create and Change Templates

Word 2007 comes with several templates that you can use to create letters, faxes, memos, and more. In addition, as you saw earlier, the Microsoft Office web site has online templates that you can make use of. You can also create your own templates.

CHANGE THE DEFAULT NORMAL TEMPLATE

The *Normal* template is the default template used by Word unless you tell it otherwise. It, like all templates, includes default styles, AutoText, and other customizations that determine the general look of your document. You can customize the Normal template to include the styles you want to use on a regular basis. To change the default styles of the Normal template:

1. With a Word document open, click the **Office button**, click **Open**, and then click **Templates** under Favorite Links.

2. If no templates are listed in the Open dialog box, click the **Files Of Type** down arrow (immediately above the Cancel button), and click **All Files (*.*)**. If you still do not see Normal.dotm (indicating a macro-enabled template), right-click **Computer** in the Favorite Links pane, click **Search**, and type Normal.dotm in the Search field. The search will begin as you type.

TIP

If the Folders pane is showing on the Open dialog box instead of Favorite Links, click the **Folders** title bar to display the Favorite Links pane.

CAUTION

Keep in mind that any changes you make to the Normal template will be applied to any future documents you create, unless you specifically apply a different template.

NOTE

If the Normal.dotm template is renamed, damaged, or moved, Word automatically creates a new version (with the original default settings) the next time you start it. The new version will not include any changes or modifications you made to the version that you renamed or moved.

NOTE

You can also create a new template based on a previously created document.

TIP

If you want to create a template based on a different type of document—for example, a web page or an e-mail message—select the relevant template instead of the Blank Document template in the Templates or Microsoft Office Online list.

3. Click **Normal.dotm** and click **Open** to open it. Ensure that you're working in the template by verifying that "Normal.dotm" appears in the Word title bar.

4. Change the template by changing the styles using the steps described in "Modify a Style" earlier in this chapter.

5. When you are finished making the changes that you want, click the **Office button**, and click **Save** to resave Normal.dotm.

CREATE A TEMPLATE

1. With Word open, click the **Office button**, and click **New**. The New Document dialog box appears, as shown in Figure 4-7.

2. Under Templates, click **Blank And Recent** to display a blank document template and the templates that you most recently used.

3. Click the **Blank Document** thumbnail.

4. Click **Create**. A new document opens.

5. Save the document with a unique name and the .dotm template file type.

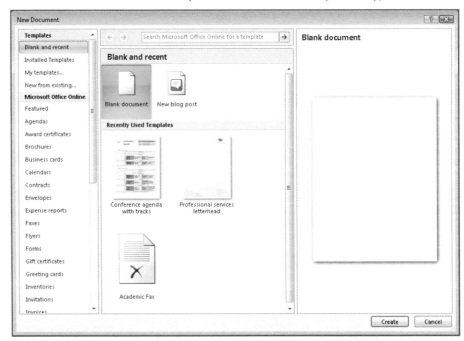

Figure 4-7: Word comes with several templates you can use to create letters, faxes, and more.

APPLY A TEMPLATE TO A NEW DOCUMENT

1. Click the **Office button**, and click **New** to open the New Document task pane.

2. Under Templates, scroll down to review the list of templates that are installed on your computer and available online.

3. Click the template you want to use, and click **Create**.

4. Save the document with a unique name, using the Word Document (.docx) file type.

Work with Documents

In addition to using styles and templates to format your documents, you can use section breaks, columns, tabs, headers and footers, tables of contents, and indexes to further refine your documents.

Create Section Breaks

A *section break* indicates the end of a section in a document. You can use section breaks to vary the layout of a document within a page or between pages. For example, you might choose to format the introduction of a magazine article in a single column and format the body of the article in two columns. You must separately format each section, but the section break allows them to be different. Section breaks allow you to change the number of columns, page headers and footers, page numbering, page borders, page margins, and other characteristics and formatting within a section.

INSERT A SECTION BREAK

1. Open the document and click where you want to insert a section break.

2. Click the **Page Layout** tab, and click **Breaks** in the Page Setup group. The Breaks context menu appears.

3. To create a new section, in the Section Breaks area, select what comes after the break. You have the following options:

- Click **Next Page** to begin a new section on the next page.
- Click **Continuous** to begin a new section on the same page.
- Click **Even Page** to start the new section on the next even-numbered page.
- Click **Odd Page** to start the new section on the next odd-numbered page.

Breaks | Watermark ▾ | Indent

Page Breaks

Page
Mark the point at which one page ends and the next page begins.

Column
Indicate that the text following the column break will begin in the next column.

Text Wrapping
Separate text around objects on web pages, such as caption text from body text.

Section Breaks

Next Page
Insert a section break and start the new section on the next page.

Continuous
Insert a section break and start the new section on the same page.

Even Page
Insert a section break and start the new section on the next even-numbered page.

Odd Page
Insert a section break and start the new section on the next odd-numbered page.

Section Break (Continuous)

Section Break (Even Page)

4. When you click the option you want, the section break is inserted. If the Show/Hide Formatting feature is turned on (in the Home tab Paragraph group), you'll be able to see the section breaks in the text.

DELETE A SECTION BREAK

When a section break is inserted on a page, you will see a note to that effect if the Show/Hide Formatting feature is turned on. You can delete the break by selecting that note.

1. Click the section break that you want to delete.

2. Press **DELETE**.

Create and Use Columns

You can format your documents in a single column or in two or more columns, like text found in newspapers or magazines. You must first create either a continuous or a page break, not a column break, before you create the columns in order to prevent columns from forming in the previous section. To create columns in a document:

1. Place the insertion point at the place where you want the columns to begin. On the Page Layout tab, click **Breaks** in the Page Setup group and click **Continuous**.

2. Click the **Page Layout** tab, and click **Columns** in the Page Setup group to display a context menu.

3. Click the thumbnail option that corresponds to the number or type of columns you want.

–Or–

If you do not see what you want, click **More Columns** to display the Columns dialog box (see Figure 4-8):

- Click an icon in the Presets area, or type a number in the Number Of Columns box to set the number of columns you want.

- Use the options in the Width And Spacing area to manually determine the dimensions of your columns and the amount of space between columns. To do this, you will have to clear the **Equal Column Width** check box. (You may have to click a thumbnail option to make it available first.)

NOTE

When you delete a section break, you also delete the specific formatting for the text above that break. That text becomes part of the following section and assumes the relevant formatting of that section.

TIP

If you don't see section breaks displayed in your document, click the **Home** tab, and click the **Show/Hide** button in the Paragraph group. ¶

TIP

You can set or change a section break from the Page Setup dialog box. In the Page Layout tab Page Setup group, click the **Page Setup Dialog Box Launcher,** and click the **Layout** tab. The section settings are at the top of the dialog box.

Columns   Hyph

One

Two

Three

Left

Right

More Columns...

Columns dialog box

Columns

Presets

One Two Three Left Right

Number of columns: 2

□ Line between

Width and spacing

Col #:	Width:	Spacing:
1:	3"	0.5"
2:	3"	

□ Equal column width

Apply to: This point forward

   This section
   This point forward
   Whole document

□ Start new column

Preview

OK   Cancel

Figure 4-8: Use the Columns dialog box to create and format columns in your documents.

TIP

The Preview area in the Columns dialog box displays the effects of your changes as you change the various column settings.

TIP

To see tabs, the ruler needs to appear on the screen. If you do not see the ruler, click the **View** tab, and click **Ruler** in the Show/Hide group.

- Click the **Line Between** check box if you want Word to insert a vertical line between columns.
- Use the **Apply To** list box to select the part of the document to which you want your selections to apply: Whole Document, This Section, or **This Point Forward**. Click **This Point Forward**, and then click the **Start New Column** check box if you want to insert a column break at an insertion point.

4. Click **OK** when finished.

Use Tabs

A *tab* is a type of formatting usually used to align text and create simple tables. By default, Word 2007 has *tab stops* (the horizontal positioning of the insertion point when you press TAB) every half-inch. Tabs are better than space characters in such instances, because tabs are set to specific measurements, while spaces may not always align the way you intend due to the size and spacing of individual characters in a given font. Word 2007 supports five kinds of tabs:

- **Left tab** left-aligns text at the tab stop.
- **Center tab** centers text at the tab stop.
- **Right tab** right-aligns text at the tab stop.
- **Decimal tab** aligns the decimal point of tabbed numbers at the tab stop.
- **Bar tab** left-aligns text with a vertical line that is displayed at the tab stop.

To align text with a tab, press the TAB key before the text you want aligned.

SET TABS USING THE RULER

To set tabs using the ruler at the top of a page:

1. Select the text, from one line to an entire document, in which you want to set one or more tab stops.

2. Click the **Left Tab** icon [L] located at the far left of the horizontal ruler until it changes to the type of tab you want: Left Tab, Center Tab [±], Right Tab [⅃], Decimal Tab [±], or Bar Tab [⅃].

3. Click the horizontal ruler where you want to set a tab stop.

Figure 4-9: From the Tabs dialog box, you can format specific tab measurements and set tab leaders.

TIP

When working with tabs, it's a good idea to display text formatting so that you can distinguish tabs from spaces. To display formatting, click the **Show/Hide** button in the Home tab Paragraph group.

4. Once you have the tabs set:

- Drag a tab off the ruler to get rid of it.
- Drag a tab to another spot on the ruler to change its position.
- Click the **First Line Indent** , and then click the top of the ruler line to insert the first line of the paragraph where you want it to start.
- Click the **Hanging Indent** , and then click the bottom of the ruler to insert a hanging indent for the rest of the lines in a paragraph.

SET TABS USING MEASUREMENTS

To set tabs according to specific measurements:

1. Double-click a tab, and the Tabs dialog box will appear, as shown in Figure 4-9.
2. Enter the measurements you want in the Tab Stop Position text box. Click **Set**.
3. Click the tab alignment option you want.
4. Repeat steps 2 and 3 for as many tabs as you want to set. Click **OK** to close the dialog box.

SET TABS WITH LEADERS

You can also set tabs with *tab leaders*—characters that fill the space otherwise left by a tab—for example, a solid, dotted, or dashed line.

1. Double-click any tab, and the Tabs dialog box appears, as shown in Figure 4-9.
2. In the Tab Stop Position text box, type the position for a new tab or select an existing tab stop to which you want to add a tab leader.
3. In the Alignment area, select the alignment for text typed at the tab stop.
4. In the Leader area, select the leader option you want, and then click **Set**.
5. Repeat steps 2–4 for additional tabs. When you are done, click **OK** to close the dialog box.

Add Headers and Footers

Headers and footers are parts of a document that contain information such as page numbers, revision dates, the document title, and so on. The header appears at the top of every page, and the footer appears at the bottom of every page. Figure 4-10 shows the buttons available on the Header And Footer Tools Design tab.

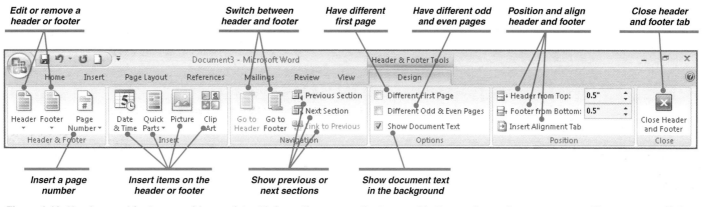

Edit or remove a header or footer

Switch between header and footer

Have different first page

Have different odd and even pages

Position and align header and footer

Close header and footer tab

Insert a page number

Insert items on the header or footer

Show previous or next sections

Show document text in the background

Figure 4-10: Headers and footers provide consistent information across the tops and bottoms of your document pages. These areas can also have unique tabs and other formatting.

CREATE A HEADER OR FOOTER

1. Open the document to which you want to add a header or footer (see Chapter 2).

2. Click the **Insert** tab, and click **Header** or **Footer** in the Header & Footer group. The header or footer area will be displayed along with the special contextual Header & Footer Design tab.

   –Or–

   Double-click in the top area of the document where a header would be, if it is visible. Or, first double-click the page break line, and then double-click the header or footer area. (If the page break and header area are hidden, you can't use the double-click method.)

3. Click **Header** or **Footer** in the Header & Footer group to select a style for the heading if you want.

4. Type the text you want displayed in the header:

   - To switch between typing text in the header and typing it in the footer, click the **Go To Header** or **Go To Footer** buttons in the Navigation group, and type the text you want.

   - Click **Date And Time** in the Insert group to insert a date or time.

   - To insert a page number, click **Page Number** in the Header & Footer group, click a location in the drop-down menu, scroll down, choose a format, and then click **OK**.

USING DIFFERENT LEFT AND RIGHT HEADERS

Different left and right pages use section breaks to allow different margins and tabs. Sometimes, you might want to create a document that has different left and right headers and/or footers. For example, you might have a brochure, pamphlet, or manuscript in which all odd-numbered pages have a title in the header and all even-numbered pages have the author's name or other information.

To create different left and right headers and/or footers:

1. Open the document to which you want to add a different left and right header or footer.

Continued . . .

- To enter a date that is left-aligned, a title that is centered, and a page number that is right-aligned, type the date (or click **Date & Time** in the Insert group), press TAB, type the title, press **TAB**, and type the page number (or click **Page Number** in the Header and Footer group and click **Current Position** to click the style you want).

- To go to the next or last section to enter a different header or footer, click **Previous Section** or **Next Section** in the Navigation group.

5. When finished, double-click in the document area or click the **Close Header And Footer** button.

EDIT A HEADER OR FOOTER

1. Open the document to which you want to add a header or footer.

2. Double-click the header or footer area, if it is visible. Or, first double-click the page break line, and then double-click the header or footer area to display the header and footer along with the Header And Footer Tools Design tab, as shown in Figure 4-10.

3. If necessary, click the **Previous Section** or **Next Section** button in the Navigation group to display the header or footer you want to edit.

4. Edit the header or footer. For example, you might revise text, change the font, apply bold formatting, or add a date or time. You can also click **Header** and select a style.

5. When finished, double-click in the document area or click the **Close Header And Footer** button in the Close group.

DELETE A HEADER OR FOOTER

1. Open the document from which you want to delete a header or footer.

2. Double-click the header or footer area of the document, if it is visible. Or, first double-click the page break line, and then double-click the header or footer area. The header or footer area will be displayed along with the Header And Footer Tools Design tab.

3. If necessary, click **Previous Section** or **Next Section** in the Navigation group to move to the header or footer you want to delete.

4. Select the text or graphics you want to delete, and press **DELETE**.

–Or–

Click **Header** or **Footer** in the Header & Footer group, and click **Remove Header** or **Remove Footer** from the bottom of the menu.

UICKSTEPS

USING DIFFERENT LEFT AND RIGHT HEADERS *(Continued)*

2. Double-click in the header area, if it is visible. Or, first double-click the page break line, and then double-click the header or footer area; or click the **Insert** tab, click **Header**, and click **Edit Header** at the bottom of the menu. The header area will be displayed, along with the special contextual Header & Footer Design tab.

3. In the Options group, click **Different First Page** to enter a separate title or no title for the first page. Create a different first page in the First Page Header area, create the normal header in the Header area of the second page, and so on.

4. Click the **Different Odd And Even Pages** check box to have a different heading on the odd- and even-numbered pages. For instance, perhaps your page number is on the left for even-numbered pages and on the right for odd-numbered pages. Create the header or footer for odd-numbered pages in the Odd Page Header or Odd Page Footer area, and create the header or footer for even-numbered pages in the Even Page Header or Even Page Footer area.

5. When finished, double-click in the document area or click the **Close Header And Footer** button in the Close group.

Add Footnotes and Endnotes

Footnotes and *endnotes* are types of annotations in a document usually used to provide citation information or to provide additional information for readers. The difference between the two is where they appear in a document. Footnotes appear either after the last line of text on the page or at the bottom of the page on which the annotated text appears. Endnotes appear either at the end of the section in which the annotated text appears or at the end of the document.

INSERT A FOOTNOTE OR ENDNOTE

1. To display the Print Layout view, click the **View** tab, and then click **Print Layout** in the Document View group.

2. In the Print Layout view, position the insertion point immediately after the text you want to annotate.

3. Click the **References** tab, and then click **Insert Footnote** or **Insert Endnote** in the Footnotes group. For a footnote, the insertion point will be positioned at the bottom of the page; for an endnote, it will be positioned at the end of the document.

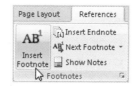

4. Type the text of the endnote or footnote.

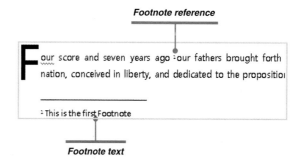

Footnote reference

Footnote text

5. To return to the text where the footnote reference was placed, right-click the footnote and click **Go To Footnote** or **Go To Endnote**.

Figure 4-11: Footnotes and endnotes provide supplemental information to the body of your document. Use the dialog box to control location and formatting.

CHANGE FOOTNOTES OR ENDNOTES

If you want to change the numbers or formatting of footnotes or endnotes, or if you want to add a symbol to the reference, use the Footnote And Endnote dialog box.

1. On the References tab, click the **Footnote & Endnote Dialog Box Launcher** in the Footnotes group. The Footnote And Endnote dialog box appears (see Figure 4-11).

2. You have these options:
   - In the Location box, click the **Footnotes** or **Endnotes** option, and click the down arrow to the right to choose where the footnote or endnote will be placed.
   - Click the **Number Format** down arrow, and select the type of numbering you want from the drop-down list.
   - To select a custom mark (a character that uniquely identifies a footnote or endnote), click the **Symbol** button, and select and insert the symbol you want. It will be displayed in the Custom Mark text box. You can also just type in a character into the text box.
   - Click the **Numbering** down arrow, and choose how the numbering is to start.
   - Click the **Apply Changes To** down arrow to select the part of the document that will contain the changes.

3. Click **Insert**. Word makes the changes as noted.

4. Type the note text.

5. When finished, return the insertion point to the body of your document, and continue typing.

DELETE A FOOTNOTE OR ENDNOTE

In the document, select the number of the note you want to delete, and then press DELETE. Word automatically deletes the footnote or endnote and renumbers the notes.

CONVERT FOOTNOTES TO ENDNOTES OR ENDNOTES TO FOOTNOTES

1. Select the reference number or symbol in the body of a document for the footnote or endnote.

2. Click the **References** tab, and click the **Footnotes Dialog Box Launcher**. The Footnote And Endnote dialog box appears.

3. Click **Convert**. The Convert Notes dialog box appears.

4. Select the option you want, and then click **OK**.

5. Click **Close**.

Create an Index

An *index* is an alphabetical list of words or phrases in a document and the corresponding page references. Indexes created using Word can include main entries and subentries as well as cross-references. When creating an index in Word, you first need to tag the index entries and then generate the index.

TAG INDEX ENTRIES

Mark Entry

1. In the document in which you want to build an index, select the word or phrase that you want to use as an index entry. If you want an index entry to use text that you separately enter instead of using existing text in the document, place the insertion point in the document where you want your new index entry to reference.

2. Click the **References** tab, and click **Mark Entry** in the Index group (you can also press **ALT-SHIFT-X**). The Mark Index Entry dialog box appears (see Figure 4-12).

3. Type or edit the text in the Main Entry box. Customize the entry by creating a subentry or by creating a cross-reference to another entry, if desired.

4. Click the **Bold** or **Italic** check box in the Page Number Format area to determine how the page numbers will appear in the index.

5. Click **Mark**. To mark all occurrences of this text in the document, click **Mark All**.

6. Repeat steps 3–5 to mark additional index entries on the same page.

7. Click **Close** to close the dialog box when finished.

8. Repeat steps 1–7 for the remaining entries in the document.

GENERATE AN INDEX

1. Position the insertion point where you want to insert the finished index (this will normally be at the end of the document).

2. Click the **References** tab, and click **Insert Index** in the Index group. The Index dialog box appears (see Figure 4-13).

3. In the Index tab of the Index dialog box, set the formatting for the index. You have these options:

- Click the **Type** option to indent subentries beneath the main entries, or click **Run-In** to print subentries in a string immediately following the main entries.

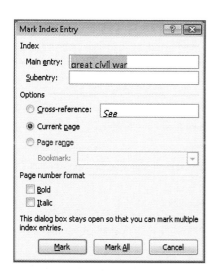

Figure 4-12: You need to tag index entries before you can generate an index.

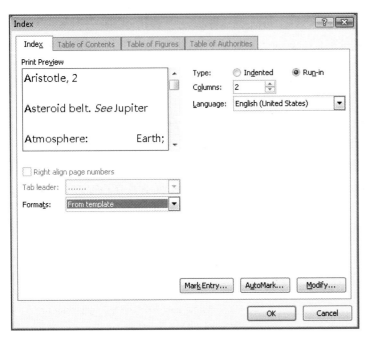

Figure 4-13: *Use the options and settings in the Index dialog box to determine how your index will look.*

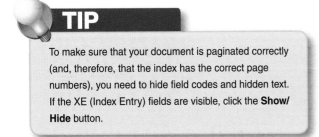

- Click the **Columns** spinner to set the number of columns in the index page.
- Click the **Language** down arrow to set the language for the index.
- Click **Right Align Page Numbers** to right-align the numbers.
- Click **Tab Leader** to print a leader between the entry and the page number.
- Click the **Formats** down arrow to use an available design template, such as Classic or Fancy.

4. Click **OK** when finished. Word generates the index.

Create a Table of Contents

A *table of contents* is a list of the headings in the order in which they appear in the document. If you have formatted paragraphs with heading styles, you can automatically generate a table of contents based on those headings. If you have not used the heading styles, then, as with indexes, you must first tag table of contents (or TOC) entries and then generate the table of contents. (See "Use Styles," earlier in this chapter.)

TAG ENTRIES FOR THE TABLE OF CONTENTS

Use the Quick Styles gallery to identify a segment of text within your document so that it can contain a consistent style for headings and other text that you want contained in a table of contents.

1. Select the text to be formatted, for example, a title or heading.
2. Click the **Home** tab, and click the **Styles More** down arrow in the Styles group.
3. Point at each thumbnail to determine which style it represents, and then click the thumbnail of the style you want to apply.

PLACE OTHER TEXT IN A TABLE OF CONTENTS

To add text other than identified headings in a table of contents:

1. Highlight the text or phrase to be shown in the table of contents.
2. Click the **References** tab, and click **Add Text** in the Table Of Contents group. A menu is displayed.

3. Click the option you want. You have these choices:

- **Do Not Show In Table Of Contents** removes the identification that something should be included in the TOC.

- **Level 1**, **Level 2**, or **Level 3** assigns selected text to a level similar to Heading1, Heading 2, or Heading 3.

USE THE OUTLINING TAB FOR THE TABLE OF CONTENTS

The outlining tab contains an easy way to tag or identify entries for the table of contents.

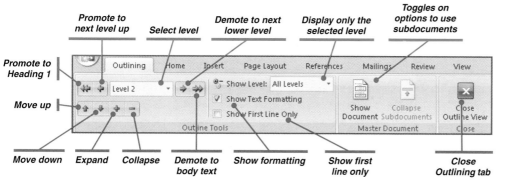

Figure 4-14: Use the Outlining tab to mark entries for a table of contents. The Outlining toolbar provides a number of ways to work with outlines.

1. Click the **View** tab, and click **Outline** in the Document Views group. An Outlining tab will become available. Figure 4-14 shows the Outlining tab. Within the Outlining tab, Figure 4-15 shows the Master Document group from which you can insert and manipulate subdocuments.

2. Click the right or left arrows to promote or demote the levels, respectively.

TIP

You can also tag TOC entries by selecting the text that you want to include in your table of contents. Press **ALT-SHIFT-O**. The Mark Table Of Contents Entry dialog box appears. In the Level box, select the level and click **Mark**. If you have multiple tables of contents, you can identify to which TOC the current entry belongs by using the Table Identifier feature. To mark additional entries, select the text, click in the **Entry** box, and click **Mark**. When you have finished adding entries, close the dialog box.

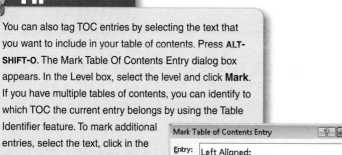

Figure 4-15: The subdocument commands appear when Show Documents on the Outlining tab is clicked. These commands allows subdocuments to be inserted and manipulated.

GENERATE A TABLE OF CONTENTS

1. Place the insertion point where you want to insert the table of contents (normally at the beginning of the document).

2. Click the **References** tab, and click **Table Of Contents** in the Table Of Contents group. A menu is displayed showing various styles for the Table of Contents plus commands at the bottom of the menu.

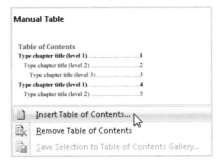

3. At the bottom of the menu, click **Insert Table Of Contents**. The Table of Contents dialog box, shown in Figure 4-16 is displayed.

4. The Print Preview and Web Preview features show how the TOC will appear based on the options selected. You have these options:

   - Clear the **Show Page Numbers** check box to suppress the display of page numbers.
   - Clear the **Right Align Page Numbers** check box to allow page numbers to follow the text immediately.
   - Clear the **Use Hyperlinks Instead Of Page Numbers** check box to use hyperlinks in place of page numbers.
   - Click the **Tab Leader** down arrow, and click **(None)** or another option for a leader between the text in the TOC and the page number.
   - Click the **Formats** down arrow to use one of the available designs.
   - Click the **Show Levels** down arrow, and click the highest level of heading you want to display in the TOC.

5. Click **OK** when finished.

Figure 4-16: Use the options and settings in the Table Of Contents dialog box to determine how your table of contents will look.

QUICKSTEPS

USING VIEW BUTTONS

Word 2007 contains five views that you can use to display your document in different ways, as you can see in Figures 4-17 and 4-18:

- **Print Layout** is the default view in Word and shows text as you will see it when the document is printed.

- **Full Screen Reading** displays the document as a "book" with facing pages. You can "flip" through the pages rather than scroll through them. It uses the full screen in order to display as much of the document as possible. On the top is a restricted toolbar with limited options for using the document.

- **Web Layout view** displays a document in a larger font size and wraps to fit the window rather than the page margins.

- **Outline view** displays the document's framework as it has been laid out with headers identified, etc.

- **Draft** suppresses headings and footers and other design elements in order to display the text in draft form so that you can have an unobstructed view of the contents.

To display any of these views, click the **View** tab, and click the view you want in the Document Views group (Figure 4-17); or click the relevant button on the View toolbar on the right of the status bar (Figure 4-18).

Create and Use Outlines

An *outline* is a framework upon which a document is based. It is a hierarchical list of the headings in a document. You might use an outline to help you organize your ideas and thoughts when writing a speech, a term paper, a book, or a research project. The Outline tab in Word makes it easy to build and refine your outlines.

1. Open a new blank document (see Chapter 1). Click the **View** tab, and click **Outline** in the Document Views group. Word switches to the Outlining tab, displayed earlier in Figures 4-14 and 4-15.

2. Type your heading text, and press **ENTER**. Word formats the headings using the built-in heading style Heading 1. Continue throughout the document. You have these ways of working with the levels:

   - Assign a heading to a different level by selecting it from the Outline Level drop-down list box.

     –Or–

     Place the insertion point in the heading, and then click the **Promote** or **Demote** button on the Outlining toolbar until the heading is at the level you want.

   - To move a heading to a different location, place the insertion point in the heading, and then click the **Move Up** or **Move Down** button ⬆ ⬇ on the Outlining tab of the Outline Tools group until the heading is where you want it. (If a heading is collapsed, the subordinate text under the heading moves with it.)

3. When you're satisfied with the organization, click **Close Outline View**, which automatically switches to Print Layout view. (See the QuickSteps "Using View Buttons" for more information.)

Figure 4-17: Click the View tab, and in the Documents Views group, click the view you want.

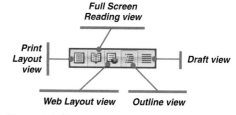

Figure 4-18: You can immediately switch to another view using the Views toolbar on the status bar.

Use Word Writing Aids

Word 2007 provides several aids that can assist you in not only creating your document, but also in making sure that it is as professional-looking as possible. These include AutoCorrect, AutoFormat, AutoText, AutoSummarize, an extensive equation-writing capability, character and word counts, highlighting, hyphenation, and a thesaurus.

Implement AutoCorrect

The AutoCorrect feature automatically corrects common typographical errors when you make them. While Word 2007 comes preconfigured with hundreds of AutoCorrect entries, you can also manually add entries.

CONFIGURE AUTOCORRECT

1. Click the **Office button**, click **Word Options**, click **Proofing** in the left column, and click **AutoCorrect Options**. The AutoCorrect: *Language* dialog box appears.

2. Click the **AutoCorrect** tab (if it is not already displayed), and select from the following options, according to your preferences (see Figure 4-19):

   - **Show AutoCorrect Options Buttons** displays a small blue button or bar beneath text that was automatically corrected. Click this button to see a menu, where you can undo the correction or set AutoCorrect options.

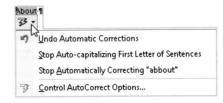

   - **Correct TWo INitial CApitals** changes the second letter in a pair of capital letters to lowercase.
   - **Capitalize The First Letter Of Sentences** capitalizes the first letter following the end of a sentence.
   - **Capitalize The First Letter Of Table Cells** capitalizes the first letter of a word in a table cell.

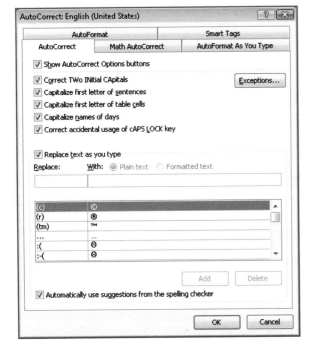

Figure 4-19: Use the AutoCorrect tab to determine what items Word will automatically correct for you as you type.

- **Capitalize Names Of Days** capitalizes the names of the days of the week.
- **Correct Accidental Usage Of cAPS LOCK Key** corrects capitalization errors that occur when you type with the CAPS LOCK key depressed and turns off this key.
- **Replace Text As You Type** replaces typographical errors with the correct words as shown in the list beneath it.
- **Automatically Use Suggestions From The Spelling Checker** tells Word to replace spelling errors with words from the dictionary as you type.

3. Click **OK** when finished.

ADD AN AUTOCORRECT ENTRY

1. Click the **Office button**, click **Word Options**, click **Proofing** in the left column, and click **AutoCorrect Options**. The AutoCorrect: *Language* dialog box appears.

2. Click the **AutoCorrect** tab (if it is not already displayed).

3. Type the text that you want Word to automatically replace in the Replace box. Type the text that you want to replace it with in the With box.

4. Click **Add I OK**.

DELETE AN AUTOCORRECT ENTRY

1. Click the **Office button**, click **Word Options**, click **Proofing** in the left column, and click **AutoCorrect Options**. The AutoCorrect: *Language* dialog box appears.

2. Click the **AutoCorrect** tab (if it is not already displayed).

3. Scroll through the list of AutoCorrect entries, and click the entry you want to delete.

4. Click **Delete I OK**.

Use AutoFormat

AutoFormat automatically formats a document as you type it by applying the associated styles to text, depending on how it is used in the document. For example, Word will automatically format two dashes (--) into an em dash (—) or will automatically format Internet and e-mail addresses as hyperlinks.

To choose the formatting you want Word to apply as you type:

1. Click the **Office button**, click **Word Options**, click **Proofing** in the left column, and click **AutoCorrect Options**. The AutoCorrect: *Language* dialog box appears. Click the **AutoFormat As You Type** tab.

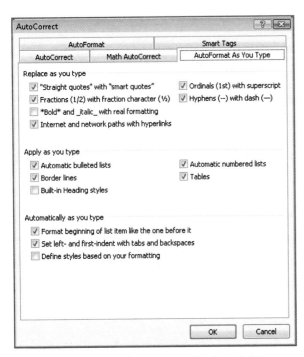

Figure 4-20: Use the AutoFormat As You Type tab to determine what items Word will automatically format for you as you type.

NOTE

The AutoFormat feature in Word 2003 that applied formatting to a document after it was written is not available in Word 2007. Also, the AutoFormat tab in the AutoCorrect dialog box does not do anything. The options have been replaced by the AutoFormat As You Type tab.

2. Select from among the following options, depending on your preferences (see Figure 4-20):

- **"Straight Quotes" With "Smart Quotes"**   Replaces plain quotation characters with curly quotation characters.

- **Ordinals (1st) With Superscript**   Formats ordinal numbers (numbers designating items in an ordered sequence) with a superscript. For example, 1st becomes 1st.

- **Fractions (1/2) With Fraction Character (½)**   Replaces fractions typed with numbers and slashes with fraction characters.

- **Hyphens (--) With Dash (—)**   Replaces a single hyphen with an en dash (–) and two hyphens with an em dash (—).

- ***Bold* And _Italic_ With Real Formatting**   Formats text enclosed within asterisks (*) as bold and text enclosed within underscores (_) as italic.

- **Internet And Network Paths With Hyperlinks**—Formats e-mail addresses and URLs (Uniform Resource Locator—the address of a web page on the Internet or an intranet) as clickable hyperlink fields.

- **Automatic Bulleted Lists**   Applies bulleted list formatting to paragraphs beginning with *, o, or – followed by a space or tab character.

- **Automatic Numbered Lists**   Applies numbered list formatting to paragraphs beginning with a number or letter followed by a space or a tab character.

- **Border Lines**   Automatically applies paragraph border styles when you type three or more hyphens, underscores, or equal signs (=).

- **Tables**   Creates a table when you type a series of hyphens with plus signs to indicate column edges.

- **Built-In Heading Styles**   Applies heading styles to heading text.

- **Format Beginning Of List Item Like The One Before It**   Repeats character formatting that you apply to the beginning of a list item. For example, if you format the first word of a list item in bold, the first word of all subsequent list items are formatted in bold.

- **Set Left- And First-Indent With Tabs And Backspaces**   Sets left indentation on the tab ruler based on the tabs and backspaces you type.

- **Define Styles Based On Your Formatting**   Automatically creates or modifies styles based on manual formatting that you apply to your document.

3. Click **OK** when finished.

Use Building Blocks

Building blocks are blocks of text and formatting that you can use repeatedly, such as cover pages, a greeting, phrases, headings, or a closing. Word provides a number of these for you, but you can identify and save your own building blocks, and then use them in different documents.

CREATE A BUILDING BLOCK

1. Select the text or graphic, along with its formatting, that you want to store as a building block. (Include the paragraph mark in the selection if you want to store paragraph formatting.)

2. Click the **Insert** tab, click **Quick Parts** [Quick Parts] in the Text group, and then click **Save Selection To Quick Parts Gallery**.

3. The Create New Building Block dialog box appears. Accept the suggested name for the building block, or type a short abbreviation for a new one. For example, I changed this one to "mt" for Matthews Technology.

4. In most cases, you will accept the Quick Parts gallery, the General category, and the Building Blocks.dotx file name, since those provide for the easiest retrieval.

5. Click the **Options** down arrow, and, depending on what you are saving in your building block, click the option that is correct for you. If you want paragraph formatting, you must include the paragraph mark.

6. Click **OK**.

    –Or–

1. After selecting the text or graphic that you want as a building block, press **ALT-F3**. The Create New Building Block dialog box appears.

2. Follow steps 3–6 in the preceding procedure.

INSERT ONE OF YOUR BUILDING BLOCKS

1. Place the insertion point in the document where you want to insert the building block.

2. Click the **Insert** tab, click **Quick Parts** in the Text group, and then double-click the entry you want, as shown in Figure 4-21.

    –Or–

    At the point in the document where you want to insert the building block, type its name or the short abbreviation you entered in place of the name, and press **F3**. For example, if I type mt and press **F3**, I get "Matthews Technology."

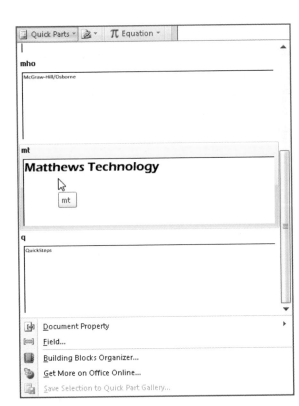

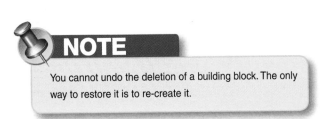

Figure 4-21: The Quick Parts feature provides direct access to your building block entries so that you can insert them in documents.

NOTE

You cannot undo the deletion of a building block. The only way to restore it is to re-create it.

INSERT ONE OF WORD'S BUILDING BLOCKS

1. Place the insertion point in the document where you want to insert the building block.

2. Click the **Insert** tab, click **Quick Parts** in the Text group, and then click **Building Blocks Organizer**. The Building Blocks Organizer dialog box appears, as shown in Figure 4-22.

3. Scroll through the list of building blocks until you find the one that you want. Click the entry to see it previewed on the right. When you are ready, click **Insert**.

DELETE A BUILDING BLOCK

1. Click the **Insert** tab, click **Quick Parts** in the Text group, and then click **Building Blocks Organizer**. The Building Blocks Organizer dialog box appears.

2. Scroll through the list of building blocks until you find the one that you want. Click the entry to see it previewed on the right. When you are ready, click **Delete**, click **Yes** to confirm the deletion, and click **Close**.

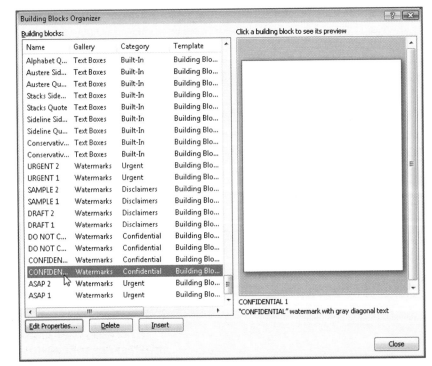

Figure 4-22: Word comes with a large number of building blocks that you can access.

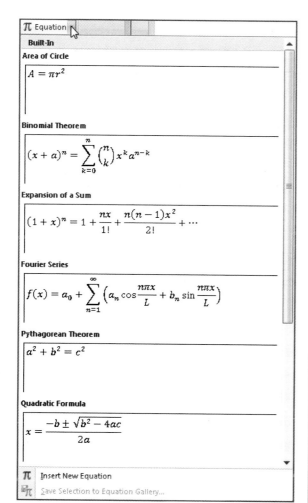

Built-In

Area of Circle

$$A = \pi r^2$$

Binomial Theorem

$$(x + a)^n = \sum_{k=0}^{n} \binom{n}{k} x^k a^{n-k}$$

Expansion of a Sum

$$(1 + x)^n = 1 + \frac{nx}{1!} + \frac{n(n-1)x^2}{2!} + \cdots$$

Fourier Series

$$f(x) = a_0 + \sum_{n=1}^{\infty} \left(a_n \cos \frac{n\pi x}{L} + b_n \sin \frac{n\pi x}{L} \right)$$

Pythagorean Theorem

$$a^2 + b^2 = c^2$$

Quadratic Formula

$$x = \frac{-b \pm \sqrt{b^2 - 4ac}}{2a}$$

π Insert New Equation

π Save Selection to Equation Gallery...

Figure 4-23: Word provides a number of ready-made equations for your use.

Enter an Equation

If you include mathematical equations in the documents you produce, Word has several helpful tools for producing them. These include ready-made equations, commonly used mathematical structures, a large standard symbol set, and many special mathematical symbols that can be generated with Math AutoCorrect. These tools allow you to create equations by modifying a ready-made equation, by using an equation text box with common mathematical structures and symbols, and by simply typing an equation as you would ordinary text.

MODIFY A READY-MADE EQUATION

1. Click at the location in the document where you want the equation.

2. Click the **Insert** tab, and click the **Equation** down arrow in the Symbols group. The list of built-in equations appears, as shown in Figure 4-23.

3. Click the equation you want to insert. An equation text box will appear, containing the equation, and the Equation Tools Design tab will display, as shown in Figure 4-24.

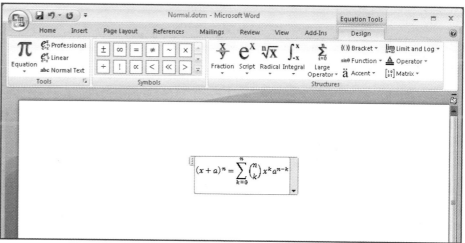

Figure 4-24: The equation text box automatically formats equations, which can be built with the structures and symbols in the Equation Tools Design tab.

NOTE

Treat an equation in its text box as you would ordinary text and the text box itself as an object in a line of text.

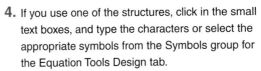

Mathematical·theorems·express·mathematically·truths·that·exist·in·the·universe.· Some·of·these·truths·are·directly·observable,·such·as·the·Pythagorean·Theorem.·¶

The·Binomial·Theorem,·$(x + a)^n = \sum_{k=0}^{n} \binom{n}{k} x^k a^{n-k}$,·Wikipedia·says,·is·an·

important·formula·giving·the·expansion·of·powers·of·sums.·It·is·often·attributed· to·Blaise·Pascal·who·described·them·in·the·17th·century.·It·was,·however,·known·

NOTE

If you save a document with an equation in any format prior to Word 2007, the equation will be converted to a .tif image and you will not be able to edit it after you reopen it.

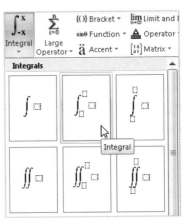

4. Click in the equation, and make any needed changes. Use the **RIGHT ARROW** and **LEFT ARROW** keys to move through the text. To save the revised equation, click the down arrow on the text box and click **Save As New Equation**.

5. When you have completed the equation, click outside the text box to close it and leave the equation looking like it is part of ordinary text.

CREATE AN EQUATION IN A TEXT BOX

You can open an equation text box and use the Equation Tools Design tab to create a professional-looking equation.

1. Click at the location in the document where you want to insert the equation.

2. Click the **Insert** tab, and click **Equation** in the Symbols group. An empty equation text box appears.

3. Either begin typing the equation or click one of the structures in the Structures group on the Equation Tools Design tab. If a drop-down menu appears, click the specific format you want.

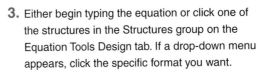

4. If you use one of the structures, click in the small text boxes, and type the characters or select the appropriate symbols from the Symbols group for the Equation Tools Design tab.

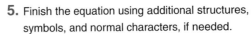

5. Finish the equation using additional structures, symbols, and normal characters, if needed.

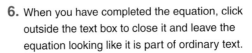

6. When you have completed the equation, click outside the text box to close it and leave the equation looking like it is part of ordinary text.

CREATE AN EQUATION FROM SCRATCH

You can also type an equation in a line of text using standard keyboard keys plus special symbols, and then convert it to a professional-looking equation.

1. Click at the location in the document where you want to insert the equation.

2. Begin typing using the keys on your keyboard, and, when needed, enter special characters by either:

● Typing one of the Math AutoCorrect text sequences, like \sqrt to get a square root symbol.

–Or–

- On the Insert tab, click **Symbol** in the Symbols group, and click the symbol you want if you see it; or click **More Symbols**, scroll through the symbols list until you see the one you want, double-click it, and click **Close**.

3. Finish the equation using the techniques in step 2. When you have completed it (Figure 4-26a shows a quadratic equation created in this manner), select the entire equation, and, in the Insert tab Symbol group, click **Equation**. An equation text box forms around the new equation.

4. In the Equation Tools tab, click **Professional** 𝑒ˣ in the upper-right area of the Tools group. Click outside the text box to close it. The professionally formatted quadratic equation looks like Figure 4-26b.

$$x=\{-b\pm\sqrt{(b^2-4ac)}\}/2a\cdot\P$$

(a)

$$x = \frac{-b\pm\sqrt{b^2-4ac}}{2a}\cdot\P$$

(b)

Figure 4-26: You can type an equation with normal text (a), and then convert it to a professional-looking equation (b).

Count Characters and Words

Word can tell you the number of characters and words in a document or in just a portion of the document you select.

On the Review tab, click **Word Count** in the Proofing group. The Word Count dialog box appears, displaying the following information about your document (see Figure 4-27):

- Number of pages
- Number of words
- Number of characters (not including spaces)
- Number of characters (including spaces)
- Number of paragraphs
- Number of lines

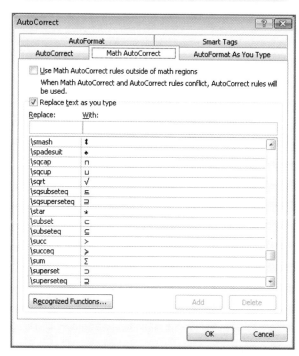

Figure 4-25: Math AutoCorrect allows you to insert math symbols by typing text sequences.

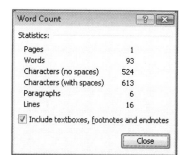

Figure 4-27: The Word Count feature is a quick and easy way to view the specifics of your document.

Use Highlighting

The Highlight feature is useful for marking important text in a document or text that you want to call a reader's attention to. Keep in mind, however, that highlighting parts of a document works best when the document is viewed online. When printed, the highlighting marks often appear gray and may even obscure the text you're trying to call attention to.

APPLY HIGHLIGHTING

1. In the Home tab Font group, click **Highlight** .

2. Select the text or graphic that you want to highlight. The highlighting is applied to your selection (see Figure 4-28.)

3. To turn off highlighting, click **Highlight** again or press **ESC**.

REMOVE HIGHLIGHTING

1. Select the text that you want to remove highlighting from, or press **CTRL-A** to select all of the text in the document.

2. In the Home tab Font group, click **Highlight**.

   –Or–

   In the Home tab Font group, click the **Highlight** drop-down arrow, and then click **No Color**.

CHANGE HIGHLIGHTING COLOR

In the Home tab Font group, click the **Highlight** drop-down arrow, and then click the color that you want to use.

FIND HIGHLIGHTED TEXT IN A DOCUMENT

1. In the Home tab, click **Find** in the Editing group.

2. If you don't see the Format button, click the **More** button.

3. Click the **Format** button, and then click **Highlight**.

4. Click **Find Next** and repeat this until you reach the end of the document.

5. Click **OK** when the message box is displayed indicating that Word has finished searching the document, and click **Close** in the Find And Replace dialog box.

Highlighting·is·best·when·viewed·online.··When·it·is·printed,·the· highlighting·often·appears·gray·and·may·obscure·the·text·you·are· trying·to·call·attention·to.¶

Figure 4-28: Highlighting is a great way to call attention to specific sections or phrases of your document.

Add Hyphenation

The Hyphenation feature automatically hyphenates words at the ends of lines based on standard hyphenation rules. You might use this feature if you want words to fit better on a line, or if you want to avoid uneven margins in right-aligned text or large gaps between words in justified text. (See Chapter 3 for information on text alignment.)

AUTOMATICALLY HYPHENATE A DOCUMENT

To automatically hyphenate a document you must be in Print Layout format:

1. In the Page Layout tab, click **Hyphenation** in the Page Setup group. A drop-down menu appears.

2. Click **Hyphenation Options** to open the Hyphenation dialog box. Select the option you want (see Figure 4-29):

   - **Automatically Hyphenate Document**   Either enables automatic hyphenation as you type or after the fact for selected text (this option is turned off in Word by default).

   - **Hyphenate Words in CAPS**   Hyphenates words typed in all uppercase letters.

   - **Hyphenation Zone**   Sets the distance from the right margin within which you want to hyphenate the document (the lower the value, the more words are hyphenated).

   - **Limit Consecutive Hyphens**   Sets the maximum number of hyphens that can appear in consecutive lines.

3. Click **OK** when finished.

MANUALLY HYPHENATE TEXT

1. In the Page Layout tab, click **Hyphenation** in the Page Setup group. A drop-down menu appears.

2. Click **Manual**.

3. Word searches for possible words to hyphenate. When it finds one, the Manual Hyphenation dialog box appears.

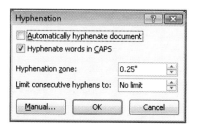

Figure 4-29: You can determine how Word will automatically hyphenate words.

QUICKSTEPS

EXPLORING THE THESAURUS

A *thesaurus* is a book or list of synonyms (words that have similar meanings), and Word contains a Thesaurus feature that will help you find just the right word to get your message across.

1. Select the word in your current document for which you want a synonym. You can also type a word later.

2. In the Review tab, click **Thesaurus** in the Proofing group. The Research task pane is displayed (see Figure 4-30.)

3. If you did not select a word in step 1, type the word you want to find synonyms for in the Search For field.

4. Click the green arrow button to start searching.

5. A list of possible words is displayed. Point to the word you want to use. Click the arrow that appears, and click **Insert**.

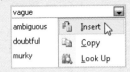

6. Close the Research pane when finished.

TIP

You can also open the Thesaurus by selecting the word you want to look up and pressing **SHIFT-F7**.

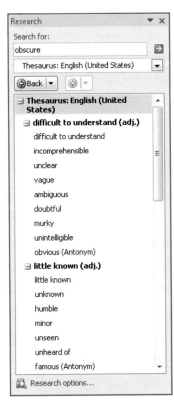

Figure 4-30: The Thesaurus feature enables you to find exactly the right word.

4. Do one of the following:

   ● Click **Yes** to hyphenate the word at the suggested blinking hyphen.

   ● Click one of the other hyphen choices, and then click **Yes**.

   ● Click **No** to continue without hyphenating the word.

5. Word will continue searching for words to hyphenate and display the Manual Hyphenation dialog box until the entire document has been searched. A message box is displayed to that effect. Click **OK**.

How to...

Chapter 5
Entering and Editing Data

Data is the heart and soul of Excel, yet before you can calculate data, chart it, analyze it, and otherwise *use* it, you have to place it in a worksheet. Data comes in several forms—such as numbers, text, dates, and times—and Excel handles the entry of each form uniquely. After you enter data into Excel's worksheets, you might want to make changes. Simple actions—such as removing text and numbers, copying and pasting, and moving data—are much more enhanced in Excel than the standard actions most users are familiar with.

In addition, Excel provides several tools to assist you in manipulating your data. You can have Excel intelligently continue a series without having to manually enter the sequential numbers or text. Automatic tools are available to help you verify accuracy and provide pop-ups—small toolbars related to the task you're working on. These, and other ways of entering and editing data, are covered in this chapter.

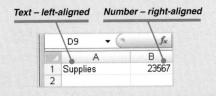
Enter Data

An Excel worksheet is a matrix, or grid, of lettered *column headings* across the top and numbered *row headings* down the side. The first row of a typical worksheet is used for column *headers*. The column headers represent categories of similar data. The rows beneath a column header contain data that is further categorized either by a row header along the leftmost column or listed below a column header. Figure 5-1 shows examples of two common worksheet arrangements. Worksheets can also be used to set up *tables* of data, where columns are sometimes referred to as *fields* and each row represents a unique *record* of data.

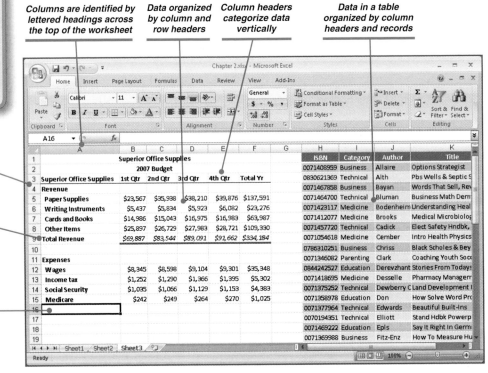

Figure 5-1: *The grid layout of Excel worksheets is defined by several components.*

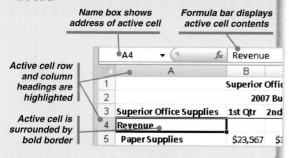

Each intersection of a row and column is called a *cell*, and is referenced first by its column location and then by its row location. The combination of a column letter and row number assigns each cell an *address*. For example, the cell at the intersection of column D and row 8 is called D8. A cell is considered to be *active* when it is clicked or otherwise selected as the place in which to place new data.

Enter Text

In an Excel worksheet, text is used to identify, explain, and emphasize numeric data. It comprises characters that cannot be used in calculations. You enter text by typing, just as you would in a word-processing program.

ENTER TEXT CONTINUOUSLY

Text (and numbers) longer than one cell width will appear to cover the adjoining cells to the right of the active cell. The covered cells have not been "used"; their contents have just been hidden, as shown in Figure 5-2. To enter text on one line:

1. Click the cell where you want the text to start.

2. Type the text. The text displays in one or more cells. (See Chapter 6 for more information on changing cell width.)

3. Complete the entry. (See the "Completing an Entry" QuickSteps later in this chapter for several ways to do that.)

WRAP TEXT ON MULTIPLE LINES

You can select a cell and wrap text at the end of its column width, much like how a word-processing program wraps text to the next line when entered text reaches its right margin.

1. Click the cell where you want to enter text.

2. Type all the text you want to appear in a cell. The text will continue to the right, overlapping as many cells as its length dictates (see row 4 in Figure 5-2).

3. Press **ENTER** to complete the entry. (See the "Completing an Entry" QuickSteps later in this chapter.) Click the cell a second time to select it.

TIP

If you are a keyboard junkie, you'll love the new KeyTips to access tools on the ribbon. Start by pressing **ALT** to place lettered KeyTips on the first level of tools on the ribbon. Press a letter corresponding to the tab or tool you want and if there are additional tools available, they will display. For example, press **ALT** to display KeyTips for the tabs on the ribbon. Press **N** to see the KeyTips available on the Insert menu. Press **T** to insert a table. Remove the KeyTips by pressing **ALT** a second time.

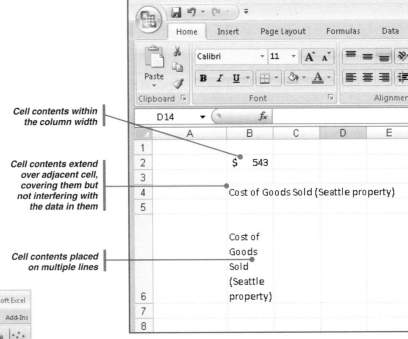

Cell contents within the column width

Cell contents extend over adjacent cell, covering them but not interfering with the data in them

Cell contents placed on multiple lines

Figure 5-2: **Text in a cell can cover several cells or be placed on multiple lines.**

NOTE

The *beginning cell* is in the same column where you first started entering data. For example, if you started entering data in cell A5 and continued through E5, pressing **TAB** between entries A5 through D5 and pressing **ENTER** in E5, the active cell would move to A6 (the beginning cell in the next row). If you had started entering data in cell C5, after pressing **ENTER** at the end of that row of entries, the active cell would move to C6, the cell below it.

4. Click the **Home** tab at the left end of the ribbon. In the Alignment group, click the **Wrap Text** button. The text wraps within the confines of the column width, increasing the row height as necessary (see row 6 in Figure 5-2).

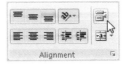

CONSTRAIN TEXT ON MULTIPLE LINES

When you want to constrain the length of text in a cell:

1. Click the cell where you want to enter text.

2. Type the text you want to appear on the first line.

QUICKSTEPS

COMPLETING AN ENTRY

You can complete an entry using the mouse or the keyboard, and control where the active cell goes next.

STAY IN THE ACTIVE CELL

To complete an entry and keep the current cell active, click Enter on the Formula bar.

MOVE THE ACTIVE CELL TO THE RIGHT

To complete the entry and move to the next cell in the same row, press **TAB**.

MOVE THE ACTIVE CELL TO THE NEXT ROW

To complete the entry and move the active cell to the next row below, press **ENTER**. The active cell moves to the beginning cell in the next row (see Note).

CHANGE THE DIRECTION OF THE ACTIVE CELL

1. Click the **Office button**, click **Excel Options**, and click the **Advanced** option.

2. Under Editing Options, click **After Pressing Enter, Move Selection** to select it if it is not already selected.

3. Click the **Direction** down arrow, and click a direction. Down is the default.

4. Click **OK** when finished.

MOVE THE ACTIVE CELL TO ANY CELL

To complete the entry and move the active cell to any cell in the worksheet, click the cell you want to become active.

3. Press **ALT-ENTER**. The insertion point moves to the beginning of a new line.

4. Repeat steps 2 and 3 for any additional lines of text. (See row 6 in Figure 5-2.)

5. Complete the entry. (See the "Completing an Entry" QuickSteps.)

Enter Numeric Data

Numbers are numerical data, from the simplest to the most complex. Excel provides several features to help you more easily work with numbers used to represent values in various categories, such as currency, accounting, dates and time, and mathematics.

ENTER NUMBERS

Enter numbers by simply selecting a cell and typing the numbers.

1. Click the cell where you want the numbers entered.

2. Type the numbers. Use decimal places, thousands separators, and other formatting as you type, or have Excel format these things for you. (See the "Formatting Numbers" QuickSteps later in this chapter).

3. Complete the entry. (See the "Completing an Entry" QuickSteps.)

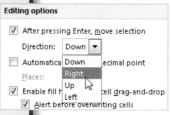

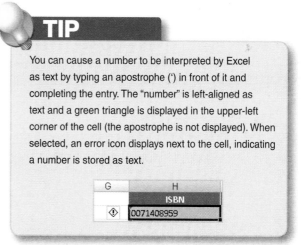

TIP

You can cause a number to be interpreted by Excel as text by typing an apostrophe (') in front of it and completing the entry. The "number" is left-aligned as text and a green triangle is displayed in the upper-left corner of the cell (the apostrophe is not displayed). When selected, an error icon displays next to the cell, indicating a number is stored as text.

ENTER NUMBERS USING SCIENTIFIC NOTATION

Exponents are used in scientific notation to shorten (or round off) very large or small numbers. The shorthand scientific notation display does not affect how the number is used in calculations or how it is stored in the computer.

1. Click the cell where you want the data entered.

2. Type the number using three components:

   - **Base** For example: 4, 7.56, -2.5.

   - **Scientific notation identifier** Type the letter "e" to represent the number is based on powers (exponents) of 10.

   - **Exponent** The number of times 10 is multiplied by itself. Positive exponent numbers increment the base number to the right of the decimal point, negative numbers to the left.

     For example, scientific notation for the number 123,456,789.0 is written to two decimal places as 1.23×10^8. In Excel you would type <u>1.23e8</u>, and it would display as: `1.23E+08`

3. Complete the entry. (See the "Completing an Entry" QuickSteps.)

Enter Dates

If you can think of a way to enter a date, Excel can probably recognize it as such. For example, Table 5-1 shows how Excel handles different ways to make the date entry using the date of March 1, 2009 (assuming you enter the date sometime in 2009) in a worksheet.

In cases when a year is omitted, Excel assumes the current year.

TYPING THIS...	DISPLAYS THIS AFTER COMPLETING THE ENTRY
3/1, 3-1, 1-mar, or 1-Mar	1-Mar
3/1/09, 3-1-09, 3/1/2009, 3-1-2009, 3-1/09, 3-1/2009, 20009/3/1, or 2009-3-1	3/1/2009
Mar 1, 09, March 1, 2009, 1-mar-09, or 1-Mar-2009	1-Mar-09

Table 5-1: *Examples of Excel Date Formats*

UICKSTEPS

FORMATTING NUMBERS

Numbers in a cell can be formatted in any one of several numeric categories by first selecting the cell containing the number. You can then use the tools available in the Home tab Number group or have the full range of options available to you from the Format Cells dialog box.

DISPLAY THE NUMBER TAB

Click the **Dialog Launcher** arrow in the lower-right corner of the Number group. The Format Cells dialog box appears with the Number tab displayed (shown in Figure 5-3).

ADD OR DECREASE DECIMAL PLACES

1. On the Number tab of the Format Cells dialog box, choose the appropriate numeric category (Number, Currency, Accounting, Percentage, or Scientific) from the Category list box.

2. In the Decimal Places text box, enter a number or use the spinner to set the number of decimal places you want. Click **OK**.

   –Or–

   In the ribbon's Home tab Number group, click the **Increase Decimal** or **Decrease Decimal** buttons.

ADD A THOUSANDS SEPARATOR

On the Number tab of the Format Cells dialog box, click the **Number** category, and click **Use 1000 Separator (,)**. Click **OK**.

–Or–

In the ribbon's Home tab Number group, click the **Comma Style** button in the Number group.

Continued . . .

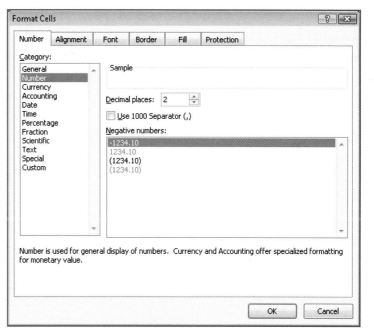

*Figure 5-3: **The Format Cells Number tab provides a complete set of numeric formatting categories and options.***

CHANGE THE DEFAULT DISPLAY OF DATES

Two common date formats (long and short) are displayed by default in Excel from settings in the Windows Regional And Language Options feature in Control Panel, shown in Figure 5-4.

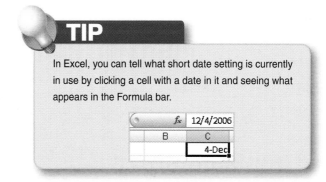

TIP

In Excel, you can tell what short date setting is currently in use by clicking a cell with a date in it and seeing what appears in the Formula bar.

 QUICKSTEPS

FORMATTING NUMBERS *(Continued)*

ADD A CURRENCY SYMBOL

1. On the Number tab, choose the appropriate numeric category (Currency or Accounting) from the Category list box.

2. Click **OK** to accept the default dollar sign ($), or choose another currency symbol from the Symbol drop-down list, and click **OK**.

   –Or–

   Click the **Accounting Number Format** button in the Number group. (You can change the currency symbol by clicking the down arrow next to the current symbol and choosing another one.)

CONVERT A DECIMAL TO A FRACTION

1. On the Number tab, click the **Fraction** category.

2. Click the type of fraction you want. View it in the Sample area, and change the type if needed. Click **OK**.

CONVERT A NUMBER TO A PERCENTAGE

1. On the Number tab, click the **Percentage** category.

2. In the Decimal Places text box, enter a number or use the spinner to set the number of decimal places you want. Click **OK**.

   –Or–

   Click the **Percent Style** button in the Number group.

FORMAT ZIP CODES, PHONE NUMBERS, AND SSNS

1. On the Number tab, click the **Special** category.

2. Select the type of formatting you want. Click **OK**.

Figure 5-4: *Use Windows to change how Excel and other Windows programs display dates.*

1. In Windows Vista, click **Start** and click **Control Panel**.

2. In Control Panel Home's Category view, click the **Clock, Language, And Region** category, and then click **Regional And Language Options**.

   –Or–

   In Classic view, double-click **Regional And Language Options**.

3. On the Formats tab, click **Customize This Format**.

4. Click the **Date** tab, click the **Short Date Format** down arrow, and select a format. Similarly, change the long date format, as necessary.

5. Click **OK** twice and close the Control Panel.

To enter the current date in a cell, click the cell and type **CTRL-;** (press and hold **CTRL** and press ;). The current date is displayed in the date format applied to the cell, the default of which is the short date.

QUICK**FACTS**

UNDERSTANDING EXCEL DATES AND TIMES

If you select a cell with a date within the last few years and open the Number Format list in the Number group, you'll notice several of the formats show examples with a number close to 40,000. Is this just an arbitrary number Excel has cooked up to demonstrate the example formats? Hardly. Dates and times in Excel are assigned values so that they can be used in calculations (Chapter 7 describes how to use formulas and functions). Dates are assigned a serial value starting with January 1, 1900 (serial value 1). The number you see on the Number Format list is the value of the date in the active cell (you can convert a date to its serial value by changing the format from Date to Number). For example, January 1, 2009, has a serial value of 39,814. Times are converted to the decimal equivalent of a day. For example, 4:15 P.M. is converted to .68. Since Excel considers dates and times as numerics, they are right-aligned in a cell. If you see what you think is a date but it is left aligned, Excel is treating it as text, not a date, and you would receive an error message if you tried to use it in a formula.

FORMAT DATES

You can change how a date is displayed in Excel by choosing a new format.

1. Right-click the cell that contains the date you want to change. (See the "Selecting Cells and Ranges" QuickSteps later in this chapter to see how to apply formats to more than one cell at a time.)

2. Click **Format Cells** on the context menu. The Format Cells dialog box appears with the Date category selected in the Number tab, as shown in Figure 5-5.

3. Select a format from the Type list. You can see how the new date format affects your date in the Sample area. Click **OK** when finished.

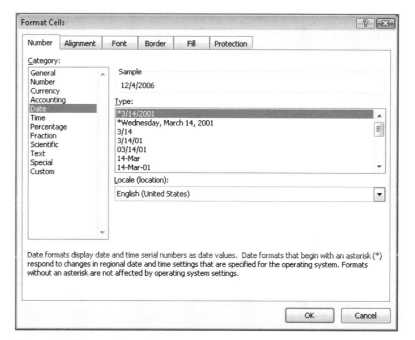

*Figure 5-5: **You can choose from among several ways to display dates in Excel.***

Use Times

Excel's conventions for time are as follows:

- Colons (:) are used as separators between hours, minutes, and seconds.
- AM is assumed unless you specify PM or, in the special case when you enter a time from 12:00 to 12:59, it is assumed to be PM.
- AM and PM do not display in the cell if they are not entered.
- You specify PM by entering a space followed by "p," "P," "pm," or "PM."
- Seconds are not displayed in the cell if not entered.
- AM, PM, and seconds are displayed in the Formula bar of a cell that contains a time.

ENTER TIMES

1. Select the cell in which you want to enter a time.
2. Type the hour followed by a colon.
3. Type the minutes followed by a colon.
4. Type the seconds, if needed.
5. Type a space and **PM**, if needed.
6. Complete the entry.

CHANGE THE DEFAULT DISPLAY OF TIMES

Times are displayed by default in Excel from settings configured in the Windows Regional And Language Options feature of Control Panel. To change the default settings:

1. In Windows Vista, click **Start** and click **Control Panel**.
2. In Category view, click the **Clock, Language, And Region** category, and then click **Regional And Language Options**.

   –Or–

   In Classic view, double-click **Regional And Language Options**.
3. On the Formats tab, click **Customize This Format**.
4. Click the **Time** tab, click the **Time Format** down arrow, and select a format. Similarly, change the AM and PM format, as necessary.

5. Click **OK** twice and close the Control Panel.

TIP

To enter the current time in a cell, click the cell and type **CTRL-SHIFT-:**. The current time in the form h:mm AM/PM is displayed.

CAUTION

Changing the *system* date/time formats in **Regional And Language Options** changes the date and time formats used by all Windows programs. Dates and times previously entered in Excel may change to the new setting unless they were formatted using the features in Excel's Format Cells dialog box.

QUICKSTEPS

ADDING DATA QUICKLY

Excel provides several features that help you quickly add more data to existing data with a minimum of keystrokes.

USE AUTOCOMPLETE

Excel will complete an entry for you after you type the first few characters of data that appears in a previous entry in the same column. Simply press **ENTER** to accept the completed entry. To turn off this feature if you find it bothersome:

1. Click the **Office button**, click **Excel Options**, and click the **Advanced** option.

2. Under Editing Options, click **Enable AutoComplete For Cell Values** to remove the check mark.

FILL DATA INTO ADJOINING CELLS

1. Select the cell that contains the data you want to copy into adjoining cells.

2. Point to the fill handle in the lower-right corner of the cell. The pointer turns into a cross.

3. Drag the handle in the direction you want to extend the data until you've reached the last cell in the range you want to fill.

4. Open the Smart tag , and select fill options.

–Or–

Select the contiguous cells you want to fill in with the data in a cell (see the "Selecting Cells and Ranges" QuickSteps later in this chapter). In the Home tab Editing group, click the Fill button.

Continued . . .

FORMAT TIMES

You can change how a time is displayed in Excel by choosing a new format.

1. Select the cell that contains the time you want to change. (See the "Selecting Cells and Ranges" QuickSteps later in this chapter for how to apply formats to more than one cell at a time.)

2. Click the **Dialog Launcher** arrow in the Home tab Number group. The Format Cells dialog box appears with the Number tab displaying the Time category.

3. Under Type, select a format. You can see how the new time format will affect your time in the Sample area. Click **OK** when finished.

TIP

You can fill data into the active cell from the cell above it or to its left by clicking **CTRL-D** or **CTRL-R**, respectively.

Edit Data

The data-intensive manner of Excel necessitates easy ways to change, copy, or remove data already entered on a worksheet. In addition, Excel has facilities to help you find and replace data and check the spelling.

Edit Cell Data

You have several choices on how to edit data, depending on whether you want to replace all the contents of a cell or just part of the contents, and whether you want to do it in the cell or in the Formula bar.

EDIT CELL CONTENTS

To edit data entered in a cell:

- Double-click the text in the cell where you want to begin editing. An insertion point is placed in the cell. Type the new data, use the mouse to select characters to be overwritten or deleted, or use keyboard shortcuts. Complete the entry when finished editing. (See the "Completing an Entry" QuickSteps earlier in this chapter.)

  –Or–

QUICKSTEPS

ADDING DATA QUICKLY *(Continued)*

CONTINUE A SERIES OF DATA

Data can be *logically* extended into one or more adjoining cells. For example, 1 and 2 extend to 3, 4...; Tuesday extends to Wednesday, Thursday...; January extends to February, March...; and 2006 and 2007 extend to 2008, 2009....

1. Select the cell or cells that contain a partial series. (See the "Selecting Cells and Ranges" QuickSteps later in this chapter for more information on selecting more than one cell.)

2. Point to the fill handle in the lower-right corner of the last cell. The pointer turns into a cross.

3. Drag the handle in the direction you want until you've reached the last cell in the range to complete the series.

   –Or–

1. Select the partial series, and continue the selection to as many contiguous cells as you want. In the Home tab Editing group, click the Fill down arrow, and click **Series**.

2. Verify the series parameters are what you want (see Figure 5-6), and click **OK**.

REMOVE THE FILL HANDLE

To hide the fill handle and disable AutoFill:

1. Click the **Office button**, click **Excel Options**, and click the **Advanced** option.

2. Under Editing Options, click **Enable Fill Handle And Cell Drag And Drop** to remove the check mark.

Continued . . .

- Select the cell to edit, and then click the cell's contents in the Formula bar where you want to make changes. Type the new data, use the mouse to select characters to overwrite or delete, or use keyboard shortcuts. Click **Enter** on the Formula bar or press **ENTER** to complete the entry.

   –Or–

- Select the cell to edit, and press **F2**. Edit in the cell or on the Formula bar using the mouse or keyboard shortcuts. Complete the entry.

REPLACE ALL CELL CONTENTS

Click the cell and type new data. The original data is deleted and replaced by your new characters.

CANCEL CELL EDITING

Before you complete a cell entry, you can revert back to your original data by pressing **ESC** or clicking **Cancel** on the Formula bar.

Remove Cell Contents

You can easily delete cell contents, move them to other cells, or clear selective attributes of a cell.

Figure 5-6: **You can fine-tune how you want a series to continue.**

TIP

To undo a data-removal action, even if you have performed several actions since removing the data, click **Undo** on the Quick Access toolbar next to the Office button (or press **CTRL-Z**) for the most recent action. For earlier actions, continue clicking **Undo** to work your way back; or click the down arrow next to the button, and choose the action from the drop-down list.

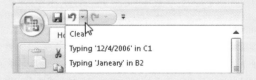

QUICKSTEPS

ADDING DATA QUICKLY (Continued)

ENTER DATA FROM A LIST

Previously entered data in a column is available to be selected from a list and entered with a click.

1. Right-click a cell in a column of data.

2. Select **Pick From Drop-Down List** from the context menu, and then click the data you want to enter in the cell.

Business
Education
Education
Business
Education
Medicine
Parenting
Technical
Business

CAUTION

If you use the Delete button in the Home tab Cells group, you delete the selected cells' contents *and* the cells themselves from the worksheet. See Chapter 6 for more information on deleting cells.

TIP

To select larger numbers of adjacent cells, rows, or columns, click the first item in the group, and then press **SHIFT** while clicking the last item in the group.

DELETE DATA

Remove all contents (but not formatting) from a cell by selecting it and pressing **DELETE**. You can delete the contents of more than one cell by selecting the cells or range and pressing **DELETE**. (See the "Selecting Cells and Ranges" QuickSteps for more information on selecting various configurations.)

MOVE DATA

Cell contents can be removed from one location and placed in another location of equal size. Select the cell or range you want to move. Then:

- Place the pointer on any edge of the selection, except the lower-right corner, until it turns into a cross with arrowhead tips. Drag the cell or range to the new location.

11	Expenses					
12	Wages	$8,345	$8,598	$9,104	$9,301	$35,348
13	Income tax	$1,252	$1,290	$1,366	$1,395	$5,302
14	Social Security	$1,035	$1,066	$1,129	$1,153	$4,383
15	Medicare	$242	$249	$264	$270	$1,025
16						
17						

–Or–

- On the Home tab Clipboard group, click **Cut**. Select the new location, and click **Paste** in the Clipboard group. (See "Copy and Paste Data" and "Use Paste Special" later in this chapter for more information on pasting options.)

REMOVE SELECTED CELL CONTENTS

A cell can contain several components, including:

- **Formats** Consisting of number formats, conditional formats (formats that display if certain conditions apply), and borders.

- **Contents** Consisting of formulas and data.

- **Comments** Consisting of notes you attach to a cell.

1. Choose which cell components you want to clear by selecting the cell or cells.

2. On the Home tab Editing group, click the **Clear** button, and click the applicable item from the menu. (Clicking **Clear Contents** performs the same action as pressing delete.)

QUICKSTEPS

SELECTING CELLS AND RANGES

The key to many actions in Excel is the ability to select cells in various configurations and use them to perform calculations. You can select a single cell, nonadjacent cells, and adjacent cells (or *ranges*).

SELECT A SINGLE CELL

Select a cell by clicking it, or move to a cell using the arrow keys or by completing an entry in a cell above or to the left.

SELECT NONADJACENT CELLS

Select a cell and then press **CTRL** while clicking the other cells you want to select.

SELECT A RANGE OF ADJACENT CELLS

Select a cell and drag over the additional cells you want to include in the range.

SELECT ALL CELLS ON A WORKSHEET

Click the **Select All** button in the upper-left corner of the worksheet, or press **CTRL-A**.

Select All

	A	B
4	**Revenue**	
5	**Paper Supplies**	$23,567
6	**Writing Instruments**	$5,437

SELECT A ROW OR COLUMN

Click a row (number) heading or column (letter) heading.

	A	B ↓
1		
2		
3		

Continued . . .

Copy and Paste Data

Data you've already entered on a worksheet can be copied to the same or other worksheets, or even to other Windows applications. You first *copy* the data to the Windows Clipboard, where it is temporarily stored. After selecting a destination for the data, you *paste* it into the cell or cells. You can copy all the data in a cell or only part of it.

1. Select the cells that contain the data you want to copy; or double-click a cell, and select the characters you want to copy.

2. In the Home tab Clipboard group, click the **Copy** button 🗐, or press **CTRL-C**. The selected data is copied to the Clipboard and the border around the cells displays a flashing dotted line.

Cards and Books	$14,986	$15,043

3. Select the new location for the data. In the Clipboard group, click **Paste** or press **CTRL-V**. The selected data is entered into the new cells. (If you click the **Paste** down arrow, you will see a menu of other paste options. Most of these options are covered in the next section, "Use Paste Special," and the others are related to features described in other chapters in this book.)

4. Click the **Smart** tag next to the pasted data, and choose the formatting or other options you want.

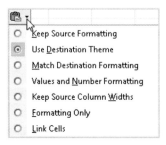

5. Repeat steps 3 and 4 to paste the copied data to other locations. Press **ESC** when finished to remove the flashing border around the source cells.

CAUTION

If you paste data into a cell that contains existing data, that existing data will be replaced with the pasted data. To avoid losing data, insert blank cells, rows, and columns to accommodate the data you are pasting. See Chapter 6 for more information on inserting cells, rows, and columns.

Use Paste Special

Paste Special allows you to selectively include or omit formulas, values, formatting, comments, arithmetic operations, and other cell properties *before* you copy or move data. (See Chapter 7 for information on formulas, values, and arithmetic operations.) This tool offers more options than the Paste Smart tag used *after* you paste.

1. Select and then copy or cut the data you want.

2. Select the destination cell or cells to where you want the data copied or moved.

3. In the Home tab Clipboard group, click the **Paste** down arrow, and click **Paste Special**; or right-click the destination cells, and click **Paste Special**. The Paste Special dialog box appears, as shown in Figure 5-8.

4. Select the paste options you want in the copied or moved cells, and click **OK**.

Find and Replace Data

In worksheets that might span thousands of rows and columns (over one million rows and over 16,000 columns are possible), you need the ability to locate data quickly, as well as to find instances of the same data so that consistent replacements can be made.

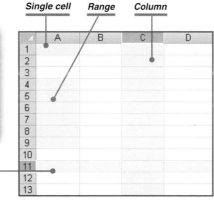

Figure 5-7: *You can include a single cell, a row, a column, and a range all in one selection.*

Figure 5-8: *You can selectively add or omit many cell properties when you move or copy data.*

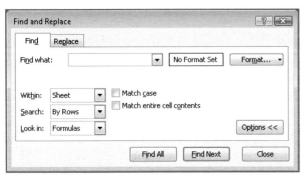

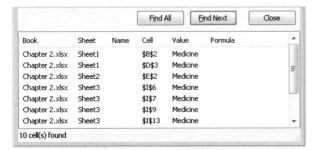

Figure 5-9: *The Find tab lets you refine your search based on several criteria.*

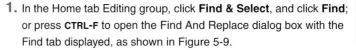

FIND DATA

1. In the Home tab Editing group, click **Find & Select**, and click **Find**; or press **CTRL-F** to open the Find And Replace dialog box with the Find tab displayed, as shown in Figure 5-9.

2. Type the text or number you want to find in the Find What text box.

3. Click **Options** to view the following options to refine the search:

   - **Format**   Opens the Find Format dialog box, where you select from several categories of number, alignment, font, border, patterns, and protection formats.

   - **Choose Format From Cell**   From the Format drop-down list; lets you click a cell that contains the format you want to find.

   - **Within**   Limits your search to the current worksheet or expands it to all worksheets in the workbook.

   - **Search**   Lets you search to the right by rows or down by columns. You can search to the left and up by pressing **SHIFT** and clicking **Find Next**.

   - **Look In**   Focuses the search to just formulas, values, or comments.

   - **Match Case**   Lets you choose between uppercase or lowercase text.

   - **Match Entire Cell Contents**   Searches for an exact match of the characters in the Find What text box.

4. Click **Find All** to display a table of all occurrences, or click **Find Next** to find the next singular occurrence.

REPLACE DATA

The Replace tab of the Find And Replace dialog box looks and behaves similar to the Find tab covered earlier.

1. In the Home tab Editing group, click **Find & Select**, and click **Replace**; or press **CTRL-H** to open the Find And Replace dialog box with the Replace tab displayed.

2. Enter the text or number to find in the Find What text box; enter the replacement characters in the Replace With text box. If formatting or search criteria are required, click **Options**. See the section "Find Data" for the options' descriptions.

3. Click **Replace All** to replace all occurrences in the worksheet, or click **Replace** to replace occurrences one at a time.

FIND SPECIFIC EXCEL OBJECTS

You can quickly locate key Excel objects, such as formulas and comments, without having to type any keywords. The objects you can directly search for are listed on the Find & Select drop-down menu.

1. In the Home tab Editing group, click **Find & Select**. The drop-down menu lists several categories of objects from which you can choose.

   Click the item whose instances you want selected. The first instance is surrounded by a thin border, and all other instances in the worksheet are selected/highlighted (see Figure 5-10).

   –Or–

   Click **Go To Special** to open a dialog box of the same name, and select from several additional objects. Click **OK** after making your selection.

2. To remove the selection/highlight from found objects, click **Find & Select** again, and click **Select Objects** to turn off that feature.

Verify Spelling

You can check the spelling of selected cells—or the entire worksheet—using Excel's main dictionary and a custom dictionary you add words to (both dictionaries are shared with other Office programs).

1. Select the cells to check; to check the entire worksheet, select any cell.

2. In the Review tab Proofing group, click **Spelling** or press **F7**. When the spelling checker doesn't find anything to report, you are told the spelling check is complete. Otherwise, the Spelling dialog box appears, as shown in Figure 5-11.

	A	B	C	D	E	F
1	Superior Office Supplies					
2	2007 Budget					
3	Superior Office Supplies	1st Qtr	2nd Qtr	3rd Qtr	4th Qtr	Total Yr
4	Revenue					
5	Paper Supplies	$23,567	$35,938	$38,210	$39,876	$137,591
6	Writing Instruments	$5,437	$5,834	$5,923	$6,082	$23,276
7	Cards and Books	$14,986	$15,043	$16,975	$16,983	$63,987
8	Other Items	$25,897	$26,729	$27,983	$28,721	$109,330
9	Total Revenue	$69,887	$83,544	$89,091	$91,662	$334,184

Figure 5-10: Certain Excel objects, such as comments, can be located and identified with just a few clicks.

Figure 5-11: *The Spelling dialog box provides several options to handle misspelled or uncommon words.*

Figure 5-12: *AutoCorrect provides several automatic settings and lets you add words and characters that are replaced with alternatives.*

3. Choose to ignore one or more occurrences of the characters shown in the Not In Dictionary text box, or change the characters by picking from the Suggestions list.

4. Click **AutoCorrect** if you want to automatically replace words in the future. (See the next section, "Modify Automatic Corrections," for more information on using AutoCorrect.)

5. Click **Options** to change language or custom dictionaries and set other spelling criteria.

Modify Automatic Corrections

Excel automatically corrects common data entry mistakes as you type, replacing characters and words you choose with other choices. You can control how this is done.

1. Click the **Office button**, then click **Excel Options** | **Proofing** | **AutoCorrect Options**. The AutoCorrect dialog box appears, as shown in Figure 5-12. As appropriate, do one or more of the following:

   - Choose the type of automatic corrections you do or do not want from the options at the top of the dialog box.

   - Click **Exceptions** to set capitalization exceptions.

   - Click **Replace Text As You Type** to turn off automatic text replacement (turned on by default).

   - Add new words or characters to the Replace and With lists, and click **Add**; or select a current item in the list, edit it, and click **Replace**.

   - Delete replacement text by selecting the item in the Replace and With lists and clicking **Delete**.

2. Click **OK** when you are done.

Chapter 6
Formatting a Worksheet

Arguably, the primary purpose of a worksheet is to provide a grid to calculate numbers, generally regarded as a rather boring display of numeric data. Excel provides you with the tools to adjust and rearrange the row-and-column grid to meet your needs, but it goes much further to bring emphasis, coordinated colors, and other features that let you add *presentation* to your data.

In this chapter you will learn how to add and delete cells, rows, and columns, and how to change their appearance, both manually and by having Excel do it for you. You will see how to change the appearance of text, how to use themes and styles for a more consistent look, and how to add comments to a cell to explain important points. Techniques to better display workbooks and work with worksheets are also covered.

UICKSTEPS

ADDING AND REMOVING ROWS, COLUMNS, AND CELLS

You can insert or delete rows one at a time or select adjacent and nonadjacent rows to perform these actions on them together. (See Chapter 5 for information on selecting rows, columns, and cells.)

ADD A SINGLE ROW

1. Select the row below where you want the new row.

2. In the Home tab Cells group, click **Insert**; or right-click a cell in the selected row, and click **Insert**.

ADD MULTIPLE ADJACENT ROWS

1. Select the number of rows you want immediately below the row where you want the new rows.

2. In the Home tab Cells group, click **Insert**; or right-click a cell in the selected rows, and click **Insert**.

ADD ROWS TO MULTIPLE NONADJACENT ROWS

1. Select the number of rows you want immediately below the first row where you want the new rows.

2. Hold down the **CTRL** key while selecting the number of rows you want immediately below any other rows.

3. In the Home tab Cells group, click the **Insert** down arrow, and click **Insert Sheet Rows**; or right-click any selection, and click **Insert**.

Continued . . .

NOTE

Don't ever worry about running out of rows or columns in a worksheet. You can have up to 1,048,576 rows and 16,384 columns in each Excel worksheet.

Work with Cells, Rows, and Columns

Getting a worksheet to look the way you want will probably involve adding and removing cells, rows, and/or columns to appropriately separate your data and remove unwanted space. You might also want to adjust the size and type of cell border and add comments to provide ancillary information about the contents of a cell. This section covers these features and more.

Adjust Row Height

You can change the height of a row manually or by changing cell contents.

CHANGE THE HEIGHT USING A MOUSE

1. Select one or more rows (they can be adjacent or nonadjacent).

2. Point at the bottom border of a selected row heading until the pointer changes to a cross with up and down arrowheads.

3. Drag the border up or down to the row height you want.

CHANGE THE HEIGHT BY ENTERING A VALUE

1. Select the rows you want to adjust.

2. In the Home tab Cells group, click **Format**, and, under Cell Size, click **Row Height**; or right-click the cell, and click **Row Height**. The Row Height dialog box appears.

3. Type a new height in *points* (there are 72 points to an inch), and click **OK**. The cell height changes, but the size of the cell contents stays the same.

CHANGE ROW HEIGHT BY CHANGING CELL CONTENTS

1. Select one or more cells, rows, or characters that you want to change in height.

2. Change the cell contents. Examples of the various ways to do this include

   - **Changing Font Size** In the Home tab Font group, click the **Font Size** down arrow, and click a size from the drop-down list. (You can drag up and down the list of font sizes and see the impact of each on the worksheet without selecting one.)

ADDING AND REMOVING ROWS, COLUMNS, AND CELLS (Continued)

ADD A SINGLE COLUMN

1. Select the column to the right of where you want the new column.

2. In the Home tab Cells group, click **Insert**; or right-click a cell in the selected column, and click **Insert**.

ADD MULTIPLE ADJACENT COLUMNS

1. Select the number of columns you want immediately to the right of the column where you want the new columns.

2. In the Home tab Cells group, click **Insert**; or right-click a cell in the selected columns, and click **Insert**.

ADD COLUMNS TO MULTIPLE NONADJACENT COLUMNS

1. Select the number of columns you want immediately to the right of the first column where you want the new columns.

2. Hold down the **CTRL** key while selecting the number of columns you want immediately to the right of any other columns.

3. In the Home tab Cells group, click the **Insert** down arrow, and click **Insert Sheet Columns**; or right-click any selection and click **Insert**.

ADD CELLS

1. Select the cells adjacent to where you want to insert the new cells.

Continued . . .

NOTE

You cannot change the width of a single cell without changing the width of all cells in the column.

- **Placing Characters on Two or More Lines Within a Cell**   Place the insertion point at the end of a line or where you want the line to break, and press **ALT-ENTER**.

- **Inserting Pictures or Drawing Objects**   See Chapter 14 for information on working with graphics.

When a selected object changes size or a new object is inserted, if its height becomes larger than the original row height, the height of all cells in the row(s) will be increased. The size of the other cell's contents, however, stays the same.

CHANGE ROW HEIGHT TO FIT SIZE OF CELL CONTENTS

Excel automatically adjusts row height to accommodate the largest object or text size added to a row. If you subsequently removed larger objects or text and want to resize to fit the remaining objects, you can do so using AutoFit.

- Double-click the bottom border of the row heading for a row or selected rows.

  –Or–

- Select the cell or rows you want to size. In the Home tab Cells group, click **Format** and click **AutoFit Row Height**.

The row heights(s) will adjust to fit the highest content.

Adjust Column Width

As with changing row height, you can change the width of a column manually or by changing cell contents.

CHANGE THE WIDTH USING A MOUSE

1. Select one or more columns (columns can be adjacent or nonadjacent).

2. Point at the right border of a selected column heading until the pointer changes to a cross with left and right arrowheads.

Width: 7.43 (57 pixels)	
E	F
4th Qtr	Total Yr
$39,876	$137,591

3. Drag the border to the left or right to the width you want. The width is displayed in a ScreenTip.

QUICKSTEPS

ADDING AND REMOVING ROWS, COLUMNS, AND CELLS (Continued)

2. In the Home tab Cells group, click the **Insert** down arrow, and click **Insert Cells**, or right-click the cell and click **Insert**.

3. In the Insert dialog box, choose the direction to shift the existing cells to make room for the new cells. Click **OK**.

REMOVING CELLS, ROWS, AND COLUMNS

1. Select the single or adjacent items (cells, rows, or columns) you wish to remove. If you want to remove nonadjacent items, hold down the **CTRL** key while clicking them.

2. In the Home tab Cells group, click the **Delete** down arrow, and click the command applicable to what you want to remove; or right-click the selection, and click **Delete**.

3. When deleting selected cells, the Delete dialog box appears. Choose from which direction to fill in the removed cells, and click **OK**.

MERGE CELLS

Select the cells you want to combine into one cell.

1. In the Home tab Alignment group, click the **Merge And Center** down arrow. (If all you want to do is merge and center, click the button.)

2. Click the applicable tool from the drop-down list.

CHANGE THE WIDTH BY ENTERING A VALUE

1. Select the columns you want to adjust.

2. In the Home tab Cells group, click **Format | Column Width**; or right-click the cell, and click **Column Width**. The Column Width dialog box appears.

3. Type a new width, and click **OK**. The cell width changes, but the size of the cell contents stays the same.

CHANGE COLUMN WIDTH TO FIT SIZE OF CELL CONTENTS

- Double-click the right border of the column header for the column or selected columns.

  –Or–

- Select the cell or columns you want to size. In the Home tab Cells group, click **Format | AutoFit Column Width**.

The column width(s) will adjust to fit the longest entry.

Hide and Unhide Rows and Columns

Hidden rows and columns provide a means to temporarily remove rows or columns from view without deleting them or their contents.

HIDE ROWS AND COLUMNS

1. Select the rows or columns to be hidden (see Chapter 5).

2. In the Home tab Cells group, click **Format | Hide & Unhide | Hide Rows** or **Hide Columns**; or right-click the selection, and click **Hide**.

   –Or–

   Drag the bottom border of the rows to be hidden *up*, or drag the right border of the columns to be hidden to the *left*.

The row numbers or column letters of the hidden cells are omitted, as shown in Figure 6-1. (You can also tell cells are hidden by the slightly darker border in the row or column headers between the hidden rows or columns.)

The default column width for a worksheet is determined by the average number of characters in the default font that will fit in the column (not in points, as is row height). For example, the default Arial 10 pt. font provides a standard column width of 8.43 characters. If you want to change the default column width, in the Home tab Cells group, click **Format I Standard Width**. Type a width and click **OK**. Columns at the original standard width will change to reflect the new value.

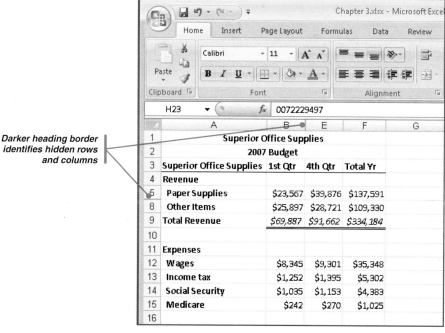

Darker heading border identifies hidden rows and columns

*Figure 6-1: **Rows 6 and 7 and columns C and D are hidden in this worksheet.***

If you hide one or more rows or columns beginning with column A or row 1, it does not look like you can drag across the rows or columns on both sides of the hidden rows or columns to unhide them. However, you can drag by selecting the row or column to the right of or below the hidden row or column and dragging the selection into the heading. Then when you click **Unhide**, the hidden object will appear. If you don't do this, you won't be able to recover the hidden row or column.

UNHIDE ROWS OR COLUMNS

1. Drag across the row or column headings on both sides of the hidden rows or columns.

2. In the Home tab Cells group, click **Format I Hide & Unhide I Unhide Rows** or **Unhide Columns**.

–Or–

Right-click the selection and click **Unhide**.

Change Cell Borders

Borders provide a quick and effective way to emphasize and segregate data on a worksheet. You can create borders by choosing from samples or by setting them up in a dialog box. Use the method that suits you best.

TIP

You can draw borders around cells on a worksheet. In the Home tab Font group, click the **Border** down arrow and click **Draw Border** to draw a perimeter border or click **Draw Border Grid** to include interior borders of selected cells. Use the pencil mouse pointer to drag over the cells you want to have a border. Click **Erase Border** and drag over a border to remove it. Also, you can change the color and line style of the borders you draw. Press **ESC** to return to the standard mouse pointer.

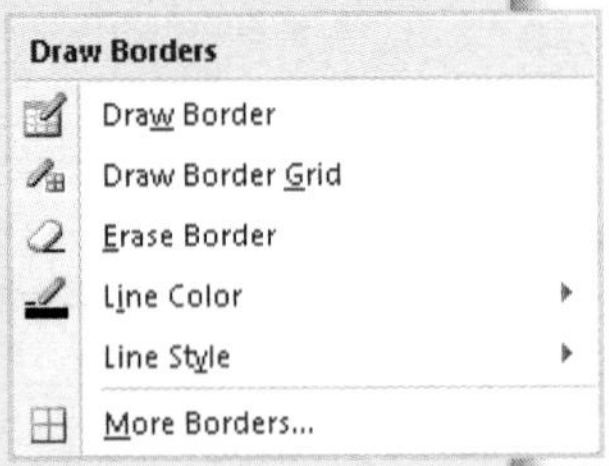

PICK A BORDER

1. Select the cell, range, row, or column whose border you want to modify.
2. In the Home tab Font group, click the **Border** down arrow, and select the border style you want. (The style you choose remains as the available border style on the button.)
3. To remove a border, select the cell(s), click the **Border** down arrow, and click **No Border**.

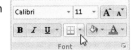

PREVIEW BORDERS BEFORE YOU CHANGE THEM

1. Select the cell, range, row, or column that you want to modify with a border.
2. In the Home tab Font group, click the **Border** down arrow, and click **More Borders**.

   –Or–

   In the Home tab Font group, click the **Dialog Box Launcher**, or right-click the selection, and click **Format Cells**. Click the **Border** tab in the Format Cells dialog box.

   In any case, the Format Cells dialog box appears with the Border tab displayed, as shown in Figure 6-2.

3. In the Border area, you will see a preview of the selected cells. Use the other tools in the dialog box to set up your borders:
   - **Presets Buttons** Set broad border parameters by selecting to have no border, an outline border, or an inside "grid" border (can also be changed manually in the Border area).
   - **Line Area** Select a border style and color (see "Change Themed Colors" later in this chapter for information on color options).
   - **Border Buttons** Choose where you want a border (click once to add the border; click twice to remove it).
4. Click **OK** to apply the borders.

Figure 6-2: ***You can build and preview borders for selected cells in the Border tab.***

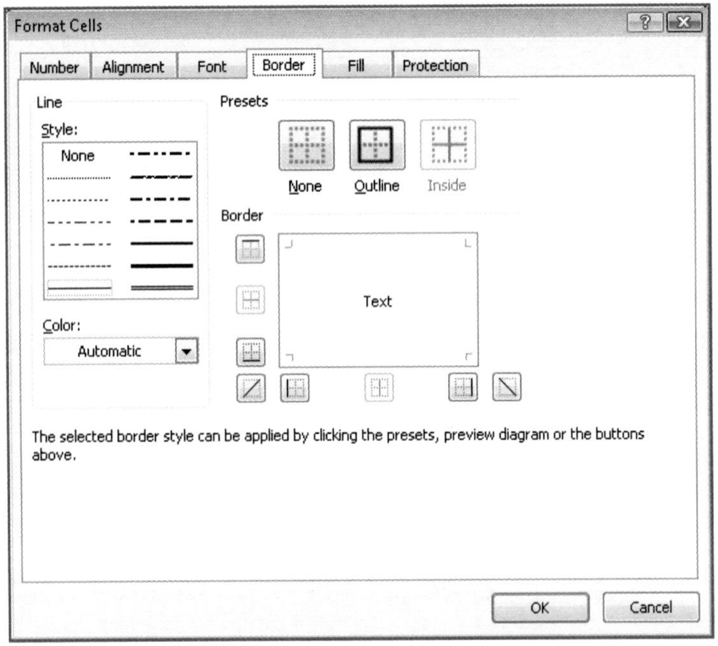

Add a Comment

A comment acts as a "notepad" for cells, providing a place on the worksheet for explanatory text that can be hidden until needed.

1. Select the cell where you want the comment.
2. In the Review tab Comments group, click **New Comment**.

–Or–

Right-click the cell, and click **Insert Comment**.

In either case, a text box labeled with your user name is attached to the cell.

3. Type your comment and click anywhere on the worksheet to close the comment. An indicator icon (red triangle) in the upper-right corner of the cell shows that a comment is attached.

> $109,330
> $334,184
> **John Cronan:**
> This has been an outstanding year!!!
> $35,348

VIEW COMMENTS

You can view an individual comment, view them in sequence, or view all comments on a worksheet:

- To view any comment, point to or select a cell that displays an indicator icon (red triangle) in its upper-right corner. The comment stays displayed as long as your mouse pointer remains in the cell.

- To view comments in sequence, in the Review tab Comments group, click **Next**. The next comment in the worksheet, moving left to right and down the rows, displays until you click another cell or press **ESC**. Click **Previous** in the Comments group to reverse the search direction.

- To keep the comment displayed while doing other work, select the cell that contains the comment. In the Review tab Comments group, click **Show/Hide Comment**; or right-click the cell, and click **Show/Hide Comments**. (Click either command to hide the comment.)

- To view all comments in a worksheet and keep the comment displayed while doing other work, in the Review tab Comments group, click **Show All Comments**. (Click the command a second time to hide all comments.)

EDIT A COMMENT

1. Select a cell that displays an indicator icon (red triangle) in its upper-right corner.

2. In the Review tab Comments group, click **Edit Comment**.

   –Or–

   Right-click the cell, and click **Edit Comment**.

3. Edit the text, including the user name if appropriate. Click anywhere in the worksheet when finished.

DELETE A COMMENT

1. Select the cell or cells that contain the comments you want to delete.

2. In the Review tab Comments group, click **Delete**.

   –Or–

   Right-click the cell, and click **Delete Comment**.

MOVE AND RESIZE A COMMENT

Open the comment (see "Edit a Comment"):

- To **Resize**, point to one of the corner or mid-border sizing handles. When the pointer becomes a double arrow-headed line, drag the handle in the direction you want to increase or decrease the comment's size.

- To **Move**, point at the wide border surrounding the comment. When the pointer becomes a cross with arrowhead tips, drag the comment to where you want it.

COPY A COMMENT

1. Select the cell that contains the comment you want to copy.

2. In the Home tab Clipboard group, click **Copy**.

   –Or–

   Right-click the cell, and click **Copy**.

   –Or–

   Press **CTRL-C**.

   In all cases, the cell is surrounded by a flashing border.

3. Select the cells to which you want the comment copied. Then, in the Clipboard group, click the **Paste** down arrow, and click **Paste Special**. In the Paste Special dialog box, under Paste, click **Comments**, and then click **OK**.

4. Repeat step 3 to paste the comment into other cells. When finished, press **ESC** to remove the flashing border.

FORMATTING COMMENTS (Continued)

CHANGE A COMMENT'S COLOR AND BORDER

1. Right-click the border of the comment, and click **Format Comment**.

2. In the Format Comment dialog box, click the **Colors And Lines** tab.

3. Click the **Fill Color** down arrow to open the gallery. Click the new color you want (see "Change Themed Colors" later in this chapter for information on color options).

4. In the Line area, change the attributes that control the comment's border. Click **OK** when finished.

Apply Formatting

Formatting gives life to a worksheet, transforming a rather dull collection of text and numbers into pleasing colors, shades, and variations in size and effects that bring attention to points you are trying to emphasize. You can apply or create *themes* (consistent use of color, fonts, and graphics effects) to give your worksheets a coordinated appearance. If you want more control, you can apply *styles* (consistent formatting parameters applicable to specific worksheet objects) and *direct formatting* (use of ribbon buttons and dialog boxes) to cells and text. (See the "Understanding Excel Formatting" QuickFacts for more information on these formatting types.) In addition, you can transfer formatting attributes from one cell to others.

UNDERSTANDING EXCEL FORMATTING

There are a plethora of ways you can change the appearance of text and worksheet elements. Without having a sense of the "method behind the madness," it's easy to become confused and frustrated when attempting to enhance your work. Excel (as well as Microsoft Word and Microsoft PowerPoint) operate on a hierarchy of formatting assistance (see Figure 6-3). The higher a formatting feature is on the stack, the broader and more automatic are its effects; the lower on the stack, the more user intervention is required, although you will have more control over the granularity of any given feature.

Continued . . .

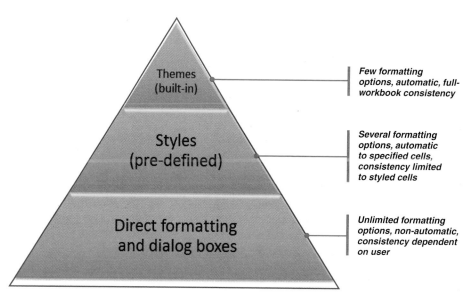

Figure 6-3: *Excel provides three levels of formatting assistance.*

UNDERSTANDING EXCEL FORMATTING *(Continued)*

- **Themes** are at the top of the formatting heap. Themes provide an efficiently lazy way to apply professionally designed color, font, and graphic elements to a workbook. Each theme (with names like Office, Currency, and Solstice) includes twelve colors (four text colors, six accent colors, and two hyperlink colors), along with six shades of each primary theme color. Theme fonts are classified for headings and the body text (the default workbook theme is Office, which is where the new Calibri font that you see in new workbooks comes from). When you switch themes, all theme-affected elements are changed. You can modify existing themes and save them, creating your own theme.

- **Styles** occupy the middle tier of Excel formatting. Styles apply consistent formatting to directed Excel components, such as cells, tables, charts, and PivotTables. Styles, similar to themes, can be modified and saved for your own design needs. Both themes and styles are supported by several galleries of their respective formatting options, and provide a live preview when you hover your mouse pointer over each choice. Certain attributes of a style are *themed*, meaning they are associated with the current theme and change accordingly.

Continued . . .

Apply Themes

Themes are the most hands-off way to add a coordinated look and feel to a worksheet. Built-in themes control the formatting of themed elements, such as the color of table headers and rows and the font used in chart text. In addition, you can change themes and modify themed elements (colors, fonts, and graphic effects).

CHANGE THE CURRENT THEME

By default, Excel applies the Office theme to new workbooks. You can easily view the effects from the other built-in themes and change to the one you prefer.

1. In the Page Layout tab Themes group, click **Themes**. A gallery of the available themes (built-in and custom) is displayed, as shown in Figure 6-4.

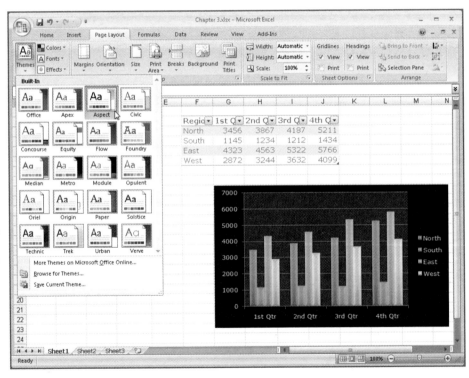

Figure 6-4: Excel provides 20 built-in professionally designed themes.

UNDERSTANDING EXCEL
FORMATTING *(Continued)*

- **Direct formatting** is the feature most of us have used to get the look we want, found in buttons on the ribbon and formatting dialog boxes divided into several tabs of options. Direct formatting provides the greatest control and access to formatting features, but even though Excel now provides live previews for many options, most still require you to accept the change, view the result in the workbook, and then repeat the process several times to get the result you want.

So how do you best put this hierarchy to work? Start at the top by applying a theme. If its formatting works for you, you're done! If you need more customization, try simply changing to a different theme. Need more options? Try applying a style to one of the style-affected components. Finally, if you need total control, use a component's formatting dialog box and ribbon buttons to make detailed changes. When you're all done, save all your changes as a new theme that you can apply to new workbooks, and also to your Word documents and PowerPoint presentations.

TIP

To quickly determine the theme currently in effect, click the **Page Layout** tab, and point to the **Themes** button in the Themes group. The ScreenTip displays the current theme (similarly, point to the **Fonts** button to see the current theme fonts in use).

Themes

Current: Office Theme

Change the overall design of the entire document, including colors, fonts, and effects.

⟳ **Press F1 for more help.**

2. Point to each theme and see how colors, fonts, and graphics change in themed elements. The best way to view changes is to create a table and associated chart, and with it displayed, point to each theme in the gallery and see how the table and chart look (see Figure 6-4).

3. Click the theme you want, and save your workbook.

CHANGE THEMED COLORS

Each theme comes with 12 primary colors (see the "Understanding Excel Formatting" QuickFacts) affecting text, accents, and hyperlinks. You can choose a theme with different colors or modify each constituent color.

1. In the Page Layout tab Themes group, click **Colors**. The drop-down list displays the built-in themes and eight of the twelve colors associated with each theme.

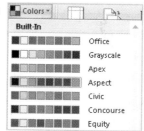

2. At the bottom of the list, click **Create New Theme Colors**. The Create New Theme Colors dialog box displays each constituent theme color and a sample displaying the current selections (see Figure 6-5).

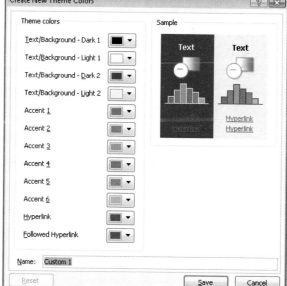
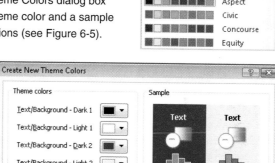

Figure 6-5: **Each theme color can be modified from an essentially infinite number of choices.**

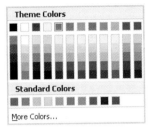

Theme Colors

Standard Colors

More Colors...

3. Click the theme color you want to change. A gallery of colors displays and provides three options from which you select a new color:

- **Theme Colors** displays a matrix of the twelve primary colors in the current theme and six shades associated with each. Click a color and see the change in the Sample area.

- **Standard Colors** displays the ten standard colors in the color spectrum (red through violet). Click the color you want.

- **More Colors** opens the Colors dialog box, shown in Figure 6-6, from where you can select a custom color by clicking a color and using a slider to change its shading, or by selecting a color model and entering specific color values. In addition, you can click the **Standard** tab, and select from a hexagonal array of Web-friendly colors.

4. Repeat step 3 for any other theme color you want to change. If you get a bit far afield in your color changes, don't panic. Click **Reset** at the bottom of the Create New Theme Colors dialog box to return to the default theme colors.

5. Type a new name for the color combination you've selected, and click **Save**. Custom colors are available for selection at the top of the theme Colors drop-down list.

TIP

To change a custom color or font, right-click the custom color or font in the respective theme Colors or Fonts drop-down list, and click **Edit**. Either Edit dialog box provides the same options as the Create New Theme Colors (or Fonts) dialog box you used to create the custom scheme.

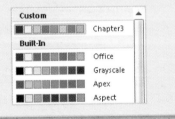

Custom

Chapter3

Built-In

Office
Grayscale
Apex
Aspect

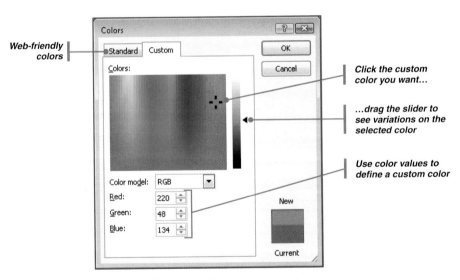

Web-friendly colors

Click the custom color you want...

...drag the slider to see variations on the selected color

Use color values to define a custom color

Figure 6-6: The Colors dialog box offers the greatest control of custom color selection, as well as a collection of standard Web-friendly colors.

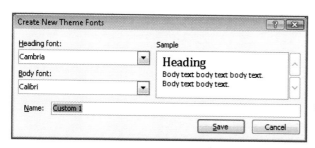

Figure 6-7: **You can choose any heading and/or body font from the fonts available in your Windows system.**

CHANGE THEMED FONTS

Each theme includes two fonts. The *body* font is used for general text entry (the Calibri font in the default Office theme is the body font). A *heading* font is also included and used in a few cell styles (see "Use Cell Styles" later in this chapter).

1. In the Page Layout tab Themes group, click **Fonts**. The drop-down list displays a list of theme font combinations (heading and body). The current theme font combination is highlighted.

2. Point to each combination to see how the fonts will appear on your worksheet.

3. Click the combination you want, or click **Create New Theme Fonts** at the bottom of the drop-down list.

4. In the Create New Theme Fonts dialog box (see Figure 6-7), click either or both the **Heading Font** and **Body Font** down arrows to select new fonts. View the new combination in the Sample area.

5. Type a new name for the font combination you've selected, and click **Save**. Custom fonts are available for selection at the top of the theme Fonts drop-down list.

CHANGE THEMED GRAPHIC EFFECTS

Shapes, illustrations, pictures, and charts include graphic effects that are controlled by themes. Themed graphics are modulated in terms of their lines (borders), fills, and effects (such as shadowed, raised, and shaded). For example,

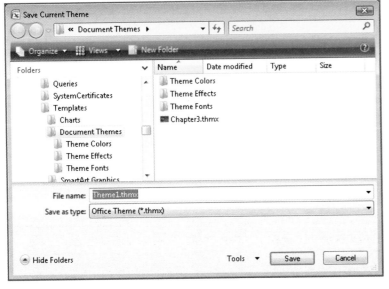

some themes simply change an inserted rectangle's fill color, while other themes affect the color, the weight of its border, and whether it has a 3-D appearance.

1. In the Page Layout tab Themes group, click **Effects**. The drop-down list displays a gallery of effects combinations.

2. Point to each combination to see how the effects will appear on your worksheet, assuming you have a graphic or chart inserted on the worksheet.

3. Click the effects combination you want.

Create Custom Themes

Changes you make to a built-in theme (or to a previously created custom theme) can be saved as a new custom theme and reused in other Office 2007 documents.

1. Make color, font, and effects changes to the current theme (see "Apply Themes" earlier in the chapter).

2. In the Page Layout tab Themes group, click **Themes I Save Current Theme**. In the Save Current Theme window, click **Browse Folders** to display the default Office themes folder, as shown in Figure 6-8.

3. Name the file and click **Save** to store the theme in the Office Document Themes folder.

   –Or–

   Name the file and browse to the folder where you want to store it. Click **Save** when finished.

Use Cell Styles

Cell styles allow you to apply consistent formatting to specific cells, and let you make changes to styled cells with a few mouse clicks instead of changing each cell individually. Excel provides dozens of predefined styles, categorized by use. One category, themed cell styles, has the additional advantage of being fully

> **CAUTION**
>
> Saved custom themes that are not stored in the default Document Themes folder will not be displayed in the Custom area of the Themes drop-down list. You will need to locate them to apply them (see the "Searching for Themes" QuickSteps).

Figure 6-8: **Custom themes are saved as individual files in the new Excel XML Office theme file format.**

integrated with the current theme. Colors associated with a theme change will automatically carry over to themed cell styles, preserving the coordinated appearance of your worksheet. Of course, you can modify any applied style and save the changes to create your own custom style.

APPLY A STYLE

1. Select the cells you want to format with a style.

2. In the Home tab Styles group, click **Cell Styles**. A gallery of cell styles displays, as shown in Figure 6-9.

3. Point to several styles in the gallery to see how each style affects your selected cells.

4. Click the style that best suits your needs. The style formatting is applied to your selected cells.

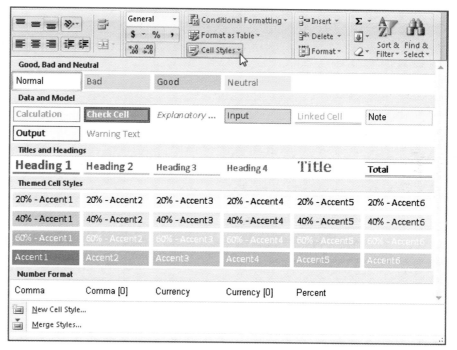

Figure 6-9: *Excel's styles provide a broad swatch of cell styling possibilities.*

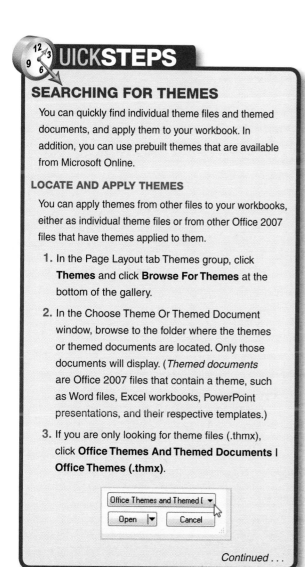

UICKSTEPS

SEARCHING FOR THEMES

You can quickly find individual theme files and themed documents, and apply them to your workbook. In addition, you can use prebuilt themes that are available from Microsoft Online.

LOCATE AND APPLY THEMES

You can apply themes from other files to your workbooks, either as individual theme files or from other Office 2007 files that have themes applied to them.

1. In the Page Layout tab Themes group, click **Themes** and click **Browse For Themes** at the bottom of the gallery.

2. In the Choose Theme Or Themed Document window, browse to the folder where the themes or themed documents are located. Only those documents will display. (*Themed documents* are Office 2007 files that contain a theme, such as Word files, Excel workbooks, PowerPoint presentations, and their respective templates.)

3. If you are only looking for theme files (.thmx), click **Office Themes And Themed Documents | Office Themes (.thmx)**.

Continued . . .

SEARCHING FOR THEMES *(Continued)*

4. Select the Office document whose theme you want to apply or the theme file you want to apply, and click **Open**.

FIND THEMES ON OFFICE ONLINE

1. In the Page Layout tab Themes group, click **Themes I More Themes On Microsoft Office Online**. Assuming you're connected to the Internet, the Microsoft Office Online Web site is displayed (see Figure 6-10).

2. Use the options on the left sidebar or the Search tool to find the theme you want and download it to your system (you might have to download a template that includes the theme you want).

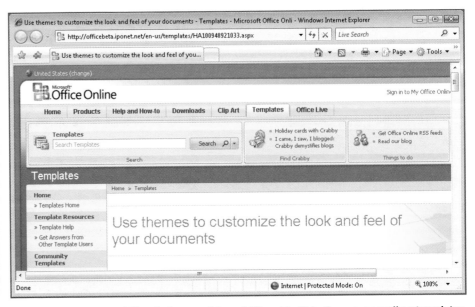

Figure 6-10: **Microsoft Office Online provides additional built-in themes, as well as templates and other professionally designed content.**

TIP

The easiest way to ensure a common look and feel to your Excel 2007 workbooks is to create or apply the theme you want and save the workbook as a template. In addition to the theme-controlled aspects of a workbook, the template allows you to consistently re-create formulas, tables, charts, and all else that Excel has to offer. Chapter 1 describes saving workbooks as templates.

NOTE

The default font used in each style is derived from the current theme. When you change themes, the font used in styled cells will change according to the font used in the new theme. Themed cell styles, unlike other cell styles, will additionally change color as applicable to the new theme.

CREATE A CUSTOM STYLE

You can create your own style by starting with a predefined style and making changes, or you can start from scratch and apply all formatting directly, using the formatting tools on the ribbon or in a formatting dialog box. In either case, you can save your changes as a custom style and apply it from the Cell Styles gallery.

1. Use one or more, or a combination, of the following techniques to format at least one cell as you want:

   • Apply a predefined style to the cell(s) you want to customize.

   • Use the formatting tools in the ribbon (Home tab Font, Alignment, and Number groups).

   • Right-click a cell to be styled, click **Format Cells**, and use the six tabs in the Format Cells dialog box to create the styling format you want. Click **OK** when finished.

2. In the Home tab Styles group, click **Cell Styles** and click **New Cell Style** at the bottom of the gallery.

3. In the Style dialog box, type a name for your style, and review the six areas of affected style formatting. If necessary, click **Format** and make formatting adjustments in the Format Cells dialog box. Click **OK** to apply formatting changes.

4. Click **OK** in the Style dialog box to create the style. The new custom style will be displayed in the Custom area at the top of the Cell Styles gallery.

CHANGE A CELL STYLE

1. In the Home tab Styles group, click **Cell Styles**.

2. Right-click a style (custom or predefined) in the gallery, and click **Modify**.

3. In the Style dialog box, click **Format** and make any formatting adjustments in the Format Cells dialog box. Click **OK** to apply the formatting changes.

4. Click **OK** in the Style dialog box to save changes to the style.

REMOVE A CELL STYLE

You can remove a style's formatting applied to selected cells, or you can completely remove the cell style from Excel (and concurrently remove all style formatting from affected cells):

- To remove style formatting from cells, select the cells, click **Cell Styles** in the Styles group, and click the **Normal** style.

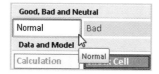

- To permanently remove a style, click **Cell Styles** in the Styles group, right-click the cell style you want removed, and click **Delete**.

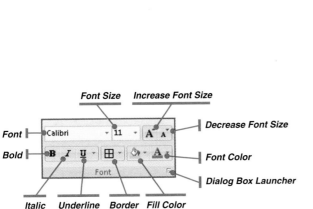

Merge Styles

Merge styles from:

Chapter 8.xlsx
My Budget.xlsx
Taxes 2007.xlsx

Choose an open workbook to copy its cell styles into this workbook.

OK   Cancel

ADD CELL STYLES FROM OTHER WORKBOOKS

1. Open any workbooks whose styles you want to add and the workbook where you want the styles to be added.

2. In the View tab Window group, click **Switch Windows** and click the workbook to which you want the styles added, making it the active workbook.

3. In the Home tab Styles group, click **Cell Styles** and click **Merge Styles**.

4. In the Merge Styles dialog box, click the workbook from which you want to add styles. Click **OK**.

Change Fonts

Each *font* is comprised of a *typeface*, such as Arial; a *style*, such as italic; and a size. Other characteristics, such as color and super/subscripting, further distinguish text. Excel also provides several underlining options that are useful in accounting applications.

1. On a worksheet, select:

   - Cells to apply font changes to all characters

   - Characters to apply font changes to just the selected text and numbers

2. Use one of the following techniques to access font tools and options:

   - On the ribbon, click the **Home** tab, and click the appropriate Font group tools (see Figure 6-11).

   - Right-click a cell or selection, and use the font tools available on the mini toolbar.

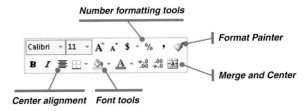

Number formatting tools

Format Painter

Merge and Center

Center alignment   Font tools

   - Click the Font group **Dialog Box Launcher** (located in the lower-right corner of group).

   - Right-click a cell or selection, click **Format Cells**, and then click the **Font** tab.

3. In the latter two cases, the Format Cells dialog box appears with the Font tab displayed, as shown in Figure 6-12. Make and preview changes, and click **OK** when finished.

Font Size   Increase Font Size

Font   Calibri   11   A A   *Decrease Font Size*

Bold   B *I* U   *Font Color*

Font   *Dialog Box Launcher*

Italic   Underline   Border   Fill Color

Figure 6-11: **Font group tools apply formatting to text.**

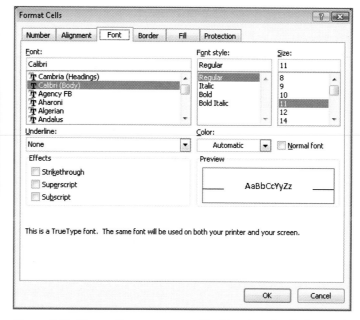

When selected, the Normal Font check box on the Font tab of the Format Cells dialog box resets font attributes to the defaults defined in the Normal template. The Normal template is an ever-present component of Excel (if you delete it, Excel will re-create another) that defines startup values in the absence of any other template.

Figure 6-12: **Change the appearance of text by changing its font and other characteristics.**

Change Alignment and Orientation

You can modify how characters appear within a cell by changing their alignment, orientation, and "compactness."

1. Select the cells whose contents you want to change.

2. Use one of the following techniques to access font tools and options:

   - On the ribbon, click the **Home** tab, and click the appropriate Alignment group tools (see Figure 6-13).

   - Click the Alignment group **Dialog Box Launcher**.

   - Right-click a cell or selection, click **Format Cells**, and then click the **Alignment** tab.

3. In the latter two cases, the Format Cells dialog box appears with the Alignment tab displayed, as shown in Figure 6-14. The specific features of the Alignment tab are described in Table 6-1.

4. Click **OK** when you are finished.

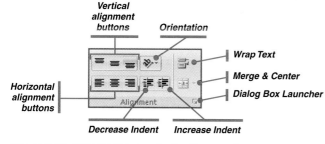

Figure 6-13: **Alignment group tools allow you to reposition text.**

FEATURE	OPTION	DESCRIPTION
Text Alignment, Horizontal	General	Right-aligns numbers, left-aligns text, and centers error values; Excel default setting
	Left (Indent)	Left-aligns characters with optional indentation spinner
	Center	Centers characters in the cell
	Right (Indent)	Right-aligns characters with optional indentation spinner
	Fill	Fills cell with recurrences of content
	Justify	Justifies the text in a cell so that, to the degree possible, both the left and right ends are vertically aligned
	Center Across Selection	Centers text across one or more cells; used to center titles across several columns
	Distributed (Indent)	Stretches cell contents across cell width by adding space between words, with optional indentation spinner
Text Alignment, Vertical	Top	Places the text at the top of the cell
	Center	Places the text in the center of the cell
	Bottom	Places the text at the bottom of the cell; Excel's default setting
	Justify	Evenly distributes text between the top and bottom of a cell to fill it by adding space between lines
	Distributed	Vertically arranges characters equally within the cell (behaves the same as Justify)
Orientation		Angles text in a cell by dragging the red diamond up or down or by using the Degrees spinner
Text Control	Wrap Text	Moves text that extends beyond the cell's width to the line below
	Shrink To Fit	Reduces character size so that cell contents fit within cell width (cannot be used with Wrap Text)
	Merge Cells	Creates one cell from contiguous cells, "increasing" the width of a cell without changing the width of the column(s)
Right To Left, Text Direction	Context	Text entry flows according to keyboard language in use
	Left To Right	Text entry flows from the left as in Western countries
	Right To Left	Text entry flows from the right as in many Middle Eastern and East Asian countries

Table 6-1: **Text Alignment Options in Excel**

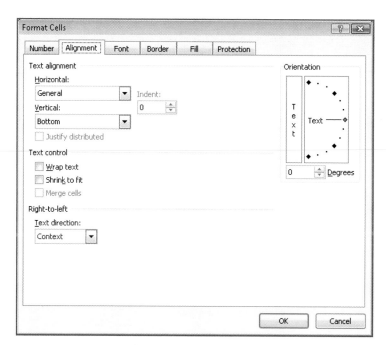

Figure 6-14: *The Alignment tab provides detailed text-alignment options.*

TIP

You can quickly add solid color and shading to selected cells from the Fill Color button in the Font group (see Figure 6-11). Click the button to apply the displayed color, or open a gallery by clicking the down arrow next to the button (see "Change Themed Colors" earlier in this chapter for information on the various gallery color options). The last color or shade selected remains on the Fill Color button until changed.

Add a Background

You can add color and shading to selected cells to provide a solid background. You can also add preset patterns, either alone or in conjunction with a solid background for even more effect.

1. Select the cell, range, row, or column that you want to modify with a background.

2. In the Home tab Alignment group, click its **Dialog Box Launcher**.

   –Or–

   Right-click the selection and click **Format Cells**.

   In either case, the Format Cells dialog box appears.

3. Click the **Fill** tab (see Figure 6-15), and choose colored and/or patterned fills.

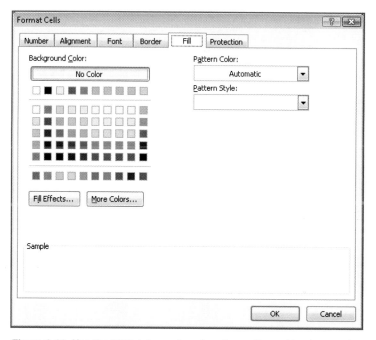

Figure 6-15: *Use the Fill tab to apply colored or patterned backgrounds to cells.*

USE SOLID COLORED BACKGROUNDS

1. In the Fill tab, click one of the color options in the Background Color area (see "Change Themed Colors" earlier in this chapter for information on the various color options), and select one of the color options.

   –Or–

   Click **Fill Effects** to apply blended fills, as shown in Figure 6-16. Preview your selections in the Sample area, and click **OK**.

2. Preview your selections in the larger Sample area at the bottom of the Fill tab, and click **OK** when finished.

USE PATTERNED BACKGROUNDS

1. In the Fill tab, click the **Pattern Style** down arrow to display a gallery of patterns. Click the design you want, and see it enlarged in the Sample area at the bottom of the Fill tab.

2. If you want to colorize the pattern, click the **Pattern Color** down arrow to display the color gallery (see "Change Themed Colors" earlier in this chapter for information on the various color options), and select one of the color options.

3. Click **OK** when finished to close the Format Cells dialog box.

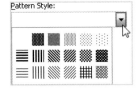

NOTE

If you choose Automatic for the Pattern Color in the Format Cells Fill tab, the pattern is applied to the background color, but if you pick both a background color and a pattern color, the colors are merged.

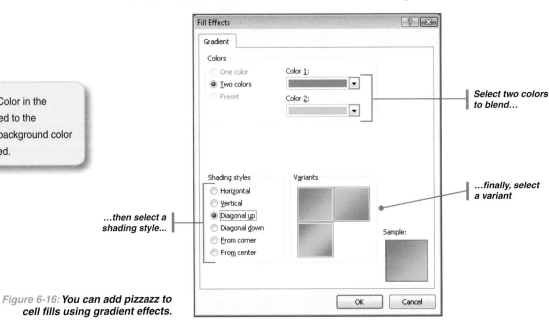

...then select a shading style...

Select two colors to blend...

...finally, select a variant

*Figure 6-16: **You can add pizzazz to cell fills using gradient effects.***

TIP

You can also copy formatting by using Paste Special and the Paste Options tag (see Chapter 5).

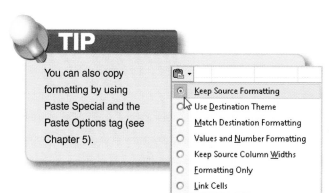

Transfer Formatting

You can manually transfer formatting from one cell to other cells using the Format Painter when you are inserting cells.

USE THE FORMAT PAINTER

1. Select the cell whose formatting you want to transfer.
2. In the Home tab Clipboard group, click the **Format Painter** once if you only want to apply the formatting one time.

   –Or–

1. Double-click the **Format Painter** to keep it turned on for repeated use.
2. Select the cells where you want the formatting applied.
3. If you single-clicked the Format Painter before applying it to your selection, it will turn off after you apply it to your first selection; if you double-clicked the button, you may select other cells to continue transferring the formatting.
4. Double-click the **Format Painter** to turn it off or press **ESC**.

ATTACH FORMATTING TO INSERTED CELLS, ROWS, AND COLUMNS

Open the **Insert Options** Smart tag (the paintbrush icon that appears after an insert), and choose from which direction you want the formatting applied, or choose to clear the formatting.

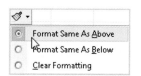

Arrange and Organize Worksheets

Excel provides several features to help you work with and view worksheets. You can retain headers at the top of the worksheet window as you scroll through hundreds of rows, split a worksheet, and view worksheets from several workbooks.

Lock Rows and Columns

You can lock (or freeze) rows and columns in place so that they remain visible as you scroll. Typically, row and column headers are locked in larger worksheets, where you are scrolling through large numbers of rows or columns. You can quickly lock the first row and/or first column in a worksheet, or you can select the rows or columns to freeze.

LOCK ROWS

- In the View tab Window group, click **Freeze Panes | Freeze Top Row**. The top row (typically, your header row) remains in place as you scroll down.

  –Or–

- Select the row below the rows you want to lock, click **Freeze Panes | Freeze Panes**. A thin border displays on the bottom of the locked row. All rows above the locked row remain in place as you scroll down.

The first nine rows are locked as you scroll the rows below them

	H	I	J	K	L	M
1	ISBN	Category	Author	Title	Publish Year	List Price
2	0071408959	Business	Allaire	Options Strategist	2003	$29.95
3	0830621369	Technical	Alth	Pbs Wells & Septic Systems	1991	$19.95
4	0071467858	Business	Bayan	Words That Sell, Revised	2006	$16.95
5	0071464700	Technical	Bluman	Business Math Demystified	2006	$19.95
6	0071423117	Medicine	Bodenheim	Understanding Health Polic	2004	$36.95
7	0071412077	Medicine	Brooks	Medical Microbiology, 23/E	2004	$52.95
8	0071457720	Technical	Cadick	Elect Safety Hndbk, 3/E	2005	$79.95
9	0071054618	Medicine	Cember	Intro Health Physics 3e	1996	$52.95
26	007146252X	Business	Krames	What The Best CEO's Know	2005	$14.95
27	0072231246	Technical	Meyers	A+ Guide To Operating Syst	2004	$60.00

LOCK COLUMNS

- In the View tab Window group, click **Freeze Panes | Freeze First Column**. The leftmost column (typically, your header column) remains in place as you scroll to the right.

  –Or–

- Select the column to the right of the columns you want to lock, click **Freeze Panes | Freeze Panes**. A thin border displays on the right side of the locked column. All columns to the left of the locked column remain in place as you scroll to the right.

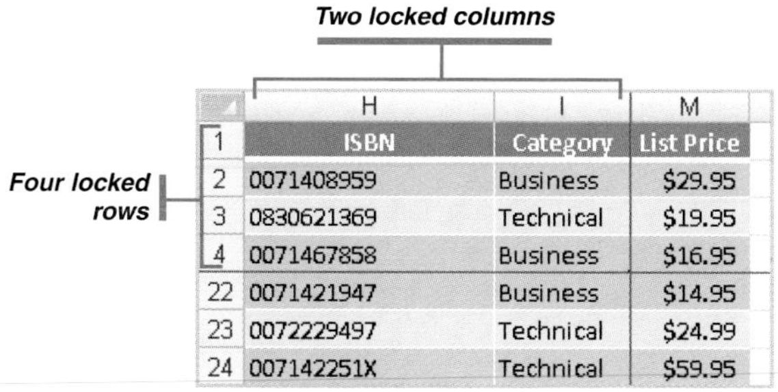

Two locked columns

	H	I	M
1	ISBN	Category	List Price
2	0071408959	Business	$29.95
3	0830621369	Technical	$19.95
4	0071467858	Business	$16.95
22	0071421947	Business	$14.95
23	0072229497	Technical	$24.99
24	007142251X	Technical	$59.95

Four locked rows

LOCK ROWS AND COLUMNS TOGETHER

1. Select the cell that is below and to the right of the range you want to lock.

2. In the View tab Window group, click **Freeze Panes | Freeze Panes**. A thin border displays below the locked rows and to the right of the locked columns. The range will remain in place as you scroll down or to the right.

UNLOCK ROWS AND COLUMNS

In the View tab Window group, click **Freeze Panes | Unfreeze Panes**.

Split a Worksheet

You can divide a worksheet into two independent panes of the same data, as shown in Figure 6-17.

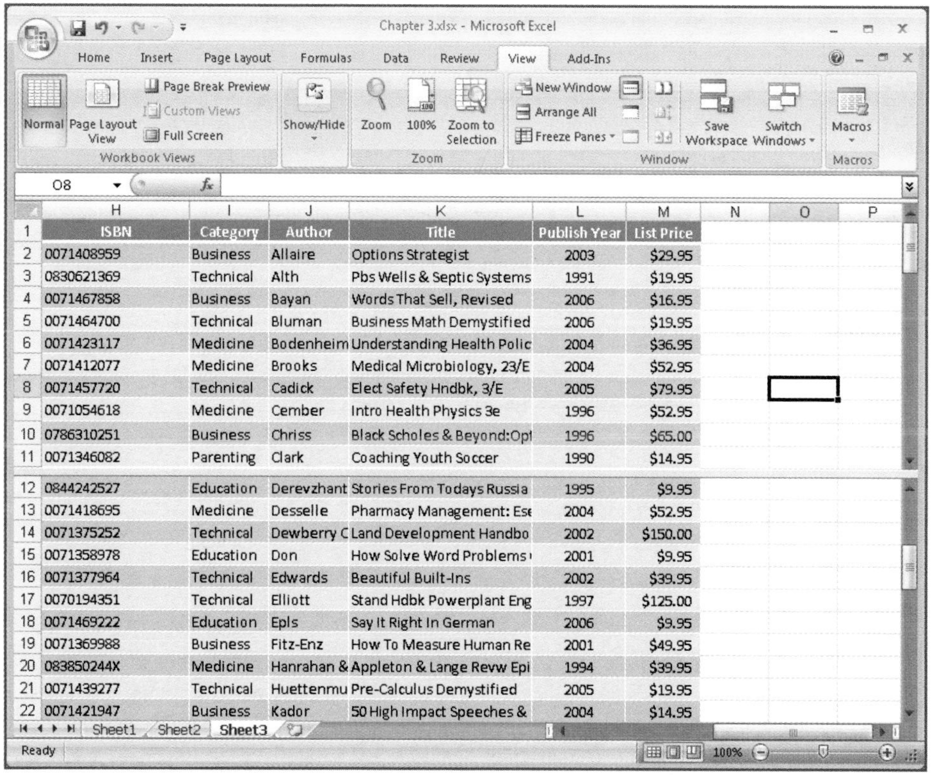

Figure 6-17: **A split worksheet provides two independent views of the same worksheet.**

QUICKSTEPS

WORKING WITH WORKSHEETS

Excel provides several tools you can use to modify the number and identification of worksheets in a workbook.

ADD A WORKSHEET

Right-click the worksheet tab to the right of where you want the new worksheet and click **Insert | OK**.

–Or–

On the worksheet bar, click **Insert Worksheet**. A new worksheet is added to the right of any current tabs.

DELETE A WORKSHEET

Right-click the worksheet tab of the worksheet you want to delete, and click **Delete**.

MOVE OR COPY A WORKSHEET

You can move or copy worksheets within a workbook or between open workbooks by dragging a worksheet's tab. (See "View Worksheets from Multiple Workbooks" earlier in this chapter for steps to arrange multiple open workbooks to facilitate dragging objects between them.)

- To move a worksheet, drag the worksheet tab to the position on the worksheet bar where you want it to appear.

Continued . . .

1. In the View tab Window group, click **Split**. Horizontal and vertical split bars are displayed across the worksheet. Remove the unwanted split bar by double-clicking it, leaving you with two panes.

2. Point at the split bar, and drag the bar up or down and/or left or right to proportion the two panes as you want.

3. Use the scroll bars to view other data within each pane. You may remove the split bar by double-clicking it.

View Worksheets from Multiple Workbooks

You can divide the Excel worksheet area so that you can view worksheets from multiple workbooks. This arrangement makes it easy to copy data, formulas, and formatting among several worksheets.

1. Open the workbooks that contain the worksheets you want to view. (See Chapter 1 for information on opening existing workbooks.)

2. In the View tab Window group, click **Arrange All**. The Arrange Windows dialog box appears.

3. Select an arrangement and click **OK**. (Figure 6-18 shows an example of tiling three workbooks.)

WORKING WITH WORKSHEETS

(Continued)

- To copy a worksheet, press and hold **CTRL**, and drag the worksheet tab to the position on the worksheet bar where you want the copy to appear.

RENAME A WORKSHEET

1. Right-click the worksheet tab of the worksheet you want to rename, and click **Rename**.

2. Type a new worksheet name, and press **ENTER**.

COLOR A WORKSHEET TAB

1. Right-click the worksheet tab of the worksheet you want to color, and click **Tab Color**.

2. Select a color from the gallery (see "Change Themed Colors" earlier in this chapter for information on using the color gallery).

CHANGE THE DEFAULT NUMBER OF WORKSHEETS IN A WORKBOOK

1. Click the **Office button**, click **Excel Options**, and click the **Popular** option.

2. Under When Creating New Workbooks, click the **Include This Many Sheets** spinner to change the number of worksheets you want.

3. Click **OK** when finished.

Continued . . .

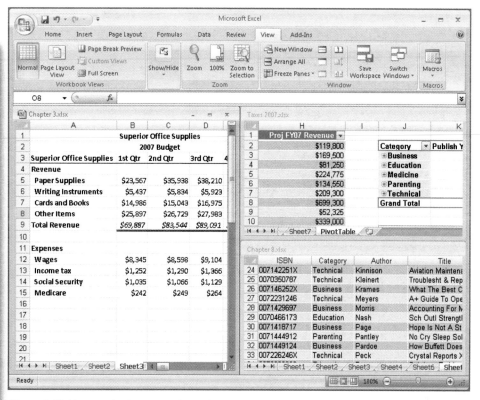

Figure 6-18: **You can look at several workbooks at the same time to compare them or to transfer information among them.**

Compare Workbooks

Excel provides a few tools that allow easy comparison of two workbooks side by side.

1. Open the workbooks you want to compare.

2. In the View tab Window group, click **View Side By Side** 🔲 . If you have only two workbooks open, they will appear next to one another. If you have more than two

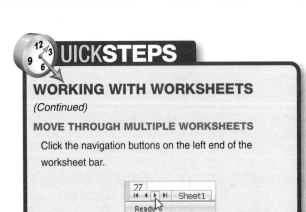

workbooks open, you can select the workbook to view along with the currently active workbook from the Compare Side By Side dialog box.

3. By default, both workbook windows will scroll at the same rate. To turn off this feature, click **Synchronous Scrolling** in the Window group.

Chapter 7

Using Formulas and Functions

Excel lets you easily perform powerful calculations using formulas and functions. Formulas are mathematical statements that follow a set of rules and use a specific syntax. In this chapter you will learn how to reference cells used in formulas, how to give cells names so that they are easily input, how to use conditional formatting to identify cells that satisfy criteria you specify, and how to build formulas. Functions—ready-made formulas that you can use to get quick results for specific applications, such as figuring out loan payments—are also covered. Finally, you will learn about several tools Excel provides to find and correct errors in formulas and functions.

Reference Cells

Formulas typically make use of data already entered in worksheets and need a scheme to locate, or *reference,* that data. Shortcuts are used to help you recall addresses as well as a *syntax*, or set of rules, to communicate to Excel how you want cells used.

Change Cell References

To change cell referencing:

1. Select the cell that contains the formula reference you want to change.

2. In the Formula bar, select the cell address, and press **F4** to switch the cell referencing, starting from a relative reference to the following in this order:

   ● Absolute (A1)

   ● Mixed (relative column, absolute row) (A$1)

   ● Mixed (absolute column, relative row) ($A1)

   ● Relative (A1)

   –Or–

   Edit the cell address by entering or removing the dollar symbol ($) in front of row or column identifiers.

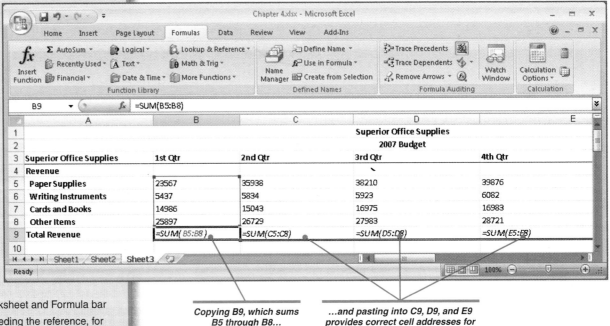

Copying B9, which sums B5 through B8...

...and pasting into C9, D9, and E9 provides correct cell addresses for each column total

*Figure 7-1: **Using relative references, Excel logically assumes cell addresses in copied formulas.***

QUICKFACTS

UNDERSTANDING CELL REFERENCING TYPES *(Continued)*

- **Mixed references** include one relative and one absolute cell reference. Such references are displayed in the worksheet and Formula bar with a dollar sign preceding the absolute reference but no dollar sign before the relative reference. For example, $A1 indicates absolute column, relative row; A$1 indicates relative column, absolute row.

- **External (or 3-D) references** are an extended form of relative, absolute, and mixed cell references. They are used when referencing cells from other worksheets or workbooks. Such a reference might look like this in the worksheet and Formula bar: [*workbook name*]*worksheet name*!A1.

TIP

To view formulas instead of cell values (see Figure 7-1), in the Formulas tab Formula Auditing group, click **Show Formulas**. Click the button a second time to return to a value display.

CAUTION

Cell names need to adhere to a set of rules. Names are case-sensitive, and no spaces are allowed in a cell name, although multiple words can be joined by an underscore or period. Also, names must start with a letter, underscore (_), or backslash (\).

Change to R1C1 References

You can change the A1 cell referencing scheme used by Excel to an older style that identifies both rows and columns numerically, starting in the upper-left corner of the worksheet, rows first, and adds a leading "R" and "C" for clarification. For example, cell B4 in R1C1 reference style is R4C2.

1. Click the **Office button**, click **Excel Options**, and click the **Formulas** option.

2. Under Working With Formulas, click **R1C1 Reference Style** to select it.

3. Click **OK** when finished.

Working with formulas

☑ R1C1 reference style ⓘ
☑ Formula AutoComplete ⓘ
☑ Use table names in formulas

Name Cells

You can name a cell (MonthTotal, for example) or a range to refer to physical cell addresses, and then use the names when referencing the cell in formulas and functions. Names are more descriptive, easier to remember, and often quicker to enter than A1-style cell references. You can name a cell directly on the worksheet or use a dialog box and provide amplifying information.

NAME A CELL OR RANGE DIRECTLY

1. Select the cells you want to reference.

2. Click the **Name Box** at the left end of the Formula bar.

3. Type a name (see accompanying Caution for naming rules), and press **ENTER**. (See the "Working with Cell Names" QuickSteps for ways to modify cell names.)

Q2TotalRevenue ▼		*fx*	=SUM(C5:C8)
	A	B	C

NAME A CELL OR RANGE IN A DIALOG BOX

1. Select the cells you want to reference.

2. In the Formulas tab Defined Names group, click **Define Name**.

   –Or–

   Right-click the selection and click **Name A Range**.

   In either case, the New Name dialog box appears, shown in Figure 7-2.

TIP

Absolute cell references are typically used when you want to copy the values of cells and are not interested in applying their formulas to other cells, such as in a summary or report where the relative references would be meaningless. Though you can apply absolute reference syntax to each cell reference, a faster way is to open the Paste Smart tag that displays next to the destination cells, and choose **Values Only** from the drop-down list. See "Copy Formulas" later in the chapter for more information on copying and pasting formulas.

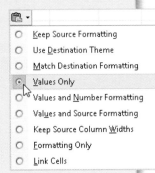

- ○ Keep Source Formatting
- ○ Use Destination Theme
- ○ Match Destination Formatting
- ◉ Values Only
- ○ Values and Number Formatting
- ○ Values and Source Formatting
- ○ Keep Source Column Widths
- ○ Formatting Only
- ○ Link Cells

QUICKFACTS

USING CELL REFERENCE OPERATORS

Cell reference operators (colons, commas, and spaces used in an address, such as E5:E10 E16:E17,E12) provide the syntax for referencing cell ranges, unions, and intersections.

REFERENCE A RANGE

A *range* defines a block of cells.

Type a colon (:) between the upper-leftmost cell and the lower-rightmost cell (for example, B5:C8).

=SUM(B5:C8)

B	C
$23,567	$35,938
$5,437	$5,834
$14,986	$15,043
$25,897	$26,729

Continued . . .

Figure 7-2: **You can easily name cells and add descriptive information.**

3. Type a name for the cell or range (see the Caution on the previous page for naming rules).

4. Click the **Scope** down arrow, and select whether the name applies to the entire workbook or to one of its worksheets.

5. If desired, type a comment that more fully explains the meaning of the named cells. Comments can be upwards of 1,000 characters and will appear as a ScreenTip when the name is used in formulas and functions.

6. If you want to modify the cell or cells to be named, click the **Refers To** text box, and type the reference (starting with the equal (=) sign), or reselect the cells from the worksheet.

7. Click **OK** when finished.

Go to a Named Cell

Named cells are quickly found and selected for you.

- Click the **Name Box** down arrow to open the drop-down list, and click the named cell or range you want to go to.

–Or–

USING CELL REFERENCE OPERATORS *(Continued)*

REFERENCE A UNION

A *union* joins multiple cell references.

Type a comma (,) between separate cell references (for example, B5,B7,C6).

=SUM(B5,B7,C6)	
B	C
$23,567	$35,938
$5,437	$5,834
$14,986	$15,043

REFERENCE AN INTERSECTION

An *intersection* is the overlapping, or common, cells in two ranges.

Type a space (press the *SPACEBAR*) between two range-cell references (for example, B5:B8 B7:C7). B7 is the common cell.

=SUM(B5:B8 B7:C7)	
B	C
$23,567	$35,938
$5,437	$5,834
$14,986	$15,043
$25,897	$26,729

TIP

Excel provides several concessions for users who are transitioning to Excel from Lotus 1-2-3. For example, when creating a formula, you can type a plus sign (+) instead of the equal sign to denote a formula. Excel will change the plus sign to an equal sign if a number follows it, or Excel will add the equal sign to a plus sign that is followed by a cell reference. In any case, be sure not to type a leading space before either the plus or the equal sign, as the characters that follow will be interpreted as text instead of as a formula. To enable Lotus transitioning, click the **Office button**, click **Excel Options**, and click the **Advanced** option. Under Lotus Compatibility Settings, click **Transition Formula Entry**, and click **OK**.

- In the Home tab Editing group, click **Find & Select** | **Go To**. In the Go To dialog box, double-click the named cell or range you want to go to.

If a cell or range name is longer than what can be displayed in the Name Box, increase the width of the Name box by dragging the circle in the arc forming its right boundary to the right.

TIP

To quickly open the Name Manager, press **CTRL-F3** or add the Name Manager icon to the Quick Access toolbar. (Chapter 1 describes how to add tools to the Quick Access toolbar.)

Build Formulas

Formulas are mathematical equations that combine values and cell references with operators to calculate a result. *Values* are actual numbers or logical values, such as True and False, or the contents of cells that contain numbers or logical values. *Cell references* point to cells whose values are to be used, for example, E5:E10, E12, and MonthlyTot. *Operators*, such as + (add), > (greater than), and ^ (use an exponent), tell Excel what type of calculation to perform or logical comparison to apply. Prebuilt formulas, or *functions*, that return a value also can be used in formulas. (Functions are described later in this chapter.)

Create a Formula

You create formulas by either entering or referencing values. The character that tells Excel to perform a calculation is the equal sign (=) and must precede any combination of values, cell references, and operators.

QUICKSTEPS

WORKING WITH CELL NAMES

Excel provides several related tools and a Name
Manager to help you manage and organize your named
cells. To open the Name Manager:

In the Formulas tab Defined Names group, click **Name
Manager**. The Name Manager
window opens, as shown in
Figure 7-3, listing all named cells
in the workbook.

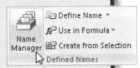

CHANGE CELL NAMES

1. Select the name of the cell reference whose
   parameters you want to change, and click **Edit**.

2. In the Edit Name dialog box, type a new name,
   add or change the comment, and/or modify the
   cell reference (you cannot change the scope).
   Click **OK** when finished.

DELETE NAMED CELLS

1. Select the name of the cell reference that you
   want to delete (to select more than one cell name
   to delete, hold down the **CTRL** key while clicking
   noncontiguous names in the list; or select the first
   name in a contiguous range, and hold down **SHIFT**
   while clicking the last name in the range).

2. Click **Delete** and click **OK** to confirm the deletion.

SORT AND FILTER NAMED CELLS

If you have several named cells in a workbook, you can
easily view only the ones you are interested in:

- To sort named cells, click a column heading to
  change the sort order from ascending (numerals
  first 0-9, then A-Z) to descending (Z-A, numerals
  last 9-0). Click the heading a second time to return
  to the original order.

Continued . . .

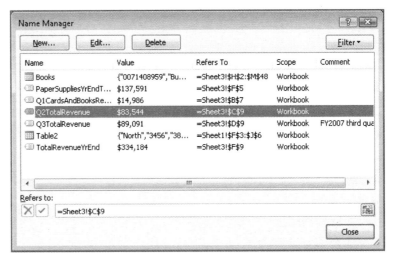

*Figure 7-3: **The Name Manager provides a central location for organizing,
creating, and modifying named cells.***

Excel formulas are calculated from left to right according to an ordered hierarchy
of operators. For example, exponents precede multiplication and division,
which precede addition and subtraction. You can alter the calculation order
(and results) by use of parentheses; Excel performs the calculation within the
innermost parentheses first. For example, =12+48/24 returns 14 (48 is divided
by 24, resulting in 2; then 12 is added to 2). Using parentheses, =(12+48)/24
returns 2.5 (12 is added to 48, resulting in 60; then 60 is divided by 24).

ENTER A SIMPLE FORMULA

1. Select a blank cell, and type an equal sign (=). The equal
   sign displays in the cell and in the Formula bar.

2. Type a value, such as 64.

3. Type an operator, such as +.

4. Type a second value, such as 96.

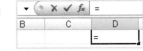

7

WORKING WITH CELL NAMES

(Continued)

- To see only specific categories of named cells, click **Filter** and click the category of named cells you want to see. Only named cells that belong in the category you select will appear in the list of cell names.

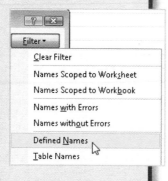

- To return a filtered list to a complete list of named cells, click **Filter | Clear Filter**.

VIEW MORE DATA

The default width of the Name Manager and its columns might not readily display longer cell names, references, or comments:

- To increase a column width, drag the right border of the column heading to the right as far as you need.

- To increase the width of the dialog box, drag either the dialog box's right or left border to the right or left, respectively.

CAUTION

When creating a formula, be careful not to click any cells that you do not want referenced in the formula. After you type the equal sign, Excel interprets any selected cell as being a cell reference in the formula.

---

5. Complete the entry by pressing **ENTER** or clicking **Enter** on the Formula bar; or add additional values and operators, and then complete the entry. The result of your equation displays in the cell. (See Chapter 5 for other methods to complete an entry.)

▼	X	✓	fx	=64+96
B			D	
			=64+96	

USE CELL REFERENCES

1. Select a blank cell, and type an equal sign (=). The equal sign displays in the cell and in the Formula bar.

2. Enter a cell reference:

   - Type a cell reference (for example, B4) that contains the value you want.

   - Click the cell whose value you want. A blinking border surrounds the cell.

   - Select a named cell. In the Formulas tab Defined Names group, click **Use In Formula**, and click the named cell you want.

fx Use in Formula ▼	Trace D
PaperSuppliesYrEndTotal
Q1CardsAndBooksRevenueTotal
Q2TotalRevenue
Q3TotalRevenue
TotalRevenueYrEnd
Paste Names...

3. Type an operator.

4. Enter another cell reference or a value.

5. Complete the entry by pressing **ENTER**; or add additional cell references, values, and operators, and then complete the entry. The result of your formula is displayed in the cell, as shown in Figure 7-4.

Edit a Formula

You can easily change a formula after you have entered one.

1. Double-click the cell that contains the formula you want to change. The formula is displayed in the cell and in the Formula bar. Cell references for each cell or range are color-coded.

X	✓	fx	=F5+F6+63987+OtherItemsYrEndTotal

D	E	F
pplies		
3rd Qtr	4th Qtr	Total Yr
$38,210	$39,876	$137,591
$5,923	$6,082	$23,276
$16,975	$16,983	$63,987
$27,983	$28,721	$109,330
$89,091	$91,662	=F5 + F6 +63987+
		OtherItemsYrEndTotal

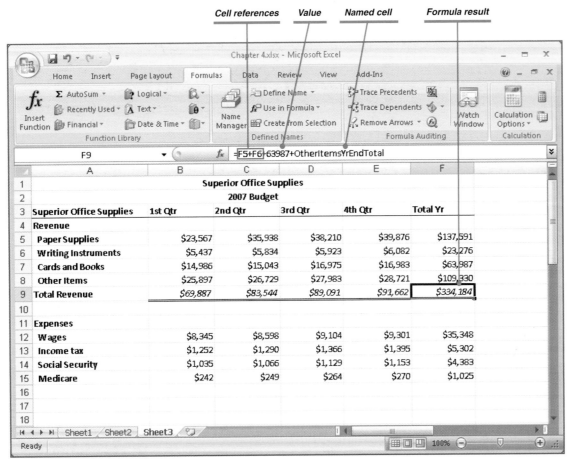

Cell references   Value   Named cell   Formula result

Formula bar: F9 fx =F5+F6-63987+OtherItemsYrEndTotal

Superior Office Supplies	1st Qtr	2nd Qtr	3rd Qtr	4th Qtr	Total Yr
Superior Office Supplies					
2007 Budget					
Revenue					
Paper Supplies	$23,567	$35,938	$38,210	$39,876	$137,591
Writing Instruments	$5,437	$5,834	$5,923	$6,082	$23,276
Cards and Books	$14,986	$15,043	$16,975	$16,983	$63,987
Other Items	$25,897	$26,729	$27,983	$28,721	$109,330
Total Revenue	$69,887	$83,544	$89,091	$91,662	$334,184
Expenses					
Wages	$8,345	$8,598	$9,104	$9,301	$35,348
Income tax	$1,252	$1,290	$1,366	$1,395	$5,302
Social Security	$1,035	$1,066	$1,129	$1,153	$4,383
Medicare	$242	$249	$264	$270	$1,025

*Figure 7-4: **A formula in Excel is comprised of cell references, values, and named cells.***

2. Edit the formula by:

- Making changes directly in the cell or on the Formula bar

- Dragging the border of a colored cell or range reference to move it to a new location

- Dragging a corner sizing-box of a colored cell or range reference to expand the reference

3. Complete the entry by pressing **ENTER**.

Move Formulas

You move formulas by cutting and pasting. When you move formulas, Excel uses absolute referencing—the formula remains exactly the same as it was originally with the same cell references. (See "Change Cell References" earlier in the chapter for more information on cell referencing.)

1. Select the cell whose formula you want to move.

2. In the Home tab Clipboard group, click Cut or press **CTRL-X**.

–Or–

Right-click the cell whose formula you want to move, and click **Cut**.

3. Select the cell where you want to move the formula.

4. In the Home tab Clipboard group, click **Paste** or press **CTRL-V**.

–Or–

Right-click the cell where you want to move the formula, and click **Paste**.

UICKSTEPS

USING FORMULAS

There are several techniques you can use to get more out of working with formulas.

REPLACE AN ENTIRE FORMULA WITH ITS VALUE

To replace an entire formula with its value:

1. Right-click the cell that contains the formula, and click **Copy**.

2. Right-click the cell a second time, click **Paste Special | Values | OK**.

REPLACE A PORTION OF A FORMULA WITH ITS VALUE

1. Double-click the cell that contains the formula.

2. In either the cell or the Formula bar, select the portion of the formula you want to replace with its value.

3. Press **F9** to calculate and insert the value, and press **ENTER** to complete the entry.

CANCEL ENTERING OR EDITING A FORMULA

Press **ESC** or click **Cancel** on the Formula bar.

=SUM(B15:E15)

DELETE A FORMULA

Select the cell that contains the formula, and press **DELETE**.

Copy Formulas

When you copy formulas, relative referencing is applied. Therefore, cell referencing in a formula will change when you copy the formula, unless you have made a reference absolute. If you do not get the results you expect, click **Undo** on the Quick Access toolbar, and change the cell references before you copy again.

COPY FORMULAS INTO ADJACENT CELLS

1. Select the cell whose formula you want to copy.

2. Point at the fill handle in the lower-right corner of the cell, and drag over the cells where you want the formula copied.

$78,086.66

COPY FORMULAS INTO NONADJACENT CELLS

1. Select the cell whose formula you want to copy.

2. In the Home tab Clipboard group, click **Copy** or press **CTRL-C**.

   –Or–

   Right-click the cell you want to copy, and click **Copy**.

3. Copy formatting along with the formula by selecting the destination cell. Then, in the Home tab Clipboard group, click **Paste** or press **CTRL-V**.

   –Or–

   Right-click the destination cell, and click **Paste**.

4. Copy just the formula by selecting the destination cell. Then, in the Home tab Clipboard group, click the **Paste** down arrow, and click **Formulas**.

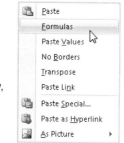

Recalculate Formulas

By default, Excel automatically recalculates formulas affected by changes to a value, to the formula itself, or to a changed named cell. You also can recalculate more frequently using the tips presented in Table 7-1.

TO CALCULATE...	IN...	PRESS...
Formulas, and formulas dependent on them, that have changed since the last calculation	All open workbooks	**F9** (or click **Calculate Now** in the Calculation group)
Formulas, and formulas dependent on them, that have changed since the last calculation	The active worksheet	**SHIFT-F9** (or click **Calculate Sheet** in the Calculation group)
All formulas, regardless of any changes since the last calculation	All open workbooks	**CTRL-ALT-F9**
All formulas, regardless of any changes since the last calculation, after rechecking dependent formulas	All open workbooks	**CTRL-SHIFT-ALT-F9**

Table 7-1: **Formula Recalculations in Excel**

To turn off automatic calculation and select other calculation options:

1. In the Formulas tab Calculation group, click **Calculation Options**.

2. In the Options drop-down menu, click **Manual**. You can also force an immediate calculation in the Calculation group by clicking **Calc Now** to recalculate the workbook or clicking **Calc Sheet** to recalculate the active worksheet.

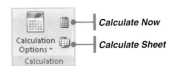

Calculate Now

Calculate Sheet

Use External References in Formulas

You can *link* data using cell references to worksheets and workbooks other than the one you are currently working in. For example, if you are building a departmental budget, you could link to each division's budget workbook and have any changes made to formulas in those workbooks automatically applied to your total budget workbook. Changes made to the *external* references in the *source* workbooks are automatically updated in the *destination* workbook when the destination workbook is opened or when the source workbooks are changed and the destination workbook is open.

CREATE EXTERNAL REFERENCE LINKS

1. Open both the source and destination workbooks in your computer.

2. Arrange the workbooks so that they are all displayed. For example, in the View tab Window group, click **Arrange All I Tiled I OK**. (See Chapter 6 for more information on arranging workbooks in the Excel window.)

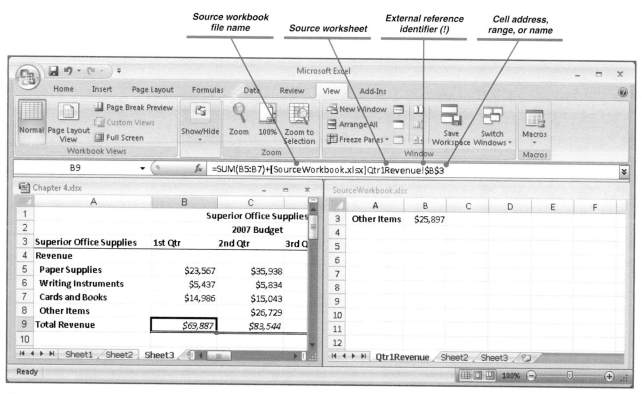

Source workbook file name · Source worksheet · External reference identifier (!) · Cell address, range, or name

B9 =SUM(B5:B7)+[SourceWorkbook.xlsx]Qtr1Revenue!B3

Figure 7-5: *An external reference in a formula is comprised of several components.*

CAUTION

If you break an external reference link in the Edit Links dialog box, all formulas using external references are converted to values. Broken links cannot be undone except by reestablishing the links.

3. In the destination worksheet, create the formula or open an existing formula.

4. Place the insertion point in the formula where you want the external reference.

5. In the source workbook, click the cell whose cell reference you want. The external reference is added to the formula, as shown in Figure 7-5.

6. Press **ENTER** to complete the entry.

UPDATE AND MANAGE EXTERNAL REFERENCES

You can control how external references are updated, check on their status, and break or change the link.

1. Open the destination workbook.

2. In the Data tab Connections group, click **Edit Links**. The Edit Links dialog box appears, as shown in Figure 7-6.

QUICKFACTS

UNDERSTANDING THE TRUST CENTER

Microsoft Office 2007 recognizes the need to provide enhanced file security against the world of viruses and other malicious code that can compromise your data and impair your computer. To provide a unified approach in applying security settings for all Office 2007 programs installed on your system, Office 2007 includes a *Trust Center* to help you manage your security settings. It also provides information on privacy and general computer security (see Figure 7-7). The Trust Center security settings window (click **Trust Center Settings**) organizes security settings in eight categories. Taking a "better safe than sorry" approach, Microsoft errs on the side of caution by limiting any automatic updates or actions without user approval. You can change these defaults to allow more or less intervention. Security settings in the Trust Center are applicable to all workbooks and "trump" the automatic link updating behavior set for individual workbooks. To allow automatic link updating for individual workbooks, you must first enable automatic link updates in the Trust Center.

To open the Trust Center, click the **Office button**, click **Excel Options**, and click the **Trust Center** option.

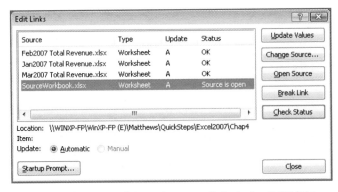

*Figure 7-6: **You can update and manage links in the Edit Links dialog box.***

3. Select a link and then use the command buttons on the right side of the dialog box to perform the action you want.

4. Click **Close** when finished.

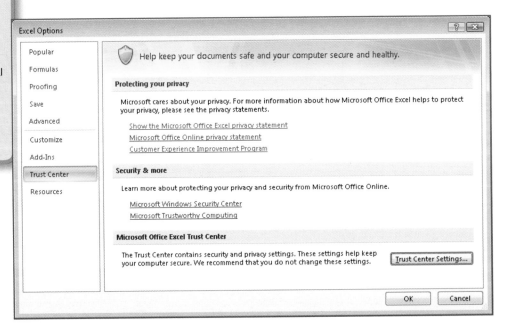

*Figure 7-7: **The Trust Center provides a focal point for accessing privacy and security information and settings for Office 2007 programs.***

TIP

If you are unsure of the origin of the source workbooks when updating links in a destination workbook, open the Edit Links dialog box to view the files involved in the links. See how in the section "Update and Manage External References" earlier in this chapter.

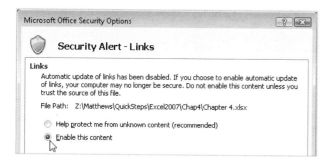

UPDATE LINKS

When you open a destination workbook with external links to source workbooks, you are potentially providing a security risk to your computer by allowing data from other sources into your system. By default, automatic updating is disabled and the user opening a destination workbook needs to provide permission to enable the links (unless the source workbooks are open on the same computer as the destination workbook).

1. Open the destination workbook. Unless default settings have been changed, a Security Warning message displays below the ribbon notifying you that automatic link updating is disabled, as shown in Figure 7-8.

2. Click **Options**. In the Security Options dialog box, click **Enable This Content**, and click **OK**. The links will be updated.

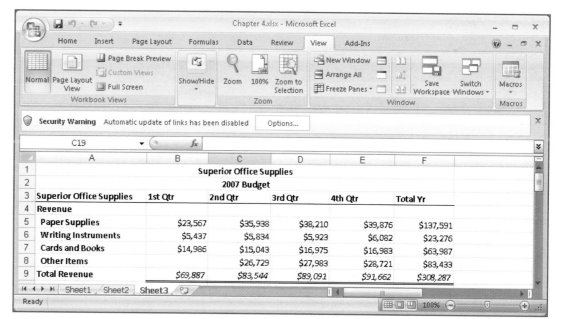

Figure 7-8: To protect you from erroneous or malicious data, Office prompts you to enable link updates.

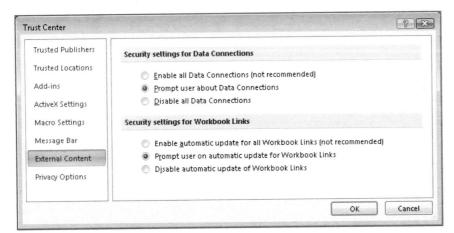

*Figure 7-9: **Trust Center privacy and security settings are organized in eight categories.***

CHANGE AUTOMATIC LINK UPDATING FOR ALL WORKBOOKS

You can change how links are updated in the Trust Center security settings window.

1. Click the **Office button**, click **Excel Options**, and click the **Trust Center** option. In the Trust Center window, click **Trust Center Settings**.

   –Or–

   If opening a destination workbook and receiving a security warning, click **Options**, and click **Open The Trust Center** in the alert.

   In either case, the Trust Center security settings window opens.

2. In the Trust Center security settings window, shown in Figure 7-9, click the **External Content** category.

3. In the Security Settings For Workbook Links area, select the automatic link updating behavior you want, and click **OK** twice.

CHANGE AUTOMATIC LINK UPDATING FOR INDIVIDUAL WORKBOOKS

You can choose to not display the security alert in a destination workbook that prompts users to update links. You can also choose to update links, or not, without user intervention.

1. Open the destination workbook whose security alert behavior you want to change.

2. In the Data tab Connections group, click **Edit Links | Startup Prompt**.

3. In the Startup Prompt dialog box, select the behavior you want, click **OK**, and click **Close**. The next time the workbook is opened, the new behavior will be enabled.

Format Conditionally

Excel 2007 has greatly improved the ease of and capabilities for identifying data in a worksheet based on rules you select. Rules are organized into several types that allow you to easily format cells that compare values against each other; meet specific values, dates, or other criteria; match top and bottom percentile values you choose; match values above or below an average; or identify unique or duplicate values. If no pre-existing rule accommodates your needs, you can use a formula to set up criteria that cells must match.

COMPARE CELLS AGAINST ONE ANOTHER

You can highlight the comparative value of selected cells by using one of three formatting styles:

- **Data bars** display in each cell colored bars whose length is proportional to their value as compared to the other values in the selection.

4	Revenue		
5	Paper Supplies		$23,567
6	Writing Instruments		$5,437
7	Cards and Books		$14,986
8	Other Items		$25,897
9	Total Revenue		$69,887

- **Color scales** blend two or three colors (such as a green-yellow-red traffic light metaphor) to differentiate among high to low values.

4	Revenue		
5	Paper Supplies		$23,567
6	Writing Instruments		$5,437
7	Cards and Books		$14,986
8	Other Items		$25,897
9	Total Revenue		$69,887

- **Icon sets** use from three to five similar icons (similar to the circles used in *Consumer Reports*) to differentiate among high to low values.

4	Revenue		
5	Paper Supplies	●	$23,567
6	Writing Instruments	○	$5,437
7	Cards and Books	◑	$14,986
8	Other Items	●	$25,897
9	Total Revenue		$69,887

To apply conditional formatting that will compare selected cells:

1. Select the cells that will be compared against one another.

2. In the Home tab Styles group, click **Conditional Formatting** and click the style you want to use to see a submenu of options.

3. Point to each option to see a live preview of its effect on your selected data, as shown in Figure 7-10. Click the option you want to use.

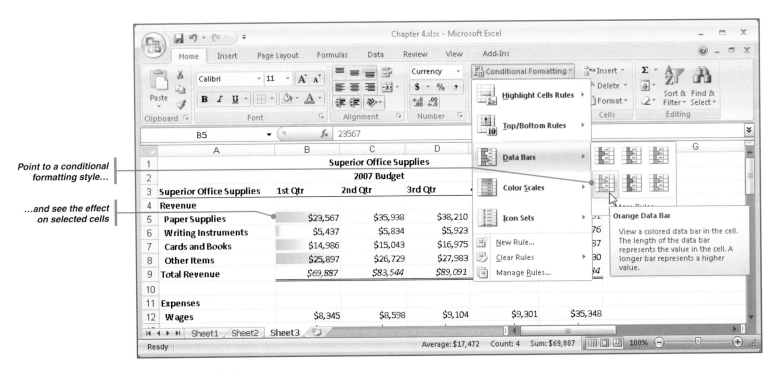

Point to a conditional formatting style...

...and see the effect on selected cells

Figure 7-10: **You can see a live preview of each formatting style on your data before selecting one.**

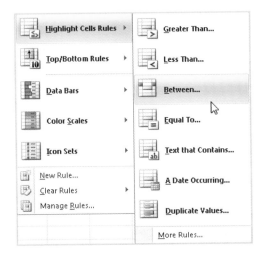

4. For more choices of each style, click **More Rules** at the bottom of each of their respective submenus.

5. In the New Formatting Rule dialog box, under Edit The Rule Description, you can change from one style to another and, depending on the style, change colors, change the values attributed to an icon or color, and make other customizations (see Figure 7-11). Click **OK** when finished.

FORMAT CELLS THAT MATCH VALUES OR CONDITIONS

Excel provides several pre-existing rules that let you easily format cells that meet established criteria.

1. Select the cells that will be formatted if they meet conditions you select.

2. In the Home tab Styles group, click **Conditional Formatting I Highlight Cell Rules** to view a submenu of rules that compare values to conditions.

–Or–

Click **Top/Bottom Rules** to view a submenu that lets you select cells based on top/bottom ranking or whether they're above or below the average of the selected cells.

3. For more choices, click **More Rules** at the bottom of each of the respective submenus.

4. In the New Formatting Rule dialog box, under Edit The Rule Description, you can change criteria and the formatting you want applied (see Chapter 6 for more information on using the Format Cells dialog box). Click **OK** when finished.

MANAGE CONDITIONAL FORMATTING RULES

Using the Conditional Formatting Rules Manager, you can view any conditional formatting rules in a workbook as well as edit, delete, re-order, and create new rules.

1. In the Home tab Styles group, click **Conditional Formatting | Manage Rules**. The Conditional Formatting Rules Manager appears, as shown in Figure 7-12.

2. Click the **Show Formatting Rules For** down arrow to select the scope of where you want to look for rules.

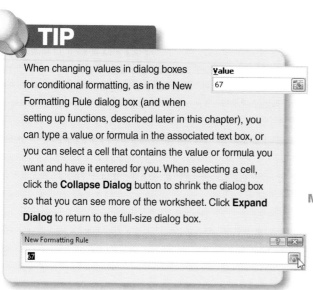

Figure 7-11: Each style has a set of customizations (or rules) that apply to how data is visually identified.

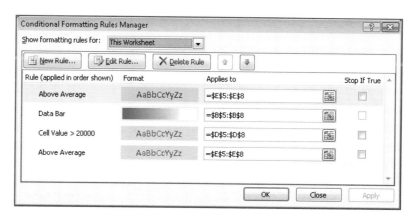

Figure 7-12: You can view and manage conditional formatting rules set up in a workbook.

3. Select a rule and perform one or more of the following actions:

- Click **Edit Rule** to open the Edit Formatting Rule dialog box and change criteria or conditions. Click **OK** to close the Edit Formatting Rule dialog box.
- Click **Delete Rule** to remove it. (Alternatively, you can click **Clear Rules** on the Conditional Formatting drop-down menu to remove all rules in the selected cells or worksheet).
- Click the up and down arrows to change the order in which rules are applied (rules are applied in order from top to bottom).
- Click the **Stop If True** check box to discontinue further rules from being applied if the selected rule is satisfied as being True.

4. Click **New Rule** to open the New Formatting Rule dialog box and create a new rule. Click **OK** to close the New Formatting Rule dialog box.

5. Click **OK** when finished.

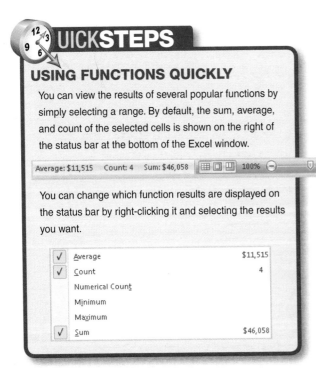

QUICKSTEPS

USING FUNCTIONS QUICKLY

You can view the results of several popular functions by simply selecting a range. By default, the sum, average, and count of the selected cells is shown on the right of the status bar at the bottom of the Excel window.

Average: $11,515   Count: 4   Sum: $46,058   100%

You can change which function results are displayed on the status bar by right-clicking it and selecting the results you want.

✓	A̲verage	$11,515
✓	C̲ount	4
	Numerical Coun̲t	
	Mi̲nimum	
	Ma̲ximum	
✓	S̲um	$46,058

Use Functions

Functions are prewritten formulas that you can use to perform specific tasks. They can be as simple as =PI(), which returns 3.14159265358979, the value of the constant pi; or they can be as complex as =PPMT(rate,per,nper,pv,fv,type), which returns a payment on an investment principal.

A function is comprised of three components:

- **Formula identifier**, the equal sign (=), is required when a function is at the beginning of the formula.
- **Function name** identifies the function, and typically is a two- to five-character uppercase abbreviation.
- **Arguments** are the values acted upon by functions to derive a result. They can be numbers, cell references, constants, logical (True or False) values, or a formula. Arguments are separated by commas and enclosed in parentheses. A function can have up to 255 arguments.

Enter a Function

You can enter functions on a worksheet by typing or by a combination of typing and selecting cell references, as described for formulas earlier in this chapter.

=PMT(

	B	C	D
	=PMT(		

PMT(**rate**, nper, pv, [fv], [type])

In addition, you can search for and choose functions from Excel's library of built-in functions.

TYPE A FUNCTION

To type a function in a cell on the worksheet:

1. Select a blank cell, and type an equal sign (=). The equal sign displays in the cell and the Formula bar.

2. Start typing the function name, such as <u>AVERAGE</u>, <u>MAX</u>, or <u>PMT</u>. As you start typing, functions with related spellings are displayed. Click any to see a description of the function.

3. Double-click the function you want. The function name and open parenthesis are entered for you. Excel displays a ScreenTip showing arguments and proper syntax for the function.

4. Depending on the function, for each argument you need to do none, one, or both of the following:

   - Type the argument.

   - Select a cell reference.

5. Type a comma to separate arguments, and repeat steps 4 and 5 as necessary.

6. Type a closing parenthesis, and press **ENTER** or click **Enter** on the Formula bar to complete the entry. A value will be returned. (If a #code is displayed in the cell or a message box displays indicating you made an error, see "Find and Correct Errors" later in this chapter.)

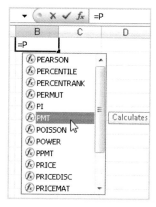

=P

	B	C	D
=P			

- PEARSON
- PERCENTILE
- PERCENTRANK
- PERMUT
- PI
- PMT — Calculates
- POISSON
- POWER
- PPMT
- PRICE
- PRICEDISC
- PRICEMAT

=PMT

INSERT A FUNCTION

You can find the function you want by using the Insert Function tool or by using the function category buttons on the ribbon.

fx Insert Function | Σ AutoSum · | Logical · | Lookup & Reference ·
| Recently Used · | A Text · | Math & Trig ·
| Financial · | Date & Time · | More Functions ·

Function Library

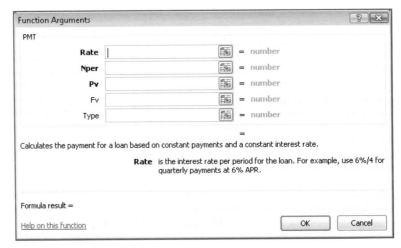

Insert Function

Search for a function:

Type a brief description of what you want to do and then click Go

[Go]

Or select a category: Financial ▼

Select a function:

ACCRINT
ACCRINTM
AMORDEGRC
AMORLINC
COUPDAYBS
COUPDAYS
COUPDAYSNC

ACCRINT(issue,first_interest,settlement,rate,par,frequency,basis,...)
Returns the accrued interest for a security that pays periodic interest.

Help on this function   [OK]   [Cancel]

Figure 7-13: *You can search for and select functions from Excel's extensive library in the Insert Function dialog box.*

In either case, Excel helps you enter arguments for the function you choose.

1. Select a blank cell. In the Formulas tab Function Library group, click the relevant function category button, and scroll to the function you want. Click the function and skip to step 5 to view its arguments.

   –Or–

   Click **Insert Function** in the Function Library group or its button on the Formula bar *fx*, or press **SHIFT-F3**. The Insert Function dialog box appears, as shown in Figure 7-13.

2. Type a brief description of what you want to do in the **Search For A Function** text box, and click **Go**. A list of recommended functions is displayed in the Select A Function list box.

   –Or–

   Open the **Select A Category** drop-down list, and select a category.

3. Click the function you want from the **Select A Function** list box. Its arguments and syntax are shown, as well as a description of what the function returns.

4. If you need more assistance with the function, click **Help On This Function**. A Help topic provides details on the function and an example of how it's used.

5. Click **OK** to open the Function Arguments dialog box, shown in Figure 7-14. The function's arguments are listed in order at the top of the dialog box, and the beginning of the function displays in the cell and in the Formula bar.

TIP

Using the AutoSum technique, you can apply other common functions to adjacent cells, such as averaging and getting a count. Click the **AutoSum** down arrow, and click the function you want; or click **More Functions** to open the Insert Function dialog box and access the full function library.

Σ AutoSum ▾   ? Logi

Σ   Sum
    Average
    Count Numbers
    Max
    Min
    More Functions...

Function Arguments

PMT

Rate [   ] 📊 = number
Nper [   ] 📊 = number
Pv   [   ] 📊 = number
Fv   [   ] 📊 = number
Type [   ] 📊 = number

=

Calculates the payment for a loan based on constant payments and a constant interest rate.

Rate   is the interest rate per period for the loan. For example, use 6%/4 for quarterly payments at 6% APR.

Formula result =

Help on this function   [OK]   [Cancel]

Figure 7-14: *Type or click cell references to enter argument values.*

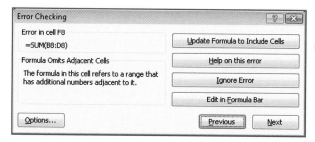

Figure 7-15: *You can manage how errors are checked and locate cells that contain errors.*

6. Enter values for the arguments by typing or clicking cell references. Click the **Collapse Dialog** button to shrink the dialog box so that you can see more of the worksheet. The formula on the worksheet is built as you enter each argument.

7. Click **OK** to complete the entry.

Enter a Sum in Columns or Rows Quickly

AutoSum uses the SUM function to add contiguous numbers quickly.

1. Select a blank cell below a column or to the right of a row of numbers.

2. In the Formulas tab Function Library group, click **AutoSum**. The cells Excel "thinks" you want to sum above or to the left of the blank cell are enclosed in a border, and the formula is displayed in the cell and in the Formula bar.

3. Modify the cells to be included in the sum by dragging a corner sizing-box, editing the formula in the cell or the Formula bar, or by selecting cells.

4. Press **ENTER** or click **Enter** on the Formula bar to complete the entry. The sum of the selected cells is returned.

–Or–

1. Select a contiguous column or row of cells, including a blank cell at the end of the column or to the right of the row.

2. Click **AutoSum**. The sum is entered in the blank cell.

Find and Correct Errors

Excel provides several tools that help you see how your formulas and functions are constructed, recognize errors in formulas, and better locate problems.

Check for Errors

Excel can find errors and provide possible solutions.

1. In the Formulas tab Formula Auditing group, click **Error Checking**. If you have an error on the worksheet, the Error Checking dialog box appears, as shown in Figure 7-15.

2. Use the command buttons on the right side of the dialog box to perform the indicated action. Click **Next** or **Previous** to check on other errors.

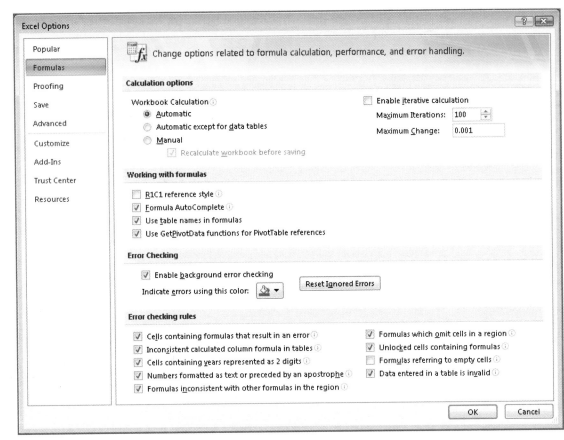

Figure 7-16: **You can customize how Excel performs error checking.**

3. Click **Options** to view the Excel Options Formulas window (see Figure 7-16), where you can customize error checking:

- **Error Checking** lets you turn error checking on or off as you enter formulas and determines the color of flagged cells that contain errors. Errors are flagged in green by default.

- **Error Checking Rules** provides several criteria that cells are checked against for possible errors.

Trace Precedent and Dependent Cells

Precedent cells are referenced in a formula or function in another cell; that is, they provide a value to a formula or function. *Dependent* cells contain a formula or function that uses the value from another cell; that is, they depend on the value in another cell for their own value.

This interwoven relationship of cells can compound one error into many, making a visual representation of the cell dependencies a vital error-correction tool.

1. Click a cell that uses cell references and/or is itself used as a reference by another cell in its formula or function.

2. In the Formulas tab Formula Auditing group, click **Trace Precedents** to display blue arrows that point to the cell from other cells.

–Or–

Click **Trace Dependents** to display blue arrows that point to other cells.

3. Click the **Remove Arrows** down arrow, and select whether to remove precedent, dependent, or all arrows.

Watch a Cell

You can follow what changes are made to a cell's value as its precedent cells' values are changed, even if the cells are not currently visible.

1. In the Formulas tab Formula Auditing group, click **Watch Window**. The Watch Window window opens.

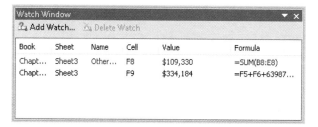

2. Click **Add Watch** to open the Add Watch dialog box.

3. Select the cell or cells you want to watch, and click **Add**. Each selected cell will be listed individually in the Watch Window window. As changes are made to a precedent cell, the value of the cells "being watched" will be updated according to the recalculation options you have set. (See "Recalculate Formulas" earlier in the chapter.)

4. Close the Watch Window window when you are done.

Evaluate a Formula in Pieces

You can see what value will be returned by individual cell references or expressions in the order they are placed in the formula.

1. Select the cell that contains the formula you want to evaluate.

2. In the Formulas tab Formula Auditing group, click **Evaluate Formula** 🔍 on the Formula Auditing toolbar. The Evaluate Formula dialog box, shown in Figure 7-17, appears.

TIP

To remove a watch you have placed, in the Formulas tab Formula Auditing group, click **Watch Window**, select the watch you want to remove, and click **Delete Watch**.

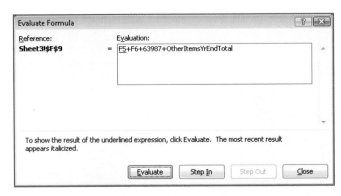

Figure 7-17: *You can dissect each expression or component of a formula to see its cell reference, its formula, and its value.*

3. Do one or more of the following:

- Click **Evaluate** to return the value of the first cell reference or expression. The cell reference or expression is underlined.

- Continue clicking **Evaluate** to return values for each of the cell references or expressions (again, underlined) to the right in the formula. Eventually, this will return the value for the cell.

- Click **Restart** to start the evaluation from the leftmost expression. (The Evaluate button changes to Restart after you have stepped through the formula.)

- Click **Step In** to view more data on the underlined cell reference.

- Click **Step Out** to return to the formula evaluation.

4. Click **Close** when finished.

How to...

- *Defining Themes, Layouts, and Master Slides*
- Create a Presentation from Another Presentation
- Create a Presentation Using a Standard Theme
- Create a Template
- *Working with Themes*
- Create a Presentation from Scratch
- Select a Layout
- *Adding Content to a Slide*
- Set Passwords for a Presentation
- Remove Password Restrictions
- Strip File Information from the Presentation
- Create an Outline
- *Understanding the Outlining Feature*
- Insert an Outline From Other Sources
- *Indenting with the Keyboard*
- Preview the Outline
- *Using the Outlining Commands*
- Print the Outline

Chapter 8
Creating the Presentation

This chapter describes how to create a presentation. You'll find that PowerPoint provides many methods for quickly and easily creating dramatic and effective presentations. Sometimes you'll find what you need in the prepackaged themes and templates that are already designed with specific presentation types in mind (for instance, an academic or business presentation, or one for healthcare professionals). These may be available from the online gallery. Sometimes, you'll find what you need in previous presentations you've created, so that you can simply borrow slides or design elements from past successful efforts. Sometimes, nothing you have in your presentation library or those offered by PowerPoint can fill your particular requirements. In this case, you create your own template from scratch or with Office-wide themes and the styling assistance of PowerPoint.

DEFINING THEMES, LAYOUTS, AND MASTER SLIDES

Themes in PowerPoint lend presentations color and design coordination. Up to 20 theme templates are available in a ribbon gallery in PowerPoint, or you can download additional choices from Microsoft's online templates. Chapter 9 explains how themes can be changed and customized to give you almost unlimited variations in how your presentation looks.

Layouts define where the objects of a slide (such as the text, spreadsheets or diagrams, pictures, or headings and footers) will be placed and formatted. Objects are positioned on a slide using *placeholders* that identify the specific object being inserted (a text placeholder vs. a chart placeholder, for instance). PowerPoint has defined several standard layout templates that you can choose when you insert a new slide. When you insert a new slide into a given theme, the slide takes on the colors and design elements of the theme, with the chosen layout attribute's placeholder positioning.

When you want to create your own themes and layouts to use in a future presentation, you create your own templates by saving them with a special file extension: .potx. Figure 8-1 explains some of the components of layouts and themes that you may have on a slide.

You can make your templates to be *master slides*—see Chapter 10 for additional information. Master slides, which are just another kind of template, define the parts of a slide that you want to be the same and in the background for a whole presentation or a group of contiguous slides.

Continued . . .

This chapter looks at how to organize and manage your slides by creating and working with a presentation outline. Finally, you will see how to protect your presentations with passwords.

Create a Presentation

There are three ways to begin creating your presentation: using a theme and standard layouts that define the design and layout of a slide, using another existing presentation and then modifying it, and starting from scratch—creating your own template in the process.

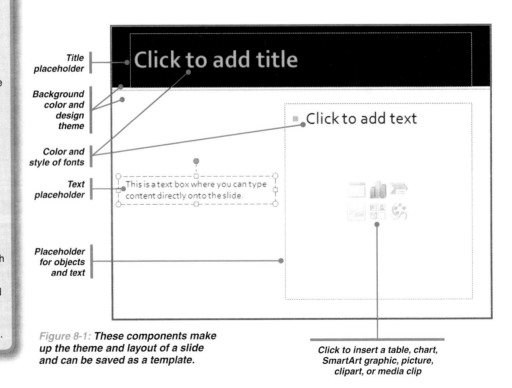

Title placeholder

Background color and design theme

Color and style of fonts

Text placeholder

Placeholder for objects and text

Click to add title

Click to add text

This is a text box where you can type content directly onto the slide.

Figure 8-1: **These components make up the theme and layout of a slide and can be saved as a template.**

Click to insert a table, chart, SmartArt graphic, picture, clipart, or media clip

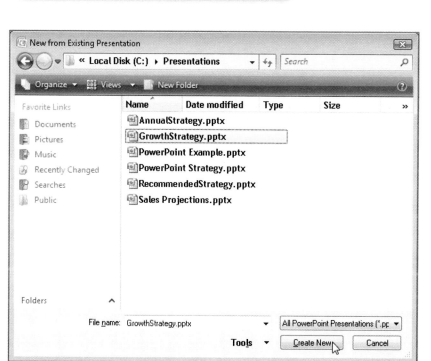

QUICKFACTS

DEFINING THEMES, LAYOUTS, AND MASTER SLIDES *(Continued)*

(You can have multiple master slides in a presentation.) In addition to any color and design elements (such as fonts) found in themes, master slides might include unique graphics (such as a logo), a specific header or footer, and options for placing placeholders for text and other objects while you are creating a presentation.

Figure 8-2: *In this window, you find the presentation you want to use as a model and create a new one.*

Create a Presentation from Another Presentation

The easiest and most direct way to create a new presentation is to start with an existing one. To copy a presentation, rename it, and then modify it according to your needs:

1. Click the **Office button** and click **New**.
2. On the New Presentation window, click **New From Existing ...**.

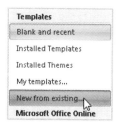

3. Find the presentation or template you want to use and click **Create New**, as shown in Figure 8-2.
4. Modify the presentation by replacing the theme, highlighting text and replacing it with your own; deleting unnecessary slides; inserting new slides; inserting your own graphics, charts, and art; and rearranging the slides according to your needs (subsequent chapters in this book describe how to do these actions in detail).
5. Click the **Office button** and click **Save As**. Enter a name for the presentation, choose the **Save As Type** option, and click **Save**.

Create a Presentation Using a Standard Theme

Themes are used to give your presentation a unified and professional look. They provide background color and design, predefined fonts, and other elements that hold a presentation together. Once you have defined the overall theme, it is a simple task to add slides with the appropriate layout for the data you wish to present. You select a theme from a predefined gallery available on the ribbon.

Blank and recent

Blank
Presentation

(See the "Defining Themes, Layouts, and Master Slides" QuickFacts.) Follow these steps to find and use one of PowerPoint's standard themes:

1. Click the **Office button** and select **New**. The New Presentation dialog box will open.
2. Click **Blank and Recent**, double-click the **Blank Presentation**, and a standard fare blank slide will open.
3. Click the **Design** tab and in the Themes group, click the **Themes More** down arrow to see thumbnails of color and design themes listed. Hold your mouse pointer over individual thumbnails to see their effects on the slide beneath. When you find the theme you want to use, click its thumbnail.

4. At this point you can either begin to add content to an actual presentation (see the "Adding Content to a Slide" QuickSteps), or you can create a template for a presentation (see "Create a Template").

All Themes ▼
This Presentation

Aa

Built-In

Aa   Aa   Aa   Aa   Aa   Aa   Aa

Aa   Aa   Aa   Aa   Aa   Aa   Aa
                                        Origin

Aa   Aa   Aa   Aa   Aa   Aa

More Themes on Microsoft Office Online...
Browse for Themes...
Save Current Theme...

Create a Template

A template contains one or more slides with attributes of the color themes and standard layouts you want to have available. First you create the slide with the desired themes and layouts. Then you save them as a template so that they can be used in formatting and adding your own color and design theme to new presentations. Template files have .potx extensions. When you create a new template, it will be displayed in the New Presentations dialog box under My Templates. To create a new presentation:

1. Click the **Office button** and click **New**. Click **Blank and Recent**, and double-click **Blank Presentation** to get the basic slide layout.
2. To prepare your slide:
   - Click the **Design** tab and click on the **Themes More** down arrow to select themes or design elements for the template.
   - Click the **Home** tab, click the **New Slide** down arrow to list possible layouts, and then click the layouts you want to use in the presentation.

 **NOTE**

In order to see the file extensions in the Save As Type list, the reader must choose that option in the Windows Explorer. In the Windows Explorer dialog box, click **Organize I Folder and Search Options**, click the **View** tab, and click **Hide Extensions for Known File Types** to remove the checkmark. By default, file extensions will not be displayed.

3. When you have a template that carries the attributes you want the presentation to have, click the **Office button** and click **Save As**.
4. In the **File Name** box, type a name for the new template.

NOTE

Unless you change the folder location, the template will be saved in the default template folder where PowerPoint design templates are stored. If you do not change the folder location, the template will appear in the Themes menu under "Custom."

QUICKSTEPS

WORKING WITH THEMES

You can search Microsoft Office resources to find other templates, apply a theme to selected or all slides in a presentation, or set a theme to be the default assigned to all future presentations, for a consistent business look, for example.

FIND OTHER MICROSOFT THEMES AND TEMPLATES

1. Click the **Design** tab and click the **More** down arrow on the **Themes** button.

2. Below the thumbnails, click **More Themes** on Microsoft Office Online.

3. On the Office Online window, click the thumbnail to the template you want. Follow the download instructions to install the template. The new template will appear on a blank slide in PowerPoint.

APPLY A THEME TO ALL SLIDES

Use the context menu for the theme thumbnail to select the option to apply the theme to all slides.

1. Right-click the theme thumbnail.

Continued . . .

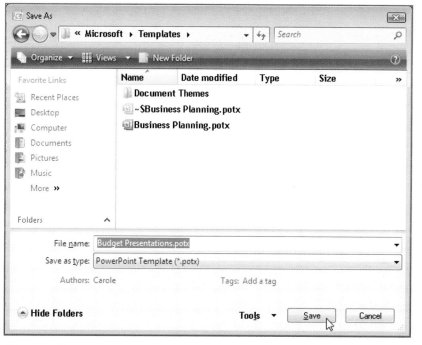

Figure 8-3: *You can save a file containing themes and layouts as a template for future presentations.*

5. In the **Save As Type** drop-down list box, click **PowerPoint Template (.potx)**, as seen in Figure 8-3.

6. Click **Save**. The templates are now available under My Templates in the New Presentation dialog box.

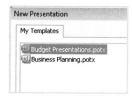

Create a Presentation from Scratch

When you create a presentation from scratch, you'll begin with blank slides and add layouts, color schemes, fonts, graphics and charts, other design elements, and text.

1. Click the **Office button** and click **New**. The New Presentation dialog box will be displayed.

2. Click **Blank and Recent**, and double-click **Blank Presentation**. A blank title page slide will be displayed.

QUICKSTEPS

WORKING WITH THEMES *(Continued)*

2. Click **Apply To All Slides**.

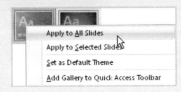

APPLY A THEME TO SELECTED SLIDES

1. First select the slides to which the themes will be applied:

   - Press **CTRL** and click the thumbnail in the Slides tab.

     -Or-

   - Press **CTRL** and click slides in the Slide Sorter view.

2. On the Design tab, click the **More** down arrow on the Themes group, and right-click the theme thumbnail to be selectively applied.

3. Click **Apply To Selected Slides**.

SET A DEFAULT THEME TO APPLY A THEME TO ALL FUTURE PRESENTATIONS

1. Under the Themes group in the Design tab, click the **More** down arrow and right-click the thumbnail you want.

2. Click **Set As Default Theme**.

NOTE

A theme can be further modified by changing its components, color, font, and graphic effects. Chapter 4 describes how to work with themes in more detail.

3. On the Design tab, select a **Theme** for the background color and design for your presentation. If none of them are acceptable, click the **More Themes on Microsoft Office Online** at the bottom of the list of thumbnails to search the themes available online.

4. Click and type over **Click To Add Title** to enter the title of your presentation. If you want to add a subtitle, click and type over **Click To Add Subtitle**.

5. When you are satisfied with that slide, click **New Slide** on the Home tab to insert another blank slide with the layout you want.

   - Click the **New Slide** button itself to get a slide with the last layout used.

   - Click the **New Slide** down arrow to get a menu of layout choices.

6. Open the **Insert** tab and click the relevant buttons to add text and other content to your slides. (See the "Adding Content to a Slide" QuickSteps.)

7. Repeat steps 5 through 6 for as many slides as you have in your presentation.

8. Save the presentation. Click the **Office button** and click **Save As**. Enter a name and click **Save**.

Select a Layout

As mentioned earlier, you can add a slide and select a layout by accessing the New Slide button in the Home tab. Here is another way:

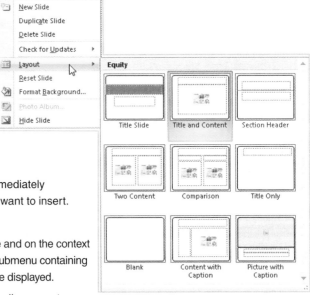

To add a slide and select a layout,

1. Right-click the slide immediately preceding the one you want to insert.

2. Click **New Slide**.

3. Right-click the new slide and on the context menu, click **Layout**. A submenu containing layout possibilities will be displayed.

4. Click the layout thumbnail you want.

ADDING CONTENT TO A SLIDE

The following elements are available to help you present the points you are making in the presentation. This is an overview of the procedures. Each element is covered in depth in later chapters of this book.

WORK WITH TEXT

Text can be added to placeholders, text boxes, and some shapes, or changed very easily. Chapter 10 deals with text in detail. To add type, you click inside of a text box, some shapes, or a placeholder, and begin to type.

1. To modify text attributes, highlight the text by dragging the pointer over it. A text toolbar will appear that you can use for simple changes.

2. Select the **Home** tab and click any of the Font group buttons. On this same tab are the Paragraph settings, which contain WordArt Styles options. (See Chapter 10 for additional information on using text.)

ADD OR CHANGE COLOR SCHEMES

Ask yourself, what color schemes might you want to use? Are there company colors that you want to use or colors you want to stay away from?

1. To see your standard options, click the **Design** tab and click the **Themes More** down arrow to list thumbnails of the standard choices. This establishes a design and color foundation for the presentation.

Continued . . .

Protecting Your Presentation

You can set two levels of passwords restricting access to your presentation: you can deny access to look at a presentation, and you can permit looking but deny modifying it. You can also strip personal information from the presentation—information that is automatically stored by PowerPoint, such as your name and certain file information.

Set Passwords for a Presentation

1. Open the presentation to be password protected.

2. Click the **Office button** and click **Save As**.

3. Click the **Tools** button and then click **General Options**. The General Options dialog box will open.

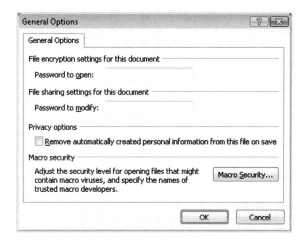

- To restrict anyone without a password from opening and looking at the presentation, type a password in the **Password To Open** text box.

- To restrict anyone from modifying the presentation, type a password in the **Password To Modify** text box.

4. Click OK.

5. In the Confirm Password dialog box, re-enter the password and click **OK**.

6. Then save the file by clicking **Save**.

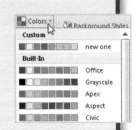

QUICKSTEPS

ADDING CONTENT TO A SLIDE *(Continued)*

2. To change the color grouping for a theme, click the **Theme Colors** button and click the color group you want. (See Chapter 9 for more information.)

3. To change color for individual slides, add a colored background (see Chapter 4).

SELECT AN ANIMATION SCHEME

To display animated text on your slide, click the **Animations** tab. Find the animation scheme you want in the Animations group and click it.

INSERT ART AND GRAPHICS

1. Click the **Insert** tab and in the Illustrations group, click the button for the art or graphic object you want to insert.

2. Find the object and drag it where you want it and resize it as needed.

   -Or-

3. Create and insert your own drawing using the Drawing group in the Home tab.

INSERT A TABLE

Insert a table to present more organized data. You can insert three types of tables: a PowerPoint-created table, one drawn by yourself, or one from Excel. On the **Insert** tab, click the **Table** down arrow and select your choice.

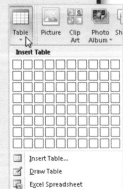

When anyone tries to open or modify a protected file, they will see a message like this:

Remove Password Restrictions

1. Click the **Office button** and click **Save As**.
2. Click **Tools | General Options**.
3. Clear any passwords in the Password To Open or Password To Modify text boxes.
4. Click **OK**.
5. Click **Save** and, if saving an existing file, confirm that you want to replace the existing file.

Strip File Information from the Presentation

When you set PowerPoint to strip personal information from a presentation, it is done when you save the file.

1. Click the **Office button** and click **Save As**.
2. Click **Tools | General Options**.
3. Under Privacy Options, place a checkmark next to **Remove Automatically Created Personal Information From This File On Save**.
4. Click **OK**.
5. Click **Save**, and if saving an existing file, confirm that you want to replace it.

Outline a Presentation

Outlining a presentation is easily done in PowerPoint. You simply bring up the Outline tab and begin typing. These sections explain how to create, manipulate, modify, and print an outline.

Create an Outline

The outline is created, modified, and viewed using the Outline tab, shown in Figure 8-4. An outline is created from scratch or by inserting text from other sources. You create an outline by indenting subtopics under topics. When you create a subtopic, or indent it under the one above it, you *demote* the point, or make it a lower level than the previous topic. It is contained within the higher level. When you remove an indent, you *promote* the point, making it a new topic. It becomes a higher level and may contain its own subtopics.

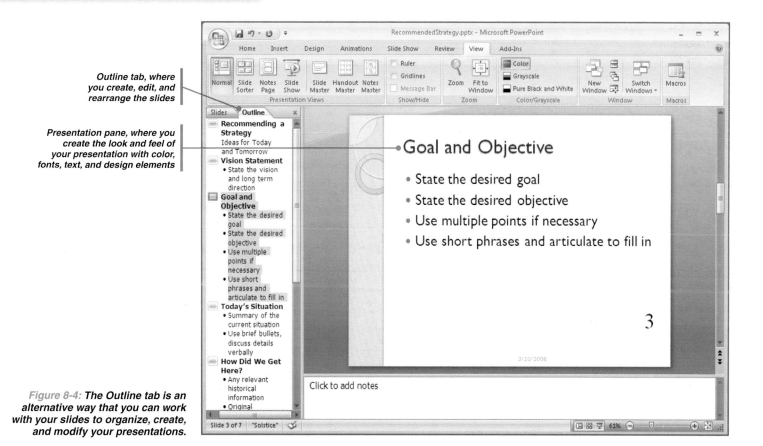

Outline tab, where you create, edit, and rearrange the slides

Presentation pane, where you create the look and feel of your presentation with color, fonts, text, and design elements

Figure 8-4: The Outline tab is an alternative way that you can work with your slides to organize, create, and modify your presentations.

UNDERSTANDING THE OUTLINING FEATURE

PowerPoint's outlining feature is not only an organizational tool, but it is a quick way to create a cohesive and logical path for your presentation. As you type the outline, you are creating the actual slides in a presentation. This is an alternative way to create a presentation from scratch. If you like to outline your presentations prior to jumping in and typing in your information, you'll like this way of building your presentation. The outline should contain:

- Main points you want to make that will become the titles of the slides
- Subsidiary points that support the main points and will become the bulleted content of each slide

Your main and subsidiary points are essential to the presentation. Although not essential at this point, certain secondary considerations are beneficial in flushing out your main points and the "feel" of your presentation, and the more you think these through initially, the more smoothly your presentation will flow. What graphics will you want to use on each slide? Do you have charts or graphs that tell the story? Are there photos that will take up part of the slide? Will you have a logo or other mandated identification on the chart?

CREATE AN OUTLINE FROM SCRATCH

To create a fresh outline, type your text into the Outline tab.

1. To open a blank presentation, click the **Office button** and click **New**. Click the type of presentation you want: **Blank and Recent**, **Installed Templates**, **My Templates**, or **New From Existing**.

2. On the **View** tab click **Normal** in the Presentation Views group. (You can also click the **Normal View** button on the View toolbar.)

3. Click the **Outline** tab so that the outline view is available, as shown in Figure 8-4.

4. Click to the right of the Outline slide icon to place the insertion point.

5. Type the title (the title of your first slide is typically the title of your presentation). Press **ENTER** to insert a new slide.

6. Type your next title, typically the first topic or main point. Press **ENTER** when you are done. Another new slide will be inserted.

   - To add points to the slide rather than to insert a new one, click **Increase List Level** on the Home tab Paragraph group to move the topic to the right. It will become a subtopic under the previous slide.

   - To move points to the left, making them a higher level, click **Decrease List Level** on the Home tab Paragraph group. It will become either a higher level point or a new slide, depending on the original level.

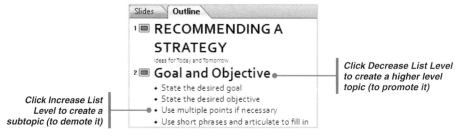

Click Increase List Level to create a subtopic (to demote it)

Click Decrease List Level to create a higher level topic (to promote it)

7. Continue typing and pressing **ENTER,** and clicking **Increase List Level** or **Decrease List Level** to move the text into headings and bulleted points until the presentation is outlined.

Instead of using the Increase List Level or Decrease List Level buttons, you can also press **ENTER** to create a new bulleted line. Pressing **CTRL-ENTER** will create a new slide. Other options for working with outlines are specific keypresses (see the "Indenting with the Keyboard" QuickSteps), and the right-click context menu (see the "Using the Outlining Commands" QuickSteps).

Insert an Outline from Other Sources

You can create slides from an outline you have previously created in another document. Depending on the format of the text, the formatting retained and used by PowerPoint will differ.

- A **Microsoft Word (.doc) or Rich Text Format (.rtf)** outline will use paragraph breaks to mark the start of a new slide. Each paragraph will become a slide title. However, if the document is formatted with headings, Heading 1 will become the title of the slide, Heading 2 will be the second level, Heading 3 the third level, and so on. (See Figure 8-5.)

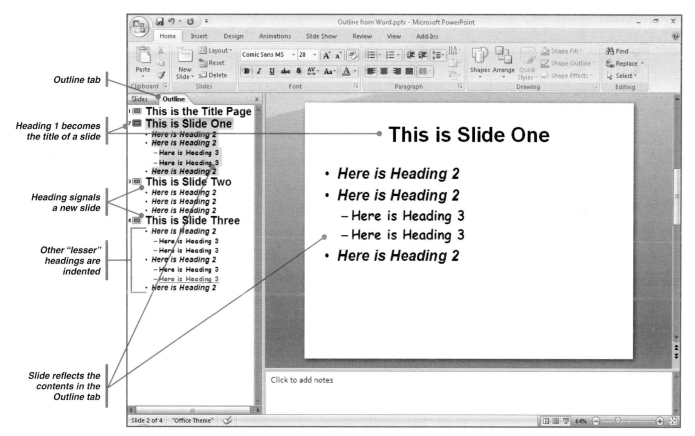

Figure 8-5: *Inserting an outline into a presentation from a Word document retains the heading level formatting to separate slides and bulleted items.*

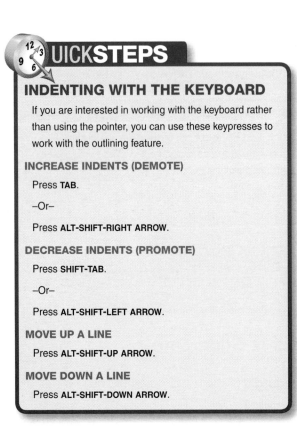

INDENTING WITH THE KEYBOARD

If you are interested in working with the keyboard rather than using the pointer, you can use these keypresses to work with the outlining feature.

INCREASE INDENTS (DEMOTE)

Press **TAB**.

–Or–

Press **ALT-SHIFT-RIGHT ARROW**.

DECREASE INDENTS (PROMOTE)

Press **SHIFT-TAB**.

–Or–

Press **ALT-SHIFT-LEFT ARROW**.

MOVE UP A LINE

Press **ALT-SHIFT-UP ARROW**.

MOVE DOWN A LINE

Press **ALT-SHIFT-DOWN ARROW**.

- An **HTML** outline will retain its formatting; however, the text will appear in a text box on the slide and can only be edited in the Presentation pane, not in the Outline tab. In addition, you must create a separate HTML file for each slide. (To see the HTML file in the Insert Outline dialog box, you may have to select .htm as the Type of File.)

- A **Plain Text** (.txt) outline will adopt the styles of the current presentation. PowerPoint will use paragraph separations to start a new slide.

To insert an outline from another source:

1. On the Home tab Slides group, click the **New Slide** down arrow and on the bottom of the menu, click **Slides From Outline**.

2. In the Insert Outline dialog box, find the location and name of the outline to be used, select it, and click **Insert**.

Preview the Outline

To preview an outline and then print it:

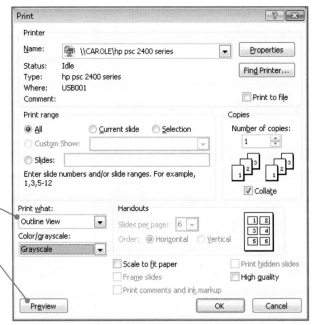

Select what is to be printed

Click to see what will be printed

Figure 8-6: The Print dialog box allows you to preview the outline before you print it.

1. Right-click the Outline tab and click **Expand**, and then **Expand All** from the submenu to expand the entire outline so that all details are showing.

2. Click the **Office button** and click **Print**.

3. Open the **Print What** drop-down list box, and click **Outline View**, as seen in Figure 8-6.

4. Click **Preview**.

5. Click **Close Print Preview** to close the preview view.

QUICKSTEPS

USING THE OUTLINING COMMANDS

Although some of the buttons available on the ribbon work well with the outlining function, you can display commands specifically for use with the Outline tab.

DISPLAY THE OUTLINING COMMANDS

1. Select the slide or line of text in the Outline tab.

2. Right-click, and select one of the following commands:

PROMOTE OR DEMOTE OUTLINE TEXT

- Click **Promote** to move the selected text in a slide up one level.

- Click **Demote** to move the selected text in a slide down one level.

MOVE UP OR MOVE DOWN OUTLINE TEXT

- Click **Move Up** to move the selected text of a slide up one line or item.

- Click **Move Down** to move the selected text of a slide down one line or item.

COLLAPSE OR EXPAND A SLIDE

- Click **Collapse** and from the menu, click **Collapse** to hide the detail beneath the title of a selected slide; or click **Collapse All** to hide all the detail lines in the outline.

- Click **Expand** and from the menu, click **Expand** to show the detail beneath a title of a selected slide; or click **Expand All** to show all the detail lines in the outline.

SHOW FORMATTING

Click **Show Text Formatting** to toggle between showing and not showing the formatting in the outline text.

Print the Outline

To print the outline without previewing it:

1. Click the **Office button** and click **Print**.

2. In the Print dialog box, open the **Print What** drop-down list box. Click **Outline View**.

3. Click **OK** to print.

Chapter 9
Working with Slides

Getting around in a presentation and being able to manipulate slides easily is a critical skill in becoming a capable PowerPoint user. In this chapter you will find how to work with presentations at the slide level. In addition to navigating through the slides in various views of PowerPoint, you will learn to insert, delete, rearrange, and copy slides, as well as to change a presentation's basic components of themes, fonts, and colors. Finally, permissions are covered.

Navigate and Manipulate Slides

Working with slides enables you to find your way around PowerPoint and to manipulate the slides, both individually and globally. This section addresses how to insert and delete slides, display slides in a variety of ways, and move and duplicate slides.

NAVIGATING WITH THE KEYBOARD

If you are more comfortable working with the keyboard, rather than the mouse pointer, you can work with slides using the keyboard.

ACCESS THE RIBBON AND RIBBON COMMANDS

- Press **ALT** to display the ribbon tags. To choose a specific tab, press the letter of the ribbon tag.
- To move among the ribbon commands, press **ALT**, and then **TAB** or **RIGHT ARROW**. Then press **ENTER** to choose a command or menu.

MOVE TO THE NEXT OR PREVIOUS SLIDE

You have two ways on the keyboard to move to the next or previous slide on the Slide pane and the Slides tab:

- To move to the previous slide, press **PAGE UP** or press the **UP ARROW**.
- To move to the next slide, press **PAGE DOWN** or press the **DOWN ARROW**.

MOVE TO FIRST OR LAST SLIDE

- Press **CTRL-HOME** to move to the first slide.
- Press **CTRL-END** to move to the last slide.

MOVE TO NEXT PLACEHOLDER (DOTTED BOX) OR WINDOW AREA

- Press **CTRL-ENTER** to move to the next placeholder.
- Press **F6** to cycle between areas of a window: ribbon, presentation pane, Slides/Outline panes, and Note pane.

OPEN AND CLOSE THE RIBBON

Press **CTRL-F1**.

Continued . . .

Navigate from Slide to Slide

To move between the slides, you can use the Slide pane, the Outline tab, or the Slides tab to select and move to the slide you want.

- On the Slides tab, click the **thumbnail** of the slide you want.
- On the Outline tab, click the **icon** of the slide you want.
- On the Slide pane or either tab, click the vertical **scroll bar** to move to the next or previous slide.
- On the Slide Sorter view, click the vertical **scroll bar** to move to the next screen of thumbnails. Click the **scroll bar** down arrow or up arrow to move more slowly. Click the up or down arrows on the **scroll bar** to move in increments. Click **each slide** to select it.

Insert a Slide

You can insert new slides in various ways in several places in PowerPoint. You can also insert slides from other presentations.

INSERT A NEW SLIDE

You can insert a new blank slide from several places in PowerPoint. The most common ways are

- In the Home tab Slides group, click **New Slide**.
- In the Outline tab, when entering bulleted text, press **CTRL-ENTER**.
- In either the Slides or Outline tabs, right-click the slide before the one you want to insert, and click **New Slide**.

  –Or–

  In either the Slides or Outline tabs, click the slide or slide icon before the one you want to insert and press **ENTER**.

- In the Slide Sorter view, right-click the slide preceding the new one, and click **New Slide** or press **CTRL-M**.

NAVIGATING WITH THE KEYBOARD

(*Continued*)

START AND END SLIDE SHOWS

- To start a slide show on the current slide, press **SHIFT-F5**.

- To start a slide show beginning with the first slide, press **F5**.

- To close the slide show and return to Normal view, press **ESC**.

- To switch between the slide show and the Normal view, press **ALT-TAB**. (You must start with the slide show.)

Microsoft PowerPoint - [Recommending a Str...

TIP

To delete a slide from the Slide Sorter view, the Outline tab, or the Slides tab: click the thumbnail slide to select it, and press **DELETE**. You can also right-click the thumbnail slide, and click **Delete Slide** from the context menu.

INSERT A SLIDE FROM ANOTHER FILE

To insert a slide duplicated from another presentation, you must find and display the slides from the source presentation, and then select the slide or slides that you want to copy into your destination presentation.

1. In the Slides tab click the slide positioned immediately before the one to be inserted.

2. Select the **Home** tab and in the Slides group, click the **New Slide** down arrow. From the drop-down menu, click **Reuse Slides** (at the bottom of the menu). The Reuse Slides task pane will be displayed.

3. Click **Browse** to find the source file containing the slide to be copied. Choose **Browse Files**. When found, select the file and click **Open**. The Reuse Slides task pane, illustrated in Figure 9-1, will contain thumbnails of the presentation.

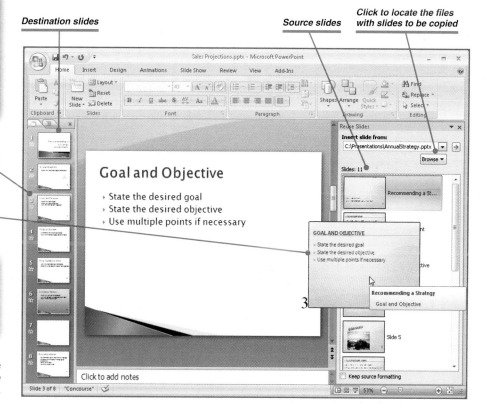

Destination slides

Source slides

Click to locate the files with slides to be copied

Click the slide positioned immediately before the one to be inserted

Click a slide to copy it into the destination slides

Figure 9-1: *The Reuse Slides task pane allows you to find and copy one or more slides from another presentation into your current one.*

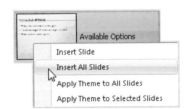

4. To insert the slides into the presentation, you must work back and forth between the Slides tab (destination) and the Reuse Slides (source) task pane:

- Scroll to the thumbnail image in the source Reuse Slides task pane and click the one to be inserted. It will be inserted when you click it.

- To insert all the slides in the source Reuse Slides task pane, right-click a thumbnail and select **Insert All Slides** from the context menu.

- To apply the formatting of the source slides to those in the destination Slides tab, right-click and choose **Apply Theme to All Slides** to copy the formatting to all of them, or select **Apply Theme To Selected Slides** to copy the format only to selected destination slides.

- To retain the formatting of the source Reuse Slides as you copy them, click the **Keep Source Formatting** checkbox at the bottom of the task pane.

- To view a larger image of the Reuse Slide task pane, place the pointer over the slide thumbnail image, but do not click.

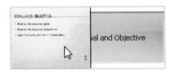

TIP

Before closing the task pane, you can Browse for other files and insert slides from them without closing the task pane.

5. When you have inserted all the slides you want, click **Close** ☒.

Display Multiple Presentations at Once

Opening and displaying two or more presentations opens many possibilities for dragging one slide from one presentation to another, copying color or formatting from one slide or presentation to another, and for comparing the presentations or slides side by side.

1. Open both presentations. Click the **Office button**, click **Open,** and complete the sequence of locating and opening the presentations.

2. Click the **View** tab and from the Window group, choose one of the following views:

- Click the **Arrange All** button to display each presentation window side by side, as seen in Figure 9-2.

–Or–

- Click the **Cascade Windows** to see the windows cascading, as seen in Figure 9-3.

Tiles all open windows

Lists windows so you can switch between them

Opens all windows in an "offset-stacked" view

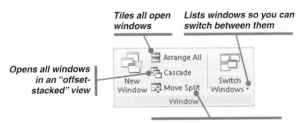

Allows you to use arrow keys to move the split between the Slide pane and the Notes pane

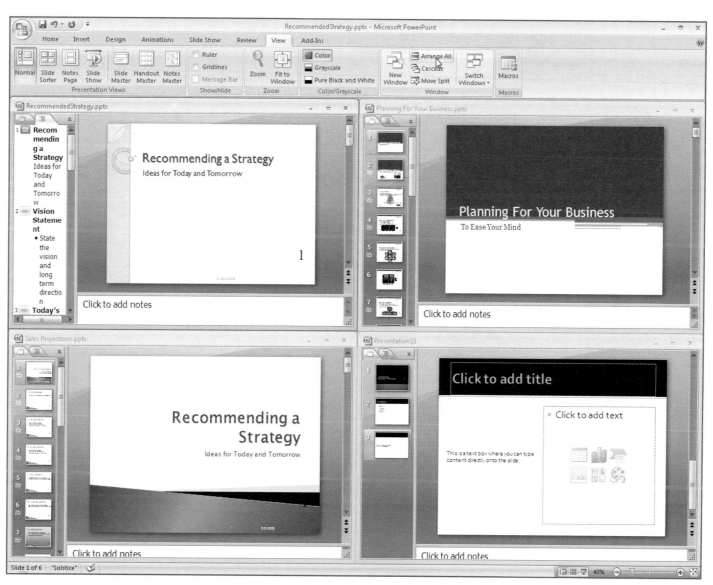

Figure 9-2: *You can see each window separately by using the Arrange All command.*

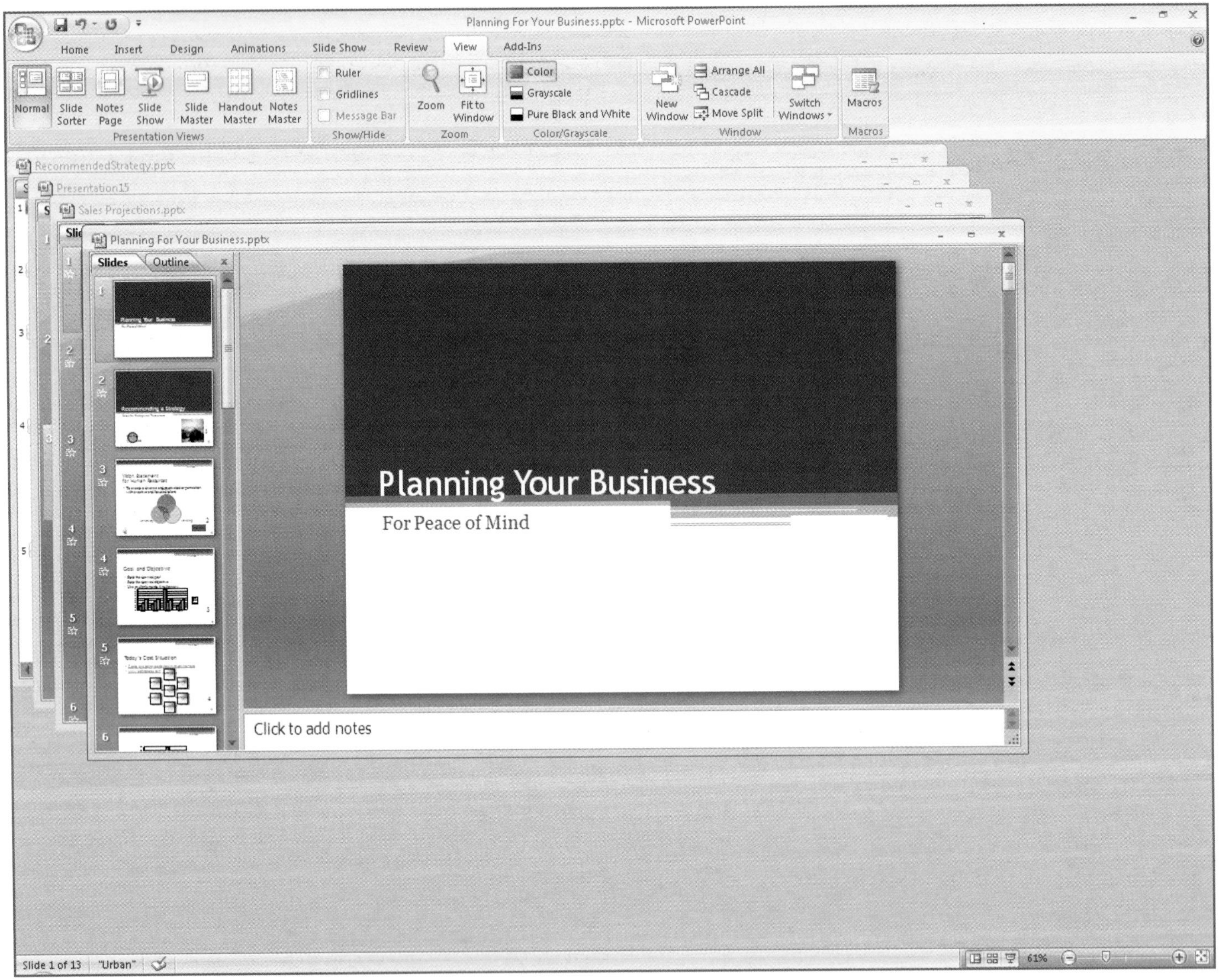

Figure 9-3: *Using the Cascade command you can arrange the presentations in a cascading sequence.*

● Click **Move Split** and then press the **UP ARROW** and **DOWN ARROW** keys to move the split between the Slide pane and the Notes pane; press the **RIGHT ARROW** and **LEFT ARROW** keys to move the split between the Slide pane and the Outline/Slides tab. Press **ENTER** to exit the Move Split mode.

● Click **Switch Windows** to go back and forth between two or more presentations.

Duplicate a Slide

An alternate way to copy or duplicate a slide uses the Duplicate Slides command:

1. In the Slide Sorter view, the Outline tab, or the Slides tab, select the slide you want to copy. To copy multiple slides in the thumbnail view or the Outline tab, press **CTRL** while you click the slides to select them. For contiguous slides, you can press **SHIFT** and click the first and last slide in the range. In Normal view, the active slide is the one that is selected.

   ● To duplicate a single slide or multiple selected slides, right-click the slide or slides, and click **Duplicate Slide** from the context menu.

   ● To duplicate multiple selected slides, click the **New Slide** down arrow (on the Home tab) and click **Duplicate Selected Slides** from the bottom of the menu.

USING A KEYBOARD WITH SLIDES

If you are more comfortable using the keyboard than a mouse pointer, you have the following commands and more. Some of the commands use a combination of pointer and keyboard commands, such as Copy.

START A NEW PRESENTATION

Press **CTRL-N**.

INSERT A NEW SLIDE

Press **ALT-H**, press **I**, then use the arrow keys to select a layout from the menu. Press **ENTER** when finished.

REMOVE A SLIDE

Press **DELETE** or press **CTRL-X**.

COPY A SLIDE

- Click a thumbnail to select it, and press **CTRL-C**.
- Click where you want the copied slide inserted, and press **CTRL-V**.

COPY THE CONTENTS OF A SLIDE

- Click a thumbnail to select it, select the text to be copied, and press **CTRL-C**.
- Move the insertion point to where you want the items copied, and press **CTRL-V**.

Where you place the insertion point will determine where the new slide will be positioned. It's possible to insert a slide into the middle of another one, splitting its contents unintentionally. Make certain you place the insertion point precisely where you want the new slide to go.

Copy a Design Using Browse

To copy just the design (and not the content) of a presentation, use the Browse feature of the Design Themes feature.

1. Open in **Normal v**iew the presentation to which you will apply the design of another presentation.

2. Click the **Design** tab, click the **Themes More** down arrow, and click **Browse For Themes**.

3. In the Choose Theme Or Themed Document dialog box, find the document or presentation containing the theme you want to copy and click it.

4. Click **Apply**, and the theme will be copied to the original presentation.

Use Zoom

You can zoom in or out of a slide, which enables you to work at a very detailed level or back off to see the total slide, respectively.

- To control the zoom with a specific percentage, click the **View** tab and click the **Zoom** button in the Zoom group. When the Zoom dialog box displays, click the percentage you want displayed or use the Percent spinner. A smaller percentage will reduce the image; a larger percentage will increase it. Click OK when finished.

- To make the slide fit in the window, click the **View** tab, then click the **Fit To Window** button in the Zoom group. The image will be reduced or increased in size to fit in the slide pane. If you are not in the View tab, a quicker way to do this is to click the **Fit Slide To Current Window** button 🔲 on the right of the status bar.

- To increase or decrease the zoom effect with a slider, drag the **Zoom** slider on the right of the status bar, or click the **Zoom In** or **Zoom Out** buttons on either side of the slider to zoom in smaller increments. The percentage of the zoom will be shown to the left of the slider.

Change the Look and Feel of Slides

At some point or another, you will want to change the look and feel of slides in a presentation. The slides may have been created from another presentation, and you want this one to be unique. You may need just to tweak a few components of the presentation. You can change the theme, color, fonts, and special effects of a presentation.

Change a Theme

As you have seen in Chapter 8, you can select a built-in (or PowerPoint standard) theme for your slides. These themes can be changed to fit your own presentation requirements. The theme can be changed for a single slide or the whole presentation by altering the fonts, color, and design elements.

CHANGE THE COLOR OF A THEME

Each theme consists of a set of four colors for text and background, six colors for accents, and two colors for hyperlinks. You can change any single color element, or all of them. When you change the colors, the font styles and design elements remain the same.

1. With your presentation open, click the **Design** tab.

2. If you want to change the theme colors on only some of the slides, select those slides now. Use **CTRL**-click to select noncontiguous slides or use **SHIFT**-click to select contiguous slides.

3. Click **Theme Colors**. The menu of color combinations will be displayed, as seen in Figure 9-4.

4. Run the pointer over the rows of color combinations to see which appeals to you.

5. When you find the one you want, right-click the row and click **Apply To All Slides** to change the colors throughout the whole presentation, or **Apply To Selected Slides** for selected slides.

9

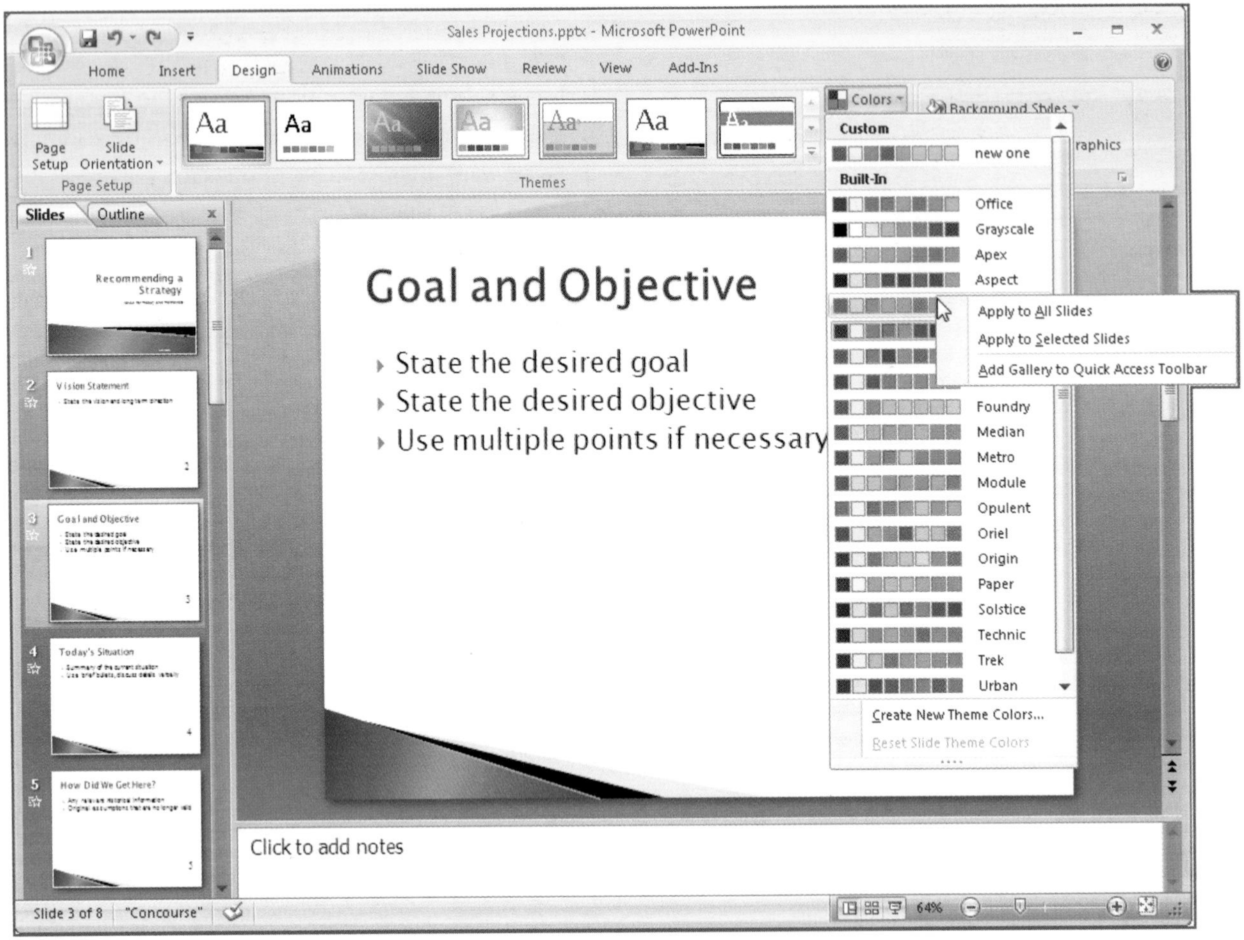

Figure 9-4: *The menu of color combinations offers alternatives for your theme colors.*

CHANGE THEME FONTS

Each theme includes two fonts. The *body* font is used for general text entry and a *heading* font is used for headings. The default font used in PowerPoint for a new presentation without a theme is Calibri for headings and body text. Once a theme is assigned to slides, the fonts may be different, and they can be changed.

TIP

You may have to drag your text placeholder to the right or left to see the effects of the fonts as you pass your pointer over them.

1. In the Design tab Themes group, click the **Theme Fonts**. The drop-down list displays a list of theme fonts. The current theme font combination, in its place in the list, is highlighted.

2. Point to each font combination to see how the fonts appear on your presentation.

3. Click the font name combination you decide upon. If you click a font name combination, the font will replace both the body and heading fonts in your presentation on one or selected slides.

CREATE A NEW THEME FONT

You may also decide that you want a unique set of fonts for your presentation. You can create a custom font set that is available in the list of fonts for your current and future presentations.

1. In the Design tab Themes group, click **Theme Fonts**.

2. Click **Create New Theme Fonts** at the bottom of the drop-down list.

3. In the Create New Theme Fonts dialog box (see Figure 9-5), click either or both the **Heading Font** and **Body Font** down arrows to select a new fonts combination. View the new combination in the Sample area.

4. Type a new name for the font combination you've selected and click **Save**. Custom fonts are available for selection at the top of the Theme Fonts drop-down list.

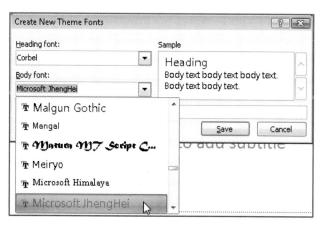

Figure 9-5: **You can choose a heading or body font from the fonts available in your Windows system.**

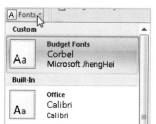

9

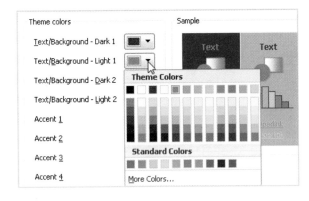

CHANGE THEMED GRAPHIC EFFECTS

Shapes, illustrations, pictures, and charts include graphic effects that are controlled by themes. Themed graphics are modulated in terms of their lines (borders), fills, and effects (such as shadowed, raised, and shaded). For example, some themes simply change an inserted rectangle's fill color, while other themes affect the color, the weight of its border, and whether it has a 3-D appearance.

1. In the Design tab Themes group, click **Theme Effects**. The drop-down list displays a gallery of effects combinations. The current effects combination is highlighted.

2. Point to each combination to see how the effects appear on your presentation, assuming you have a graphic or chart inserted on the slide (see Chapter 14 for information on inserting pictures, shapes and graphics).

3. Click the effects combination you want.

Create a Custom Theme

You can create a new theme, save it, and use it in your presentations. You select a group of text, background, accent, and hyperlink colors and give them a name.

1. Click the **Design** tab and then in the Themes group, click **Theme Colors**.

2. At the bottom of the menu of colors, click **Create New Theme Colors**. The Create New Theme Colors dialog box will be displayed, as shown in Figure 9-6.

3. To select a color for one of the color groups, click the down arrow for the Text/ Background/Accent/ and/or Hyperlink group and click the color you want to test. It will be displayed in the Sample pane.

4. Go through each set of colors that you want to change.

5. When you find a group of colors that you like, type a name in the **Name** text box and click **Save**.

USE CUSTOM COLORS

Using a similar technique to creating your own themes, you can create your own unique color mix for text, background accents, and hyperlinks. Here is how you work with custom colors.

TIP

To restore the original colors in the Create New Theme Colors dialog box Sample pane and start over, click **Reset**.

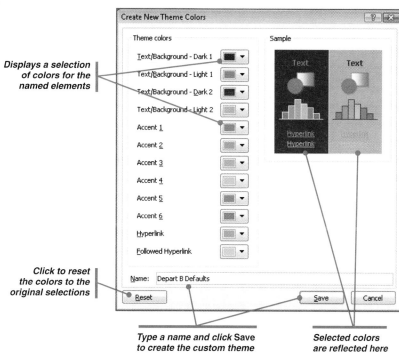

Displays a selection of colors for the named elements

Click to reset the colors to the original selections

Type a name and click **Save** to create the custom theme

Selected colors are reflected here

*Figure 9-6: **The Create New Theme Colors dialog box** allows you to create new themes to use in presentations.*

1. Select the slides to be affected with the new colors, whether all of them or a selected few.

2. Click the **Design** tab and click **Theme Colors**. At the bottom of the rows of color combinations, click **Create New Theme Colors**. The Create New Theme Colors dialog box will appear.

3. Click the Theme Color group that you want to work with. The Theme Colors submenu will be displayed. Click **More Colors**.

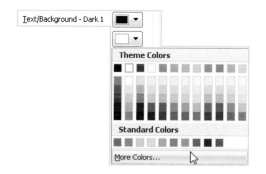

4. In the Colors dialog box you have two options.

- Click the **Standard** tab to see the dialog box shown in Figure 9-7. Click the color unit you want and see it displayed in the New preview pane. When you want to see it in the Sample pane, click **OK**.

NOTE

You may find you want to change something in a custom theme after you've been using it for awhile. To edit a custom theme, in Normal view click the **Theme Colors** button in the Design tab Themes group and right-click the custom theme you want to edit. From the context menu, click **Edit**, and the Edit Theme Colors dialog box, similar to that shown in Figure 9-6, will be displayed.

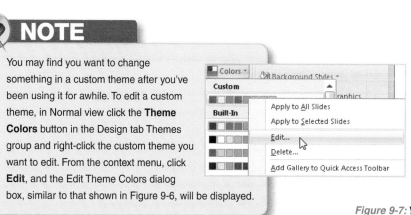

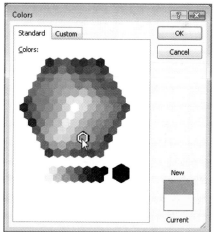

*Figure 9-7: **You can change the color very precisely by clicking the specific color shade you want.***

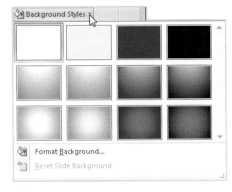

Figure 9-8: *You can create unique colors by "mixing" the combination of red, green, and blue.*

- Click the **Custom** tab to see the dialog box shown in Figure 9-8. Click somewhere on the color rainbow to get the approximate color. Then drag the slider to get precisely the color you want. You will see it displayed in the New preview pane.

  –Or–

- Click the **Red**, **Green**, or **Blue** up arrows or down arrows to get the precise color mix you want. Displayed is RGB (Red, Green, Blue color standard) color, but you can also select HSL (Hue, Saturation, and Luminosity color standard). When you are finished, click **OK**.

5. When you get the colors you want, type a name in the Name text box and click **Save** for a custom theme color.

CHANGE THE BACKGROUND STYLE

You can change the slide background on one or all slides in a presentation. When you change the background style when you have a theme already assigned to the slides in your presentation, the design elements from the theme will remain—only the background color or shading changes.

1. If you want only some of the slides changed, select those that are to be changed with a new background style.

2. Click the **Design** tab and in the Background group, click **Background Styles**. A menu of styles will open.

3. Run your pointer over the thumbnails to see which appeals to you. As you do this, the slides in the Slide pane will reflect the selection.

4. When you find the style you want, click it to change all the slides. Or right-click the thumbnail and click **Apply To Selected Slides** to change only the selected slides. The menu will close and the slides in the presentation will be changed.

Copy Attributes with Format Painter

The Format Painter can be used to copy all attributes (such as fonts, alignment, bullet styles, and color) from one slide to another as well as from one presentation to another.

1. Display the source slides in the Slides tab or Slide Sorter view. Click the **Home** tab.

2. Find and click the source slide containing the color to be copied.

NOTE

To copy attributes in one presentation to all the slides in another, open both presentations and display them in Arrange All mode. Open each in Master Slide view (for each presentation window, open the **View** tab, choose **Slide Master,** and then click **Edit Master**). Click the source master slide to select it, then click **Format Painter** in the Slides group, and click (select) the destination Slide Master to copy the attributes. Check that the attributes have been copied appropriately in Normal view. See "Working with Slide Masters" in Chapter 10 for additional information.

UICKSTEPS

USING FOOTERS ON SLIDES

To work with any aspect of footers, you need to display the Headers and Footers dialog box (shown in Figure 9-9). (Headers are available for Notes and Handouts only.) To display this dialog box, follow these three steps; then do the fourth one to complete the selection.

1. Select the slide or slides that need footers.

2. Open the **Insert** tab and click **Header & Footer** in the Text group.

3. Click the **Slide** tab for footers for slides. (See "Using Headers and Footers on Notes and Handouts" in Chapter 10.)

4. When you have finished making your selections, described next, click **Apply** to apply the choices to selected slides only, or click **Apply To All** for all slides.

Continued . . .

3. Click **Format Painter** in the Clipboard group once to copy the source format to one slide. If you want to use the source slide to reformat several other slides, double-click **Format Painter** to turn it on until you click it again to turn it off (or press **ESC**).

4. Find the destination slide and click it to receive the new attributes.

5. If you are copying the source attributes to multiple slides, continue to find the destination slides and click them.

6. When you are finished, click **Format Painter** to turn it off or press **ESC**.

Work with Hyperlinks

Inserting hyperlinks in a presentation allows you to link to other files or presentations, to a web site, to an e-mail address, or to another slide within the current presentation.

INSERT A HYPERLINK

To insert a hyperlink in the presentation:

1. On your slide, highlight the text by dragging the pointer over the characters that you want to contain the hyperlink.

2. Click the **Insert** tab and in the Links group, click the **Hyperlink** button.

Figure 9-9: **You can add footers to selected slides or to the whole presentation.**

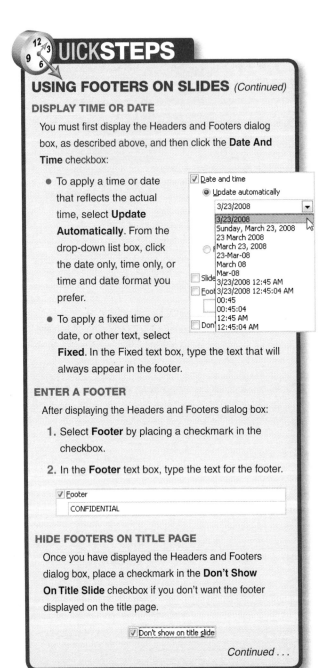

USING FOOTERS ON SLIDES *(Continued)*

DISPLAY TIME OR DATE

You must first display the Headers and Footers dialog box, as described above, and then click the **Date And Time** checkbox:

- To apply a time or date that reflects the actual time, select **Update Automatically**. From the drop-down list box, click the date only, time only, or time and date format you prefer.

- To apply a fixed time or date, or other text, select **Fixed**. In the Fixed text box, type the text that will always appear in the footer.

☑ Date and time
  ◉ Update automatically
    3/23/2008 ▼
    | 3/23/2008 |
    | Sunday, March 23, 2008 |
    | 23 March 2008 |
    | March 23, 2008 |
    | 23-Mar-08 |
    | March 08 |
    | Mar-08 |
    | 3/23/2008 12:45 AM |
    | 3/23/2008 12:45:04 AM |
    | 00:45 |
    | 00:45:04 |
    | 12:45 AM |
    | 12:45:04 AM |

ENTER A FOOTER

After displaying the Headers and Footers dialog box:

1. Select **Footer** by placing a checkmark in the checkbox.

2. In the **Footer** text box, type the text for the footer.

  ☑ Footer
  CONFIDENTIAL

HIDE FOOTERS ON TITLE PAGE

Once you have displayed the Headers and Footers dialog box, place a checkmark in the **Don't Show On Title Slide** checkbox if you don't want the footer displayed on the title page.

  ☑ Don't show on title slide

Continued . . .

3. In the Insert Hyperlink dialog box, find the destination for the link.

- If the destination is within the presentation outline itself, click **Place In This Document** and click the slide, as seen in Figure 9-10.

- If the destination is on an existing document or web page, click **Existing File Or Web Page** and follow the prompts to the destination.

- If you must create a new document for the hyperlink to point to, click **Create New Document** and proceed as prompted.

- If you want to place a hyperlink to an e-mail address, click **E-mail Address**.

4. Click **OK**.

REMOVE A HYPERLINK

To remove a hyperlink from text or an object:

1. Right-click the text or object containing the hyperlink.

2. Select **Remove Hyperlink** from the context menu.

CHANGE A HYPERLINK COLOR

To change the color of hyperlinks in a presentation:

1. Highlight the link to be changed.

2. Open the **Design** tab and click the **Theme Colors** button on the Themes group.

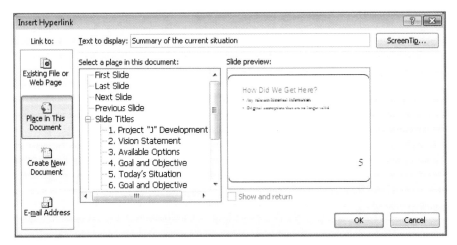

Figure 9-10: Hyperlinks can provide a means to "jump" from one part of an outline to another.

USING FOOTERS ON SLIDES (Continued)

REMOVE HEADERS OR FOOTERS

Once you have displayed the Headers and Footers dialog box:

1. Clear the checkboxes for **Date And Time**, **Slide Number**, and **Footer.**

2. To remove the footer for selected slides, click **Apply.**

   –Or–

   To remove the footer for all slides, click **Apply To All.**

TIP

To remove both the text and the hyperlink, select the text, and press **DELETE.**

NOTE

The hyperlink only works in the Slide Show view.

3. At the bottom of the list of color combinations, click **Create New Theme Colors**. The Create New Theme Colors dialog box will be displayed with your current theme's color selected in each of the sets.

4. Click the hyperlink color you want to change to open the colors gallery, and click the new color. As you click a color, you'll see it reflected in the Sample box.

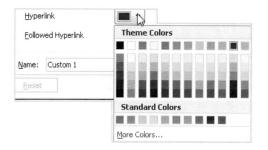

5. Type a name in the **Name** text box and click **Save** to make the change to the hyperlinks in the presentation. Your changed color will be applied to the links in your presentation, and a custom theme color will be listed in the Theme Colors list. By default it will be named "Custom 1," unless you rename it.

Chapter 10

Working with Notes, Masters, and Slide Text

This chapter covers three important features that make a presentation more effective: notes, slide masters, and slide text. Using notes for preparing speaker and handout notes allows you to fully prepare a presentation so that you remember all you wanted to say and so that the audience remembers your important points as well. Slide masters allow you to make changes to your presentations that are reflected on each slide or on only some of them.

This chapter also addresses how to work with text, from selecting a layout or inserting a placeholder, to modifying text by editing, positioning, moving, copying, and deleting it. The Office Clipboard is covered, as is checking the spelling of standard and foreign languages. Special features, like AutoFit and AutoCorrect, are also discussed.

Work with Notes

Notes are used to create speaker notes that aid a speaker during a presentation and to create handouts given to the audience so that it can follow the presentation easily. The notes do not appear on the slides during a slide show presentation; they are only visible for the presenter's benefit.

Create a Note

To create speaker notes, which can also be used as handouts, you can either use the Notes pane in Normal view (as shown in Figure 10-1) or the Notes Page

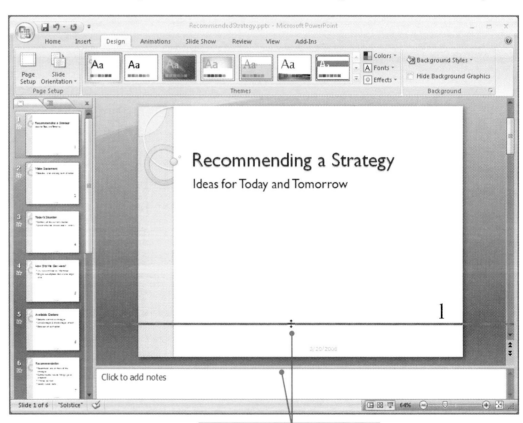

Figure 10-1: In the Notes pane of the Normal view, you can expand the area where you add your notes by dragging the border of the Notes pane upward to increase its size.

Drag the border to enlarge the Notes pane

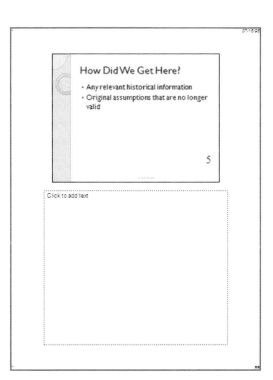

Figure 10-2: *The Notes Page displays what the printout will look like before entering your notes and allows you to zoom in on the image to have more room for editing.*

TIP

To create a note in the Notes pane, open Normal view and click in the **Click To Add Notes** text box. Then add your notes.

TIP

If you use more of the Notes pane than is available, PowerPoint will reduce the font size and line spacing so that the text will fit.

(shown in Figures 10-2 and 10-3). In both views, you can see a thumbnail of the slide with your notes pertaining to it. Each slide has its own Notes Page. You can also add charts, graphs, or pictures to the notes. To add or change attributes or text to all notes in a presentation, make changes to the notes master.

CREATE A NOTE IN THE NOTES PAGE

1. To open the Notes Page, click the **View** tab, and, in the Presentation Views group, click **Notes Page**. The Notes Page opens, as shown in Figure 10-2.

2. To increase the size of the notes area, click the **View** tab, and, in the Zoom group, click **Zoom**.

3. Click the zoom magnification you want, and click **OK**.

4. To move to another slide, click the scroll bar.

Preview Speaker Notes

To preview your notes:

1. Click the **Office button** , and click **Print**. The Print dialog box appears.

2. Click the **Print What** down arrow, and click **Notes Pages.**

TIP

You can add an object, such as a picture, graph, chart, or organizational chart, to the notes. Click in the Notes Page where the object is to be inserted. Click the **Insert** tab, and, in the Illustrations group, click the button of the object to be inserted from the ribbon. Resize the image, if needed, and drag the object to where you want it on the page. See Chapter 14 for additional information.

TIP

To change the background of one or all notes, click the **View** tab, and, in the Presentation Views group, click **Notes Page**. Right-click the Notes Page, and select **Format Shape** from the context menu. Click the **Fill** option, and in the Fill area, click the **Solid Fill** option, and then click the **Color** button to choose your color.

TIP

In the Print Preview window, the pointer will become a Zoom tool. Place the tool on an area of the slide image, and click. Click a second time to return the image to the original size.

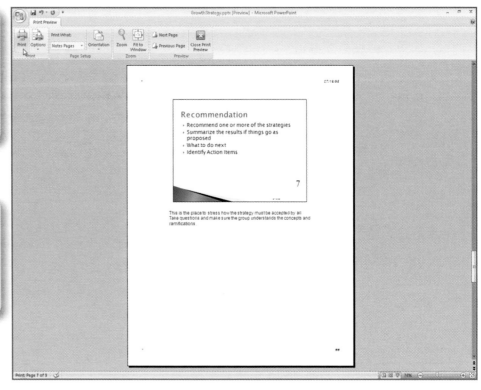

Figure 10-3: The Print Preview Notes Page displays speaker notes with the accompanying slide and allows you to print from this view.

Points to cover:
- Applies to time period 2008 to 2011
- Includes new marketing strategies and sales techniques
- Goal is to raise revenue and reduce expenses
- Mention Strategy Team

Before Zoom applied

Points to cover:
- Applies to time period 2008 to 2011
- Includes new marketing strategies and sales techniques
- Goal is to raise revenue and reduce expenses
- Mention Strategy Team

After Zoom applied

3. Then click **Preview**. The Print Preview window, shown in Figure 10-3, opens with the slide and notes showing as they will be printed. (You may have to reset the Print What option.)

4. Click **Print** to print notes (see "Print Notes and Handouts" later in this chapter), or click **Close Print Preview** to return to the Notes Page.

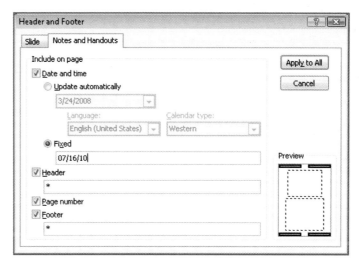

Figure 10-4: You can create a header and footer to display on note and handout pages.

Print Notes and Handouts

Speaker notes and handouts are printed in a similar way.

PRINT SPEAKER NOTES

To print your notes:

1. Click the **Office button**, and click **Print**. The Print dialog box will appear, an example of which is displayed in Figure 10-5.

2. Click the **Print What** down arrow, and click **Notes Pages**. You have these options:

   - Click **Preview** to see the Notes Page as it will be printed.

   - Under Print Range, click **All**, **Current Slide**, or **Selection**; or enter the slide numbers for specific slides or slide ranges.

   - Enter the number of copies.

   - Click the **Color/Grayscale** down arrow, and choose **Color**, **Grayscale**, or **Pure Black And White**.

3. Click **OK** to print.

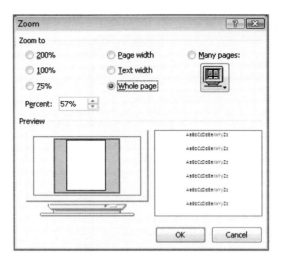

Figure 10-6: A preview of the printed handouts contains thumbnails of slides and allows you to select the number of slides displayed on a page.

Figure 10-5: The Print dialog box allows you to select specific slides and speaker notes to print and to preview before printing.

TIP

To add or remove borders that are placed around the handout thumbnail slides, click the **Frame Slides** checkbox in the Print dialog box to add or clear the checkmark. The border will be added when a checkmark is present.

☐ Frame slides

PRINT HANDOUTS

A printed handout contains a number of thumbnail slides, an example of which is shown in Figure 10-6.

1. Click the **Office button**, and click **Print**. The Print dialog box appears.

2. Click the **Print What** down arrow, and click **Handouts**.

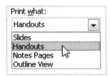

3. To print only some of the slides, click **Slides** and enter the slide numbers or ranges.

4. Click the **Slides Per Page** down arrow, and select a number to set the number of slides on a page if the default number is incorrect.

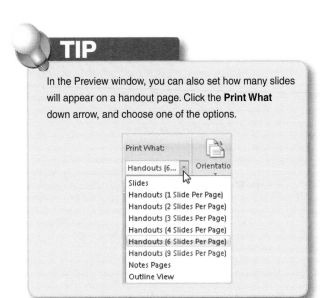

In the Preview window, you can also set how many slides will appear on a handout page. Click the **Print What** down arrow, and choose one of the options.

To specify what will be included on the printed page, use the Headers And Footers dialog box. (Click **Options** in the Print Preview window, Print group, then click **Header and Footer**.) Click the **Notes And Handouts** tab, and click to remove the checkmark next to the items you want to remove from the page. Click **Apply To All**.

5. Set the number of copies, and make other adjustments as needed.

6. Click **Preview** to see what the printout will look like, and then click **Print** to return to the Print dialog box.

7. Click **OK** to print.

Work with Slide, Note, and Handout Masters

Working with masters gives you an opportunity to change a presentation globally. PowerPoint gives you a set of master slides for slides, notes, and handouts: the slide master controls the slides of a presentation; the notes master controls the global aspects of notes; and the handout master controls the handouts. Note and handout masters are not automatically created: they are only created if you want to use global attributes for them.

Manage Slide Appearance

A presentation has a *slide master* containing formatting and other design elements that apply to all slides in a presentation (or to a set of slides with the same "look"). Usually associated with that slide master are up to ten *layout masters* that apply to other slides in a presentation. The title slide, for example, has a layout master for unique positioning of page components, formatting, headings, and design elements. The slide master may get its specific formatting from a theme template that you used, and you can change the master without changing the original template. This is one way that you can customize your presentation even after using a suggested theme to get you going. The original theme is not changed—only the theme as it is in your presentation. It becomes a custom theme.

CHANGING FONT ATTRIBUTES

You can change font attributes either by changing the fonts or by applying WordArt styles to title text, for example.

MAKE FONT CHANGES

You can change the attributes of text on only one type of slide by changing a layout master, or you can change attributes throughout the whole presentation by changing the font or character in the master slide. The following font commands are found in the Font group of the Home tab. (When you highlight text, a mini toolbar appears with additional commands available.) Figure 10-7 shows the possibilities for changing font attributes.

Use these commands to change text attributes:

- **Font** Changes the font face. Click the down arrow, and a list of font names is displayed.

- **Font Size** Changes the point size of fonts. Click the down arrow, and select a point size.

- **Increase Font Size** Increases the point size in increments. Click the button to increase it.

- **Decrease Font Size** Decreases the point size in increments. Click the button to decrease it.

- **Clear All Formatting** Removes all formatting from a selection and retains only plain text.

- **Bold** Applies boldface to selected text.

- **Italic** Applies italics to selected text.

- **Underline** Applies an underline to selected text.

- **Shadow** Applies a shadow effect to selected text.

- **Strikethrough** Applies a strikethrough to selected text.

Continued . . .

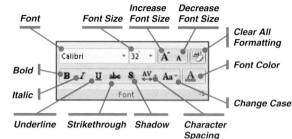

Figure 10-7: **This group of text-editing commands can be found on the Home and Edit Master tabs.**

EDIT A SLIDE MASTER OR MASTER LAYOUT

In a set of slide masters is one slide master that sets the standards for all slides in the presentation. Editing a slide master changes all the slides to which it applies. The set of associated layout masters, about ten of them, will, by default, carry the slide master's theme and other formatting. The layout masters are specific to a type of layout that might be part of the presentation. For example, perhaps you will have one particular layout for all slides containing graphs. Another example for a specific type of layout is the title layout master. A layout master usually carries the same color, design elements, and formatting as the theme assigned to a master slide. You can change particular layouts to be different from the slide master, and then the overall theme will become a custom theme.

1. Click the **View** tab, and click **Slide Master**. The slide master is displayed (see Figure 10-8).

2. Add headings or subheadings and dates or slide numbers. Add graphics, themes, or background color. Add headers or footers or other elements of the master, just as you would a normal slide. Editing and formatting changes you can make include the following:

- To change the overall font style, click the first thumbnail to select the slide master. Either click the placeholder for the text you want to change or highlight the actual heading or body text. Click the button in the Font group for the attribute you want to modify—for example, Font for the font face. See the "Changing Font Attributes" QuickSteps.

CHANGING FONT ATTRIBUTES

(Continued)

- **Character Spacing** Increases or decreases the space between the characters of a word. Choose Very Tight, Tight, Normal, Loose, Very Loose, or More Spacing—where you can set specific points between characters and set *kerning,* a more sophisticated method of setting the space between characters.

- **Change Case** Changes the case of a word between several alternatives: Sentence Case, lowercase, UPPERCASE, Capitalize Each Word, and tOGGLE cASE.

- **Font Color** Changes the color of the font. Point at each of the colors to see the effect on the background slide.

MAKE WORDART CHANGE

You can also change the text to WordArt styles. When you double-click a text or title placeholder, the Drawing Tools Format tab becomes available. On it are the WordArt Styles that can be applied to selected placeholders or text.

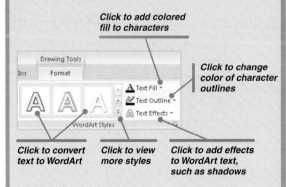

Click to add colored fill to characters

Click to change color of character outlines

Click to convert text to WordArt

Click to view more styles

Click to add effects to WordArt text, such as shadows

- To change the bullets for bulleted text, double-click the placeholder containing the bullets to change them all, or select a specific level of bullet to change one level. Click the **Home** tab, and in the Paragraph group, click the **Bullets** down arrow, and click the style of bullets you like. You can point at each bullet type to see the results in the background master slide. To insert a picture that serves as a bullet, click **Bullets And Numbering** on the bottom of the list to display a dialog box. Click the **Bulleted** tab, click **Picture**, and click the bullet picture you want. To insert a new picture, click **Import** and then find the picture you want. Click **OK** on the Picture Bullet dialog box.

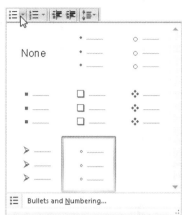

- To change the appearance of numbers for numbered lists, double-click the placeholder containing the numbered lists. Click the **Numbering** down arrow in the Paragraph group, and click the style of numbers you like. You can point at each item in the list to see the results in the background master slide. To get a size or color that isn't in the menu of choices, click **Bullets And Numbering** on the bottom of the list to display a dialog box. Click the **Numbered** tab, and click the **Size** spinner to increase or decrease the size. Click **Start At** to reset the beginning number. Click the **Color** down arrow to select a new color for the set of numbers. Click **OK** to close the Bullets and Numbering dialog box.

- By clicking the **Insert** tab and selecting **Header & Footer** in the Text group, you can include a footer, slide number, or time and date on the slide. Then, to change the format for the time or date, click a text placeholder to select it (you may have to click directly on the placeholder text to select it, such as on <date/time> in the Date Area placeholder). Then click the **Home** tab, and in the Font group, click the **Font** or **Font Size** down arrow, and select the font or size you want from the drop-down list.

3/20/2008

When you apply a new theme to a presentation, slide masters are automatically created.

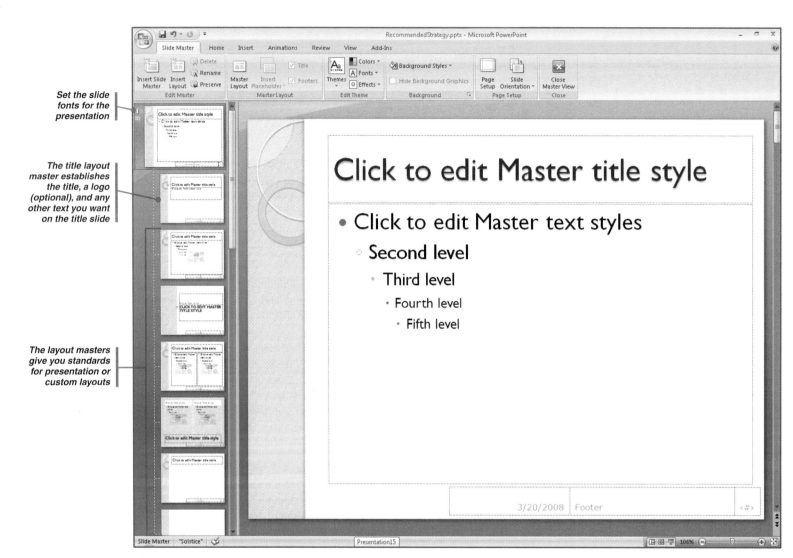

Set the slide fonts for the presentation

The title layout master establishes the title, a logo (optional), and any other text you want on the title slide

The layout masters give you standards for presentation or custom layouts

Click to edit Master title style

- Click to edit Master text styles
  - Second level
    - Third level
      - Fourth level
        - Fifth level

3/20/2008   Footer   <#>

Figure 10-8: The masters for a new presentation contain a slide master (no. 1) and several layout slides, with the default "Office Theme."

WORKING WITH SLIDE MASTERS

You can duplicate masters, create title masters that vary from the other masters, protect your masters from being accidentally or intentionally changed, or create multiple new title and slide masters.

DUPLICATE A SLIDE MASTER

To duplicate a slide master:

1. Click the **View** tab, and click **Slide Master**.

2. Right-click the master slide thumbnail to be duplicated. It may be a master slide or a layout master slide. The options on the context menu will vary depending on the type of master you select:

   • For a slide master, click **Duplicate Slide Master**. The slide master and all the sets of layouts it carries will be duplicated.

   • For a layout master, click **Duplicate Layout**, and just the layout master will be duplicated.

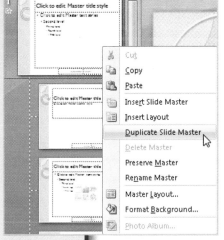

Continued . . .

NOTE

When multiple themes are used to create more than one section in order to create multiple "looks" for the presentation, a set of slide masters will be automatically created for each section. You can then modify the masters as needed to create an even more unique look.

CREATE MULTIPLE SLIDE AND TITLE MASTERS

Multiple slide masters and their associated sets of layout masters are used in a presentation to create different looks in layout or formatting for different sections of the presentation.

To create additional new slide masters:

1. Click the **View** tab, and click **Slide Master**.

2. Right-click the slide master, and click **Insert Slide Master**. A new slide master and its associated layout masters will be inserted.

3. Make any changes or incorporate different design templates to the new masters as needed.

4. Click the **Slide Master** tab, and then click **Close Master View** in the Close group to close the Slide Master view.

Work with the Notes Master

To make global changes to all notes in a presentation, use the notes master. Here you can add a logo or other graphics, change the positioning of page components, change formats, and add headings and text design elements for all notes.

1. Click the **View** tab, and click **Notes Master**. The notes master will be displayed, as shown in Figure 10-9.

2. To adjust the zoom so that you can see the notes area better, click the **View** tab, and click **Zoom**. Choose the magnification and click **OK**.

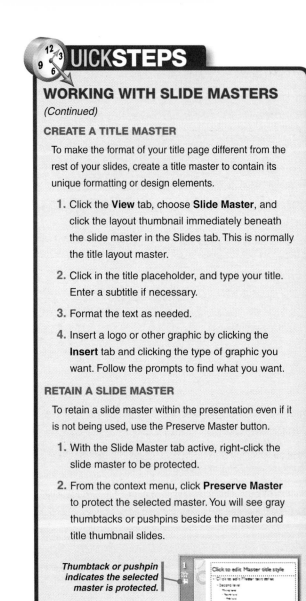

UICKSTEPS

WORKING WITH SLIDE MASTERS

(Continued)

CREATE A TITLE MASTER

To make the format of your title page different from the rest of your slides, create a title master to contain its unique formatting or design elements.

1. Click the **View** tab, choose **Slide Master**, and click the layout thumbnail immediately beneath the slide master in the Slides tab. This is normally the title layout master.

2. Click in the title placeholder, and type your title. Enter a subtitle if necessary.

3. Format the text as needed.

4. Insert a logo or other graphic by clicking the **Insert** tab and clicking the type of graphic you want. Follow the prompts to find what you want.

RETAIN A SLIDE MASTER

To retain a slide master within the presentation even if it is not being used, use the Preserve Master button.

1. With the Slide Master tab active, right-click the slide master to be protected.

2. From the context menu, click **Preserve Master** to protect the selected master. You will see gray thumbtacks or pushpins beside the master and title thumbnail slides.

Thumbtack or pushpin indicates the selected master is protected.

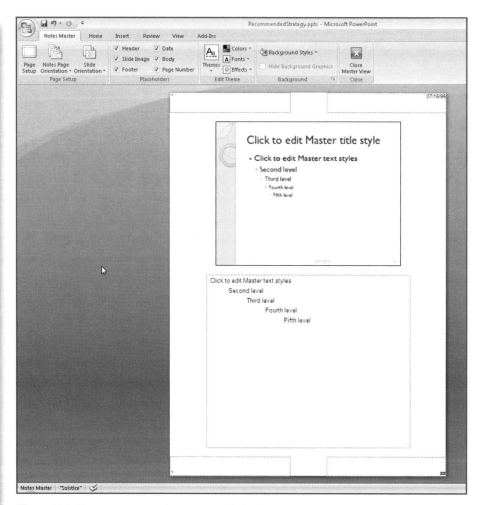

Figure 10-9: The notes master is used to globally change such note features as headers, footers, logos, or graphics; note text formatting; and placement of note elements.

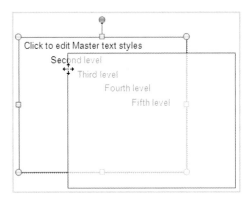

TIP

To add a text placeholder to the Notes pane, click the **Insert** tab, and click the **Text Box** button. Then drag the icon where you want the text box to be created, and type in the box. You can drag the text box to another location.

3. You can change the notes master as follows:

- Change the formatting of the text elements, such as font size or style, or change the bullets or indents.

- Drag the position of the slide or note text placeholder (the dotted box) to a different location by placing the pointer over the border until you see a four-headed arrow and then dragging.

- Change the size of the slide or note text placeholder by placing the pointer over the border until you see a two-headed arrow and then dragging the border of the placeholder to resize it.

- Add a logo by clicking the **Insert** tab and clicking the **Picture**, **Shapes**, **Clip Art**, or other graphic button. Resize the graphic as needed, and drag it where you want it to appear on all notes.

- Add text that will appear on all notes, such as page number, date, or title.

4. Click the **Notes Master** tab, and then click **Close Master View** in the Close group to close the notes master.

Change the Handout Master

Handouts display thumbnails of the slides on a printed page. You can have one, two, three, four, six, or nine slides per page. To prepare your handouts for printing with titles and other formatting, use the handout master.

1. Click the **View** tab, and click **Handout Master**. The handout master will be displayed, as shown in Figure 10-10.

2. On the handout master ribbon in the Page Setup group, click **Slides Per Page** to set the number of slides to be displayed in the handout: one, two, three, four, six, or nine, or the slide outline.

3. Make changes to the handout master as needed:

- Click **Page Setup** in the Page Setup group to set the slide size, initial numbering of slides, and orientation of slides and notes, handouts, and outline.

- Click **Handout Orientation** in the Page Setup group to give the handout a portrait or landscape orientation.

- Click **Slide Orientation** in the Page Setup group to give the slides on the handout a portrait or landscape orientation.

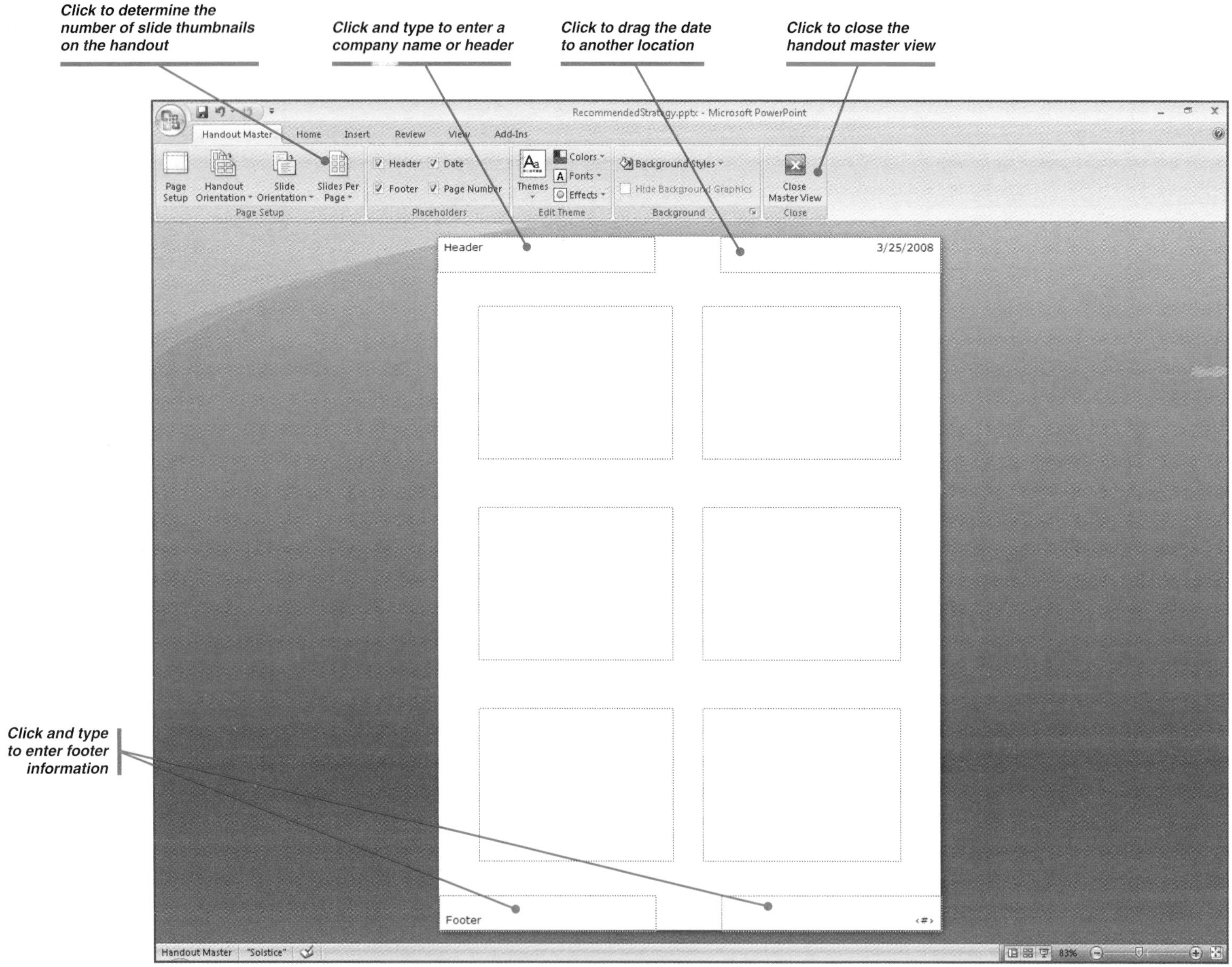

Click to determine the number of slide thumbnails on the handout

Click and type to enter a company name or header

Click to drag the date to another location

Click to close the handout master view

Click and type to enter footer information

Figure 10-10: The handout master allows you to add titles for handouts, vary the number of slides displayed in the handout, and add other text or objects as needed.

- Click **Header**, **Date**, **Footer**, or **Page Number** in the Placeholders group to remove the checkmarks if you do not want them to appear on the handouts. They are selected by default. If you choose for them to be there, enter the text in the text boxes for the header and footer information.

- To format the date, click in the date text box, click the **Insert** tab, and click **Date & Time**. Choose a format and click **OK**. Return to the Handout Master tab.

- To select a style for the background, click **Background Styles** in the Background group and choose one.

- If you want graphics to be hidden when printed, click the **Hide Background Graphics** checkbox in the Background group.

4. To close the handout master, click **Close Master View** in the Close group on the ribbon.

Work with Text

Entering and manipulating text is a major part of building a presentation. Text is not only titles and bulleted lists. It is also captions on a picture or a legend or labels on a chart. Text can be inside a shape or curved around it on the outside. Text communicates in a thousand ways. Here is how you work with text in PowerPoint.

Use a Text Layout

To create the "look" of your presentation, you will want to insert text, columns, graphics, charts, logos, and other pictures in a consistent way. PowerPoint provides standard layouts that position text or graphics in consistent ways. Chapter 9 discussed layouts in more detail. In this chapter, we are concerned with text layouts.

When you create a new blank slide, you must choose whether to use an existing layout that Microsoft provides or to create your own layout (see Figure 10-11).

1. In Normal view, click the slide immediately preceding the one you want to insert.

2. Click the **Home** tab, and click the **New Slide** down arrow.

3. Look for the placement of text, titles, and content. Examples of text placeholders are shown in Figure 10-11.

The text box will be applied to the current slide. If you have not created a new slide, the layout will be applied to whichever slide is selected.

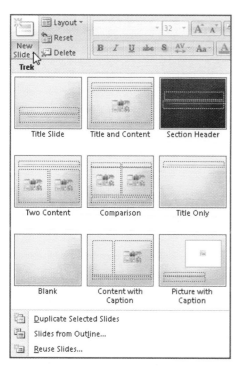

Figure 10-11: You can choose among several standard layouts containing text boxes.

4. Click the layout you want.

5. Click within the title or text placeholders to begin entering text.

Insert a New Text Box

Even when you use a predefined layout that Microsoft provides, you will find times when you want to insert a new text box.

1. Display the slide within which you will place the text box.

2. Click the **Insert** tab, and click **Text Box** in the Text group. The pointer first turns into a line pointer.

3. Place the pointer where you want to locate the text box, and drag it into a text-box shape. As you drag, the pointer will morph into a crosshair shape. Don't worry about where the box is located; you can drag it to a precise location later. When you release the pointer, the insertion point within the text box indicates that you can begin to type text.

4. Type the text you want.

5. When you are finished, click outside the text box.

Work with Text Boxes

You work with text and text boxes by typing text into a text box, moving or copying the text box, resizing the text box, positioning the text box, deleting it, rotating it, filling it with color, and more.

ENTER TEXT INTO A TEXT BOX

To enter text into a text box, simply click inside the text box; the insertion point will appear in the text box, indicating that you can now type text. Begin to type.

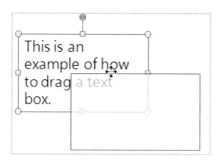

MOVE A TEXT BOX

To move a text box, you drag the border of the placeholder.

1. Click the text within a text box to display the text box outline.
2. Place the pointer over the border of the text box and between the handles. The pointer will be a four-headed arrow.
3. Drag the text box where you want.

RESIZE A PLACEHOLDER

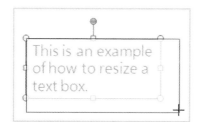

To resize a placeholder, you drag the sizing handles of the text box.

1. Click the text to display the text box border.
2. Place the pointer on the border over the handles so that it becomes a two-headed arrow.
3. Drag the sizing handle in the direction you want the text box expanded or reduced. As you drag, the pointer will morph into a crosshair.

DELETE A TEXT BOX

To delete a text box:

1. Click the text within the text box to display the border.
2. Click the border of the text box again to select the text box, not the text (the insertion point will disappear and the border will be solid).
3. Press **DELETE**.

COPY A TEXT BOX

To copy a text box with its contents and drag it to another part of the slide:

1. Click the text within the text box.
2. Place the pointer on the border of the text box (not over the handles), where it becomes a four-headed arrow.
3. Drag the text box while pressing **CTRL**.

ROTATE A TEXT BOX

When you first insert a text box (or click it to select it), a rotate handle allows you to rotate the box in a circle.

1. Place the pointer over the rotate handle.
2. Drag it in the direction it is to be rotated.
3. Click outside the text box to "set" the rotation.

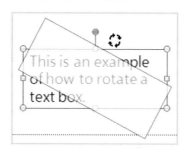

Arrange

TIP

If none of the colors is exactly right, click the **Color** down arrow, and then click **More Colors** and click the **Standard** tab. Click a color unit to select it. In the preview box, you can see the new color compared to the current color. Click **OK** and then click **Close**.

POSITION A TEXT BOX PRECISELY

To set the position of a text box precisely on a slide:

1. Click the text box to select it. A Drawing Tools Format tab will appear.

2. Click the **Format** tab, in the **Arrange** group, click **Rotate**.

3. On the Rotate menu, click **More Rotation Options**. The Size And Position dialog box will appear.

4. Click the **Position** tab.

5. Click the **Horizontal** or **Vertical** spinners to enter the exact measurements in inches of the text box. Click the drop-down list boxes to select the originating location of the text box between the upper-left corner and center.

6. Click **Close**.

CHANGE THE FILL COLOR IN A TEXT BOX

To change the background color of a text box, you use the Drawing Tools Format Shape dialog box.

1. Right-click the text box, and click **Format Shape** from the context menu. The Format Shape dialog box appears.

2. Click **Fill** and then select the type of fill you want to see. A group of options will appear, depending on your choice.

3. Click the **Preset Colors**, **Color**, or other drop-down list box to select a color. Set other attributes as you wish. Drag the dialog box to one side so that you can see the changes in the text box as you try out different shades or types of fill, as illustrated in Figure 10-12.

4. When finished, click **Close**.

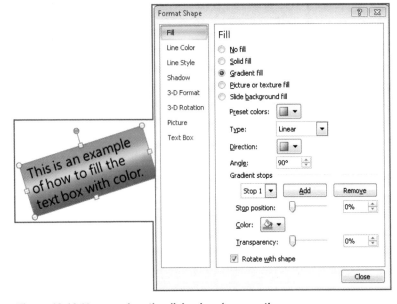

Figure 10-12: You can drag the dialog box (or sometimes the text box) to the side so that you can see the effects of settings as you work with the options.

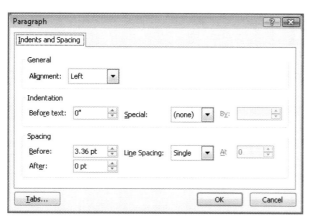

Figure 10-13: *The Paragraph dialog box allows you to change paragraph and tab settings.*

SET PARAGRAPH AND TAB SETTINGS

To change the default paragraph spacing and tab settings, you can use the Paragraph dialog box, as seen in Figure 10-13.

1. Click the paragraph text in a placeholder or text box to be changed. Click the **Home** tab, and click the **Paragraph Dialog Box Launcher** on the lower right of the Paragraph group.

   –Or–

   Right-click the paragraph text in a placeholder or text box to be changed, and click **Paragraph**. The Paragraph dialog box appears.

2. Set the settings as required:

   - Set the General positioning by clicking the **Alignment** down arrow, and then click **Left**, **Centered**, **Right**, **Justified**, or **Distributed** (which forces even short lines to be justified to the end of the line), depending on how you want the text aligned.

   - Set the indentation. Click the **Before Text** spinner to set the spacing before the text begins on a first line; click the **Special** down arrow to allow for hanging indents, an indented first line, or no indents.

   - Set the spacing. Click the **Before** spinner to set spacing before the line starts (in points); click the **Line Spacing** down arrow, and click **Single**, **Double**, **1.5**, **Exactly** (where you set the exact spacing in points in the At box), or **Multiple** (where you enter the number of lines to space in the At box).

   - Click the **Tabs** button to set tabs precisely in the Tabs dialog box. Click **OK**.

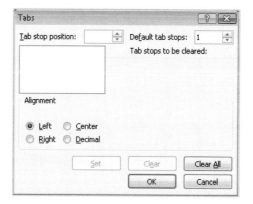

3. Click **OK**.

CAUTION

When you adjust the line spacing, the AutoFit feature, which is on by default, may cause the text to be resized to fit within the text box. See "Setting Margins, Word Wrap, AutoFit, and Columns" to change the default.

QUICKSTEPS

SETTING MARGINS, WORD WRAP, AUTOFIT, AND COLUMNS

All of the procedures in this section make use of the Drawing Tools Format Shape dialog box. To display it, right-click the text box and select **Format Shape**. Select **Text Box** from the menu on the left, as shown in Figure 10-14.

SET MARGINS IN A TEXT BOX

To change the margins in a text box, change the *Internal* Margin setting to **Left**, **Right**, **Top**, or **Bottom**.

DISABLE WORD WRAP FOR TEXT

To disable (or enable) the word wrap feature for text in a text box, click **Wrap Text In Shape**. A checkmark in the checkbox indicates that word wrap is turned on.

☑ Wrap text in shape

ANCHOR TEXT IN A TEXT BOX

To anchor the text layout within a text box, select the position where the text will start, click the **Vertical Alignment** down arrow, and click the position to which you want the text anchored. Your choices are: Top, Middle, Bottom, Top Centered, Middle Centered, and Bottom Centered.

ROTATE TEXT WITHIN A TEXT BOX

To rotate text within a text box, click the **Text Direction** down arrow, and choose an option: Horizontal, Rotate All Text 90°, Rotate All Text 270°, or Stacked.

SET UP COLUMNS WITHIN A TEXT BOX

To set up columns within a text box, click the **Columns** button. The Columns dialog box appears. Click the **Number** spinner and the **Spacing** spinner to set your column attributes, and click **OK**.

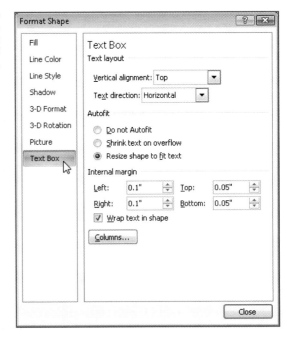

Figure 10-14: A text box can have its own margins and alignment. You can set defaults for AutoFit and automatic word wrap features and establish columns.

CHANGE CAPITALIZATION

To set your capitalization standard or to correct text typed in the wrong case:

1. Select the text on which you want to change the case.

2. Click the **Home** tab, and click the **Change Case** Aa▾ button in the Font group.

3. Select one of the following options:

   a. **Sentence case** capitalizes the first word in a sentence.

   b. **lowercase** makes all text lowercase.

   c. **UPPERCASE** makes all text uppercase.

   d. **Capitalize Each Word** capitalizes all words.

   e. **tOGGLE cASE** switches between uppercase and lowercase letters, for instance, when you have accidentally typed text in the wrong case.

USING LISTS

Lists are either numbered or bulleted. You can choose the shapes of bullets, change the style of numbering, and use SmartArt for your lists.

CHOOSE BULLET SHAPES

1. Select the text to be bulleted.

2. Right-click the text and point to **Bullets**. The context menu opens.

   –Or–

   On the Home tab, click the **Bullets** down arrow. A context menu will open.

3. Use the options presented, or, to display more options, click **Bullets And Numbering** at the bottom of the menu. The Bullets And Numbering dialog box appears, as shown in Figure 10-15.

4. To select the bullet appearance, click one of the seven options:

   - To change the size, adjust the **Size** spinner to the percentage of text you want the bullet to be.

   - To change the color, click the **Color** down arrow, and click a color.

   - To select or import a picture to use as a bullet shape, click **Picture** and select one of the menu images, or click **Import** to find your own. Then click **OK**.

   - To select a character from a variety of symbol fonts, click **Customize**. Make your selection, and then click **OK**.

5. Click **OK** to close the dialog box.

Continued . . .

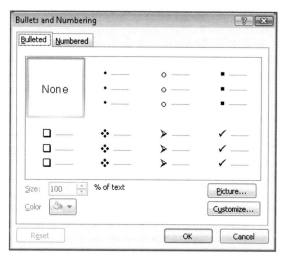

Figure 10-15: The Bullets And Numbering dialog box offers ways to change the appearance, size, and color of bullets or numbers in a list.

Use the Font Dialog Box

To set multiple font and character attributes at once or to set the standard for a slide, it is easier to use the Font dialog box than individual buttons (See the "Changing Font Attributes" QuickSteps earlier in this chapter.)

1. Select the text to be changed.

2. Click the **Home** tab, and click the **Font Dialog Box Launcher** in the lower-right area of the Font group. The Font dialog box will appear, as shown in Figure 10-16.

3. Click the **Latin Text Font** down arrow, and select the type of theme text (Heading or Body) or font name. This establishes what will be changed in the selected text.

4. Choose the options you want, and click **OK**.

USING LISTS *(Continued)*

CHANGE NUMBERING STYLES

1. Select the text to be numbered.

2. Right-click the text and point to **Numbering**. A context menu opens.

   –Or–

   On the Home tab, click the **Numbering** down arrow. A context menu will open.

3. Use the options presented, or, to display more options, click **Bullets And Numbering**. The Bullets And Numbering dialog box will appear. Click the **Numbered** tab.

   - To change the **size**, adjust the Size spinner to the percentage of the text size you want the numbering to be.

   - To change the color, click the **Color** down arrow, and click a color.

   - To set a beginning number or letter, change **Start At**.

4. Click **OK**.

USE SMARTART FOR LISTS

To make your lists artistic and professional-looking, you can choose some of the SmartArt options offered by PowerPoint 2007. These dramatically change the look and feel of lists.

1. Select the list.

2. On the Home tab, click the **Convert To SmartArt Graphic** down arrow in the Paragraph group.

   –Or–

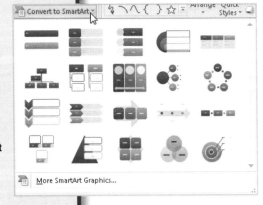

Continued . . .

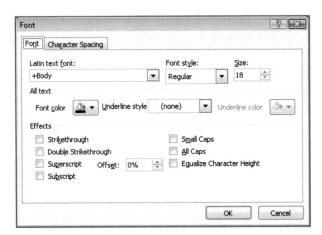

Figure 10-16: Using the Font dialog box, you can change all occurrences of certain fonts within selected text.

Align Text

You have several ways to align text: horizontally on a line, vertically on a page, or distributed horizontally or vertically. This section describes how to use these aligning techniques.

ALIGN TEXT ON A LINE

You align text by centering (placing text in the center of the horizontal margins), left-justifying, right-justifying, or justifying it (where the left and right edges are equal). All four options are available on the Home tab Paragraph group.

1. Select the text to be aligned, and click the **Home** tab.

2. From the Paragraph group, choose one of these options:

- To center text, click the **Center** button.

- To left-align text, click the **Align Left** button.

- To right-align text, click the **Align Right** button.

- To justify text, click the **Justify** button.

USING LISTS *(Continued)*

Right-click the list or place on the slide where you want special effects applied, and in the context menu point to **Convert To SmartArt**. A gallery of styles is displayed.

3. Click an option, and you will see the SmartArt effect on the slide plus a text box enabling you to enter the text into the list, as displayed in Figure 10-17. Type your text into the text box, and it will appear in the SmartArt object. Drag the shape to resize it.

4. To change shapes, right-click the SmartArt icon, and point to **Change Shape**. A gallery of shapes will display. Click the one you want.

5. When you are finished, click outside the text box.

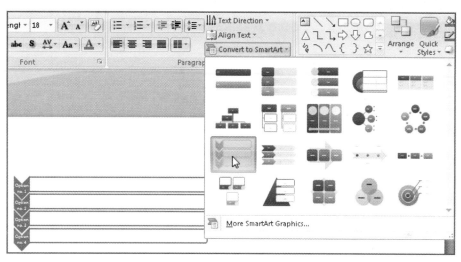

Figure 10-17: *SmartArt effects can make your lists dramatic and professional-looking.*

ALIGN TEXT IN A PLACEHOLDER

To align text with the top, middle, or bottom of a text box or placeholder, click the **Align Text** button (Home tab, Paragraph group), and click your choices from the menu. Click **More Options** to precisely specify measurements.

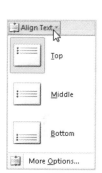

ALIGN TEXT TO THE SLIDE

You can align a placeholder or text box horizontally or vertically on a slide—that is, the spacing on the top and bottom will be equal or the spacing from the left and right edges of the slide will be distributed evenly.

1. Click the placeholder or text box to select it.

2. On the Drawing Tools Format tab, click the **Align** button in the Arrange group. A menu will appear.

3. Click one of these options:

   • Click **Distribute Horizontally** to align the object horizontally to the slide.

   • Click **Distribute Vertically** to align the object vertically on the slide.

EDITING WITH THE KEYBOARD

Working with text in PowerPoint is similar to working with text in Microsoft Word. This section presents familiar ways to move the pointer and to select, delete, and insert text.

MOVE THE POINTER WITHIN YOUR TEXT

- To move to the beginning of the line, press **HOME**.
- To move to the end of a line, press **END**.
- To skip to the next word, press **CTRL-RIGHT ARROW**.
- To skip to the previous word, press **CTRL-LEFT ARROW**.

SELECT TEXT

- To select all text contained within a text box, press **CTRL-A**.
- To select a word, double-click it.
- To select a paragraph, click within the paragraph three times.
- To select all text from where your cursor is to the end of the line, press **SHIFT-END**.
- To select all text from where your cursor is to the beginning of the line, press **SHIFT-HOME**.
- To select multiple lines, press **SHIFT-UP ARROW** or **DOWN ARROW**.
- To select one character at a time, press **SHIFT-LEFT ARROW** or **RIGHT ARROW**.

DELETE TEXT

- To delete the character to the right, press **DELETE**.
- To delete the character to the left, press **BACKSPACE**.
- To delete other text as needed, select text using the keyboard, highlighting it, and press **DELETE**.

INSERT TEXT

To insert one or more characters within a text box, click within the text box, place the pointer where you want to type, and then type.

Copy Formatting with Format Painter

To copy all formatting attributes from one placeholder to another, you use Format Painter. With it, you can copy fonts, font size and style, line and paragraph spacing, color, alignment, bullet selection, and character effects.

1. Select the text containing the formatting attributes to be copied.
2. On the Home tab, click **Format Painter** in the Clipboard group.
3. Find the destination text to contain the copied attributes, and drag the paintbrush pointer over the text to be changed.

Use AutoCorrect

AutoCorrect is a feature that helps you type information correctly. For example, it corrects simple typing errors and makes certain assumptions about what you want to type. You can turn it off or change its rules.

TURN AUTOCORRECT OPTIONS ON OR OFF

The AutoCorrect feature assumes that you will want certain corrections always to be made while you type. Among these corrections are: change two initial capital letters to the first one only, capitalize the first letter of each sentence, capitalize the first letter of table cells and names of days, correct accidental use of the **CAPS LOCK** key, and replace misspelled words with the results it assumes you want. (See "Change AutoCorrect Spelling Corrections" to retain the correction of misspelled words but to change the correction made.) To turn off the automatic spelling corrections that PowerPoint makes:

1. Click the **Office button**, and click **PowerPoint Options**.
2. Click **Proofing**, and the dialog box shown in Figure 10-18 will appear.
3. Find the option you want to turn off or on, and click the relevant checkbox. If a checkmark is in the box, the option is enabled. If it is not, the option is turned off.

MOVING OR COPYING TEXT

There are at least four ways you can move text. You can use the cut-and-paste technique, use the ribbon, right-click from a context menu, or use the drag-and-drop technique.

CUT AND PASTE TEXT WITH THE KEYBOARD

1. Select the text to be moved, and press **CTRL-X** to cut the text.

2. Click the pointer to place the insertion point, and press **CTRL-V** to paste the text in the new location.

CUT AND PASTE WITH THE RIBBON

1. Select the text to be moved.

2. Click the **Home** tab, and click **Cut** in the Clipboard group.

3. Click where you want the text inserted, and click **Paste** in the Clipboard group.

CUT AND PASTE WITH A CONTEXT MENU

1. Select the text to be moved.

2. Right-click and click **Cut**.

3. Right-click the new location, and click **Paste**.

USE THE DRAG-AND-DROP TECHNIQUE

To use the drag-and-drop technique to move text within the same text box, to other text boxes, or to other slides (when moving to other slides, you can only use the Outline tab):

1. Select the text to be moved.

2. Using the pointer, drag the text to the new location. An insertion point shows you where the text is about to be moved.

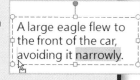

A large eagle flew to the front of the car, avoiding it narrowly.

3. Release the pointer when the insertion point is in the correct location.

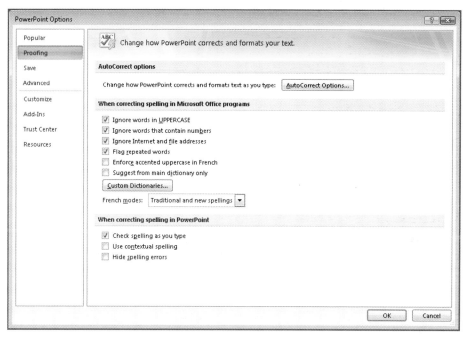

Figure 10-18: The AutoCorrect dialog box is where you change the automatic corrections made to text and spelling.

USE AUTOFIT

AutoFit is used to make text fit within a text box or AutoShape. It often resizes text to make it fit. You can turn it on or off.

1. Click the **Office button**, click **PowerPoint Options**, and then click **Proofing**.

2. Under AutoCorrect Options, click **AutoCorrect Options**. The AutoCorrect dialog box appears.

3. Click the **AutoFormat As You Type** tab.

4. Under the Apply As You Type section, choose these options:

- To remove the AutoFit feature for titles, clear the **AutoFit Title Text To Placeholder** checkbox.

- To remove the AutoFit feature for body text, clear the **AutoFit Body Text To Placeholder** checkbox.

5. Click **OK** twice.

CHANGE AUTOCORRECT SPELLING CORRECTIONS

PowerPoint may automatically correct spellings that are not really incorrect. You can add a new spelling correction, replace a current spelling correction with a new one, or replace the result that is now used. You do this by replacing one word with another in the AutoCorrect dialog box. When you first open the dialog box, both the Replace and With boxes are blank. In this case, you simply add what you want. To replace an entry, you first delete an entry—one that is not a mistake you typically make—and then you replace it with a typing error you commonly make. To replace a current spelling result, you type over the current result with the correction you want.

1. Click the **Office button**, and click the **PowerPoint Options** button. Then click **Proofing**.

2. Click the **AutoCorrect Options** button, and the AutoCorrect dialog box appears. If it is not already selected, click the **AutoCorrect** tab. Figure 10-19 shows this dialog box.

   - To add new entries when both the Replace and With boxes are blank, fill in the **Replace** and **With** boxes, and click **Add**.

   - To replace entries in the Replace and With boxes, click the text in either box, and replace it with your new entries. Click **Add**. The "old" text will not be deleted; it is still in the list. You must use the **DELETE** button to actually get rid of an entry in the list.

   - To delete and replace an entry, click the entry to be replaced, and press **DELETE**. Then type the new spelling option. Click **Add**.

NOTE

The Exceptions button in the AutoCorrect dialog box is used to provide exceptions to the capitalization rules. Clicking the button provides an opportunity to add to a list of either initially capitalized exceptions or exceptions about when to capitalize a word, such as after an abbreviation.

NOTE

All the cut-and-paste techniques can also be used to copy information. Just select **Copy** instead of Cut from the context or ribbon menus, or press **CTRL-C**. To copy using the drag-and-drop technique, right-drag the text (drag with the right mouse button depressed), and click **Copy Here**.

Figure 10-19: The AutoCorrect dialog box is where you control which spelling errors are automatically corrected and insert your own corrections.

UICKSTEPS

USING THE OFFICE CLIPBOARD

The Office Clipboard is shared by all Microsoft Office products. You can copy objects and text from any Office application and paste them into another. The Clipboard contains up to 24 items. The 25th item will overwrite the first one.

OPEN THE CLIPBOARD

To display the Office Clipboard, click the **Home** tab, and then click the **Clipboard Dialog Box Launcher** in the Clipboard group. The Clipboard task pane will open.

Clipboard	⌐

ADD TO THE CLIPBOARD

When you cut or copy text, it is automatically added to the Office Clipboard.

COPY CLIPBOARD ITEMS TO A PLACEHOLDER

To paste one item:

1. Click to place the insertion point in the text box or placeholder where you want the item on the Office Clipboard inserted.

2. Click the item on the Clipboard to be inserted.

   –Or–

   With the Clipboard item selected but no insertion point placed, right-click where you want the item.

3. Select **Paste** from the context menu.

To paste all items:

1. Click to place the insertion point in the text box or placeholder where you want the items on the Office Clipboard inserted.

2. Click **Paste All** on the Clipboard. 🔲 Paste All

Continued . . .

Use the Spelling Checker

One form of the spelling checker automatically flags words that it cannot find in the dictionary as potential misspellings. It identifies these words with a red underline. However, even when the automatic function is turned off, you can still use the spelling checker by manually opening it.

TIP

To quickly use the spelling checker, right-click the misspelled word. A context menu will display several options for correct spellings. Click the correct word if it is on the list. You can also click **Ignore All** to ignore all usages of the misspelling or click **Add To Dictionary**. You can display the Spelling dialog box by clicking **Spelling** on the context menu.

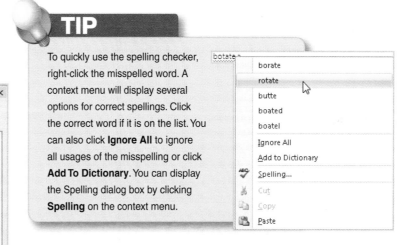

CHECK THE SPELLING IN A PRESENTATION

The spelling checker goes through all text in all placeholders on a slide looking for words that are not in the spelling dictionary. When it finds one, it displays the Spelling dialog box, seen in Figure 10-20.

1. Click in the presentation where the spelling checker should begin.

2. To display the spelling checker, press **F7**. The Spelling dialog box will appear when the spelling checker finds a word that is not in the dictionary.

3. Choose any of these options to use the spelling checker:

   ● If the word is incorrect, look at the Suggestions list, and click the one you want to use. It will appear in the Change To box. Click **Change** to change the one occurrence of the word, or click **Change All** to change all occurrences of that same word.

10

QUICKSTEPS

USING THE OFFICE CLIPBOARD
(Continued)

DELETE ITEMS ON THE CLIPBOARD

- To delete all items, click **Clear All** on the Clipboard task pane. [🗶 Clear All]

- To delete a single item, click the arrow next to the item, and click **Delete**.

SET CLIPBOARD OPTIONS

1. On the Clipboard task pane, click the **Options** down arrow at the bottom. A context menu is displayed.

2. Click an option to select or deselect it:

- **Show Office Clipboard Automatically** always shows the Office Clipboard when copying.

- **Show Office Clipboard When CTRL-C Pressed Twice** shows the Office Clipboard when you press **CTRL-C** twice to make two copies (in other words, copying two items to the Clipboard will cause the Clipboard to be displayed).

- **Collect Without Showing Office Clipboard** copies items to the Clipboard without displaying it.

- **Show Office Clipboard Icon On Taskbar** displays the icon 🖿 when the Clipboard is being used.

- **Show Status Near Taskbar When Copying** displays a message about the items being added to the Clipboard as copies are made.

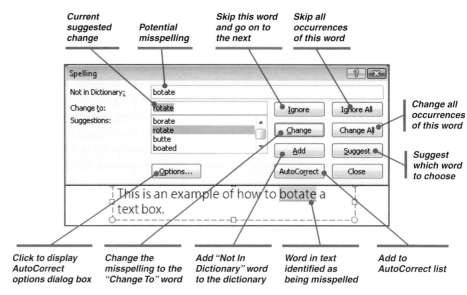

Current suggested change   *Potential misspelling*   *Skip this word and go on to the next*   *Skip all occurrences of this word*

Change all occurrences of this word

Suggest which word to choose

Click to display AutoCorrect options dialog box   *Change the misspelling to the "Change To" word*   *Add "Not In Dictionary" word to the dictionary*   *Word in text identified as being misspelled*   *Add to AutoCorrect list*

Figure 10-20: Use the Spelling dialog box to look for misspellings, correct them with suggested words or your own, and add words to the dictionary.

- If the identified word is correct but not in the dictionary, you can add the word to a custom dictionary by clicking **Add**, or you can skip the word by clicking **Ignore** or **Ignore All** (to skip all occurrences of the same word). The spelling checker will continue to the next misspelled word.

- Click **AutoCorrect** to add the word to the AutoCorrect list of automatic spelling changes that will be made as you type. Immediately the word will be placed in the AutoCorrect list.

- Click **Suggest** if you are unsure of the correct spelling and want PowerPoint to suggest the most likely spelling.

- Click **Options** to open the AutoCorrect Options dialog box.

4. Click **Close** to end the search for spelling errors. When the spelling checker is finished, a message will be displayed to that effect. Click **OK**.

SET SPELLING DEFAULTS

Set these options to determine how the spelling checker works.

1. Click the **Office button**, click **PowerPoint Options**, and click **Proofing**. The AutoCorrect Options dialog box appears, shown in Figure 10-21.

2. Select or deselect these options to best meet your needs. The defaults already have checkmarks in the checkboxes. Click to remove them. Click to select any that have no checkmark.

3. Click **OK** to accept your changes.

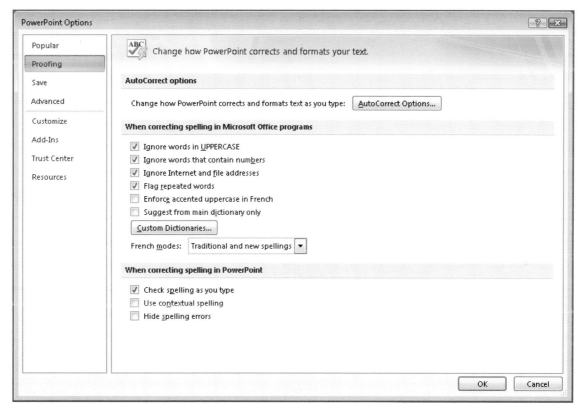

Figure 10-21: *The AutoCorrect Options dialog box sets the defaults for the changes PowerPoint will make to your text as you type.*

How to...

- *Explore the Outlook Window*
- *Change Views*
- *Display the Advanced Toolbar*
- *Using Outlook Toolbars*
- *Use the Navigation Pane*
- *Use Outlook Today*
- *Customize the To-Do Bar*
- *Find a Message*
- *Get Online*
- *Get a Hotmail Account*
- *Collecting Account Information*
- *Install Accounts in Outlook*
- *Check for E-mail*
- *Read E-mail*
- *Download Sender and Subject Information Only*
- *Filtering Out Spam*
- *Filter Junk Mail*
- *Mark Messages as Read or Unread*
- *Change the Time for Being Read*
- *Flag Your Messages for Follow-up*
- *Arrange Messages in a Folder*
- *Manipulating the Rules*
- *Make Up Your Own Rules*
- *Delete Messages*
- *Archiving Messages*
- *Manage Attachments*
- *Print Messages*

Chapter 11

Using Outlook and Receiving E-mail

When someone mentions Outlook, the first thought is generally the sending and receiving of e-mail. Outlook does handle e-mail quite competently, but it also does a lot more, including managing contacts, scheduling activities, tracking tasks, keeping a journal, and using notes. In this chapter you will familiarize yourself with Outlook; use the windows, panes, ribbons, toolbars and menus in Outlook; learn how to create e-mail accounts, receive e-mail, and deal with the messages that come in.

Upgrade from Outlook Express

If you have been using Outlook Express and you install Office 2007, when the Outlook 2007 Startup Wizard runs, you may be asked if you want to upgrade from Outlook Express. If you choose to upgrade, you will be asked if you want to import your Outlook Express messages and addresses. Click **Yes**, and you

TIP

NOTE

If you want to import Outlook Express or Windows Mail files from another computer, locate the files by starting Outlook Express on the other computer, click **Tools | Options**, click the **Advanced** tab (the Maintenance tab in Outlook Express), click the **Maintenance** button (skip this in Outlook Express), and click **Store Folder**. Drag across the entire address line, press **CTRL-C**, and click **OK** to close the Store Location dialog box. Then click **Start | Computer**, click the computer icon at the left end of the Address bar, press **CTRL-V** to copy the contents into the address bar, and click the **Go To** button or press **ENTER**. This will show you the Outlook Express files. Copy these files to the new computer, import them into Outlook

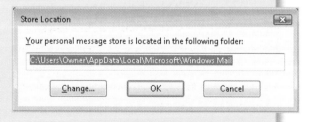

Express on that computer, and then use the instructions under "Upgrade from Outlook Express" to import the files into Outlook.

will see the progress as the files are being imported and will get a summary upon completion.

If you have been using Outlook Express and were not asked by the Outlook 2007 Startup Wizard if you want to upgrade, you can still import your Outlook Express files into Outlook.

1. Start **Outlook** in one of the ways described in Chapter 1.

2. Click **File | Import And Export**.

3. Click **Import Internet Mail And Addresses | Next**.

4. Click **Outlook Express** and make sure that the **Import Mail**, **Import Address Book**, and **Import Rules** checkboxes are all selected, as shown in Figure 11-1.

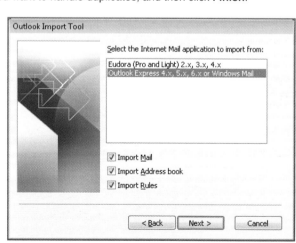

5. Click **Next**, choose how you want to handle duplicates, and then click **Finish**.

You will be told the progress as the files are being imported and will get a summary upon completion.

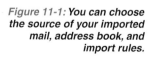

Figure 11-1: **You can choose the source of your imported mail, address book, and import rules.**

OUTLOOK FEATURES	DESCRIPTION
Title bar	Name of the open folder; contains the controls for the window.
Menu bar	Contains the primary controls for Outlook.
Standard toolbar	Changes to contain the controls needed for the open folder.
Advanced toolbar	Provides additional controls to those on the Standard toolbar.
Minimize button	Minimizes the window to an icon on the taskbar.
Maximize button	Maximizes the window to fill the screen. When maximized, this becomes the Restore button; clicking it returns the window to its previous size.
Close	Exits Outlook and closes the window.
Collapse/Expand button	Collapses or expands the current list box, whatever it might contain.
Scroll arrow	Moves the contents of the pane in the direction of the arrow.
Scroll button	Moves the contents of the pane in the direction it is dragged.
Scroll bar	Moves the contents of the pane in the direction it is clicked.
Navigation pane	Contains the means for selecting what you want to do and look at.
Reading pane	Displays the contents of the selected message in the open folder.
Folder pane	Displays the contents of the selected folder.
To-Do Bar	Contains the current month's calendar and appointments for the day.
Folder List	Contains the folders within the selected view.
Outlook view bars	Provides selection of the various views.
Control menu	Contains controls for the window itself.
Status bar	Displays information about what is selected.

Table 11-1: Principal Features of the Outlook Window

Explore Outlook

Outlook 2007 does not use the Office 2007 ribbon in its primary window (it does use a ribbon in the e-mail message window). Instead, the primary Outlook window uses a wide assortment of windows, toolbars, menus, and special features to accomplish its functions. Much of this chapter and the next couple of chapters explore how to find and use all of those items. In this section you'll see the most common features of the primary Outlook window, including the parts of the window, the buttons on the principal toolbars, and the major menus. Also, you'll see how to use the Navigation pane and Outlook Today.

Explore the Outlook Window

The Outlook window takes on a different appearance depending on the function you want Outlook to perform. The initial view when you first start Outlook is for handling mail, as shown in Figure 11-2. However, this view changes as soon as you start to do anything else, even create e-mail, as you'll see in this chapter. Other functions are described in their corresponding chapters. The principal features of the Outlook window are described in Table 11-1.

Change Views

The view you will have on the main Outlook window can be changed, depending on what you want to see. Typically, as shown in Figure 11-2, you will see the Navigation pane, Folder pane, Reading pane, and To-Do Bar. You may change these by clicking another view on the Outlook View bar.

Click the **View** menu, and select the pane or bar you want to change. Select the appropriate option from the menu.

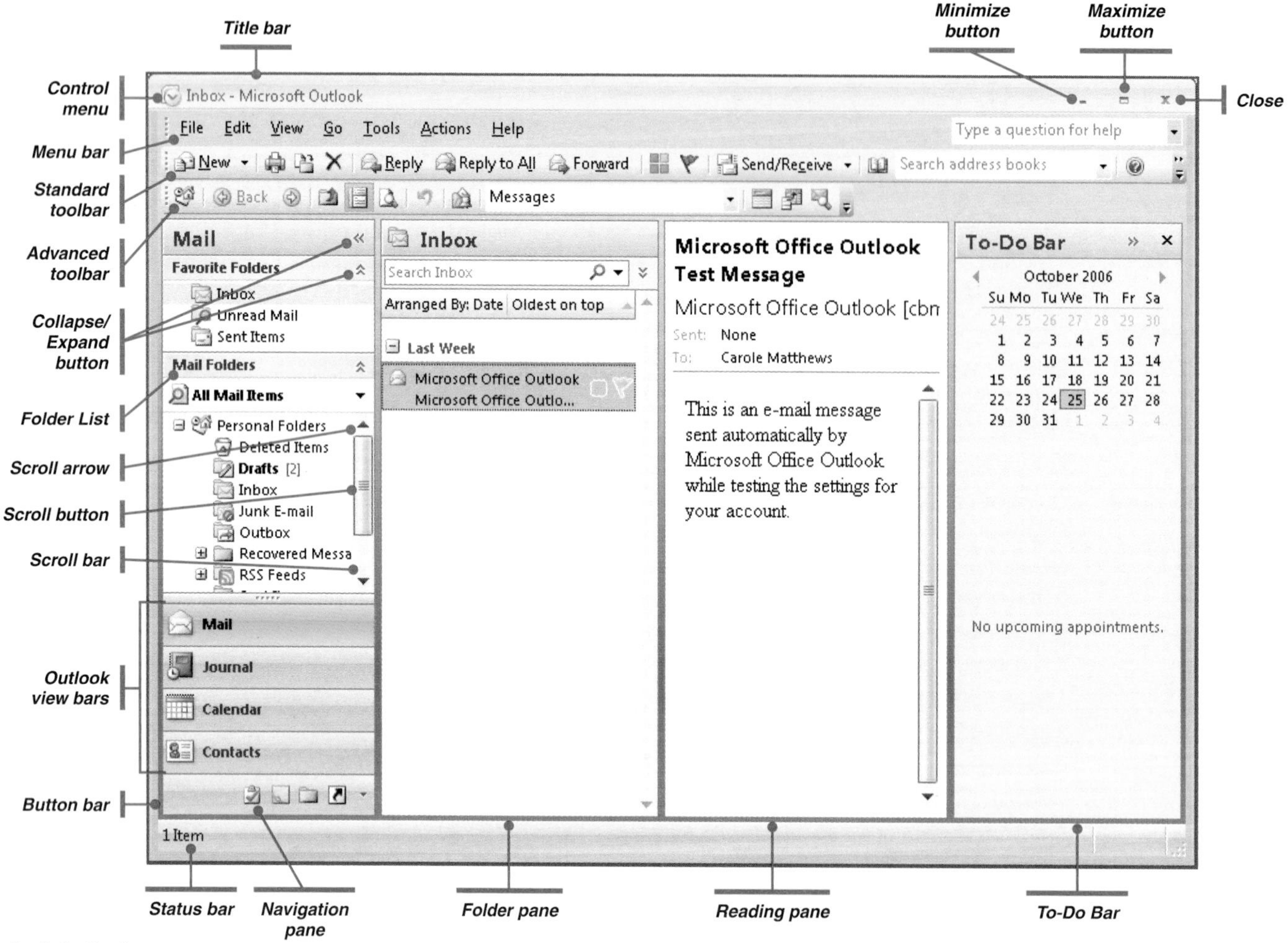
Title bar
Minimize button
Maximize button
Close
Control menu
Menu bar
Standard toolbar
Advanced toolbar
Collapse/ Expand button
Folder List
Scroll arrow
Scroll button
Scroll bar
Outlook view bars
Button bar
Status bar
Navigation pane
Folder pane
Reading pane
To-Do Bar

Figure 11-2: ***The default Outlook window is used for handling mail.***

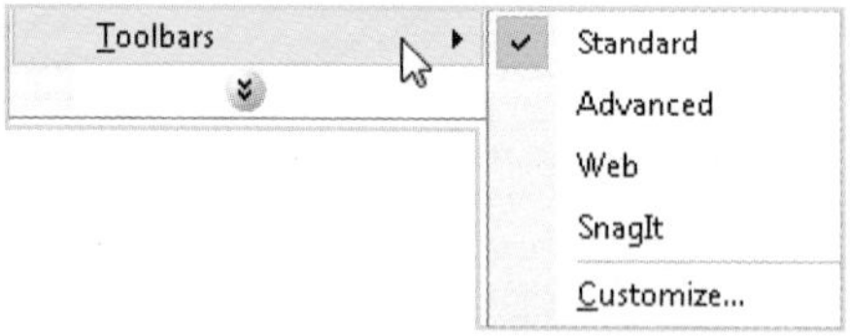
Toolbars
Standard
Advanced
Web
SnagIt
Customize...

Display the Advanced Toolbar

By default, the Advanced toolbar is not displayed. You can display it at any time, however.

1. In the initial Outlook view, click **View | Toolbars**. The Toolbars menu will be displayed.
2. Click the **Advanced** toolbar. A checkmark appears next to it, and the toolbar is displayed on the screen.

TIP

Another way to display a toolbar is to click **Tools** I **Customize**, and click the **Toolbars** tab. Click the checkbox next to the Advanced toolbar, and click **Close**.

QUICKSTEPS

USING OUTLOOK TOOLBARS

SEE WHAT A TOOL DOES

Hold the mouse pointer over the tool. A *ScreenTip* will appear, telling you what the tool does.

USE A TOOL

Click the button with the icon that represents the tool.

DISPLAY A TOOLBAR

Right-click a toolbar or the menu bar, and click the toolbar you want displayed.

MOVE A TOOLBAR

- When the toolbar is docked (attached to the edge of a window), place your pointer on the handle to the left of the toolbar (the column of four dots), and drag it to the new location.

- When the toolbar is floating (see Figure 11-3), place your pointer on the title bar of the toolbar, and drag it to the new location.

Continued . . .

Use the Navigation Pane

There are three main areas of the Navigation pane, as shown in Figure 11-4:

- **Folder List**, at the top, is where you can select the folder you want to open.
- **Outlook view bars**, in the middle, are where you can select the view in which to work.
- **Button bar**, at the bottom, lets you access views not available in the view bars.

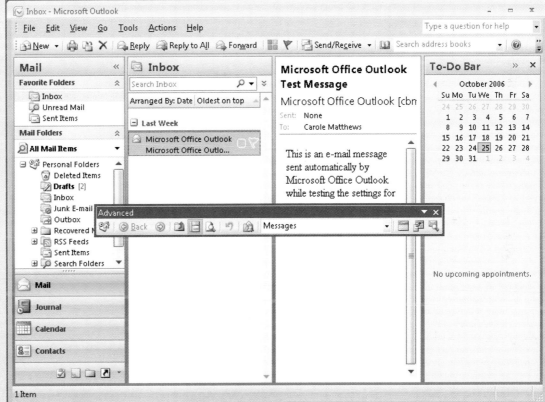

Figure 11-3: A toolbar can be attached to any edge of the Outlook window, or it can be floating in or out of the window.

USING OUTLOOK TOOLBARS

(Continued)

HIDE A TOOLBAR

1. Right-click the toolbar you want to hide.

2. In the context menu, click to remove the checkmark next to the toolbar.

TIP

When you drag a toolbar next to the top or bottom edge of the window, it automatically attaches itself to the window and becomes docked.

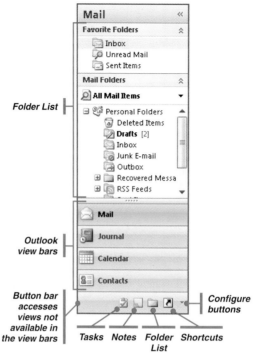

Figure 11-4: *The Navigation pane provides the primary control over which area and which folder you are working with.*

SELECT A VIEW

The Outlook view determines which area of Outlook you will work in—for example, Mail, Calendar, or Contacts. To select a view:

● Click the appropriate view bar.

–Or–

● Click the appropriate button in the button bar; see Figure 11-4.

–Or–

● Click the **Go** menu, and then click the desired view.

OPEN A FOLDER

The folder that is open determines which specific documents you will work on, for example, incoming messages in the Inbox folder or notes in the Notes folder. To open a folder:

● Click the appropriate folder in the Folder List.

–Or–

● Click the related view in the view bar, button in the button bar, or view in the Go menu.

DISPLAY VIEW BARS

The number of view bars displayed depends on the size of the Outlook window and the size of the area dedicated to the view bars. To change the number of view bars displayed:

● Drag the bottom window border up or down.

–Or–

● Drag the handle between the top view bar and the bottom of the Folder List.

DISPLAY BUTTONS

The buttons in the button bar are just an extension of view bars. When you reduce the number of view bars, the options become buttons on the button bar. To change the buttons on the button bar, in addition to changing the number of view bars that are displayed:

1. Click the **Configure button** on the right of the button bar.

2. Click **Add Or Remove Buttons**, and then click the button you want to add or remove.

REORDER NAVIGATION PANE BUTTONS

To change the buttons or the order of the buttons in the Navigation pane:

1. Click **Tools | Options**.

2. Click the **Other** tab, and under Outlook Panes, click **Navigation Pane**. The Navigation Pane Options dialog box will open.

3. Highlight a button, and click **Move Up** or **Move Down** to reorder the list. Click **OK** twice.

CLOSE THE NAVIGATION PANE

If you need more room to display a folder and its contents, you can close the Navigation pane:

● Click **View | Navigation Pane**.

–Or–

● Click the **Collapse** button at the top of the Navigation pane to reduce its size. Click it again (it's now the Expand button) to restore the Navigation pane to its regular size.

Use Outlook Today

Outlook Today gives you a summary of the information in Outlook for the current day. You can see a summary of your messages, your appointments and meetings, and the tasks you are slated to do, as shown in Figure 11-5.

⬆	Show **M**ore Buttons
⬇	Show Fe**w**er Buttons
	Na**v**igation Pane Options...
	Add or Remove Buttons

✉	**M**ail
🗓	**C**alendar
👤	Co**n**tacts
✓	**T**asks
🗒	**N**otes
📁	**F**older List
🔲	Short**c**uts
📓	**J**ournal

12

13

14

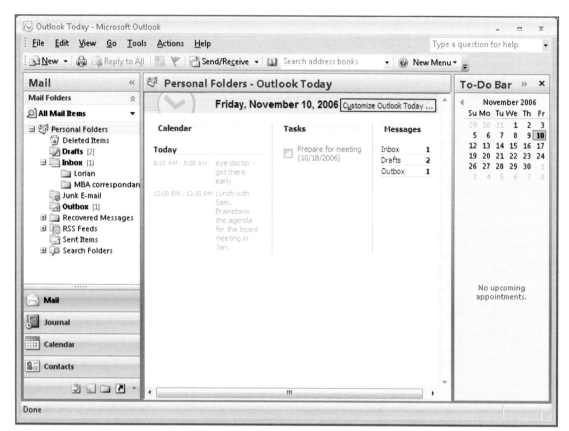

Figure 11-5: *Outlook Today provides a summary of information for the current day, such as appointments and tasks.*

OPEN OUTLOOK TODAY

If the Advanced toolbar is open, click the **Outlook Today** icon. (If it is not open, click **View | Toolbars**, and click **Advanced** so that a checkmark is in the checkbox.)

CHANGE OUTLOOK TODAY

Click **Customize Outlook Today** in the upper-right corner of the Outlook Today folder. Customize Outlook Today will open, as shown in Figure 11-6.

MAKE OUTLOOK TODAY YOUR DEFAULT PAGE

To display Outlook Today by default when you open Outlook:

1. In the Customize Outlook Today pane, opposite Startup, click **When Starting, Go Directly To Outlook Today**.

2. Click **Save Changes**.

Customize the To-Do Bar

To customize the To-Do Bar and determine what is displayed in it:

1. Click **View | To-Do Bar**, and click **Options** in the flyout menu.

2. Click the checkboxes next to the options you want.

3. Click **OK**.

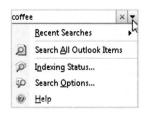

Figure 11-6: *You can tailor Outlook Today to contain only the information you want.*

Find a Message

No matter how many messages your e-mail folders contain, Outlook can help you find a specific one. You can perform instant searches for large sized files, related messages, or messages from a particular sender. You can further qualify the search by having Outlook search only certain folders, or by specifying content for which you're searching.

PERFORM INSTANT SEARCHES

Click in the search text box in the Inbox Folder pane (or whichever folder you want to search in) and type the text for which you want to search. The search will immediately display beneath the search text box the found messages with the search text highlighted. See Figure 11-7.

You have these options:

- Click **Clear Search** to clear the text box and restore the previous contents. You can enter a new search.
- Click **Show Instant Search Pane Menu** to select from a menu of search options.
- Click **Expand the Query Builder** to refine and add other search criteria.
- Click **Arranged By** to change the order for search results from the context menu.
- Click **Oldest/Newest On Top** to toggle the date ascending/descending sequence.
- Click **Try Searching Again In All Outlook Items** to expand the search to additional folders.

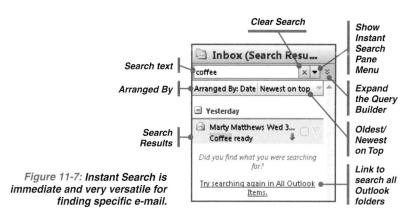

Figure 11-7: *Instant Search is immediate and very versatile for finding specific e-mail.*

EXPLORE ADVANCED SEARCHES

In addition to the Instant Search found on the Folder pane, you can also use the menu system to perform other, more advanced searches.

1. Click **Tools I Instant Search**. The flyout menu contains the following options for conducting a search:

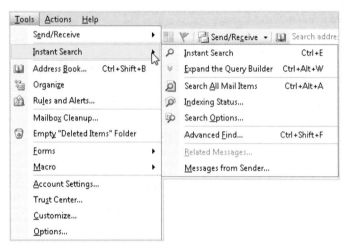

- **Instant Search**   Displays a search pane so that you can search for a phrase in the selected folder. Instant Search builds an index to search.

- **Expand The Query Builder**   Displays a search pane where you can build detailed search criteria.

- **Search All Mail Items**   Searches all mail items based on the detailed criteria set in the Search pane.

- **Indexing Status**   Reports on an indexing function performed by Outlook and returns a status. This must show that all indexing is complete before Instant Search can be relied upon.

- **Search Options**   Displays the Search Options dialog box, where you can set options for indexing files and indexing during searches, displaying search results faster and in color, searching deleted items, and, in the Instant Search, including only a selected folder or all folders.

- **Advanced Find**   Displays the Advanced Find dialog box where search criteria can include even more detail.

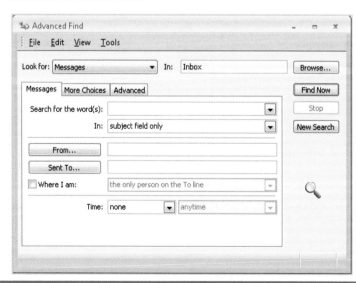

NOTE

Reference tools provided with Outlook, such as a thesaurus, are available with Outlook message windows, but not from the main Outlook window.

- **Related Messages**   Searches for messages related to the selected one.
- **Messages From Sender**   Searches for messages from selected senders.

2. Click your choice and type the information needed. Click **OK** if needed. (If your choice of option does not require a dialog box, you will not need to click **OK**.)

CHANGE SEARCH OPTIONS

To change some of the search defaults, use the Search Options dialog box, shown in Figure 11-8.

1. Click **Tools | Instant Search | Search Options**. The Search Options dialog box is displayed.

2. Under **Indexing** select the data files to be indexed (so that searches can be faster), and if you choose, deselect the default to display a message if the indexing is incomplete for a selected file. If this message is displayed, it tells you that the indexing is still in process and that results will be incomplete.

3. Under **Search**, you can determine whether you want to change the defaults to display results as you type the search text, to limit the number of results so that the searches are faster, or to highlight the search text in results and change the highlight color.

4. Under **Deleted Items**, click the option to include messages in the Deleted Items folder in the data files being searched.

5. Under **Instant Search Pane**, choose between searching the currently selected folder (the default), or all folders in the Instant Search feature.

6. Click **OK**.

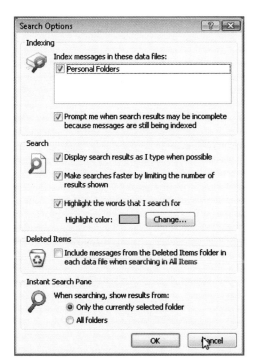

Figure 11-8: **In the Search Options dialog box, you can change search defaults that assist you during your search activity.**

Set Up E-mail

The Internet provides a global pipeline through which e-mail flows; therefore, you need a connection that lets you tap into that pipeline. Both local and national Internet service providers (ISPs) offer e-mail with their Internet connections. At your work or business, you may have an e-mail account over a local area network (LAN) that also connects to the Internet. You can also obtain e-mail accounts on the Internet that are independent of the connection.

You can access these Internet accounts (Hotmail, for example) from anywhere in the world. These three ways of accessing Internet e-mail—ISPs, corporate connections, and Internet e-mail—use different types of e-mail systems:

- **POP3 (Post Office Protocol 3)**   Used by ISPs, retrieves e-mail from a dedicated mail server, and is usually combined with SMTP (Simple Mail Transfer Protocol) to send e-mail from a separate server.

- **MAPI (Messaging Application Programming Interface)**   Lets businesses handle e-mail on Microsoft Exchange Servers and LANs.

- **HTTP (Hypertext Transfer Protocol)**   Transfers information from servers on the World Wide Web to browsers (that's why your browser's address line starts with "http://") and is used with Hotmail and other Internet mail accounts.

Get Online

Whether you choose dial-up or a high-speed service like DSL (digital subscriber line) or cable Internet, getting online requires hardware, software, and some system configuration. It's possible that everything you need is already installed or that your computer came with extra disks for getting online. First, find an ISP:

- **Get a recommendation** from satisfied friends.

- **Look in the yellow pages** under "Internet Service Providers" or "Internet Access Providers."

- **Look on your computer**. Many computer manufacturers include software from nationwide Internet providers, such as AOL, EarthLink, and others.

If you find what you want in an Internet provider already on your computer, double-click the provider's icon, or click the link and follow the instructions. If you have a disk that came with your computer or from an ISP, pop it in and follow the instructions. If you use a local provider, their tech support people will usually walk you through the entire setup process on the phone.

TIP

To find out where your e-mail data files are located and what their folder is named, in the initial Outlook window, click **Tools I Options**, and on the Options dialog box, click **Data Files**. On the Data Files tab, you will see the name and location of the Personal Folders.

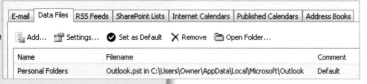

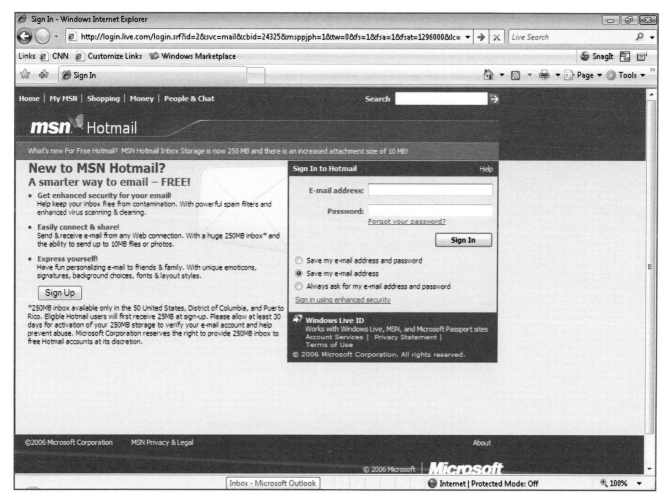

Figure 11-9: *The Microsoft Passport account lets you remember a single user name and password to log on to many secure Web sites.*

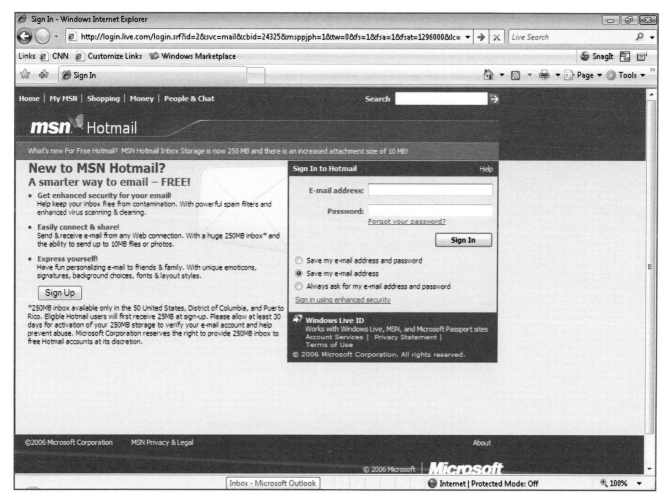
NOTE

To get a Hotmail account, you must already have a way to get on the Internet, and the instructions here assume you can do that.

Get a Hotmail Account

Hotmail, one of many Internet-based HTTP services, is free, and you can access it from any Internet connection in the world, so you don't even need to own a computer. The easiest way to set up Hotmail is to get a Microsoft Passport account just for Hotmail (see Figure 11-9).

QUICKFACTS

COLLECTING ACCOUNT INFORMATION

The information needed to install an e-mail account in Outlook depends on the type of e-mail you choose.

ISP ACCOUNTS

- **Type of server:** POP3 or IMAP
- **E-mail address**
- **User name**
- **Password**
- **Incoming mail server name**
- **Outgoing mail server name**

HTTP ACCOUNTS (LIKE HOTMAIL)

- **Type of server:** HTTP
- **E-mail address:** Microsoft Live ID or other user ID
- **User name**
- **Password**
- **Your mail service Internet address, if not Hotmail or MSN, which are provided**

TIP

To remove an e-mail account, click **Tools | Account Settings** to open the Account Settings dialog box. Click the account to select it, and then click **Remove**. Click **Yes** to confirm the removal of the account, and click **Close**.

SET UP HOTMAIL

1. Click **Start | Internet**, and/or follow any steps needed for you to open your Internet browser and get on the Internet. In your browser's address bar, type www.hotmail.com, and press **ENTER**.

2. Ignore the Microsoft Passport Sign-In box, and click the **Sign Up** button. Click the e-mail solution that is right for you. You may select a free service or one for an annual or monthly price.

3. Fill in every field on the registration form. For the Windows Live ID, enter the name you want for the account, leaving out the "@hotmail.com" part. You can click **Check Availability** to check whether the ID you want is available. You'll have to read and accept the Windows Live Service Agreement and the Privacy Statement. Click **I Accept**.

4. Scroll your way through a few pages of pitches, selecting any items you want delivered to your Inbox, until you can click **Continue**. You will see information about the mailbox usage and your current messages. At this point, your Hotmail account has been created.

Install Accounts in Outlook

Once you have an e-mail account, you need to tell Outlook where to find the server that stores your mail. As you proceed through the E-mail Accounts Wizard, you will need some information about the account. See the QuickSteps "Collecting Account Information" for the information you'll need to enter. When you have the information handy:

1. Open Outlook and click **Tools | Account Settings**. The Account Settings dialog box appears.

2. Click **New**, and The Add New E-Mail Account wizard starts. This short wizard will lead you through the process of configuring an account in Outlook. Continue as detailed in Chapter 1 on how to work through the steps.

TIP

If you like where the old Preview pane was located in earlier versions of Outlook, you can place the Reading pane beneath the Folder pane: Click **View | Reading Pane | Bottom**. (You can also turn it off.)

Receive E-mail

With at least one e-mail account installed in Outlook, you're ready to receive mail. Everything is done from the Outlook Mail folder, shown in Figure 11-10. Be sure to share your e-mail address with the friends you'd like to hear from.

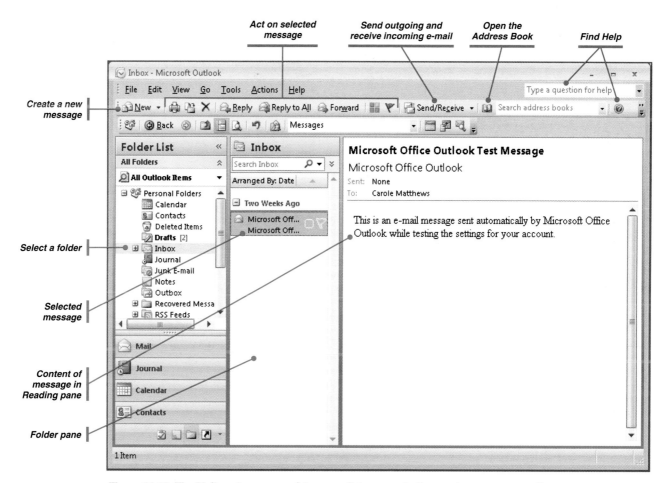

Figure 11-10: *The Mail workspace provides one-click access to the most common operations.*

NOTE

If you don't see the Send/Receive button on your toolbar, click **Toolbar Options** at the right end of the toolbar, and click the **Send/Receive** button you see there. After you do that once, it will appear in its normal place.

TIP

You can download messages from a particular e-mail provider, if you prefer. Click **Tools**, point to **Send/ Receive**, click the desired account, and click **Inbox**.

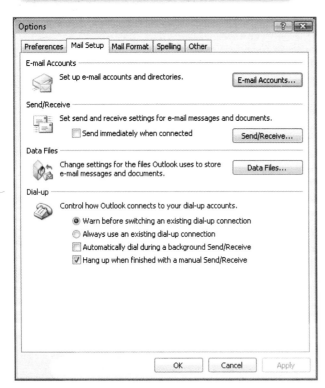

Check for E-mail

Once you are set up, it's easy to download mail.

1. Make sure you're connected to the Internet or can be automatically connected, and that **Mail** is selected in the Outlook Navigation pane.

2. Click **Send/Receive** on the toolbar.

3. If it is not already open, click the **Inbox** icon in the Navigation pane, and watch the mail come in.

RECEIVE E-MAIL AUTOMATICALLY

Not only can Outlook periodically check your e-mail provider for you, but it can also do it automatically. Desktop alerts are subtle, given the way they quietly fade in and out.

1. Click **Tools | Options**.

2. Click the **Mail Setup** tab, shown in Figure 11-11, and click **Send/Receive**.

3. Under the section Setting For Group, check Schedule An Automatic Send/Receive Every, type or click the spinner to enter the number of minutes to elapse between checking, and click **Close**.

4. If you also want to create a desktop alert telling you when mail arrives, click the **Preferences** tab, click **E-mail Options**, and click **Advanced E-mail Options**. Check **Display A New Mail Desktop Alert**, and click **OK** twice.

5. Click **OK** to close the Options dialog box.

Figure 11-11: **The Options dialog box is where you can customize many Outlook processes.**

Read E-mail

Besides being easy to obtain, e-mail messages are effortless to open and read.
There are two ways to view the body of the message:

- Double-click the message and read it in the window that opens, as shown in
  Figure 11-12.

  –Or–

- Click the message and read it in the Reading pane, scrolling as needed.

Of course, you can also control which accounts you check, what kinds of e-mail
you let in, and how it is presented to you.

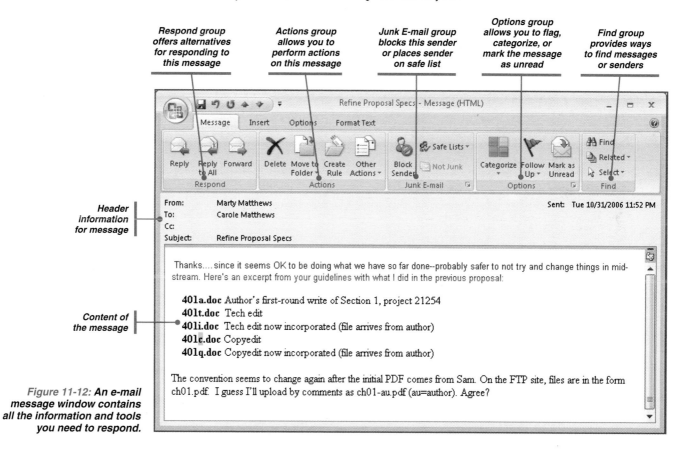

Respond group offers alternatives for responding to this message

Actions group allows you to perform actions on this message

Junk E-mail group blocks this sender or places sender on safe list

Options group allows you to flag, categorize, or mark the message as unread

Find group provides ways to find messages or senders

Header information for message

Content of the message

Figure 11-12: **An e-mail message window contains all the information and tools you need to respond.**

Download Sender and Subject Information Only

If you are inundated with e-mail, or if messages contain really large files (like lots of photos), you might want to choose among your messages for specific ones to download to Outlook. You can save time downloading e-mail, especially with large files—which you may want to download at a later time. This only works on your POP server e-mail (not on HTTP server e-mail, such as Hotmail). First, you instruct Outlook to download only the headers, and then you mark the headers for which you want to download the messages.

RECEIVE HEADERS MANUALLY

1. Click **Inbox** (or whatever folder you prefer).

2. Click the **Send/Receive** down arrow on the toolbar, click the account for which you want to download the headers, and click **Download** *foldername* **Headers**.

   –Or–

   Click the **Tools** menu, point at **Send/Receive**, click the account for which you want to download headers, and click **Download** *foldername* **Headers**.

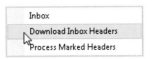

The headers, assuming you have e-mail waiting to be downloaded, will be downloaded to your selected folder. It will have an identifying icon:

MARK HEADERS TO DOWNLOAD, COPY, OR DELETE

1. Right-click a header-only message in the folder to open the context menu.

   –Or–

   Double-click a header-only message in the Inbox folder to open the Remote Item Header dialog box.

2. In either case, click one of these options:

   - **Open** Displays the Remote Item Header dialog box, which allows you to unmark the header, mark it to be downloaded and/or copied on the server, or deleted.

   - **Mark To Download Message(s)** Downloads the whole message the next time you click **Send/Receive**.

QUICKSTEPS

FILTERING OUT SPAM

Begin by setting the options for the Junk E-mail folder.

1. Click **Tools | Options**.

2. Click the **Preferences** tab, and click the **Junk E-mail** button.

SELECT A LEVEL OF PROTECTION

Click the **Options** tab, and click the desired level of protection.

BUILD ADDRESS LISTS

The Safe Senders, Blocked Senders, and Safe Recipients tabs let you manually create lists of e-mail addresses and domain names.

For each entry, click **Add**, type the information, and click **OK** twice.

UPDATE LISTS QUICKLY

Sender and recipient addresses can be added quickly to the Safe Senders, Blocked Senders, and Safe Recipients lists from an Outlook folder.

1. Right-click a message whose sender you want to put on a list.

2. Point at **Junk E-mail**, and click the appropriate option.

UNBLOCK PICTURE DOWNLOADS

By default, picture downloads are blocked to speed up the downloading of e-mail. To change that for specific items:

- For a **single opened message**, click **Click Here To Download Pictures** in the information bar at the top of the message.

Continued . . .

- **Mark To Download Message Copy** Downloads the whole message the next time and leaves the original on the server (this is handy when checking e-mail on the road).

- **Delete** Removes the message from the server and from Outlook the next time you click **Send/Receive**.

3. Repeat the process for all headers, and click **Send/Receive** to perform the actions selected.

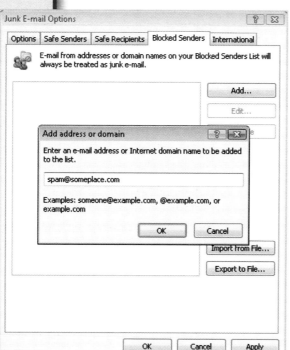

RECEIVE HEADERS AUTOMATICALLY

If you want to download only headers from your POP server accounts every time, you can set up Outlook to do so.

1. Click the **Send/Receive** down arrow on the toolbar, point at **Send/Receive Settings**, and click **Define Send/Receive Groups**.

   –Or–

   Click the **Tools** menu, point at **Send/Receive**, point at **Send/Receive Settings**, and click **Define Send/Receive Groups**.

2. Make sure **All Accounts** is selected, and click **Edit**. All your e-mail accounts are listed on the left.

3. Click the desired POP account.

4. Under Folder Options, click **Download Headers Only**, as shown in Figure 11-13, click **OK**, and click **Close**.

PROCESS HEADERS

When your headers have been marked, you can download them.

1. Click the **Send/Receive** down arrow.

2. Click **Process All Marked Headers** or **Process Marked Headers In This Folder**.

QUICKSTEPS

FILTERING OUT SPAM (Continued)

- For **all mail from the source of the open message**, right-click a blocked item, point at **Junk E-mail**, and click **Add Sender's Domain To Safe Senders List**.

- For **all HTML mail** (not recommended), click **Tools I Trust Center**, click the **Automatic Download** option on the left, and clear the **Don't Download Pictures Automatically In HTML E-Mail Messages Or RSS Items** checkbox. Click **OK**.

NOTE

The domain in a person's e-mail address is the part of the address after "@." In an Internet address (URL, or uniform resource locator) the domain is the part after the "http://www"—for example, "whidbey.net" (a local ISP) or "loc.gov" (the Library of Congress Web site).

NOTE

One easy way to reduce the junk e-mail you get is to avoid replying to any suspicious message. If you reply and tell them to go away, they learn that they reached a valid address, which they will hit again and again.

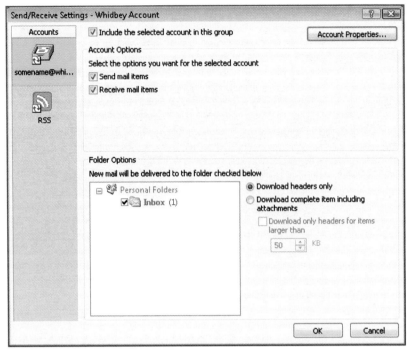

Figure 11-13: **Outlook can be set up to download only headers for all messages.**

Filter Junk Mail

Outlook can automatically filter out a lot of annoying spam before you ever see it, and it can set aside suspicious-looking messages in a Junk E-mail folder. It does this in two ways: by analyzing message content based on a protection level you choose, and by having you identify good and bad senders.

Outlook also prevents pictures and sounds from being downloaded into messages that contain HTML formatting. Up to now, savvy spammers have been able to design messages that only download images when you open or preview the message. They plant *Web beacons* in the messages, which tell their server that they have reached a valid address so that they can send you even more junk.

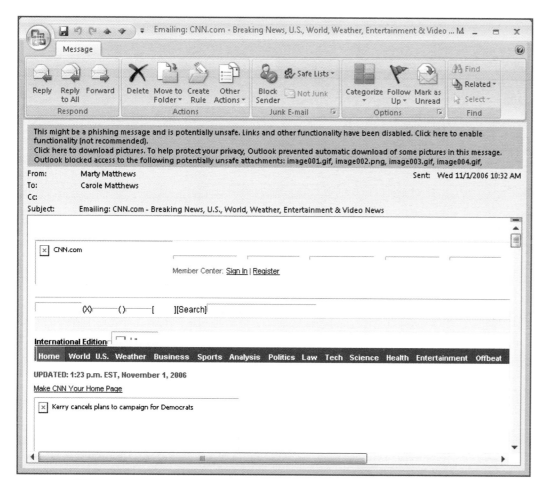

Figure 11-14: *Blocking image and sound files protects your computer, but you can easily unblock a message by clicking in its top banner.*

Outlook blocks both the external content, as shown in Figure 11-14, and the beacon, unless you tell it to unblock it.

CHOOSE A PROTECTION LEVEL

The amount of junk e-mail you receive suggests the level of protection you need. By default, Outlook sets the level at Low, but you might decide that another option would work better for you. Table 11-2 shows some considerations in choosing a level.

To set the protection level:

1. Click **Tools | Options**, and click the **Junk E-mail** button.

2. Beneath Choose The Level Of Junk E-mail Protection You Want, click the desired protection level. See Table 11-2 for explanations.

ADD ADDRESSES TO FILTER LISTS

The four other tabs in the Junk E-mail Options window provide a means for you to specifically identify good and bad e-mailers:

- **Safe Senders** Specifies e-mail senders from whom you always want to receive messages. This list automatically contains your contacts, so Outlook never identifies their messages as junk, no matter how silly their jokes are. If you subscribe to a newsgroup or some other mass mailing, you might need to specifically add it to the list.

- **Safe Recipients** Ensures that mailing lists you subscribe to treat you as a safe sender when you contribute messages to the list.

OPTION	RESULT	PROS	CONS
No Automatic Filtering	Only mail from blocked senders goes to the Junk E-mail folder.	You have total control.	Your Inbox could be stuffed; you or others might see unsolicited pornography.
Low (default)	Outlook scans messages for offensive language and indications of unsolicited commercial mailings.	The worst of the junk gets caught.	Some canny spammers will still find ways around the protections.
High	Pretty much all the junk e-mail gets caught.	Considerably fewer rude shocks in the Inbox.	Some regular mail will inadvertently get sent to the junk folder.
Safe Lists Only	Only mail from Safe Senders and Safe Recipients lists goes to the Inbox.	Complete protection.	Lots of friendly mail will be junked.
Permanently Delete Suspected Junk E-Mail Instead Of Moving It To The Junk E-Mail Folder	Filtered junk mail never gets onto your computer.	You never have to inspect the Junk E-Mail folder.	Unless you chose the No Automatic Filtering option, you are sure to lose some friendly mail.

Table 11-2: Junk E-mail Protection Levels

TIP

If you aren't satisfied with the way junk e-mail filtering is being handled, click **Help** and type troubleshoot junk in the **Search** text box (you can be offline to do this), and scroll down to "Ten Tips on How to Help Reduce Spam," guidelines explaining easy solutions to common issues.

- **Blocked Senders**   Sends messages from specified senders straight to the Junk E-mail folder. It's especially useful to add obnoxious domains to this list so that no address from that source makes it to your Inbox.

- **International**   Allows you to block international e-mails by foreign domain codes or by language.

Handle E-mail Messages

E-mail has a way of building up fast. Outlook lets you sort your messages just about any way you want. You learned all about managing folders in Chapter 8. Now we'll consider ways to sort and mark messages so that they don't get lost in the crowd.

Mark Messages as Read or Unread

A message is marked as "read" after you have selected it so that its contents display in the Reading pane for a designated time (see "Change the Time for Being Read"). The header in the Folder list changes from boldface to plain type.

A message can get lost in the pile if it's accidentally selected and you don't notice or forget about it. You can easily mark it as unread again by right-clicking the message and clicking **Mark As Unread**.

Change the Time for Being Read

To change the time that a message must be selected before it is marked as read:

1. Click **Tools | Options**, and click the **Other** tab.
2. In the Outlook Panes area, click the **Reading Pane** button. The Reading Pane dialog box will appear.
3. Click one of these options:
   - **Mark Items As Read When Viewed In The Reading Pane**   Allows you to set the number of seconds that a message must be selected before being marked as read.
   - **Mark Item As Read When Selection Changes**   Marks the message as read as soon as the pointer selects another message in the Folder pane. This is the default setting.
4. Click **OK** to close the dialog box.

Flag Your Messages for Follow-up

You can place colored flags beside messages you want to do something with later. The flag will appear in the flag column of the Folder pane.

- Select the message you want to flag, click the **Flag** button in the standard toolbar, and click the type of flag you want to insert.

  –Or–

- Right-click the flag column of the selected message, and on the context menu, click the type of flag you want to insert.

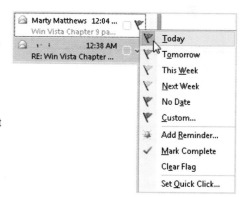

TIP

You can scroll through a selected message by pressing **SPACEBAR**. To disable this feature, click **Tools | Options**, click the **Other** tab, click the **Reading Pane** button, and clear the **Single Key Reading Using Space Bar** checkbox.

NOTE

If you want to insert a Today red flag beside a message, just click in the flag column. A red flag displays. Or you can press **INSERT** on the keyboard. (Press again to toggle between the Follow-Up red flag and a Complete checkmark.)

TIP

To group all of your flagged messages, click **View | Arrange By | Flag: Start Date** or **Flag: Due Date**.

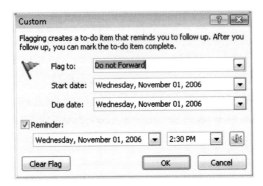

FINE-TUNE YOUR FLAGS

You can fine-tune the follow-up actions of the flags and specify that a reminder be given so that an e-mail message can be responded to in a timely manner.

1. In the Folder pane, right-click the flag column, and click **Add Reminder** or **Custom**.

   –Or–

   In the open message window, click the **Follow Up** button in the Options group on the toolbar, and click **Add Reminder** or **Custom**.

2. In the Custom dialog box, click the **Flag To** down arrow, and click an action.

3. Click the **Start Date** down arrow, and click a date to indicate when the message is to be flagged.

4. Click the **Due Date** down arrow, and click a date that indicates when the response to the e-mail is to be completed.

5. Click **Reminder** to place a checkmark in the checkbox and to display the date when the reminder is to begin. Click the date down arrow, and click a date. Click the time down arrow, and click a time for the reminders to begin.

6. Click the **Sound** icon to remove the default setting in which a sound file is played when the reminder displays on the screen.

7. Click **OK**.

8. At the designated time, a reminder will be displayed, as shown in Figure 11-15. To repeat the reminder, click the snooze down arrow, click an interval until the next sound, and then click Snooze.

NOTE

To remove a flag, or to indicate that the e-mail no longer needs to be handled, right-click the flag and click either **Clear Flag** or **Mark Complete**.

TIP

At times, you will receive e-mail tagged with an exclamation point to get your attention. If you disagree with the priority the sender gave it, right-click the message, click **Options**, and pick another level of importance. Click **Close**.

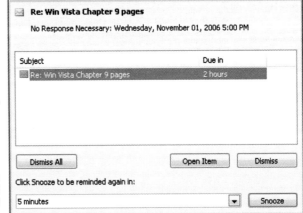

Figure 11-15: **You can set a flag to display a reminder with a sound that alerts you that an important e-mail has not been handled.**

Arrange Messages in a Folder

Outlook contains 13 types of Inbox arrangements, as seen in Figure 11-16. You can have Outlook organize messages by the date they were sent, which Outlook uses by default; alphabetically by who sent them or by first word in the subject line; or by clustering those with attachments, colored flags you give them, or categories you created for your own use. Outlook can even group *conversations*, e-mail exchanges in which senders clicked Reply, thus preserving the subject line. To arrange messages:

1. Click **Inbox** or another specific mail folder in the navigation bar on the left side.

2. Click **View I Arrange By**, and click one of the arrangements listed.

The next two illustrations show both how the expansion button works and what the full list of items on the menu is. So, I see the menus displayed outside the note box directly beneath it.

Figure 11-16: **You can arrange the messages in a folder in many different ways to more easily find one message or to group messages in a meaningful way.**

NOTE

Whenever a menu displays the expansion arrow at the bottom of the list, pointing at it will expand the list.

NOTE

A plus (+) or minus (–) sign to the left of an item indicates that you can expand or contract a list by clicking the sign.

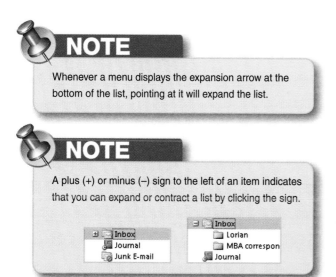

ADD COLORED CATEGORIES

Assigning categories to mail is one way of separating your messages with a colored code that you determine. You might categorize by project, priority, sender, etc. You determine what a color will mean when it is assigned to a message. Once your e-mail contains categories, it can be sorted and arranged so that you can find or track it more efficiently. The colors make the categories highly visible in lists. Mail is only one kind of item that you can categorize. You can assign categories to whatever you create in Outlook—tasks, appointments,

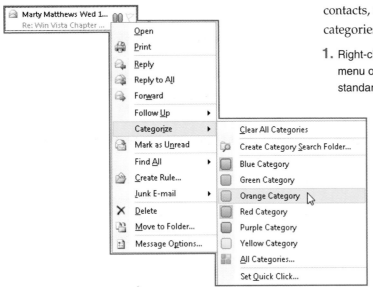

Figure 11-17: The Categorize menu shows colors, which you can define as categories according to your needs.

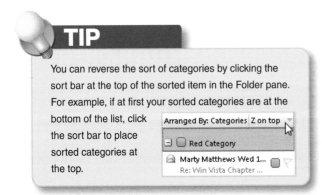

TIP

You can reverse the sort of categories by clicking the sort bar at the top of the sorted item in the Folder pane. For example, if at first your sorted categories are at the bottom of the list, click the sort bar to place sorted categories at the top.

contacts, notes, journal entries, and documents. You can also create new categories in the list.

1. Right-click a message (or other item), and click **Categorize**. The categories context menu opens, shown in Figure 11-17. (You can also click the **Categorize** button in the standard toolbar.)

2. Do one of the following:

- Click **Create Category Search Folder** to create a folder that tracks all categorized e-mails. You can create a folder for all categories or for specific ones. When created, you can find this folder under Search Folders in the Navigation pane's Folder List, and quickly scan your categorized and sorted e-mail.

- Click a color category for the item.

- Click **All Categories** to assign more than one category to a name (or to edit a category—see the next section, "Edit a Category"). Click a color to select it (place a checkmark in the checkbox), and then click **OK**.

3. View items sorted into categories by clicking **View | Arrange By | Categories**.

EDIT A CATEGORY

You can edit a category to change its name, its color, or assigned shortcut.

1. Right-click a message to be categorized, click **Categorize** from the context menu, and click **All Categories**.

2. Select from among these options:

- To create a new category, click **New**. In the Add New Category dialog box, type a name; click the **Color** down arrow, and click a color; click the **Shortcut** key down arrow, and click a shortcut key if you want one. Click **OK**.

- To rename a category, click a category, click **Rename**, and type the new name in the category name text box.

- To delete a category, click the category and click **Delete**.

- To change the color, click the Color down arrow, and click a replacement color.

- To assign a shortcut key, click the **Shortcut Key** down arrow, and click a shortcut key combination.

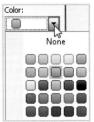

3. Click **OK** to close the Color Categories dialog box.

MANIPULATING THE RULES

To get to the Rules And Alerts Wizard, click the **Rules And Alerts** button in the Advanced toolbar 🔳 (or click **Tools | Rules And Alerts**). The first page of the Rules And Alerts Wizard lists current rules under the names you gave them.

LEARN THE RULES

Select a rule in the list, and review it in the description pane below it.

CHANGE THE RULES

1. Click a rule in the list, click **Change Rule**, and click an action from the drop-down list.

   –Or–

   Double-click the rule to open the Rules And Alerts Wizard.

2. If you opened the wizard, change the contents as needed, click **Next | Finish | OK**.

3. If you selected an option under Change Rules with an icon beside it, add any requested information or fill in any new underlined variable in the description, and click **OK** until the window is closed.

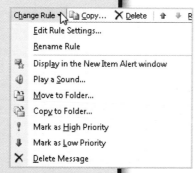

MAKE A SIMILAR RULE

1. Click a rule in the list, click **Copy**, accept the default folder or type a folder name to copy the rule to, and click **OK**. ☑ Copy of MBA

2. Double-click the copy.

Continued . . .

Make Up Your Own Rules

When it comes to sorting e-mail, you can make up the rules as you go along, and Outlook will follow them. Or you can pick from a list of predefined rules for common situations, like having Outlook send a message to your cell phone if you win an eBay auction or flagging all messages from your son at college for follow-up. (This only works for POP3 server accounts.)

1. With Mail selected, click **Tools | Rules And Alerts**. The Rules And Alerts Wizard is displayed, as shown in Figure 11-18.

2. Click **New Rule** and click one of the options in the list under Step 1 (it displays in the description box below Step 2) in one of these categories:

   - **Stay Organized**   Lets you manipulate e-mail in a variety of ways.
   - **Stay Up To Date**   Alerts you when new mail arrives by displaying it in a special window, playing a sound, or alerting your mobile device.

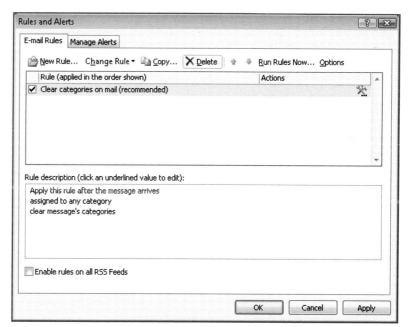

*Figure 11-18: **The Rules And Alerts Wizard is where you establish rules for handling e-mail, including being alerted to the arrival of e-mail.***

MANIPULATING THE RULES (Continued)

3. Step through the wizard, changing settings as necessary and clicking **Next** as you go.

4. Give the rule a new name, and click **Finish**.

CANCEL A RULE

1. Select a rule in the list, and click **Delete**.

2. Click **Yes**.

REARRANGE THE RULES

You might want rules to be applied in a certain order.

1. Select a rule in the list that you want to move.

2. Click the **Move Up** or **Move Down** arrow until the rule resides where you want it in the sequence.

BASE A RULE ON A MESSAGE

1. In the Mail Folder pane, right-click the message and click **Create Rule**.

2. Check the desired options in the Create Rule dialog box.

3. To use the more detailed specifications in the Rules And Alerts Wizard, click **Advanced Options**, step through the wizard (with information from the dialog box supplying some of the underlined values), click **Next** as needed, and then click **Finish**.

4. If using the Create Rule dialog box, click **OK** twice.

- **Start From A Blank Rule**   Lets you build a completely custom rule for receiving or sending messages.

3. Click **Next**. Click all conditions under which you want the rule applied, clicking any underlined value and changing it as needed. The information is added to the scenario. Click **Next**.

4. Step through the wizard, selecting circumstances and actions, changing values as needed, and clicking **Next**.

5. Type a name for the rule where requested, click an option specifying when the rule goes into effect, click **Finish**, and click **OK**.

Delete Messages

Outlook creates two stages for deleting messages by providing a Delete folder, which holds all the things you deleted from other folders.

DELETE MESSAGES FROM THE INBOX

Start by clicking a message in the Inbox. Then perform one of the following actions:

- **Delete one message** by selecting a message and clicking **Delete** on the toolbar. ✕

- **Delete a block of messages** by clicking the first message, holding down **SHIFT**, clicking the last message (all the messages in between are selected as well), and clicking **Delete** on the toolbar.

- **Delete multiple noncontiguous messages** by pressing **CTRL** while clicking the messages you want to remove and then clicking **Delete** on the toolbar.

EMPTY THE DELETED ITEMS FOLDER

1. Click the **Deleted Items** folder.

2. Choose one of the following actions:

- Select files to be permanently deleted as you did earlier, click **Delete**, and click **Yes**.

–Or–

Create Rule dialog box:

When I get e-mail with all of the selected conditions

- ☑ From NYTimes.com
- ☑ Subject contains   Today's Headlines
- ☐ Sent to   me only ▼

Do the following

- ☐ Display in the New Item Alert window
- ☑ Play a selected sound: Windows Notify.wav ▶ ■ Browse...
- ☑ Move the item to folder: RSS Feeds   Select Folder...

OK   Cancel   Advanced Options...

ARCHIVING MESSAGES

Archiving is for people who have a hard time throwing things away. Outlook is set up on a schedule, which you can see by clicking **Tools | Options**, clicking the **Other** tab, and clicking **AutoArchive**.

The AutoArchive dialog box allows you to set the time interval between archive functions, when to delete old messages, the path to the archived file, and other settings.

By default, a dialog box appears, asking if you are ready to archive files; you can click **Yes** and be assured of finding the messages later. They are saved in a file structure that mirrors your Personal folders yet compresses the files and cleans up the Inbox. To open archived files, use one of these methods:

- Click ⊞ beside Archive Folders in the Navigation pane, and click a folder.

  –Or–

- Click **File | Open | Outlook Data File**, and click a file.

Either way, archived files, saved in .pst format, display in the Reading pane. You can search them to find the message you want.

NOTE

Remember to delete the contents of the Sent folder on a regular basis. It can get huge.

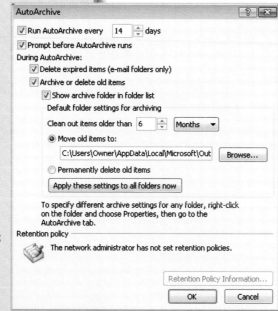

- Press **CTRL-A** to select all items in the folder, click **Delete**, and click **Yes**.

  –Or–

- Right-click the Deleted Items folder, and click Empty "Deleted Items" Folder.

Manage Attachments

Messages that contain files, such as pictures and documents, display a paper clip icon in the second message line within the Folder pane to show that there's more to see. Attachments are listed in the message itself in the Reading pane, as shown in Figure 11-19. Since computer vandals like to broadcast debilitating viruses by way of attachments, you should be sure that you are dealing with a trusted source before you open any attachments. Also, it's important to have an up-to-date antivirus program running on your system, as well as any protection provided by your ISP. Make sure you have it, and keep your virus definitions up-to-date. If you are running Windows Vista, there are several Internet and e-mail protections built into it.

When a message comes in with an attachment, you can preview the attachment, open it, or save it first.

Marty Matthews 1:07 AM
Illustration

OPEN ATTACHMENTS

In the Reading pane:

- Double-click the attachment icon.

  –Or–

- Right-click the attachment and click either **Preview** or **Open**.

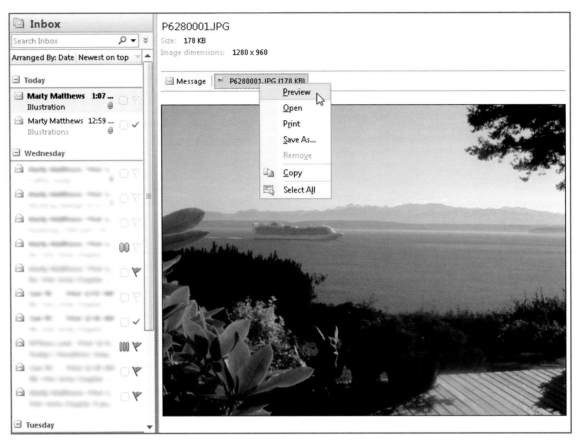

Figure 11-19: A single message can contain one or many attachments, consisting of all kinds of files, which may be previewed before opening.

SAVE ATTACHMENTS

If you have My Computer or Windows Explorer open to the folder where you want to save the attachment, you can drag the attachment there. Otherwise:

1. Right-click the attachment icon, and click **Save As**.

2. Use the Save Attachment dialog box to navigate to the desired folder.

3. Type a name in the File Name text box, and click **Save**.

OPEN SAVED ATTACHMENTS

1. Navigate to the folder where you saved the file.

2. Double-click the file.

Print Messages

Occasionally, you might receive something that you want to print and pass around or save as a hard copy. Outlook lets you print in a hurry with the default print settings, or you can control certain parts of the process.

PRINT QUICKLY

Right-click the message or an attachment, and click **Print**.

CHOOSE PRINT SETTINGS

1. Select or open the message.

2. Click **File | Print**. The Print dialog box appears.

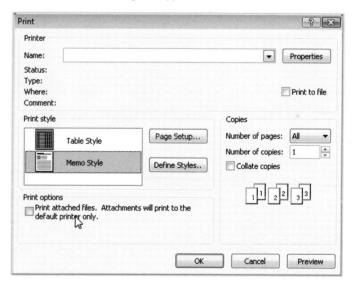

3. Enter your preferences in the Print dialog box.

4. If desired, click **Properties**, select the layout or quality, and click **OK**.

5. Click **OK** to begin printing.

Chapter 12

Creating and Sending E-mail

As the saying goes, you have to send mail to get mail. The beauty of Outlook e-mail is that the messages are so easy to send and respond to that you can essentially carry on conversations. Outlook also makes it just as easy to send a message to one person or to 50, bedeck messages with fancy backgrounds known as *stationery,* insert links to Internet sites, include pictures—even add a distinctive signature. In this chapter you will learn how to create and enhance messages, as well as how to send copies, respond to others, and control how and when e-mail is sent.

Write Messages

Creating an e-mail message can be as simple as dispatching a note or as elaborate as designing a marketing poster. It's wise to get used to creating simple messages before making an art project of one. Without your having to impose any guidelines, however, Outlook is set to create an attractive basic e-mail message.

Create a Message

One click starts a message, and the only field you have to complete is the address of the recipient. Normally, at least three fields are filled in before you send the message:

- **Recipient**   One or more e-mail addresses or names in your Address Book
- **Subject**   Words indicating the contents of the message (used by the Find tool in a search)
- **Message Body**   Whatever you want to say to the recipient

To start a message, with Outlook open and Mail selected in the Navigation pane, click the **New** button on the standard toolbar. The new Message window opens, as shown in Figure 12-1.

Address a Message

Outlook is the lazy person's dream for addressing messages. Of course, the address itself is simple: *username@domain.suffix* (such as ".com"). Once you have entered names in the Contacts workspace, however, you can address your messages with almost no typing. In this chapter we will focus on what happens to the e-mail itself. The following alternatives come into play as soon as you create a new message by clicking **New** on the toolbar.

TYPE THE ADDRESS

This is the most basic addressing technique. As soon as you click **New**, the cursor blinks in the To field on the message.

| To... | |

- For **a single recipient**, type the address.
- For **multiple recipients**, type each address, separating them with semicolons (;) or commas (,).

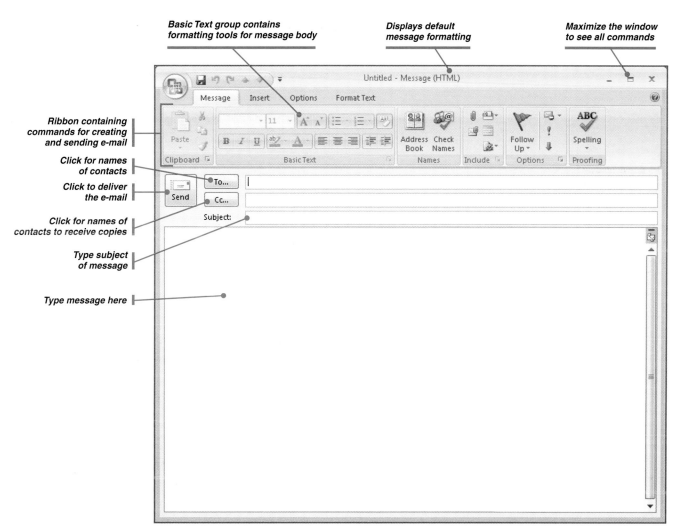

Basic Text group contains formatting tools for message body

Displays default message formatting

Maximize the window to see all commands

Ribbon containing commands for creating and sending e-mail

Click for names of contacts

Click to deliver the e-mail

Click for names of contacts to receive copies

Type subject of message

Type message here

Figure 12-1: *The window for creating a message contains important differences from the one in which you read them.*

SELECT FROM THE ADDRESS BOOK

1. Click **To**. The Select Names dialog box displays your Address Book.

2. Choose one of the following:

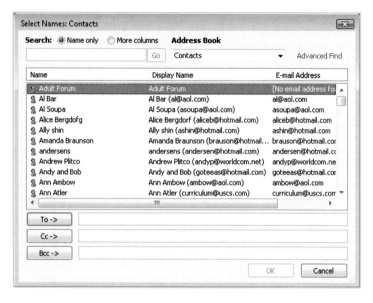

- Type the first few letters of the recipient's name in the Name text box, or select a name from the list box, and double-click it in the list.

- Scroll through the list, and double-click the name you want.

- For multiple names, type ; or , and a space between names or e-mail addresses or hold down **CTRL** while you click all desired names in your address book (Outlook will add the semi-colon), and then click **To**.

- Repeat step 2 as needed until all desired names are listed in the To text box.

3. Click **OK**.

COMPLETE ADDRESSES AUTOMATICALLY

Outlook runs AutoComplete by default. As soon as you type the first letter of a contact's name, Outlook begins searching for matches among names and addresses you've typed in the past.

NOTE

Even if a name appears in your Address Book, the name won't be suggested with AutoComplete unless you have used it to send e-mail.

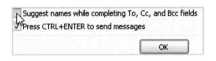

NOTE

You can turn off AutoComplete if you wish: In the initial Outlook window, click **Tools I Options**, and click the **Preferences** tab. Then click the **E-mail Options button**, click **Advanced E-mail Options**, and clear the **Suggest Names While Completing To, Cc, And Bcc Fields** checkbox. Click **OK** three times to close.

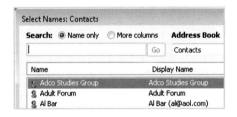

☐ Suggest names while completing To, Cc, and Bcc fields
☑ Press CTRL+ENTER to send messages

[OK]

Select Names: Contacts

Search: ● Name only ○ More columns   **Address Book**

[   ] [Go]   Contacts

Name | Display Name
Adco Studies Group | Adco Studies Group
Adult Forum | Adult Forum
Al Bar | Al Bar (al@aol.com)

1. Begin typing a name or address in the To field in the Message window. The closest name(s) to what you have typed will be displayed in a list.

2. If the name you want appears in the list, press **DOWN ARROW** (if necessary) until the name is highlighted.

3. Press **ENTER** to accept the address. The name displays, a semicolon follows it, and the cursor blinks where the next name would appear.

4. If you wish to add another recipient, begin typing another name (a new set of suggestions will be displayed), and repeat steps 2 and 3 as needed.

5. Press **TAB** to go to the next desired field.

Use a Distribution List

In Contacts you can group your contacts into distribution lists, giving you an even quicker way to add multiple addresses to messages. Use any of the preceding procedures, and enter or select the name of the distribution list as it appears in the Address Book. When you send it, the message will go to everyone on the list.

Add Carbon and Blind Copies

You may never have seen a real carbon copy, but Outlook keeps the concept alive by way of this feature located just below the To field in the new Message window. Persons who receive a message with their e-mail address in the *Cc* (carbon copy) line understand that they are not the primary recipients—they got the message as an FYI (for your information), and all other recipients can see that they got it (see Figure 12-2). A *Bcc* (blind carbon copy) hides addresses entered in that line from anyone else who receives the message.

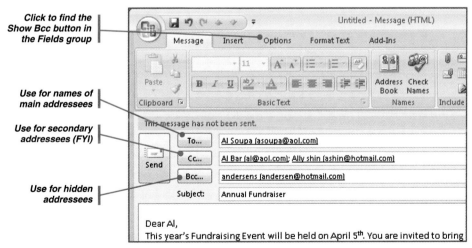

Click to find the Show Bcc button in the Fields group
Use for names of main addressees
Use for secondary addressees (FYI)
Use for hidden addressees

Figure 12-2: *The way a message is delivered suggests different roles for the various recipients.*

INCLUDE OR REMOVE BCC ON NEW MESSAGES

1. In the Message window, click the **Options** tab.

2. In the Fields group, click **Show Bcc** to toggle the Bcc field on and off.

ADDRESS THE COPIES

Type addresses in the Cc and Bcc fields completely or with the aid of AutoComplete. You can also use the Address Book: click **Cc** or **Bcc** in the Message window, scroll through the names, and double-click the name(s) in the Address Book you want to be copied.

Edit a Message

E-mail can be created in any of three formats and has the additional option of using the powerful formatting capability of Microsoft Word for composing messages. Outlook handles all three formats quite easily, but sometimes you need to consider your recipients' computer resources and Internet connections:

- **HTML** (Hypertext Markup Language), the default format, lets you freely use design elements, such as colors, pictures, links, animations, sound, and movies (though good taste and the need to control the size of the message file might suggest a little discretion).

- **Plain Text** format lies at the other extreme, eliminating embellishments so that any computer can manage the message.

- **Rich Text Format** (RTF) takes the middle ground, providing font choices—including color, boldface, italics, and underlining—basic paragraph layouts, and bullets.

With Outlook, you can edit messages you create as well as those you receive. Regardless of which of the three formats you choose, some editing processes are always available. Using HTML or Rich Text Format provides a wide range of options for enhancing the appearance of a message. Finally, you can also create the message in another program and copy and paste it into a message body. HTML will preserve the formatting exactly, and Rich Text Format will come close.

NOTE

The Outlook Message window uses most of the selection techniques and formatting tools that are available in Microsoft Word 2007. If you are in doubt of how to do an editing task in an Outlook message, see Chapter 3 for a rundown on formatting.

SELECT A MESSAGE FORMAT

The message format displays in the title bar of the new Message window. You can either set a format for an individual message, or you can set a default for all message formats.

Figure 12-3: You can create personal message designs that distinguish you as the sender.

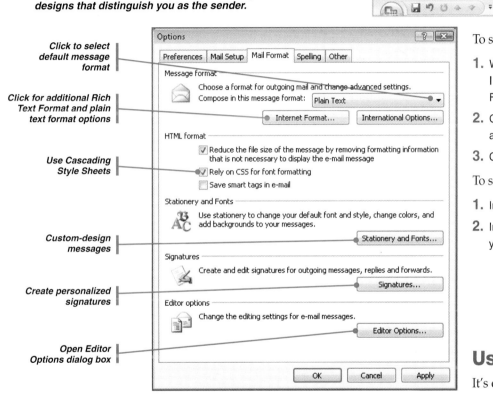

Click to select default message format

Click for additional Rich Text Format and plain text format options

Use Cascading Style Sheets

Custom-design messages

Create personalized signatures

Open Editor Options dialog box

To set a default format for all e-mail:

1. With Outlook open (not in a message), click **Tools I Options**, and click the **Mail Format** tab, shown in Figure 12-3.

2. Click the **Compose In This Message Format** down arrow, and select one of the choices.

3. Click **OK** to close the Options dialog box.

To set formatting for an individual message:

1. In the Message window, click the **Options** tab.

2. In the Format group, click the formatting button you want.

Use Stationery

It's easy to choose stationery for a message. You can pick a different type of stationery for every new message or set a default style for all messages (until you change it).

SET A DEFAULT STATIONERY THEME

You can set a default for your stationery that will be used each time you write a new e-mail. You can also select a theme for your stationary and still have your own unique fonts. You can vary fonts as well, either for new e-mails or for

TIP

You can also edit received messages. This can be handy when printing them. You might want to print only the final comment and eliminate the original message text in exchanges where participants replied a number of times.

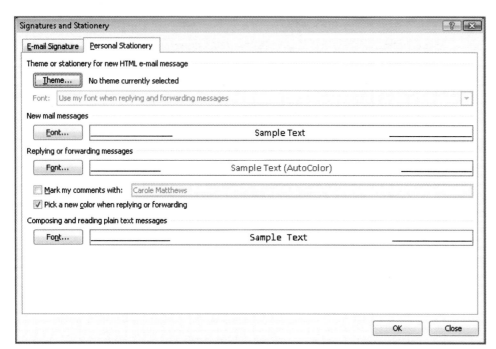

Figure 12-4: *You can design custom stationery for your e-mail with your own theme, fonts, and colored replies and forwards.*

those you reply to or forward. To set a default stationery:

1. Click **Tools | Options**, and click the **Mail Format** tab.

2. Make sure that **HTML** has been selected as the message format.

3. Click the **Stationery And Fonts** button. Click the **Personal Stationery** tab to open the dialog box shown in Figure 12-4. Select from these choices:

   ● Click the **Theme** button, and under Choose A Theme, click the theme you want, and click **OK**. When you choose a theme, the fonts will be automatically defined for you, and those buttons will become unavailable or grayed.

   ● If, after choosing a theme, you want to use another font, click the **Font** down arrow, and click either **Always Use My Fonts** or **Use My Font When Replying Or Forwarding Messages**. This will enable you to select a font for all new messages or for replying to and forwarding e-mails.

   ● If you want to use your fonts, click the appropriate **Font** button, and select the font, font style, size, and color you want.

   ● If you want to insert your name, click the **Mark My Comments With** checkbox. Type over the default text, if desired.

   ● If you want your replies or forwards to be in a different color, click **Pick A New Color When Replying Or Forwarding**.

4. Click **OK** twice to close the Options dialog box.

APPLY STATIONERY TO A SINGLE MESSAGE

1. Click the **Insert** tab in the Outlook new Message window, and click the **Signature** button in the Include group. Click **Signatures** on the menu. The Signature And Stationery dialog box appears.

2. Click the Personal Stationery tab.

3. Change the theme and fonts, as described in "Set a Default Stationery Theme."

4. Click **OK**.

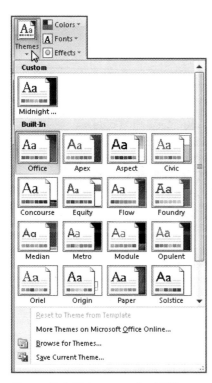

Figure 12-5: *Using a standard Office theme allows you to coordinate your e-mail and regular Word correspondence.*

NOTE

In the Message window, when you click the **Themes** button in the Themes group on the Options tab, you will see additional options at the bottom of the gallery of theme thumbnails. You can search for additional themes online by clicking **More Themes On Microsoft Office Online** or search for your own custom theme by clicking **Browse For Themes**. If you alter a standard theme with new colors, fonts, or effects, you can save these changes as a custom theme to use again later by clicking **Save Current Theme**.

USE A STANDARD MICROSOFT OFFICE THEME

You can use a standard Microsoft Office theme in your e-mail that differs from the Outlook themes used for stationery. You might use these to coordinate your regular Word correspondence with your e-mail, thus creating a consistent and professional look. These themes are easy to use and available in your new Message window.

1. In the new Message window, click the **Options** tab if it is not already selected.

2. In the Themes group, if you can't see Colors, Fonts, and Effects, click **Themes**. Then, in any case, click the **Themes** down arrow, and click the standard theme you'd like to use for your e-mail, as shown in Figure 12-5:

   ● Click **Colors** and click a combination of colors to change the color scheme.

   ● Click **Fonts** and click a font style to change the fonts used.

   ● Click **Effect** and click an effect to change the special effects of the graphics.

3. Type your new message and send it.

REMOVE STATIONERY

To remove stationery from a single message: In Outlook, click **Actions | New Mail Message Using**, and select **HTML (No Stationery)**.

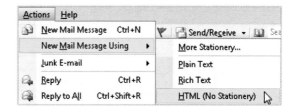

To stop having standard stationery as a default:

1. Click **Tools | Options**, and click the **Mail Format** tab.

2. Click the **Stationery And Fonts** button.

3. On the Personal Stationery tab, click **Theme** and click **(No Theme)** at the top of the theme list.

4. Click **OK** three times.

INCLUDING HYPERLINKS

You can add hyperlinks (whether links to an Internet site, to other locations in the current document, or to other documents) to your e-mail by typing them into the message body or by copying and pasting them. Outlook creates a live link, which it turns into blue, underlined text when you type or paste any kind of Internet protocol (http://, mailto:, www.*something.com*:), regardless what mail format you use. Only HTML, however, will make a live link out of an e-mail address: *something@ something .com*. Also, only in HTML can you substitute different text for the actual Uniform Resource Locator (URL) or e-mail address and still retain the link—by dragging to select the hyperlink and typing something different. In addition to typing the hyperlink address, you can also click the **Insert** tab and click **Hyperlink** in the Links group. Then find the location of the link—in an existing file or Web page, a place in a document, a new document, or an e-mail address—and click **OK**.

Attach Files

Sometimes you will want to send or receive a message that is accompanied by other files: pictures, word-processed documents, sound, or movie files. Creating attachments is like clipping newspaper stories and baby pictures to a letter. If you are editing or otherwise working on the item you want to attach, make sure that you save the latest version before you proceed. After that, click **New** to open the new Message window, and use one of the following attachment procedures.

DRAG A FILE TO A MESSAGE

Find the file to be attached by using My Computer or Windows Explorer, and drag it to the message.

INSERT A FILE

When you attach a file to an e-mail message, it can either be attached as a file or entered as text into the body of the message. In some cases, it may be attached as a hyperlink. The attached file and its commands are identified with a paper clip icon.

1. To display the Insert File dialog box:

- Click the **Insert** tab, and then click **Attach File** in the Include group.

  –Or–

- In the Message tab, click the **Attach File** icon in the Include group.

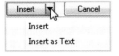

2. The Insert File dialog box appears. Find and select the file to be attached. Then:

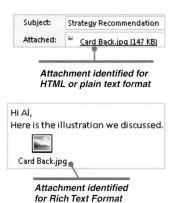

**Attachment identified for
HTML or plain text format**

Hi Al,
Here is the illustration we discussed.

Card Back.jpg

**Attachment identified
for Rich Text Format**

- Click **Insert** to insert the file as an attachment. If the e-mail format is HTML or plain text, it will be attached in a field labeled "Attached" beneath the Subject field. If the format is Rich Text Format, the file attachment will be in the body of the message.

- Click the **Insert** down arrow, and choose between inserting the file as an attachment and inserting it as text in the body of the message. If you choose **Insert As Text**, the file is entered as text in the message. The file content of certain file types, such as .txt, .doc, and .eml, and the source code of others, such as HTML or HTA (HTML Application), will become part of the message. Everything else—pictures, sound, and movie—will generate nonsense characters in the message body.

- Click **Insert As Hyperlink** to insert the selected file as a hyperlink. (This option is not always available from the Attach File command.)

3. Complete and send the e-mail message.

EMBED A PICTURE INTO A MESSAGE

Though any kind of file you save on your computer or on a disk can be sent by following the previous steps, you have the added option of placing pictures (.gif, .jpg, .bmp, .tif, and so on) right into the message body.

1. Click in the message body to set the insertion point.

2. Click the **Insert** tab, and click **Picture** in the Illustrations group. The Insert Picture dialog box appears, as shown in Figure 12-6.

3. Find the picture file you want, and click **Insert**.

Figure 12-6: You can insert a picture or a link to it using the Insert Picture dialog box.

From the submenu:

- Click **Insert** to embed the picture in the message. You can then drag it to size it correctly for your message or right-click to display the Format Picture dialog box and edit the photo.

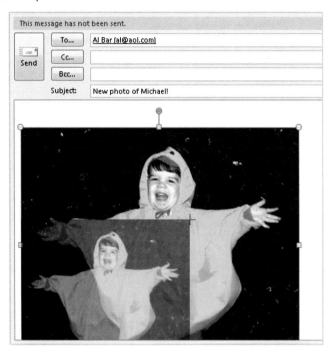

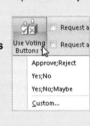

NOTE

If you link a picture to your message rather than embed it, you will need to either send the picture with the document or store the picture in a shared network folder available to the message recipient. Otherwise, your e-mail will be seen with a red X where the photo should be.

TIP

If you are on a Microsoft Exchange Server network, you can even insert voting options that the recipient has only to click for a response. To do this, create a message, click the **Options** tab, and click the **Use Voting Buttons** down arrow in the Tracking group. Select the kind of reply you need or click **Custom** to type new options separated by semicolons (;) in the Use Voting Buttons text box.

- Click **Link To File** to send a link to where the file is stored. This reduces the size of the message.

- Click **Insert And Link** to both embed the photo and send a link to its location.

- Click **Show Previous Versions** to list the previous versions of the files so that you can select the version you want to attach.

4. Complete and send the e-mail message.

Sign Messages

You can create closings, or signatures, for your e-mail messages. Outlook signatures can contain pictures and text along with your name. You can create

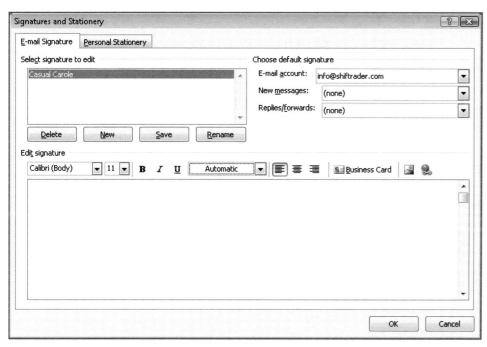

Figure 12-7: *You can create one or more signatures with custom-designed characteristics that will be included in the bottom of your e-mail.*

signatures in different styles for the different kinds of messages you write: friendly, formal, or business.

CREATE A SIGNATURE

With Outlook open:

1. Click **Tools I Options**. The Options dialog box appears. Click the **Mail Format** tab.

2. Click **Signatures** in the Signatures panel, and then click **New**.

3. Type a name for your signature, and click **OK**. The Signatures And Stationery dialog box appears and the E-mail Signature tab is selected, as shown in Figure 12-7.

4. In the Edit Signature text box, type (or paste from another document) any text you want to include in your closing, including your name.

5. To apply formatting, select the text and click any of the formatting buttons in the toolbar. You can even insert a business card, picture, or hyperlink. Use the steps in Chapter 3 that discussed formatting in Word, since Outlook uses the same techniques. Plain text messages, by definition, cannot be formatted.

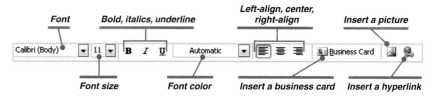

6. Click **OK** twice to close the dialog boxes.

QUICKSTEPS

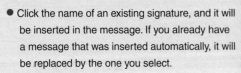
Use Digital Signatures

A *digital signature* certifies that everything contained in the message—documents, forms, computer code, PowerPoint presentations, whatever—originated with the sender. Computer programmers and people engaged in e-commerce use them a lot. To embed a formal digital signature, you need to acquire a *digital certificate*, which is like a license, from a certificate authority, such as VeriSign, Inc (http://www.verisign.com).

Alternatively, you can create your own digital signature, although it is not administered by a certificate authority. A self-signed certificate is considered unauthenticated and will generate a security warning if the recipient has his or her security set at a high level.

ACQUIRE A DIGITAL CERTIFICATE

If you do not already have a digital certificate, Outlook can lead you to a Web site where you can find a commercial certification authority to issue one. Make sure you are online before you begin.

1. Click **Tools | Trust Center**. The Trust Center dialog box appears. Click **E-mail Security**.

2. Under Digital IDs (Certificates), click **Get A Digital ID**.

3. Follow the instructions on the Digital ID Web page to obtain a certificate.

IMPORT OR EXPORT A DIGITAL ID

1. Click **Tools | Trust Center**. The Trust Center dialog box appears. Click **E-mail Security**.

2. Under Digital IDs (Certificates), click **Import/Export**. The Import/Export Digital ID dialog box appears.

3. Click **Import Existing Digital ID From A File** to import a digital ID, or click **Export Your Digital ID To A File** to export your own digital ID.

4. Fill in the requested information, and click **OK**.

ADD A DIGITAL SIGNATURE TO MESSAGES

1. In the initial Outlook window, click **Tools | Trust Center**. The Trust Center dialog box appears.

2. Click the **E-mail Security** option.

3. Under Encrypted E-mail, click the **Add Digital Signature To Outgoing Messages** checkbox.

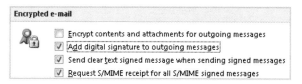

4. To make sure that recipients can read the message if they don't have Secure/ Multipurpose Internet Mail Extensions (S/MIME) security, click the **Send Clear Text Signed Message When Sending Signed Messages** checkbox.

5. To receive a message confirming that your message got to the recipient, click the **Request S/MIME Receipt For All S/MIME Signed Messages** checkbox.

6. Click **OK**.

Check Spelling

For all the hip abbreviations that have emerged with e-mail and instant messaging, unintentional spelling errors still can be a problem. You can have Outlook check the spelling of your message when you finish, or you can have it automatically check messages before you send them.

CHECK A MESSAGE

Create a message and keep the cursor in the body when you are finished. Any spelling errors will be automatically flagged for you with a red wavy line. You will have these options:

Can you stilb make it?
Let me knw.

- Right-click the flagged word, and if a correct spelling is suggested, click it.

- If you do not see the correct spelling, then the flagged word cannot be found in the dictionary. Either look it up in a reference and type it in, or type another spelling to see if it is correct.

- If you know the flagged word is correct and you want to add it to the dictionary, use the Spelling And Grammar dialog box. See "Add a Word to the Dictionary," next.

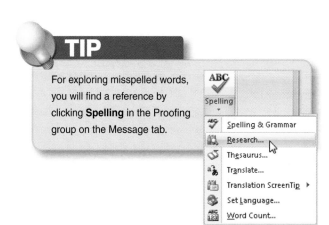

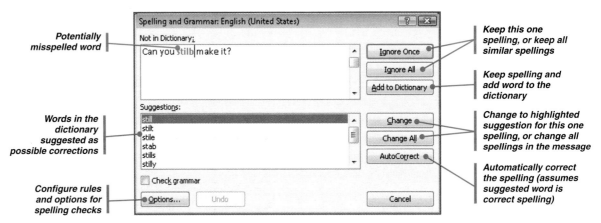

Potentially misspelled word — Can you stilb make it?

Keep this one spelling, or keep all similar spellings — Ignore Once / Ignore All

Keep spelling and add word to the dictionary — Add to Dictionary

Words in the dictionary suggested as possible corrections — still, stilt, stile, stab, stills, stilly

Change to highlighted suggestion for this one spelling, or change all spellings in the message — Change / Change All

Automatically correct the spelling (assumes suggested word is correct spelling) — AutoCorrect

Configure rules and options for spelling checks — Options... / Undo / Cancel

Figure 12-8: The default spelling dictionary contains everyday words rather than technical or scientific terms. You can add special words to it.

ADD A WORD TO THE DICTIONARY

To add a flagged word to the dictionary so that it will not continue to be flagged as a potential misspelling:

1. Highlight the flagged word, and click **Spelling** in the Proofing group of the Message tab. Click **Spelling & Grammar**. The Spelling And Grammar dialog box will appear, as seen in Figure 12-8.

2. Click Add To Dictionary.

3. Click Close.

CHECK MESSAGES BEFORE SENDING

To automatically check spelling in messages before sending them:

1. With Outlook open, click **Tools | Options**, and click the **Spelling** tab.

2. Click **Always Check Spelling Before Sending**, and click **OK**.

TIP

The personal, or custom, dictionary can get long, and misspellings can be added accidentally. To edit the dictionary from Outlook, click **Tools | Options**, and click the **Spelling** tab. Click **Spelling And AutoCorrection**. In the Editor Options dialog box, click **Custom Dictionaries**. In the Custom Dictionaries dialog box, click **Edit Word List**. Remove a word by clicking it, pressing **DELETE** (to fix it, type the correct spelling instead), and then clicking **OK**.

CUSTOM.DIC

Word(s):

Dictionary:
Al
Ann
Bartlett
Marty
Matthews
Morrow

Add / Delete / Delete all

OK / Cancel

Send Messages

No extra postage, no trip to the post office, no running out of envelopes. What could be better? Once a message is ready to go, you can just click a button. Outlook provides features that let you exercise more control over the process than you could ever get from the postal service, or "snail" mail.

Make sure that your message is complete and ready to send, and then click **Send** on the message toolbar.

When you have more than one account, your Message window contains an Account button that is not available otherwise. To send a message from a particular account:

Click **Accounts** beneath the Send button on the Message window, select an account, and click **Send**.

Reply to Messages

When you receive a message that you want to answer, you have three ways to initiate a reply:

- Open the message and click **Reply** in the Respond group on the Message tab.

  –Or–

- Right-click the message in the folder pane, and select **Reply** from the context menu.

  –Or–

- Click the message in the folder pane, and click **Reply** on the standard toolbar.

Whichever way you use, a reply Message window opens, as illustrated in Figure 12-9. The message will be formatted using the same format the sender used, the subject will be "Re:" plus the original subject in the Subject line. By default, the pointer blinks in the message body above the original message and sender's address (see also "Change the Reply Layout" later in this chapter). Treat it like a new Message window: type a message, add attachments or links, and click **Send**.

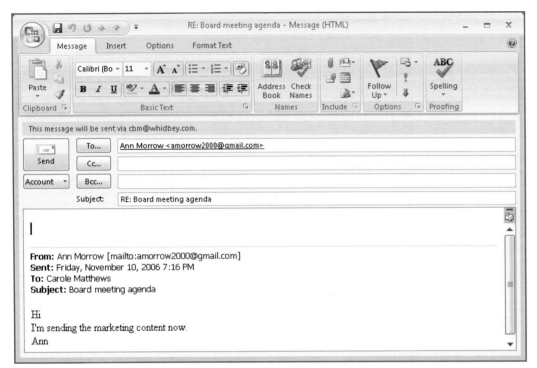

Figure 12-9: *The Reply window uses the sender's message format and subject to make the e-mail conversation easy to track and respond to.*

REPLY TO ALL RECIPIENTS

If the To field in the message contains several recipients, all of whom should read your reply, Outlook makes it simple. Using any of the three ways just listed, select **Reply To All**. The reply Message window will list all original recipients in the To and Cc fields. Send the message as usual.

Reply to All

CHANGE THE REPLY LAYOUT

You can select from five different ways to incorporate the original message. Also, if you'd rather just insert your responses into the original text, Outlook lets you decide how to identify your remarks.

1. With Outlook open, click **Tools | Options**, and, at the top of the Preferences tab, click the **E-mail Options** button.

2. Click the **When Replying To A Message** down arrow, and select how you want the original message included.

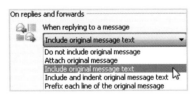

3. Click the **Mark My Comments With** checkbox, and type the label you want.

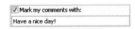

4. Click **OK** twice.

SET AUTOMATIC REPLY

Organizations that use Microsoft Exchange Server for e-mail can create an automatic reply during times when you are not available to answer messages. Each sender will receive only one notification, no matter how many messages he or she sends before you return. This procedure explains how to set up the Out Of Office Assistant with Exchange 2007. If you are using an earlier version of Exchange Server, there is a slightly different set of options.

1. With Outlook open, click **Tools | Out Of Office Assistant**. (If this command is not on your Tools menu, you are not using an Exchange account.)

2. Click **Send Out Of Office Auto-Replies**.

3. If useful, click **Only Send During This Time Range**, and click the **Start Time** and **End Time** down arrows for the date and times you'll be gone.

4. In the Auto Reply Only Once panel, type the message you want in your reply, both for inside and outside your organization.

5. To turn it off, click **Tools | Out Of Office Assistant | Do Not Send Out Of Office Auto-Replies**.

6. Click **OK** to close the assistant.

Forward Messages

When you forward a message, you send an incoming message to someone else. You can send messages to new recipients, using the same techniques as with the Reply feature.

When you receive a message that you want to forward to someone else, use one of these techniques:

- Open the message and click **Forward** in the Respond group on the Message tab.

  –Or–

- Right-click the message in the Folder pane, and select **Forward** from the context menu.

  –Or–

- Click the message in the Folder pane, and click **Forward** on the standard toolbar.

A forward Message window opens, with the cursor blinking in the To field and a space above the original message for you to type your own. Once the

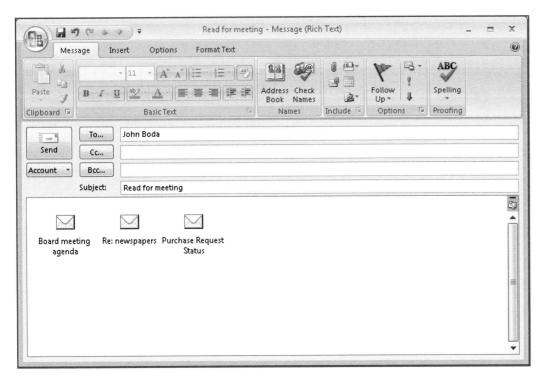

forward Message window opens, the simplest action is to enter the recipient(s) address(es), insert attachments as needed, and send as usual.

FORWARD MULTIPLE MESSAGES

Rather than forward a bunch of messages one by one, you can bundle them and forward them in one message.

1. Press **CTRL** while you click each message in the message list that you want to forward.

2. Right-click one of the messages in the group, and click **Forward Items**. A new mail message opens with the messages included as attachments, as seen in Figure 12-10. You may also see the attachments in the Attached box rather than in the message area.

3. Complete the message and send as usual.

Figure 12-10: *You can group and forward e-mails as attachments.*

Set Message Priority

If your recipient gets a lot of messages, you might want to identify your message as important so that it will stand out in his or her Inbox. Outlook includes a red exclamation point in the message list to call attention to messages with high importance and a blue down arrow to indicate messages with low importance. In the Message window, you flag your e-mail messages with the appropriate flag.

1. Create a message. In the Options group on the Message tab, select one of these options:

   • Click **High Importance** to insert a red exclamation point to indicate high importance.

   • Click **Low Importance** to insert a blue down arrow to indicate low importance.

2. Send the message as usual.

SENDING MESSAGES

You can fire off your messages now or later or on a schedule.

SEND MESSAGES MANUALLY

By default, as long as you are connected to the Internet, clicking **Send** in the Message window sends the completed message. You can turn this off so that clicking **Send** in the Message window only puts the message in the Outbox folder. You must then additionally click **Send/ Receive** in the Outlook standard toolbar to send all the messages in the Outbox folder.

TURN OFF AUTO-SEND

To prevent a message from being automatically sent unless you click **Send** in the Message window:

1. Click **Tools | Options**, and click the **Mail Setup** tab.

2. Under Send/Receive, clear the **Send Immediately When Connected** checkbox.

3. Click **Send/Receive**. Under Settings For Group "All Accounts," clear the **Schedule An Automatic Send/Receive Every** checkbox. Also clear the **Perform An Automatic Send/Receive When Exiting** checkbox.

4. Click **Close** and then click **OK**.

SEND MESSAGES AT A CERTAIN TIME

1. Create the message and click the **Options** tab.

2. Click the Delay Delivery button in the More Options group. The Message Options dialog box appears. Delay Delivery

3. Under Delivery Options, click **Do Not Deliver Before**.

Continued . . .

Request Receipts

Anyone who has sent an important message and has not heard a peep from the recipient can appreciate receipts. When the addressee receives or reads the message, you are notified. You can request receipts for all your messages or on a message-by-message basis.

OBTAIN RECEIPTS FOR ALL MESSAGES

1. Click **Tools | Options**, and click the **E-mail Options** button.

2. In the E-mail Options dialog box, click the **Tracking Options** button.

3. On the lower half of the dialog box, click **Read Receipt**, **Delivery Receipt**, or both.

4. If you like, choose an option for responding to other senders' requests for a receipt— **Always Send A Response**, **Never Send A Response**, or **Ask Me Before Sending A Response** (the default).

5. Click **OK** three times.

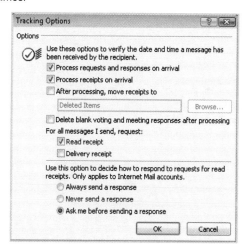

OBTAIN A SINGLE RECEIPT

1. Create a message and click the **Options** tab in the Message window.

2. In the Tracking group, click **Request A Delivery Receipt**, **Request A Read Receipt**, or both. (If you have set these options for all mail, this message will reflect those settings.)

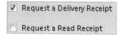

3. Click **Close**.

⏱ QUICKSTEPS

SENDING MESSAGES *(Continued)*

4. Click the date and time down arrows, and select a day and time.

5. Click **Expires After** and click the date and time down arrows to set the end time.

Delivery options

- ☐ Have replies sent to: [   ]
- ☑ Do not deliver before: [11/17/2006 ▼] [2:00 AM ▼]
- ☑ Expires after: [11/30/2006 ▼] [5:00 PM ▼]

6. Click **Close**.

SAVE A SENT MESSAGE

You can select the folder within which a sent message will be saved.

1. On the Message window, on the Options tab in the More Options group, click **Save Sent Item**.

   Save Sent Item · | Delay Delivery | Direct Replies To

   - 📋 Other Folder...
   - ✓ Use Default Folder
   - Do Not Save

2. In the submenu, select whether you want to save the message to the default folder, to another folder (which you find and select in the Select Folder dialog box), or to not save the message at all.

Delay Delivery with a Rule

You can create a rule to control when messages leave your system after you click **Send**.

1. With Outlook open, click **Tools | Rules And Alerts**.

2. If you are told that messages sent and received with HTTP (such as Hotmail, Gmail, and Yahoo) cannot be filtered using Rules And Alerts, click **OK**.

3. In the Rules And Alerts dialog box, click **New Rule**.

4. In the Rules Wizard, under Start From A Blank Rule, click **Check Messages After Sending**, and click **Next**.

5. Click to select any desired conditions that limit which messages the rule applies to, and then click the link in the description panel (as you can see in Figure 12-11), which may display a dialog box to specify the exact criteria. Click **OK** and click **Next**.

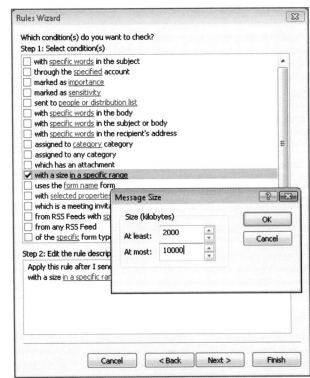

Figure 12-11: Outlook's rule-making feature has a large number of conditions that you can organize into rules.

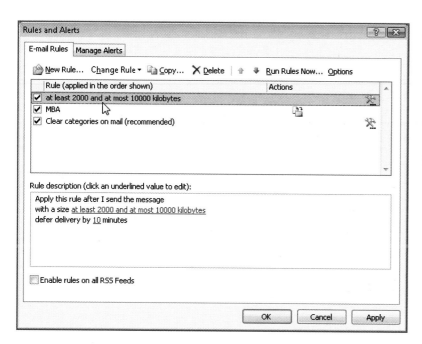

Figure 12-12: *The Rules And Alerts dialog box, opened from the Tools menu, provides for the creation and management of rules.*

6. Under Select Action(s), click **Defer Delivery By A** *number* **Of Minutes**.

7. In the description box, click the link for *a number of* minutes, and in the Deferred Delivery dialog box, type the total minutes (up to 120) that you want messages delayed, click **OK**, and click **Next**.

8. Click any exceptions, specify them in the description panel, click **OK** if necessary, and click **Next**.

9. Type a name for the rule, and click **Finish**. You are returned to the Rules And Alerts dialog box, which will now show your new rule, as shown in Figure 12-12.

Chapter 13

Scheduling and the Calendar

The Calendar is second only to mail in its importance in Outlook. The Calendar works closely with contacts and tasks to coordinate the use of your time and your interactions with others. The Calendar lets you schedule appointments and meetings, establish recurring activities, and tailor your calendar to your area, region, and workdays.

In this chapter you will see how to use and customize the Calendar, schedule and manage appointments, and schedule and track meetings and resources.

Use the Calendar

The Calendar has a number of unique items in its Outlook window, as seen in Figure 13-1:

- Buttons allow you to quickly switch the view of your Calendar between daily, weekly, and monthly views, as well as to show or hide details of your activities.

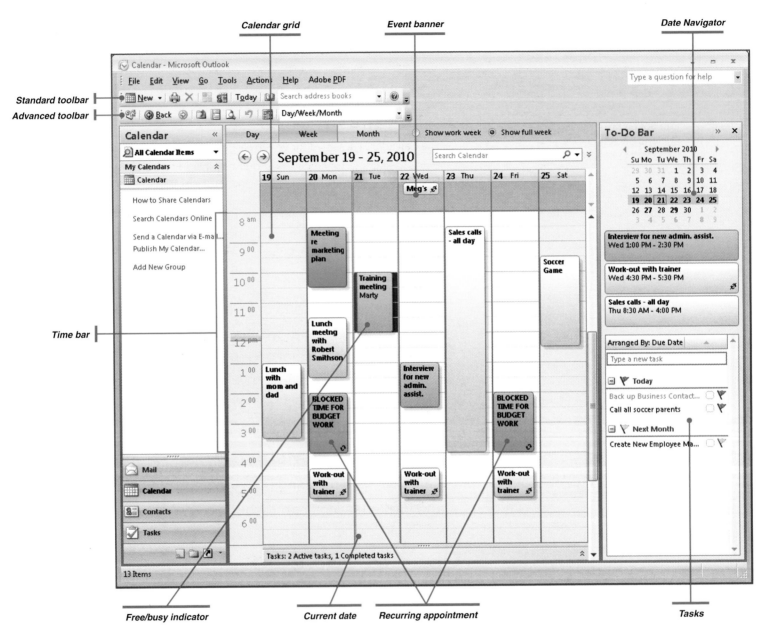

Figure 13-1: The Calendar provides an easy way to track meetings, appointments, and due dates.

ACTIVITY	DESCRIPTION	ICON
Appointments	Appointments only involve you.	
Meetings	Meetings happen at a scheduled time, just like an appointment. The difference is that other people are involved. You invite others via e-mail, and the Meeting displays in your Calendar with the location and meeting organizer's name.	
Events	Events last all day long. Events that you put on your Calendar do not block out time like a meeting or an appointment, so you can have other entries for that day display on your Calendar.	
Tasks	Tasks are activities that do not need time scheduled for them and involve only you. Your tasks will display in the Day and Week views of your Calendar, as well as on your To-Do Bar.	

Table 13-1: Common Calendar Activities

NOTE

When your Calendar is in Day or Week view, the Tasks area appears both under the To-Do Bar and underneath the Calendar.

- Forward and Back buttons let you move quickly to the next month, week, or day.
- The To-Do Bar displays the Date Navigator, an Appointments section, your Task list, and the Task Input panel. In Outlook 2007, your Daily Task list displays in the Day and Week views of the Calendar as well.

Explore the Calendar

The Calendar is designed for you to easily keep track of appointments, meetings, events, due dates, anniversaries, birthdays, and any other date-related happenings. You can schedule several different types of activities, as shown on Table 13-1.

To open your Calendar, start Outlook in one of the ways described in Chapter 1. Then:

1. Click **Calendar** in the Navigation pane.

   –Or–

   Press **CTRL-2** on the keyboard

2. Once the Calendar is open, you can start entering your activities. Double-click in any date in the Calendar. A new Appointment window will open, as shown in Figure 13-2. See "Create Appointments" later in this chapter for more information.

3. Click **Close** to close the Appointment window.

4. Double-click in the Tasks area below the To-Do Bar to open a Task window. In Outlook, a task involves only you, but it does not have a set block of time.

5. Click **Close** to close the Task window.

6. Double-click a date in the Date Navigator section of the To-Do Bar. If the Calendar is in either Day or Month view, the date you click will be displayed by itself in your center Calendar section and the view is changed from Month view to Day view. If the Calendar is in Week view, the week in which you've chosen the date displays in the center Calendar section.

Customize the Calendar

As you have seen with the rest of Outlook, there are many ways you can customize the Calendar to meet your needs. You can change the way the Calendar displays time intervals, the font size and face, the background color, and any additional options as you require.

QUICKSTEPS

NAVIGATING THE CALENDAR

The Date Navigator, which by default is in the upper-right corner of the Calendar window in the To-Do Bar, allows you to pick any date from April 1, 1601, to August 31, 4500. To cover this almost 2,900-year span, Outlook provides several efficient tools:

To-Do Bar » X

◄   September 2010   ►
Su Mo Tu We Th Fr Sa
29 30 31 1 2 3 4
5 6 7 8 9 10 11
12 13 14 15 16 17 18
19 20 21 22 23 24 25
26 27 28 29 30 1 2
3 4 5 6 7 8 9

- **Display a day** by clicking it in the Date Navigator, and then clicking the **Day** or **Month** button. Or, from anywhere in Outlook, click **Calendar** on the Navigation pane.

- **Display a day with appointments** by clicking a boldface day in the Date Navigator.

- **Display several days** by holding down **CTRL** while clicking the days.

- **Display a week** by clicking to the left of the first day of the week.

- **Display several weeks** by holding down **CTRL** while clicking to the left of the weeks.

- **Display a month** by dragging across the weeks of the month.

- **Change the month from one to the next** by clicking the left or right arrow in the month bar.

- **Scroll through a list of months** by dragging the heading up or down for an individual month.

- **Directly display any date** by clicking the **Go** menu and clicking **Go To Date** or pressing **CTRL-G**.

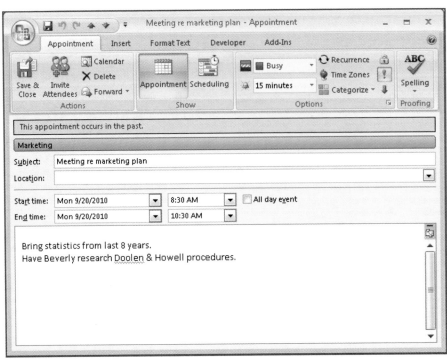

Figure 13-2: An appointment or an all-day event can be any date-related activity, such as due dates or birthdays.

CHANGE THE TIME SCALES

The default display of time intervals, or *scales*, on your Calendar grid is 30 minutes. If you want to change these scales to reflect another time interval:

1. In the Calendar grid, right-click any blank area.

2. Click **Other Settings**.

3. Click the **Time Scale** down arrow to display a list of choices.

4. Click the scale you want to show in the Calendar.

5. Click **OK** to close the dialog box.

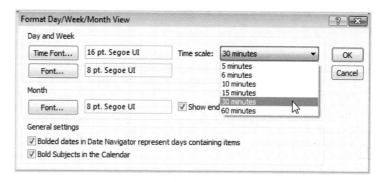

CHANGE THE FONT FACE AND SIZE

You can change the font in both your Calendar and your Daily Task list.

1. Right-click any blank area in the Calendar grid.

2. Click **Other Settings**.

3. Click **Time Font** to change the font in your Daily Task list in the Day and Week views.

   –Or–

   Click **Font** under Day and Week to change the font as it displays in the Day and Week views.

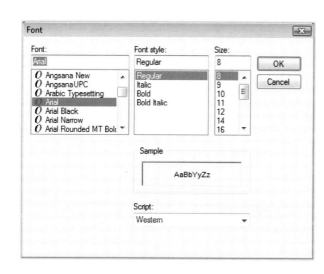

4. Choose **Font** to change the font face.

5. Choose **Font Style** to have the font appear as bold, italic, or bold italic, depending on the font you have chosen in step 4.

6. Click **Size** to choose a size from the drop-down box, or type another font size in the Size field.

7. Click **OK** to close the Font dialog box and save your choices.

8. Click **Font** under Month, and follow steps 4–7.

9. Click **OK** to close the Format Day/Week/Month dialog box.

SET ADDITIONAL SETTINGS

From the Other Settings dialog box, you can tell the Calendar how to display items in your Calendar and Date Navigators.

1. Under General Settings, click **Bolded Dates In Date Navigator** to have dates with activities display in bold type on the Date Navigator.

13

2. Click **Bold Subjects In The Calendar** to have the headings or subjects of your activities appear in bold type in your Calendar grid.

3. Click **OK** to close the dialog box.

CUSTOMIZE WITH THE VIEW MENU

The View menu includes several options that are available on the standard or advanced toolbars, and those options will be discussed with their respective sections. Some of the options are also available when you display a menu by right-clicking in a blank area of the Calendar grid, as discussed previously.

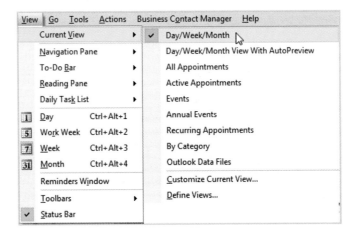

1. Click the **View** menu.

2. Click **Current View** to display the options available:

- **Day/Week/Month** is the default view. Each view has its own button on the Calendar grid.

- **Day/Week/Month View With AutoPreview** displays detailed information about each appointment in Day view.

- **All Appointments** displays all the appointments you have set on this Calendar, both past and present.

- **Active Appointments** lists all current and future appointments.

- **Events** lists all events you have scheduled.

- **Annual Events** and **Recurring Appointments** list only those events that happen either annually or recur more than one time.

- **Category** lists all of your events and appointments by the category you have assigned. Those activities without a category are listed first.

- **Outlook Data Files** lists all of the data files you have created in Outlook if you use a Microsoft Exchange Server account. Exchange Server accounts are used primarily in a business, rather than in a home or personal setting.

USE THE STANDARD AND ADVANCED TOOLBARS

BUTTON	TOOLBAR	VIEW WHERE AVAILABLE	DESCRIPTION
Today	Standard	Day/Week/Month. Day/Week/Month with AutoPreview.	This button places your cursor on today's date.
Categorize	Standard	All list views, such as All Appointments. In Day/Week/Month views, this button is only available when an activity is selected.	This button allows you to assign a color category to an activity you have scheduled.
Group By Box	Advanced	All list views, such as All Appointments or Events.	This button allows you to filter your list by a specific column header.
Field Chooser	Advanced	All list views.	This button allows you to customize your lists. See the "Using Field Chooser" QuickSteps later in this chapter.
AutoPreview	Advanced	All list views.	This button turns on the AutoPreview feature in list views that displays the notes and other information you have entered into an activity.

Table 13-2: Available Buttons on the Standard and Advanced Toolbars

Both the standard and advanced toolbars have several buttons that are unique to the Outlook Calendar. In the standard toolbar, only one button, the View Group Schedules button, is available all the time. This button allows you to view the combined schedules of several people, as well as other resources from a public folder. Group scheduling requires a Microsoft Exchange 2000 or later account. See the "Creating a Group Schedule" QuickSteps later in this chapter.

The two buttons that are available all the time on the advanced toolbar are the Reading pane and the Current View buttons.

- Click **Reading Pane** and an activity in any view to display information about that activity in the Reading pane at the bottom of the Calendar grid.

- Click the **Current View** button to change the Calendar view.

- Buttons on the standard and advanced toolbars that are used by the Calendar in various views are shown in Table 13-2.

NOTE

Columns in Calendar views are also called *fields*.

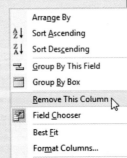

QUICKSTEPS

USING FIELD CHOOSER

The Field Chooser allows you to customize your list views, such as All Appointments or Events.

1. In any list view, on the advanced toolbar, click **Field Chooser**.

2. The Field Chooser dialog box appears.

3. Click the **Frequently-Used Fields** down arrow to display a list of other field choices.

4. Drag the column header you have chosen to a place on your list.

5. Click **Close** to close the Field Chooser dialog box.

You can remove columns from your list views as well.

1. Right-click the column header you want to remove.

2. On the menu that appears, click **Remove This Column**. The column is removed from your list.

The column header will appear on the Field Chooser list. If you want to put it back on your list, follow the first set of steps (1–5) in this QuickSteps.

Customize Calendar Views

As with mail and contacts, you can create customized views, either by modifying an existing view or by creating a new one. The Day, Week, and Month views have fewer choices than the various list views.

MODIFY A DAY, WEEK, OR MONTH VIEW

1. Click **View | Current View**, and click the view you want to change.

2. Click **View | Current View | Customize Current View** to open the Customize View: Day/Week/Month dialog box, as seen in Figure 13-3.

3. Click **Fields** to open the Date/Time Fields dialog box:

   a. Click the field you want to add or change.

   b. Click **Start** if the new field is to replace the Start field.

   c. Click **End** if the new field is to replace the End field.

   d. Click **OK** to close the dialog box.

4. Click **Filter** to open the Filter dialog box:

   a. In the Appointments And Meetings tab, enter any words by which you want to filter your Calendar entries.

   b. Make additional choices, if necessary, in each of the other three tabs.

   c. Click **OK** to close the dialog box.

Figure 13-3: Outlook provides a comprehensive set of tools to modify what you see on the screen so that it can it almost any need.

5. Click **Other Settings** to open the Format Day/Week/Month View dialog box:

   a. Click **Time Font** or **Font** to open the Font dialog box.

   b. Click the **Font**, **Font Style**, and **Size** options you want.

   c. Click **OK** twice to save your changes and return to the Customize View dialog box.

6. Click **Automatic Formatting** to open the Automatic Formatting dialog box:

   a. Click **Add** to create a new rule.

   b. Click in the **Name** text box, and type a name for this rule.

   c. Click the **Color** down arrow to choose a color for this rule.

   d. Click **Condition** to open the Filter dialog box. Type the word or words to create this filter.

   e. Click **In** to choose where Outlook is to find the words you are searching for.

   f. Enter any additional filter information you require.

   g. Click **OK** to close the Filter dialog box.

   h. Click **OK** to close the Customize View dialog box.

7. Click **OK** to save your changes.

8. If you want to undo a change you made to the current view, click **Reset Current View** in the Customize View dialog box.

NOTE

You can also open the Customize View dialog box from a Day, Week, or Month view by right-clicking an empty part of your Calendar grid and clicking *Customize Current View*.

MODIFY A LIST VIEW

1. Click **View I Current View**, and click the list view you want to change.

2. Click **View I Current View I Customize Current View** to open the Customize View dialog box.

3. The Customize View dialog box will appear for the selected list view. For example, Figure 13-4 shows the dialog box for the All Appointments view.

4. Follow the same steps as described in "Modify a Day, Week, or Month View" earlier in this chapter.

5. Click **OK** to close the Customize View dialog box.

Customize View: All Appointments	
Description	
Fields...	Icon, Attachment, Subject, Location, Start, End, Recurrenc...
Group By...	Recurrence (ascending)
Sort...	Start (ascending)
Filter...	Off
Other Settings...	Fonts and other Table View settings
Automatic Formatting...	User defined fonts on each message
Format Columns...	Specify the display formats for each field
Reset Current View	OK Cancel

Figure 13-4: The Customize View dialog box in list views offers more choices than the Day, Week, and Month views.

Figure 13-5: The Custom View Organizer gives you a list and summary of the current view, as well as the ability to modify the current view and create new ones.

CREATE A NEW VIEW

1. Click the **View | Current View | Define Views**. The Custom View Organizer will open, as shown in Figure 13-5.

2. Click **New** to open the Create A New View dialog box:

   a. Type a name for this new view.

   b. Click the type of view this will be from the six options displayed.

   c. Click **This Folder, Visible To Everyone** if you want to make your new view available in this folder to everyone. Choose one of the other two options, if required.

   d. Click **OK** to open the Customize View dialog box.

   e. Follow the steps outlined in "Modify a Day, Week, or Month View" earlier in this chapter.

   f. Click **OK** to save the new view and close the dialog box.

3. Your new view will appear on the Custom View Organizer.

4. Click **Apply View** to immediately see the new view, or click **Close** to close the dialog box and stay in the current view.

Set Up the Calendar

The Calendar allows you to define your normal work week in terms of the days it contains and when it starts, the normal start and end of your working day, the holidays you observe, and what you consider the first week of the year. To set up your Calendar:

1. In Outlook 2007, click **Calendar** in the Navigation pane, and click **Tools | Options**.

2. In the Options dialog box that appears, click **Calendar Options** to display the Calendar Options dialog box, as shown in Figure 13-6.

3. Click the days of the week you consider work days if they are different from the default of Monday through Friday.

4. Click the **First Day Of Week** down arrow to select the day of the week you want considered the first day of the week if it is a day other than Sunday. The weeks in the Date Navigator will begin with this day.

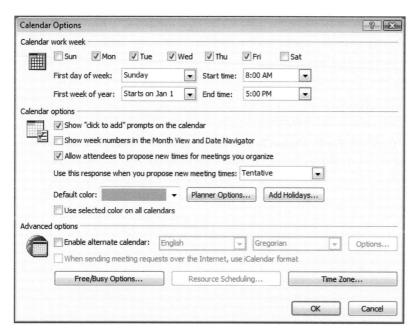

Figure 13-6: You can set Calendar options, such as defining your work week and displaying week numbers, the time zone, and holidays.

5. Click the **First Week Of Year** down arrow to choose a definition for the first week of the year if it does not begin January 1. If you turn on week numbering, week number 1 is defined in this manner.

6. Click the **Start Time** down arrow to choose the normal start time for your working day if it is other than 8:00 A.M. Click the **End Time** down arrow to change the end of your working day if it is other than 13:00 P.M. In the Day and Week views, non-working hours are blue, while working hours are pale blue by default.

7. Clear **Show "Click To Add" Prompts On The Calendar** if you do not want this default prompt to display.

8. Click **Show Week Numbers In The Month View And Date Navigator** to display week numbers.

9. Click **Allow Attendees To Propose New Times For Meetings You Organize** if you choose to allow this.

10. Click the **Use This Response When You Propose New Meeting Times** down arrow to change the automatic response to new meetings.

11. Click the **Default Color** down arrow to choose from a list of colors other than the default blue for the background on your Calendar grid.

12. Click **Use Selected Color On All Calendars** if you want this new color to be used on all Calendars you create.

13. Click **Planner Options** to display the Planner Options dialog box:
    a. Make your choices in both the Meeting Planner and the Group Schedule as they pertain to your use.
    b. Click **OK** to close the Planner Options dialog box.

14. Click **Add Holidays** to open the Add Holidays To Calendar dialog box:
    a. Click the checkbox for the country and/or religious holidays you want added.
    b. Click **OK** to close the dialog box.

15. Click **Enable Alternate Calendar**, if desired, and use the drop-down lists to choose them.

16. Under most circumstances, leave the **When Sending Meeting Requests** checkbox selected.

NOTE

Setting up a group schedule is discussed in the "Creating a Group Schedule" QuickSteps later in this chapter.

SETTING FREE/BUSY OPTIONS

If you and your coworkers are part of a Microsoft Exchange network, are willing to share your schedules over the Internet, or can all access a common server, you can store your free/busy times and make them available to each other to schedule meetings and other times together. In this case, requests for meetings will be handled automatically. The request will be matched against the group's free/busy schedule and meetings will be scheduled at available times. For an individual to set up his or her free/busy options:

1. From the Calendar Options dialog box, click **Free/Busy Options**. The Free/Busy Options dialog box appears.

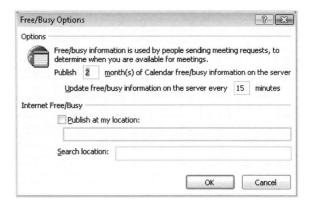

2. Click in the **Publish** box to type the number of months of free/busy information you want to store on the server.

3. Click the **Update Free/Busy Information** text box to enter how often you want the server to update your information.

4. Click **Publish At My Location**, and enter the URL (Web address) of your Internet Calendar if that applies to your situation. See "Understand Internet Calendars" later in this chapter.

5. Click **Search Location** and type the URL of servers you want Outlook to search for the free/busy information of others.

6. Click **OK** to return to the Calendar Options dialog box.

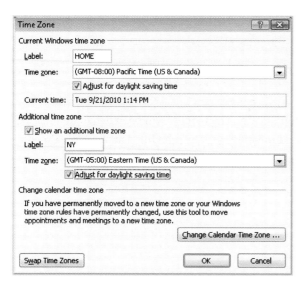

September 20 - 24, 2010

	20 Mon	21 Tue
NY	HOME	
11 am	8 am	
12 pm	9 00	Meeting re marketing plan
1 00	10 00	Training meeting Marty
2 00	11 00	

SETTING TIME ZONES

You can choose up to two time zones to display. You can define and name your current time zone, as well as an additional one, if you choose.

1. From the Calendar Options dialog box, click **Time Zone**. The Time Zone dialog box appears.

2. If you are going to use two time zones, click in the **Label** text box, and type a name that will identify the current time zone appearing in the Time Zone drop-down list.

3. Click **Show An Additional Time Zone** to add a second time zone.

4. Click in the **Label** text box, and type a name identifying this second time zone.

5. Click the **Time Zone** down arrow to display a list of time zones from which you can choose.

6. Click **Adjust For Daylight Saving Time** if it applies to either time zone you've selected.

7. Click **Change Calendar Time Zone** if you've permanently moved to a new time zone.

8. Click **Swap Time Zones** to swap time zone is on the left.

9. Click **OK** to close the Time Zone dialog box.

10. Click **OK** to close the Calendar Options dialog box, and click **OK** a second time to close the Outlook Options dialog box. Both time zones appear on your Calendar grid.

Maintain Multiple Calendars

If your Calendar is becoming cluttered and hard to use, you might try separating it into two side-by-side Calendars. For example, create one for business appointments and one for family appointments.

1. In Outlook 2007, click **Calendar** in the Navigation pane, and click the **New** down arrow on the standard toolbar.

2. Click **Calendar** to open the Create New Folder dialog box.

3. Click **Name** and type a name for your new calendar.

4. Click **Calendar** and select where to place the new folder.

5. Click **OK** to close the Create New Folder dialog box. Your new Calendar is displayed in the Navigation pane.

6. Click the checkbox to the left of your new Calendar to display it side-by-side with your original Calendar, as seen in Figure 13-7.

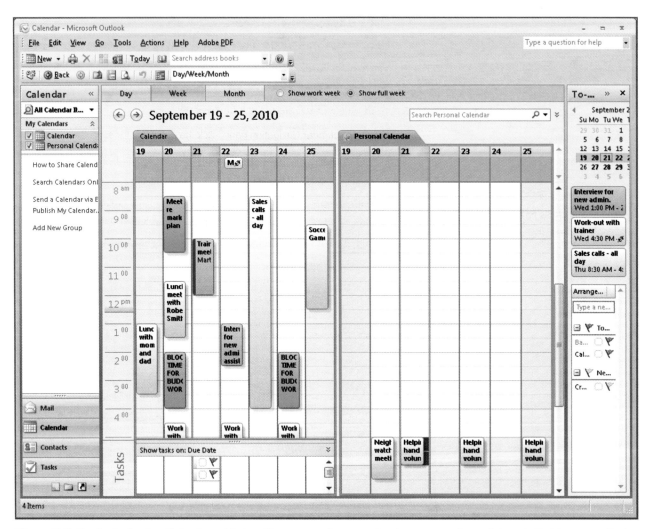

Figure 13-7: By displaying two Calendars side-by-side, you can, for example, show personal appointments that have no effect on your work Calendar.

VIEW MULTIPLE CALENDARS

You can view a Calendar in a new window, side-by-side, or stack transparent Calendars over each other to find a common free time slot on several different Calendars.

CAUTION

At least one Calendar must always be displayed, but you can create up to 30 Calendars if you choose.

To view a second Calendar in a new window:

1. From Outlook 2007, with the Calendar open, right-click the name of the second Calendar in the Navigation pane under My Calendars.

2. In the resulting menu, click **Open In New Window**.

To open several Calendars side-by-side:

1. In the Calendar Navigation pane, click the checkbox for each Calendar you want to view.

2. All the Calendars will be displayed next to each other in your Calendar grid.

To overlay your Calendars:

1. In the Calendar, from the Navigation pane, click the checkbox for each Calendar you want to stack. The Calendars display next to each other in your Calendar grid.

2. On the tab of each Calendar you want to stack, click the arrow that points to the left.

3. All of the Calendars are stacked atop each other, and you can see any dates that may be free on all Calendars.

4. To undo the stack, click the right-pointing arrow on the tab of each Calendar. The Calendars are once again displayed side by side.

Share a Calendar

There are several ways to share your Outlook 2007 Calendar with others. You can send a Calendar via e-mail, publish your Calendar to Microsoft Office Online, or share your default Microsoft Exchange Calendar with others on the same server.

SEND A CALENDAR IN E-MAIL

You can send any Calendar you own to another in the body of an e-mail message. The person receiving the Calendar will see a snapshot of your Calendar at a given moment in time. If the recipient uses Outlook 2007, he or she can open the Calendar snapshot as an Outlook Calendar and display it either side by side or as an overlay with any other Calendars. The downside of using a Calendar snapshot is that the Calendar you send is not automatically updated when you make changes. If the e-mail recipient needs a regularly updated Calendar, consider publishing your Calendar to Microsoft Office Online, using a calendar-publishing Web service, or, if your work has it, sharing your Calendars via an Exchange server.

To share a Calendar:

1. In the Calendar's Navigation pane, click **Send A Calendar Via E-mail**.

   –Or–

   In a minimized Navigation pane, right-click the Calendar you want to share. From the context menu, click **Send Via E-mail**.

   In either case, an e-mail message box opens with the Send A Calendar Via E-Mail dialog box in the message portion of the e-mail window.

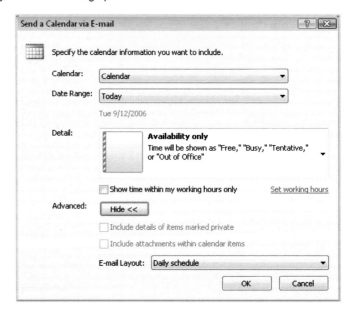

2. Click the **Calendar** down arrow, and click the Calendar you want to e-mail.

3. Click the **Date Range** down arrow, and click the time period for which you want to send the Calendar.

4. Click the **Detail** down arrow, and click the type of Calendar information you want to send.

5. If you chose Availability Only, click **Show Time Within My Working Hours Only** if that is what you want.

6. Click **Set Working Hours** to display the Calendar Options dialog box and change your working hours. Close the Calendar Options dialog box if you opened it.

7. Click **Show** (located opposite Advanced), and, if desired, click **Include Details Of Items Marked Private** and/or **Include Attachments**.

8. Click **E-mail Layout** and click either the **Daily Schedule** or **List Of Events** format.

9. Click **OK** to close the dialog box.

10. Click **To** and type the recipient's e-mail address.

11. Click **Send** to send the e-mail.

PUBLISH A CALENDAR TO MICROSOFT OFFICE ONLINE

Microsoft offers a publishing service for your Calendars. This method does not require Microsoft Exchange for either the user or the owner of the Calendar. The first time you use the service, you must register using your Microsoft Windows Live ID account. If you don't yet have an account, you may follow the instructions on the screen to obtain one for free.

1. In the Calendar's Navigation pane, click **Publish My Calendar**. Go through the registration procedure, if needed. The Publish Calendar To Microsoft Office Online dialog box appears.

2. Follow steps 4–6 in "Send a Calendar in E-mail."

3. Click **Restricted Access** if you want to allow only invited users to see your Calendar.

4. Click **Unrestricted Access** if you want to share your Calendar with anyone.

5. Click **Automatic Uploads** if you want Outlook 2007 to periodically update your published Calendar automatically.

6. Click **Single Upload** if you do not want to have your Calendar updated.

7. Click **Show** (located opposite Advanced), and, if desired, click **Include Details Of Items Marked Private** and/or **Update This Calendar** to use the server's recommended frequency for updates.

8. Click **OK** to publish your Calendar.

CAUTION

Be careful when you set the date range of a Calendar snapshot. If you set it for a long period of time, the e-mail file might be too big for the recipient's e-mail box.

9. After your Calendar has been successfully published, you are prompted to create an e-mail announcing this fact. Click **Yes** to create the e-mail or click **No** to close the dialog box.

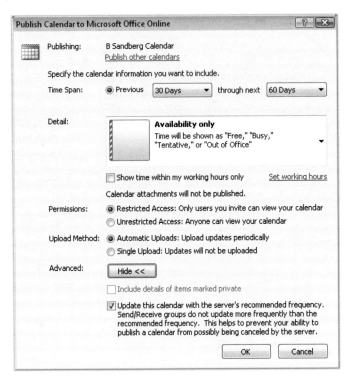

SHARE AN EXCHANGE CALENDAR

If you are connected to a Microsoft Exchange server, you can share your Calendars with others and they can share theirs with you.

1. In the Calendar, from the Navigation pane, click **Share My Calendar**.

2. In the e-mail message box that opens, click **To** and type the name of the person to whom you are granting access to your Calendar.

3. Click **Subject** and type a subject for your e-mail.

4. Click **Allow Recipient To View Your Calendar**.

5. Click **Request Permission To View Recipient's Calendar** if you want access to their Calendar as well.

NOTE

If Share My Calendar is not available in the Navigation pane, you are not connected to a Microsoft Exchange network.

QUICK**FACTS**

UNDERSTAND INTERNET CALENDARS

There are several types of Internet calendars. We've discussed the Calendar snapshot and Calendars published using both Exchange servers and Microsoft Office Online. There is another type of Internet calendar that is downloaded from calendar publishing services or special Web sites that host calendars. This downloaded calendar is created and saved in Outlook. Most Internet calendar companies charge a fee for a subscription. While Calendar snapshots are not updated with any regularity, a subscription to an Internet calendar means that your calendar is synchronized on a regular basis with a calendar saved on a Web server. The updates that result from the synchronization are downloaded to your Internet calendar.

TIP

Try using text dates, as described in the "Entering Dates and Times" QuickSteps, and you'll be amazed at how Outlook can interpret what you enter.

TIP

Combine direct entry and window entry to get the benefits of both.

6. Click in the body of the e-mail, and type any additional information.

7. Click **Send**.

8. A confirmation dialog box will appear. If all appears correct, click **OK** to close the dialog box.

Use the Calendar

Within the Calendar, you can enter several types of activities:

- **Appointments** take time on your calendar, are less than 24 hours long, and do not require inviting others within Outlook to attend. Examples include a sales call, lunch with a buyer, or time you want to set aside to write a report.

- **Meetings** are appointments that require that others be invited and/or that resources be reserved. Meetings are set up using e-mail.

- **Events** are 24 hours or longer, do not occupy time on your Calendar, and appear as a banner on each day's calendar. Examples are conferences, birthdays, or your vacation.

- **Tasks** are activities that do not need time scheduled for them and involve only you. Your tasks display in the Day and Week views of your Calendar as well as your To-Do Bar.

All types of activities can be entered in several ways and with a number of options.

Create Appointments

Appointments can be entered in any view and in several different ways. Independent of the view, the different ways can be grouped into direct entry and window entry. *Direct entry* means simply typing directly on the Calendar, while *window entry* uses a window to gather the information, which is then displayed on the Calendar. Direct entry is fast if you want to make a quick notation. Window entry allows you to select and set a number of options.

ENTER APPOINTMENTS DIRECTLY

You can directly enter an appointment on the Calendar in Day, Week, or Month view by clicking a time and typing the description. If you want the entry longer or shorter than the default half hour (or whatever standard duration you have selected), just drag the top or bottom border up or down to change the time.

⏰ QUICKSTEPS

ENTERING DATES AND TIMES

The Outlook Calendar allows you to enter dates and times as text and convert that text to numeric dates and times. For example, you can type next tue and be given next Tuesday's date, or you can type sep ninth and see that date. You can type this way in any date or time field in Outlook, such as the Go To Date dialog box, reached by pressing **CTRL-G** or right-clicking any empty spot on the Calendar grid while in Day, Week, or Month view. Likewise, you can type in the Start and End date and time fields in the appointment and event views or the Meeting dialog box. You can also:

- Abbreviate months and days (for example, *Dec* or *fri*).

- Ignore capitalization and other punctuation (for example, *wednesday, april,* and *lincolns birthday*).

- Use words that indicate dates and times (for example, *noon, midnight, tomorrow, yesterday, today, now, next week, last month, five days ago, in three months, this Saturday,* and *two weeks from now*). Words you can use include: *after, ago, before, beforehand, beginning, end, ending, following, for, from, last, next, now, previous, start, that, this, through, till, tomorrow, yesterday, today,* and *until.*

- Spell out specific dates and times (for example, *August ninth, first of December, April 19th, midnight, noon, two twenty pm,* and *five o'clock a.m.*).

- Indicate holidays that fall on the same date every year (for example, *New Year's Eve, New Year's Day, Lincoln's Birthday, Valentine's Day, Washington's Birthday, St. Patrick's Day, Cinco de Mayo, Independence Day, Halloween, Veterans' Day, Christmas Eve, Christmas Day,* and *Boxing Day*).

If you want to move the appointment, simply drag it to where you want it in the current day or to another day in the Date Navigator. To change the properties of an appointment, right-click the appointment, which opens the context menu, where a number of properties can be set.

To directly enter appointments:

1. In Outlook 2007, click any date and time in the Calendar grid in the Day, Week, or Month view. Type a short description of the appointment, and press **ENTER**.

2. Place the mouse pointer on the sizing handle at the bottom border of the appointment. Drag the border down until the end of the appointment time.

3. If you need to change the beginning time of your appointment, drag the top border up or down until the proper time is reflected in the Calendar.

ENTER EVENTS DIRECTLY

An event is an activity that normally lasts at least 24 hours (although you can designate something as an event that lasts less than 24 hours but takes most of your time that day, such as a company picnic). Examples of events are conferences, seminars, and holidays. If events are tied to specific dates, they are considered annual events, such as a birthday or holiday. When you enter an event, it is considered free time, not busy. You create events differently than appointments. All events appear in the banner at the top of the daily schedule, while all appointments are on the Calendar itself. To directly enter an event:

1. With the Outlook Calendar open in Day, Week, or Month view, select a day in the Calendar grid when the event will take place.

2. Click in the dark blue area at the top of the daily schedule, just under the date header, type the event name, and press **ENTER**.

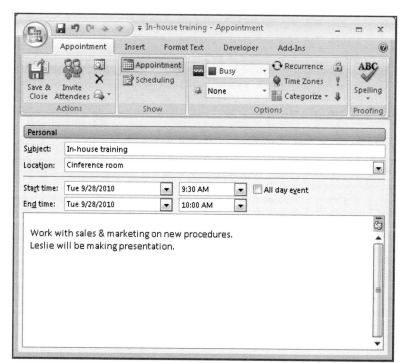

Figure 13-8: The Appointment window is used to set up or change an appointment.

NOTE

You can move an appointment without changing the duration by dragging it in any direction. This will change your start and end times but leave the duration constant.

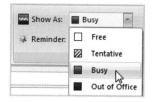

ENTER APPOINTMENTS IN A WINDOW

As an alternative to directly entering appointments and events, you can use a New Appointment window, as seen in Figure 13-8, to accomplish the same objective and immediately be able to enter a lot more information. To open a New Appointment window:

1. In the Outlook Calendar, click the **New** down arrow on the standard toolbar, and click **Appointment** to open the New Appointment window.

2. In the Appointment tab Show group, click **Appointment** if it is not already selected.

3. Click **Subject** and type the subject of the appointment. This text becomes the description in the Calendar, with the location added parenthetically and the date and time determining where the appointment goes on the Calendar.

4. Press **TAB**. Type the location, if relevant, in the Location text box.

5. Click the **Start Time** down arrow on the left to display a small calendar in which you can choose a date.

6. Click the down arrow on the right, and select a start time.

7. Click the **End Time** down arrow and select the end date and time. By default, the end date for an appointment is the same date as the start date.

8. Press **TAB** twice and type any notes or other information necessary.

9. In the Appointment tab Options group, click the **Show As** down arrow, and tell Outlook how to display this time slot on your Calendar:

   - Free
   - Tentative
   - Busy
   - Out Of Office

10. In the Appointment tab Options group, click the **Reminder** down arrow, and set the reminder time. See "Use Reminders" later in this chapter for more information.

11. In the Appointment tab Actions group, click **Save & Close** to save your appointment.

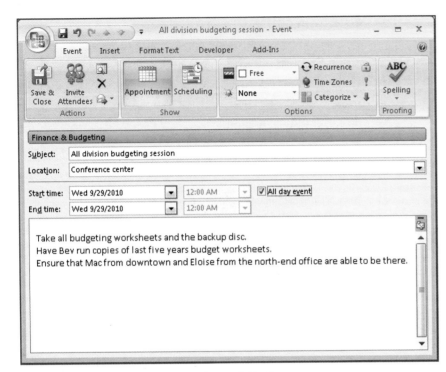

Figure 13-9: A New Event window looks much like the New Appointment window, except All Day Event is selected.

NOTE

Depending on what is selected on the Calendar grid, the window that opens when you click *New* may be either an Appointment window or an Event window. The only difference, other than the title, is that All Day Event is selected and the free/busy indicator is set to Free for an event. If you get an Event window when you want an Appointment window, simply clear the All Day Event checkbox.

ENTER AN EVENT IN A WINDOW

To enter an all-day event:

1. In the Outlook Calendar, right-click any blank date in any Calendar view.
2. Click **New All Day Event**. The New Event window opens.
3. Click **Subject** to enter text describing the event as it will appear on your Calendar.
4. Click **Location** to type information about the location. By default, All Day Event is selected.
5. Repeat steps 8–11 from "Enter Appointments in a Window." The start and end times disappear; the reminder, by default, goes to 18 hours, and Show Time As changes to Free, as seen in Figure 13-9.

Enter Recurring Appointments

Often you'll have appointments and events that recur predictably, for example, a weekly staff meeting, a monthly planning meeting, a monthly lunch with a friend, and birthdays. You obviously do not want to re-enter these every week, month, or year. Outlook has a feature that allows you to enter these activities once and have them reappear on a given frequency for as long as you want.

1. Create a new appointment as described in "Enter Appointments in a Window."
2. In the Appointments tab Options group, click **Recurrence**. The Appointment Recurrence dialog box appears, as shown in Figure 13-10.

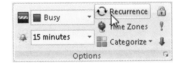

3. Click the **Start** down arrow, and select the start time of this recurring appointment.
4. Click the **End** down arrow, and select the end time.
5. Click the **Duration** down arrow, and select the length of time this appointment lasts.

13

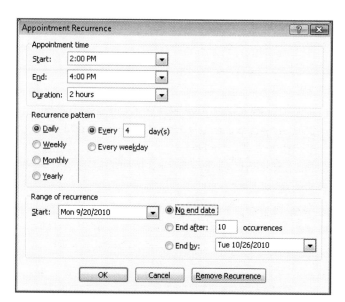

Figure 13-10: Use the Appointment Recurrence dialog box to schedule recurring appointments automatically.

NOTE

Recurring appointments and events can save you a lot of time re-entering activities, but they can also generate a lot of entries, which may unnecessarily fill your Calendar. Enter only the recurring appointments that you want to remember.

TIP

You can delete a single instance of a recurring activity without affecting the rest of the series. If you choose to delete a recurring activity, the dialog box asks if you want to delete the current instance of the activity or the entire series.

6. Click **Recurrence Pattern** and choose how often this appointment occurs.

7. Under Range of Recurrence, click the down arrow, select the date this appointment starts, the number of times it occurs, and its ending date.

8. Click **OK** to close the Appointment Recurrence dialog box.

EDIT RECURRING APPOINTMENTS

To change one instance of a recurring appointment:

1. In the Outlook Calendar, locate and double-click a recurring appointment in any Calendar view. The Open Recurring Item dialog box appears.

2. Click **Open This Occurrence** if you want to make a change to only this instance of the appointment.

3. Click **OK** to open the Appointment window and make the necessary changes to this occurrence of the appointment.

4. In the Recurring Appointment tab Actions group, click **Save & Close**.

To change all instances of a recurring appointment:

1. In the Calendar, locate and double-click the recurring appointment in any Calendar view. The Open Recurring Item dialog box appears.

2. Click **Open The Series** if you want to make a change to the recurring appointment itself.

3. Click **OK** to open the Appointment window.

4. In the Recurring Appointment tab Options group, click **Recurrence** (if you forgot to click **Open The Series** in step 2, you will see "Edit Series" in place of "Recurrence). The Appointment Recurrence dialog box appears.

5. Make the necessary changes to this appointment, and click **OK**.

6. In the Recurring Appointment tab Actions group, click **Save & Close**.

Move Appointments

If an appointment changes times within a day, you can move it to its new time by simply dragging it to that new time, as you saw earlier. If you entered an event on the wrong day, or if an appointment changes days, you can drag it to the correct or new day in the Week or Month view or in the Date Navigator. You cannot drag a recurring appointment to a date that skips over another occurrence of the same appointment. You can, however, change a recurring appointment to another date before the next one occurs. The different ways to move appointments or events are

- Drag the appointment to the day you want in a Week or Month view Calendar or the Date Navigator.

- You can drag an appointment anywhere in the Calendar grid by dragging from anywhere in the appointment, except at the expansion points on the middle of the sides.

- When you drag an appointment to a new day, it will be placed in the same time slot. You can change the time by dragging it to the new time, either before or after you move it to the new day.

TIP

You can copy an activity by right-dragging it (use the right mouse button) to where you want the copy and selecting **Copy** from the context menu that appears when you release the right mouse button.

Use Reminders

When you have set a reminder for an appointment, the Reminder dialog box appears at the time you have set before the appointment. You have several choices in the dialog box.

- Click **Dismiss All** to close the reminder and tell it not to appear again.

- Click **Snooze** to tell the dialog box when to remind you again but close the reminder for now.

- Click **Open Item** to open the Appointment window so that you can make changes to the appointment, the reminder, or both.

- Click **Dismiss** to close only the highlighted reminder.

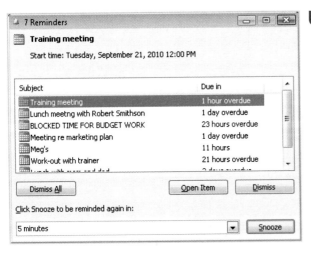

Print Calendars

When you have completed making entries on your Calendar, you may want to take it with you, away from your computer, for reference and to jot new appointments on. For this reason, Outlook includes a number of printed formats to fit your needs.

To print your calendar:

1. In any view in Outlook Calendar, choose the day, week, or month you want to print.

2. Click the **File** menu.

3. Click **Page Setup** and click the **Style** you want to print. Your choices are determined by the Calendar view you have chosen. Figure 13-11 shows an example of the weekly style and the related options from which you can choose.

4. Click the **Format** tab, and make any changes in the Options and Fonts sections.

QUICKSTEPS

CREATING A GROUP SCHEDULE

A group schedule tracks the free/busy status of several people in one place. It is like the in/out board at a reception desk. To use group schedules, all the members of the group must be on a Microsoft Exchange network.

1. In the Calendar, click the **Actions** menu.

Continued . . .

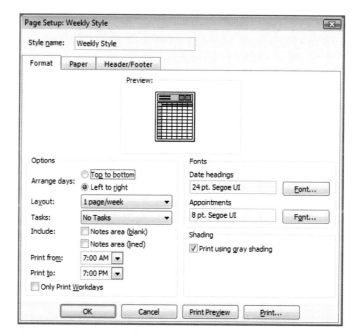

Figure 13-11: *The Page Setup dialog box gives you considerable flexibility with regards to the print style, the format, paper specifications, and header/footer information.*

13

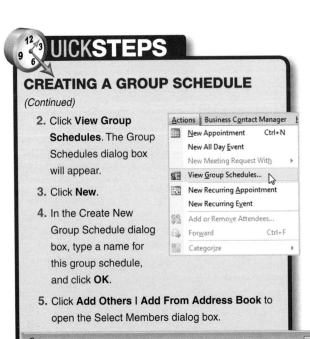

CREATING A GROUP SCHEDULE
(Continued)

2. Click **View Group Schedules**. The Group Schedules dialog box will appear.

3. Click **New**.

4. In the Create New Group Schedule dialog box, type a name for this group schedule, and click **OK**.

5. Click **Add Others I Add From Address Book** to open the Select Members dialog box.

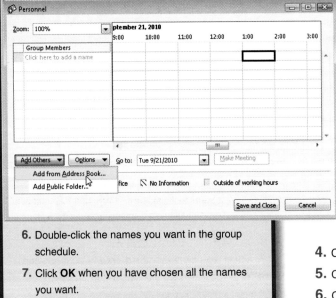

6. Double-click the names you want in the group schedule.

7. Click **OK** when you have chosen all the names you want.

8. Click **Save And Close** to close the Group Schedule dialog box.

5. Click the **Shading** checkbox if you want gray shading to be used in your printed Calendar.

6. Click **Paper** to choose the paper specifications.

7. Click **Header/Footer** to add the professional touch of a header and/or a footer.

8. When you are ready, click **Print Preview** to see how your printed Calendar will look.

9. Click **Print** to print your Calendar.

Plan Meetings and Request Attendance

In addition to using Outlook 2007 for scheduling appointments and events, you can use Outlook to plan and schedule meetings. In Outlook, a meeting is an appointment to which others are invited.

Schedule a Meeting

You create a meeting by identifying the people you want to invite and picking a meeting time. You e-mail a meeting request to people in your Outlook Contacts who you want to attend.

1. In Outlook 2007, click **File I New I Meeting Request**.

   –Or–

   Press **CTRL-SHIFT-Q**.

   In either event, the New Meeting window opens, as seen in Figure 13-12.

2. Click **To**, double-click your attendees from your Contacts list, and click **OK**.

3. Click in the **Subject** text box, and type a description for your meeting. This description will appear on all Calendars.

4. Click in the **Location** text box, and type the location information, if necessary.

5. Click the **Start Time** down arrow, and select the date and time the meeting is to start.

6. Click the **End Time** down arrow, and select the date and time the meeting is scheduled to end.

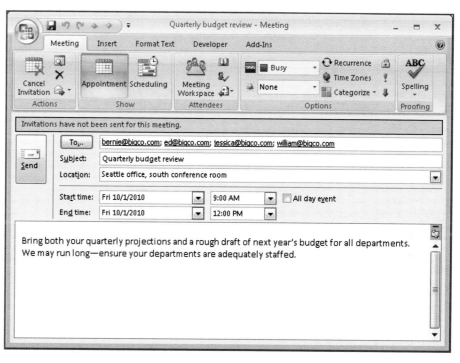

Figure 13-12: The Meeting window allows you to send out invitations, track who can attend, and schedule resources for the meeting.

7. Click **All Day Event**, if necessary.

8. Enter any additional information in the Notes section of the Meeting window that may be needed by the attendees.

9. In the Meeting tab Show group, click **Scheduling Assistant**. If you use Outlook 2007 with Business Contact Manager, in the Meeting tab Show group, click **Scheduling**.

10. If necessary, click Add Others to include others in the meeting.

11. If you want to change the meeting times, you can enter the start and ending times, or you can drag the edges of the vertical meeting line, as shown in Figure 13-13.

12. After you have entered all of your information, click Send.

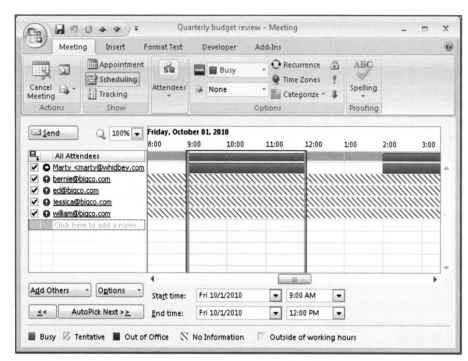

Figure 13-13: *The Scheduling Assistant determines when a meeting will be held and helps you select attendees.*

Respond to an Invitation

When you receive a meeting request, a message appears in your Inbox with an icon that is different from the normal e-mail icon.

1. In Outlook, open the meeting notification or request.

2. On the Message tab Respond group, click one of the following:

   - Accept

   - Tentative

   - Decline

3. To send your response with no comments, click **Send The Response Now**. Click **OK**.

4. To include comments with your response, click **Edit The Response Before Sending**.

5. Type your comments and click **Send**.

6. To send no response, click **Don't Send A Response**, and click **OK**. The meeting is added to your Calendar.

How to...

Chapter 14

Printing, Using Mail Merge, and Graphics

The printing capabilities provided by Office 2007 go beyond just printing a document. In this chapter you will learn how to preview your document before printing it and set specific parameters with regards to what is printed. Office also includes a convenient feature called Mail Merge within Word that you can use to merge mailing lists into documents, including letters or envelopes.

Graphics is a term used to describe several forms of visual enhancements that can be added to a document. In this chapter you will learn how to insert, format, and manage graphic files (*pictures*), such as digital photos and clip art images. In addition, you will see how to embed products of other programs (*objects*) alongside your text and how to produce organizational charts and other business-oriented *diagrams*.

NOTE

Due to the wide variety of printers available, this chapter cannot cover them all. The examples and figures in this chapter use an HP Photosmart 2600 printer. Depending on your printer model and how it's configured, you may see differences between your screen and what is shown in the figures and illustrations here.

NOTE

If there is a checkmark next to the Printer icon, that printer is already set as the default printer.

Print Documents

While printing documents may seem like a fairly basic function, there are several tasks associated with it that deserve attention, including setting up the default printer, using Print Preview, and printing envelopes and labels.

Set a Default Printer

1. From Windows Vista, click **Start** | **Control Panel**, and then, under Hardware And Sound, click **Printer**.

2. Right-click the icon for the printer you want to use as the default printer, and then click **Set As Default Printer** from the context menu that appears. A checkmark is displayed next to the icon you have selected.

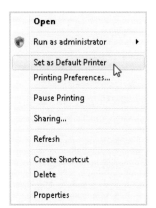

Define How a Document Is Printed

The Properties dialog box for your printer defines how your document will be printed. From here, you set such things as orientation, number of copies to print, effects, and so on. An example of a Properties dialog box for an HP Photosmart 2600 printer is shown in Figure 14-1. Keep in mind that the Properties dialog box for your printer will probably have some different options, and can even be different for the same printer, depending on whether the printer is connected directly to the computer or is accessed over the network. Consult the documentation that came with your printer for specific instructions.

To open the Properties dialog box for your printer:

1. In an Office program, such as Word, click the **Office Button**, and click **Print**. The Print dialog box appears.

2. Click **Properties**. The Properties dialog box for your printer appears. This particular printer model has seven tabs in its dialog box.

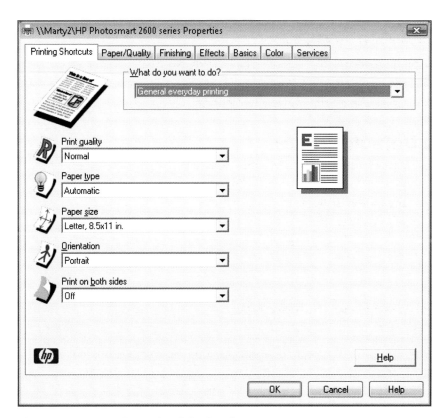

Figure 14-1: Use the Properties dialog box for your printer to define how your documents will be printed.

NOTE

Print Layout view, set in the View tab Documents Views group, provides almost the exact same view as Print Preview view, and the View tab provides many of the same options.

3. The Printing Shortcut tab for the HP Photosmart 2600 has the following options, as shown in Figure 14-1. Other printers will have different tabs and different options, but within the Properties dialog box, they will generally cover the same functions. Make your selections accordingly.

4. Other tabs will have a variety of options, depending on your printer.

5. When you have the settings the way you want them, click **OK** to close the dialog boxes.

Preview What You'll Print

You can use the Print Preview feature to view your document on the screen before you print it. Print Preview displays the page(s) of your document exactly as they will appear when printed. You can also set page breaks and margins using this feature.

To use Print Preview:

1. Click the **Office Button**, point at the **Print** arrow, and click **Print Preview**. Your document is displayed in Print Preview view, as shown in Figure 14-2. The options available to you may differ between the applications. For example, the options in the PowerPoint Print Preview window are different than those in Word.

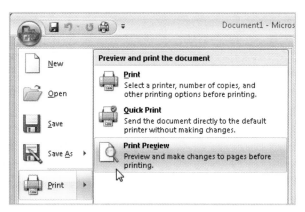

14

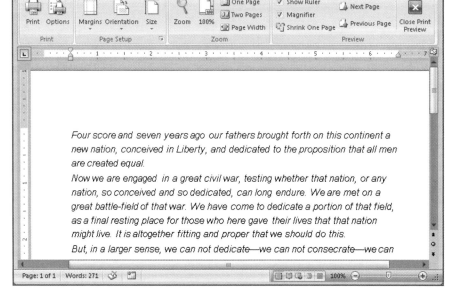

You have these options:

- Click **Zoom** on the Print Preview tab. The Zoom dialog box appears. Click one of the preset percentages, directly enter a percent, or use the spinner to set the level of magnification you want.

TIP

In Word the Magnifier, which is turned on by default in the Preview group, allows you to quickly toggle between 100 percent and full-page views by simply clicking the page.

NOTE

In Word you can display either one or two pages at a time. Click Two Pages in the Zoom group to display a two-page view. When using Print Preview, your document is automatically displayed one page at a time.

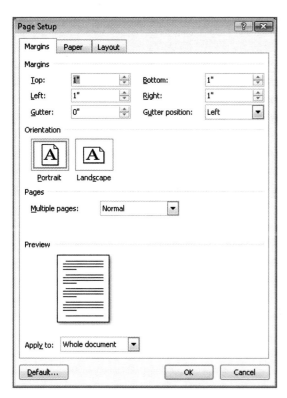

Figure 14-3: You can either select preset margins from the Margin drop-down menu or enter the custom margins you want in the Page Setup dialog box.

- You can change margins in a couple of ways, depending on the Office application. In Word's Print Preview tab, click **Show Ruler** in the Preview group. A ruler is displayed on the left and on the top of the document, as you saw in Figure 14-2. The margins are shown as the shaded areas on the ends of the rulers. In Excel, click **Page Setup** in the Print group. A Page Setup dialog box will be displayed, as shown in Figure 14-3. Click the **Margins** tab and set the margins as you wish.

- In the Print Preview tab, click **Previous Page** or **Next Page** in the Preview group to move forward or backward one page at a time.

- Click **Shrink One Page** in the Preview group on the Print Preview tab to reduce the number of pages in Word. Word reformats the document onto one less page by making slight adjustments to font size and paragraph spacing. You can keep doing this to reduce the number of pages one at a time.

2. Click **Close Print Preview** on the right of the Print Preview tab.

VIEW YOUR DOCUMENT IN FULL-SCREEN MODE

NOTE

In Excel and Word you can view a document in full-screen mode without the ribbon, status bar, or scroll bars present, as shown in Figure 14-4. This view, however, is available in Office 2007 from the View tab Document Views group. Click **Full Screen Reading**. When you are finished, click **Close** on the far right of the title bar to return to the regular window.

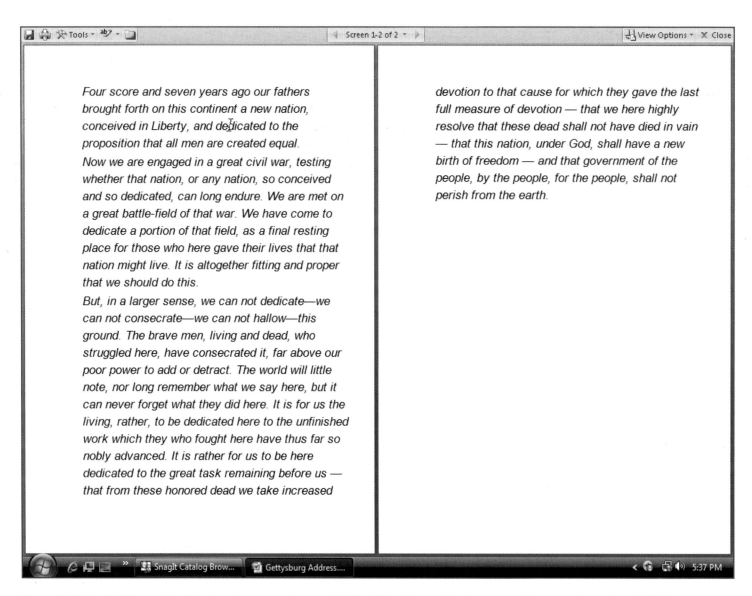

Figure 14-4: Use Full-Screen Reading view to see your document without the ribbon, status bar, or scroll bars, as shown here in Word.

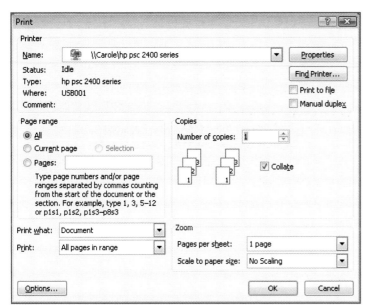

Figure 14-5: The Print dialog box provides many options for printing your document.

Print a Document

If you're in a hurry, or if you don't care about changing margins, then printing a document can be as easy as clicking a **Print** icon on the Quick Access toolbar. By default, that icon isn't on that toolbar, but you can add it. To set specific options before printing your document, you need to use the Print dialog box.

CUSTOMIZE A PRINT JOB

Customizing the print settings is done in the Print dialog box, shown in Figure 14-5.

1. Click the **Office Button**, and click **Print**. The Print dialog box appears.

2. If more than one printer is available to you, select the printer you want to use from the Name drop-down list. Usually, the default printer is displayed automatically in the Name list box.

3. Select an option in the Page Range area, choosing between All, Current Page, Selection for the text you've selected, and Pages for a range of pages. To print contiguous pages, use a hyphen (for example, 1-4); to print noncontiguous pages, use commas (for example, 1, 3, 5).

4. Select an option from the Print What drop-down list (or in Excel, click a radio button). Your options will differ between Office applications.

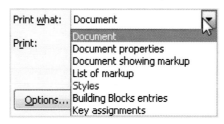

5. Select an option from the Print drop-down list. Again, the options will differ between Office applications.

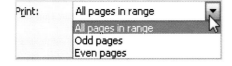

6. Type or use the spinner to select the number of copies you want to print in the Number Of Copies box.

7. When you have selected all the options you want and are ready to print your document, click **OK**. Your document is printed.

Figure 14-6: Printed envelopes give your correspondence a professional look.

Print an Envelope in Word

You can print a mailing address on an envelope to give your correspondence a more professional look. If you have a business letter with an address in the normal location, Word will pick up that address and suggest it for the envelope. If you don't have a letter, you can still create and print an envelope.

1. In the Mailings tab Create group, click **Envelopes**. The Envelopes And Labels dialog box appears with the Envelope tab selected, as shown in Figure 14-6.

2. In the Delivery Address box, if an address wasn't picked up from a letter, enter the mailing address.

3. In the Return Address box, accept the default return address, or enter or edit the return address. (If you are using preprinted envelopes, you can omit a return address by clicking the **Omit** checkbox.)

4. Click the **Add Electronic Postage** checkbox if you have separately installed electronic postage software and want to add it to your envelope.

5. To set options for the electronic postage programs that are installed on your computer, click **E-Postage Properties**.

6. To select an envelope size, the type of paper feed, and other options, click **Options**, select the options you want, and then click **OK**.

7. To print the envelope now, insert an envelope in the printer, as shown in the Feed box (see the accompanying Note), and then click **Print**.

8. To attach the envelope to a document you are currently working on and print it later, click **Add To Document**. The envelope is added to the document in a separate section.

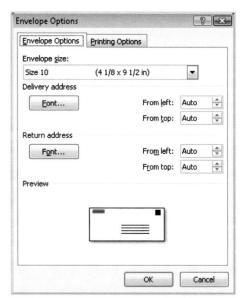

NOTE

The Feed box shows a default view that may be totally wrong for your printer. You need to use trial and error (which you can do on plain paper to save envelopes) to find the correct way to feed envelopes. When you find the correct pattern, click the feed image, select the correct image, and click **OK**.

TIP

For many HP ink-jet printers, the envelopes are fed with the flap facing up on the left of the envelope and positioned on the far right of the feed tray, like this:

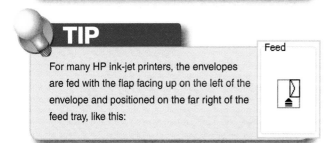

Figure 14-7: You can print a sheet of labels one at a time by specifying the row and column to be printed.

Print Labels in Word

You can print labels for a single letter or for a mass mailing, such as holiday cards, invitations, or for marketing purposes. You can also create labels for a mass mailing using the techniques described later in the chapter under, "Merge Lists with Letters and Envelopes."

To print a single label:

1. In the Mailings tab Create group, click **Labels**. The Envelopes And Labels dialog box appears with the Labels tab displayed, as shown in Figure 14-7.

2. In the Address box, do one of the following:

   • If you have a business letter open in Word with an address in the normal location, that address will appear in the Address box and can be edited.

   • If you are creating a mailing label, enter or edit the address.

   • If you want to use a return address, click the **Use Return Address** checkbox, and then edit the address if necessary.

   • If you are creating another type of label, type the text you want.

3. In the Print area, do one of the following:

   • Click the **Single Label** option to print a single label. Then type or select the row and column number on the label sheet for the label you want to print.

   • Click **Full Page Of The Same Label** to print the same information on a sheet of labels.

4. To select the label type, the type of paper feed, and other options, click **Options**, select the options you want, and then click **OK**. If the type of label you want to use is not listed in the Product Number box, you might be able to use one of the listed labels, or you can click **New Label** to create your own custom label.

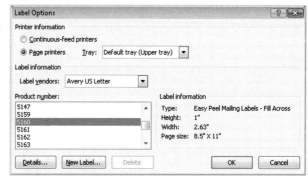

QUICKSTEPS

E-MAILING

You can e-mail documents that you create in Word, Excel, or PowerPoint as attachments to e-mail messages. To attach and send a document in an e-mail:

1. Click the **Office button**, then click **Send | E-mail** to send your document as an attachment to your e-mail message.

   A new e-mail message is opened with your document title automatically filled in the Subject line and the document automatically attached to the e-mail.

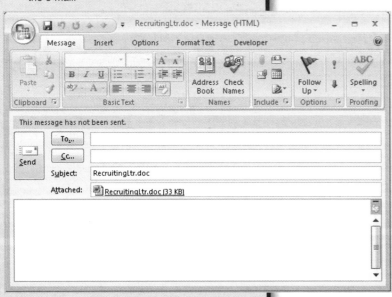

2. Fill in the To and Cc fields (if you are sending the document to multiple recipients), add anything you want to the body of the message, and click **Send**. Your e-mail message with the document attached is sent.

5. To print one or more labels, insert a sheet of labels into the printer, and then click **Print**.

6. To save a sheet of labels for later editing or printing, click **New Document** and save the labels document.

NOTE

You can also send a document in the body of an e-mail message using copy and paste. While in Word, Excel, or PowerPoint, select as much of the document as you want to send, and use the Copy command or press **CTRL-C** to copy it. In your e-mail program, open a new message form; fill in the To, Cc, and Subject fields; click in the message field; and use the Paste command or press **CTRL-V** to paste the document in the message field. When ready, click **Send**.

Merge Lists with Letters and Envelopes

The *Mail Merge* feature allows you to combine a mailing list with a document to send the same thing to a number of people. You can merge a mailing list to letters, e-mail messages, envelopes, and labels. A mail merge combines two kinds of documents: the *main document*, which is the text of the document—for example, the body of a letter—and the *data source*, which is the information that changes with each copy of the document—for example, the individual names and addresses of the people who will be receiving the letter.

The main document has two parts: static text and merge fields. *Static text* is text that does not change—for example, the body of a letter. *Merge fields* are placeholders that indicate where information from the list or data source goes. For example, in a form letter, "Dear" would be static text, while <<First Name>> <<Last Name>> are merge fields. When the main document and the data source are combined, the result is "Dear John Doe," "Dear Jane Smith," and so on.

The following sections will show you how to create a data source, create a main document, and then merge them together.

TIP

You cannot use the Mail Merge feature unless a document is open, although it can be a blank document.

NOTE

Word also allows you to take a list other than a mailing list—a parts list, for example—and merge it with a document to create a catalog or directory.

Begin a Mail Merge

You can compose the static text in a document first and then insert the merge fields, or you can compose the static text and insert the merge fields as you go. You cannot insert merge fields into a main document until you have created the data source and associated it with your main document.

To create a merge document:

1. In Word, open the document you want to use as your primary document, or open a new document.

2. Click the **Mailings** tab, click **Start Mail Merge** in the Start Mail Merge group, and click **Step By Step Mail Merge Wizard**. The Mail Merge task pane is displayed, as shown in Figure 14-8.

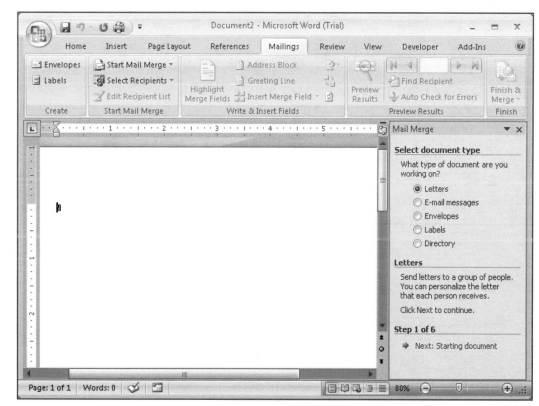

Figure 14-8: The Mail Merge task pane is where you begin the merge process.

3. In the Select Document Type area, select one of the following options:

- **Letters** are form letters designed to be sent to multiple people.

- **E-mail Messages** are form letters designed to be sent to multiple people via e-mail.

- **Envelopes** are envelopes addressed to multiple people.

- **Labels** are labels addressed to multiple people.

- **Directory** is a collection of information regarding multiple items, such as a mailing list or phone directory.

4. Click **Next: Starting Document** at the bottom of the task pane.

5. In the Select Starting Document area, select one of the following options:

- **Use The Current Document** uses the currently opened document as the main document for the mail merge.

- **Start From A Template** uses a template you designate as the main document for the mail merge.

- **Start From Existing Document** uses an existing document you designate as the main document for the mail merge.

6. See the following section, "Set Up a Name and Address List," to create a data source.

Select starting document

How do you want to set up your letters?
- ⦿ Use the current document
- ◯ Start from a template
- ◯ Start from existing document

Set Up a Name and Address List

A name and address list is a data source. A data source has two parts: fields and records. A *field* is a category of information. For example, in a mailing list, First Name, Last Name, and Street Address are examples of fields. A *record* is a set of fields for an individual. For example, in a mailing list, the record for John Doe would include all the relevant fields for this individual—his first and last name, street address, city, state, and ZIP code.

To set up a name and address list:

1. Follow steps 1–6 in the previous section, "Begin a Mail Merge."

2. Click **Next: Select Recipients** at the bottom of the task pane. In the Select Recipients area, click **Type A New List**.

3. Click **Create** in the middle of the pane in the Type A New List area. The New Address List dialog box appears, as shown in Figure 14-9.

Select recipients

- ⦿ Use an existing list
- ◯ Select from Outlook contacts
- ◯ Type a new list

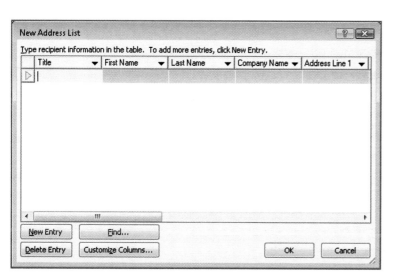

Figure 14-9: Use the New Address List dialog box to create your mailing list.

Sort the merge recipients by clicking the field name at the top of the list that will provide the sort order. For example, if you want the list ordered alphabetically by last name, click **Last Name**.

4. Enter the information for the first record in the fields you want to use. You may want to delete some of the columns or reorder them to facilitate entering data. Click **Customize Columns** to do that. Press TAB to move to the next field, or press **SHIFT-TAB** to move back to the previous field.

5. When you have completed all the fields you want for the first record, click **New Entry** and provide information for the second record.

6. Repeat steps 4 and 5 until you have added all the records you want to your list. When you are done, click **OK**.

7. A Save Address List dialog box appears. Type a file name for the list, select the folder on your computer where you want to save it, and click **Save**.

8. The Mail Merge Recipients dialog box appears, as shown in Figure 14-10. Clear the checkboxes next to the recipients you do not want to include in the list. To make further changes to the name list, select the file name in the Data Source list box, and click **Edit**.

9. Click **OK** when finished. See the following section, "Create a Merge Document."

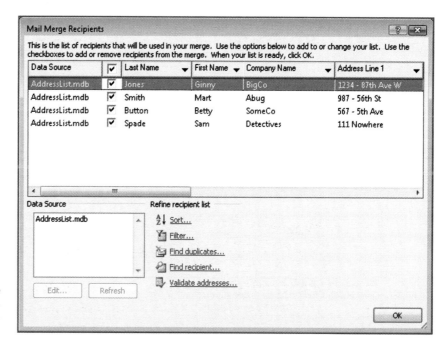

Figure 14-10: Use the Mail Merge Recipients dialog box to manage your mailing list prior to completing the merge.

Create a Merge Document

After creating the data source, you need to write the letter and insert the merge fields. This section will tell you how, after creating the main document, to insert merge fields in general. The example uses a letter; additional sections will show you how to use merge fields when creating envelopes and labels.

1. Follow the steps in the previous two sections, "Begin a Mail Merge" and "Set Up a Name and Address List."

2. Click **Next: Write Your Letter** at the bottom of the Mail Merge task pane. In the document pane, write the body of the letter—don't worry about the addressee and the greeting.

3. Place the cursor in the document where you want to insert a merge field, such as the addressee. Do one of the following:

   - Select one of the three items in the top of the Mail Merge task pane if you want to insert a predefined block of merge fields, such as an address or a greeting. If you select anything other than More Items, a dialog box will appear and ask you to select options and formatting for that item (see Figure 14-11).

Write your letter

If you have not already done so, write your letter now.

To add recipient information to your letter, click a location in the document, and then click one of the items below.

📄 Address block...

📄 Greeting line...

📑 Electronic postage...

🔢 More items...

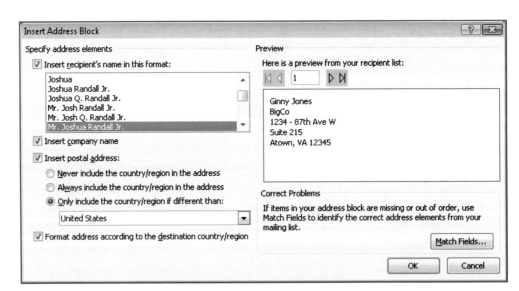

Figure 14-11: You can customize the predefined field blocks to meet your mail-merge needs.

QUICKSTEPS

USING RULES

Rules (also called *Word Fields*) apply merge fields or static text if certain conditions are met. One of the most common variable fields is the If…Then…Else rule. The If rule performs one of two alternative actions, depending on a condition you specify. For example, the statement "If the weather is sunny, we'll go to the beach; if not, we'll go to the museum," specifies a condition that *must* be met (sunny weather) for a certain action to take place (going to the beach). If the condition is not met, an alternative action occurs (going to the museum).

This is how an example of using an If rule in Word looks with the field codes turned on:

{IF { MERGEFIELD City } = "Seattle" "Please call our office." "Please call our distributor." }

This works as follows: If the current data record contains "Seattle" in the City field, then the first text ("Please call our office.") is printed in the merged document that results from that data record. If "Seattle" is not in the City field, then the second set of text ("Please call our distributor.") is printed. Using a rule is easy and doesn't require writing such a complex statement at all.

To insert a variable field into a merge document:

1. Position the insertion point where you want the rule.

2. In the Mailings tab, click **Rules** 📝▾ in the Write & Insert Fields group. A drop-down list appears.

3. Select the rule you want, for example, **If… Then…Else**.

4. The Insert Word Field dialog box appears. Fill in the text boxes with your criteria, and click **OK** when finished.

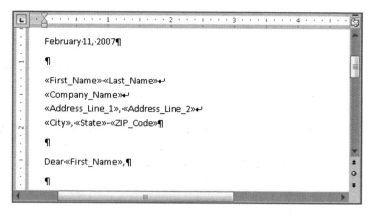

Figure 14-12: Merge fields are a convenient way to create a form letter for multiple recipients.

- Click **More Items** (the fourth item in the list) to insert an individual merge field. The Insert Merge Field dialog box appears. Verify that **Database Fields** is selected, and then select the field that you want to insert (for example, First Name and Last Name). Click **Insert** to insert the merge field into your document. Click **Close** when you are done inserting all the fields you need.

4. Add commas, spaces, and other punctuation marks to the address as needed. Figure 14-12 shows an example of a letter with merge fields inserted. See the following section, "Preview a Merge."

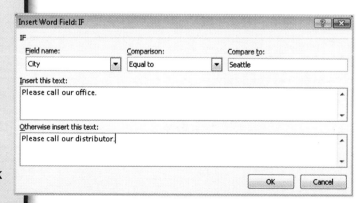

Preview a Merge

Prior to actually completing the merge, the Mail Merge task pane presents you with an opportunity to review what the merged document will look like. This way, you can go back and make any last-minute changes to fine-tune your merge.

To preview a merge:

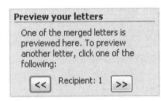

1. Follow the steps in the previous three sections, "Begin a Mail Merge," "Set Up a Name and Address List," and "Create a Merge Document."

2. Click **Next: Preview Your Letters** at the bottom of the Mail Merge task pane.

3. Use the right and left arrow buttons under Preview Your Letters in the Mail Merge task pane to scroll through the recipient list.

4. If you want to exclude a particular recipient from the merge, click **Exclude This Recipient**.

   –Or–

   Click **Edit Recipient List** to edit a particular recipient's information. If you click this link, the Mail Merge Recipients dialog box appears again (see Figure 14-12). Click the file name under Data Source, click **Edit**, modify the information, and click **OK**. Click **OK** again to close the Mail Merge Recipients dialog box.

Complete a Merge

The last step in performing a mail merge is to complete the merge—that is, to accept the preview of how the merge will look and direct Word to perform the merge.

To complete a merge:

1. Follow the steps in the previous four sections, "Begin a Mail Merge," "Set Up a Name and Address List," "Create a Merge Document," and "Preview a Merge."

2. Click **Next: Complete The Merge** at the bottom of the Mail Merge task pane.

3. Click **Print** in the Merge area. The Merge To Printer dialog box appears.

LINKING PICTURE FILES

Pictures are *embedded* by default when inserted in a document. Embedding means that the picture files become part of the Office file and their file size is added to the size of the saved document. In a document with several high-resolution pictures, the document's size can quickly rise into several megabytes (the greater the number of pixels in a picture, the higher the resolution and the larger the file size). To dramatically reduce the size of a document that contains pictures, you can *link* to the picture files instead. In this case, the addresses of picture files are retained in the document file, not the pictures themselves. (Alternatively, you can reduce the resolution and compress embedded pictures, although the reduction in file size won't be as large as with linked files. Another characteristic of linked picture files is that any changes made and saved in the source file will be updated in the Office document. Linking does have the downside of requiring the picture files to remain in the same folder location they were in when the link was created. In addition, documents with linked files are not suitable for sharing outside your local network.

1. To link a picture file when you are inserting a picture into a document, click the **Insert** tab, and click **Picture** in the Illustrations group to open the Insert Picture dialog box.

2. Click the **Insert** down arrow in the lower-right corner, and click **Link To File**.

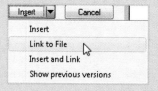

4. Select one of the following options:

   - **All** prints all records in the data source that have been included in the merge.
   - **Current Record** prints only the record that is displayed in the document window.
   - **From/To** prints a range of records you specify. Enter the starting and ending numbers in the text boxes.

5. Click **OK** when finished. The Print dialog box appears.

6. Select the print options you want, and click **OK**. Your merged document is printed.

7. If you wish, save your merge document.

Work with Pictures

Pictures can be manipulated in a number of ways once you have them within Word. You can organize your clip art collections, resize images, and move them into the exact positions that you want.

Add Pictures

You can browse for picture files, use the Clip Art task pane to assist you, drag them from other locations, or import them directly from a scanner or digital camera.

Pictures are files that are produced by a device, such as a digital camera or scanner, or that are created in a painting or drawing program, such as Microsoft Paint or Adobe Illustrator. In either case, the files are saved in a graphic format, such as JPEG or GIF (popular formats used on the Internet) or TIF (used in higher-end printing applications).

BROWSE FOR PICTURES

1. Place your insertion point in the paragraph, slide, cell, or table where you want to insert the picture.

2. In the Insert tab, click **Picture** in the Illustrations group. The Insert Picture dialog box appears.

3. Browse to the picture you want, and select it. (If you do not see your pictures, click the **Views** down arrow on the dialog box toolbar, and click **Medium Icons** or a larger size.)

4. Click **Insert**. The picture is displayed in the document.

ADD CLIP ART

1. Place your insertion point in the paragraph, slide, cell, or table where you want to insert the clip art.

2. In the Insert tab Illustrations group, click **Clip Art**. The Clip Art task pane opens.

3. In the Search For text box, type a keyword.

4. Click the **Search In** down arrow, and refine your search to specific collections. (The Web Collections category includes thousands of clips maintained at Office Online; therefore, it can take considerable time to find what you're looking for.)

5. Click the **Results Should Be** down arrow, and clear all file types other than clip art.

6. Click **Go**. In a few moments, thumbnails of the search results will appear, as shown in Figure 14-13.

7. Click the thumbnail to insert it in your document.

NOTE

Often, when you insert a picture, it is not the size that you want it to be or placed where you want it to be. You can easily make a picture the size you want by dragging the corners of the picture to resize it. You can drag the picture itself to other locations.

TIP

Besides using the Insert Pictures command in Word to add pictures, you can drag picture files from the desktop or Windows Explorer into an open document. To best use Windows Explorer, close or minimize all windows other than your Office document and Windows Explorer. Right-click a blank area of the Windows taskbar, and click either **Show Windows Stacked** or **Show Windows Side By Side** on the context menu. Locate the picture file you want in the right pane of Windows Explorer, and drag it to the location in the document where you want it.

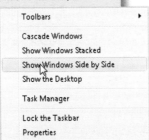

USING THE PICTURE TOOLS FORMAT TAB

Pictures are manipulated primarily by using the Picture Tools Format tab, shown in Figure 14-14. This tab on the ribbon differs slightly in PowerPoint and Excel. The Format tab automatically appears when a graphic image is selected in a document. The tab has four groups that allow you to adjust the characteristics of an image, determine its style, arrange an image on a page or in relation to other images or to text, and size an image. In addition, the two Dialog Box Launchers in the Picture Styles and Size groups provide a number of other settings.

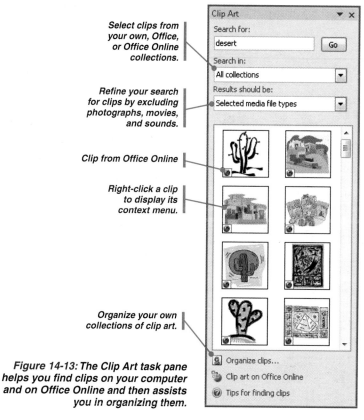

Select clips from your own, Office, or Office Online collections.

Refine your search for clips by excluding photographs, movies, and sounds.

Clip from Office Online

Right-click a clip to display its context menu.

Organize your own collections of clip art.

Figure 14-13: The Clip Art task pane helps you find clips on your computer and on Office Online and then assists you in organizing them.

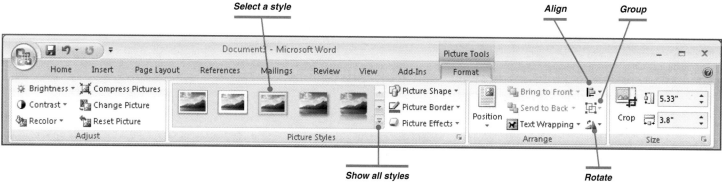

Select a style

Align

Group

Show all styles

Rotate

Figure 14-14: The Picture Tools Format tab, from Word in this case, is your one-stop shopping venue for accessing picture-related options.

Remove Unwanted Areas

You can remove areas from a picture that you do not want by using the Crop tool on the Picture toolbar.

1. Open and select the picture you want to crop. See "Add Pictures" earlier in this chapter.

2. On the Picture Tools Format tab, click **Crop** in the Size group. The picture redisplays with eight sizing handles on the corners and sides, and the mouse pointer becomes a cropping icon when outside the picture, as shown in Figure 14-15.

Figure 14-15: Cropping removes the area of a picture outside the dashed area.

TIP

In Word, you can add a caption to inserted pictures to give a uniform appearance to your picture identifiers. Right-click a picture and click **Insert Caption**. In the Caption dialog box, choose a label (create your own labels by clicking **New Label**), where you want the caption, and a numbering format. You can also have Word use AutoCaption to automatically add a caption based on the type of picture or object inserted.

TIP

Pictures in Word that are in-line with text are, in a sense, treated like a big character and have paragraph-formatting characteristics. These can be identified by the square sizing handles that surround them. Pictures that can be positioned independently of text display round sizing handles on the corners, similar to drawings.

ng·of·a·picture:

TIP

Several other shapes are available from clip art collections. Type <u>autoshapes</u> in the **Search For** text box in the Clip Art task pane. Choose to search in all collections, and click **Go** (see "Add Clip Art" earlier in the chapter).

NOTE

You can fill a drawing or shape with a picture. Click **Picture** on the Shape Fill drop-down menu. The Select Picture dialog box appears. Browse for the picture you want, select it, and click **Insert**. The picture will be inserted into the background of the drawing shape.

---

3. Place the cropping tool over one of the eight sizing handles (it will morph into an angle or T icon), and drag the tool so that the area of the picture is cut away or cropped by what you have dragged over.

4. Release the mouse button. The area of the picture is cropped. Press **ESC** or click outside of the image to turn off the Crop tool.

Add Shapes

Shapes are small, pre-built drawings that you can select, or you can create your own by modifying existing shapes or drawing your own freeform shapes. The pre-built shapes and tools for creating your own are added either from the Insert tab Illustrations group or from the Drawing tools Format tab Insert Shapes group.

1. In the Insert tab Illustrations group, click **Shapes** to open the Shapes drop-down menu.

2. Choose a shape:

   Click a shape from one of the several categories.

   –Or–

   Click one of the lines or basic shapes to begin your own shape.

3. Drag the mouse crosshair pointer in the approximate location and size you want.

Create a Diagram

You can quickly create and modify several different types of diagrams, some of which are easily interchangeable. One type, an organization or hierarchy chart, provides special tools and features that streamline the structuring of this popular form of charting.

1. In the Insert tab Illustrations group, click **SmartArt**. The Choose A SmartArt Graphic dialog box appears, as shown in Figure 14-16.

SmartArt

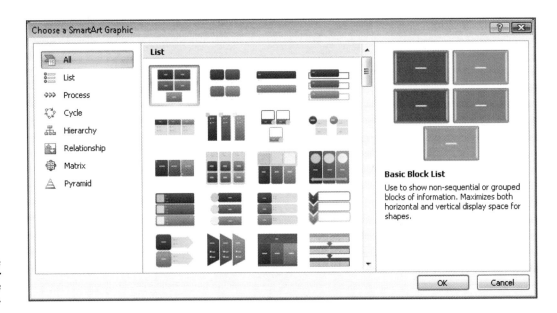

Figure 14-16: SmartArt allows you to easily create a number of diagram types, such as organizational charts.

2. Click **Hierarchy** in the left column, and then double-click the upper-leftmost diagram to display the start of an organization chart and the SmartArt Tools Design tab, shown in Figure 14-17. Then personalize your chart by doing one or more of the following:

- Click the highest level, or *manager* position, and in the SmartArt Tools Design tab, click **Layout** in the Create Graphic group to open a menu of hierarchical options. Click the structure that best matches your organization.

- Click a current box on the chart, click **Add Shape**, and select the type of new position you want to add to the current structure. For a higher level, click **Add Shape Above**; for a subordinate level, click **Add Shape Below**; for a co-worker level, click either **Add Shape Before** or **Add Shape After**.

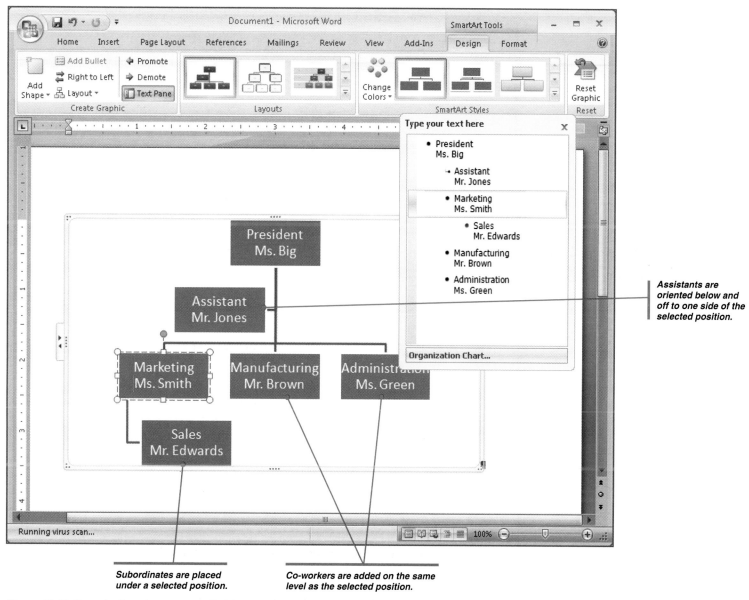

Figure 14-17: Organization charts are easily laid out and formatted using SmartArt in Word.

Assistants are oriented below and off to one side of the selected position.

Subordinates are placed under a selected position.

Co-workers are added on the same level as the selected position.

- To place text in a shape after adding a new shape, simply start typing. You can also click the insertion point in either the text pane ("Type Your Text Here" or "Text") or the organization chart shape, and then add new or edit existing text. Type the name, title, or other identifier for the position. The font size will change to fit the text box. Press **SHIFT-ENTER** after each line for a subordinate line (like a name after a position), or press **ENTER** for a second but equal line. Format text in the shapes as you would standard text, using the Home tab and its associated options.

- Click **Right To Left** to flip the names and shapes on the right with the ones on the left.

- Click **Promote** or **Demote** in the Create Graphic group to move a shape and its text up or down in the organization chart.

- Click **Text Pane** in the Create Graphic group to turn the text pane on or off.

- Point at any of the layouts, colors, or SmartArt styles to see how your chart would look with that change. Click the layout, color, or style to make the change permanent.

- If you make a "permanent" change, as just described, you can return to the previous layout, color, or style by clicking **Reset Graphic** in the Reset Graphic group.

- To select a group of shapes and their text so that they can be acted upon all at once, hold down **CTRL** while clicking each shape (including the connecting lines). Or draw a selection area around the group of shapes by moving the mouse pointer to just outside the upper-left shape and then dragging the mouse to just outside the lower-right shape.

- Click the **SmartArt Tools Format** tab to display several options for changing the shape and its text, as shown in Figure 14-18.

NOTE

Diagrams are really just combinations of shapes that fit a specific need. As such, you can, for example, delete an element of a diagram by selecting it and pressing **DELETE**. Or you can delete the entire diagram by selecting its border and pressing **DELETE**. See "Modify Graphics" to learn how to format the overall diagram, as well as how to change various components of shapes.

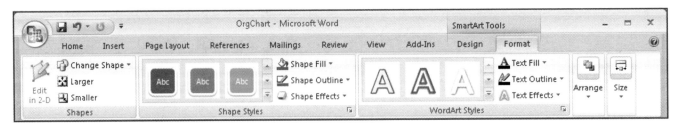

Figure 14-18: Quickly redesign the overall appearance of your organization chart.

Modify Graphics

Pictures (those that use an absolute positioning layout) and shapes or drawings share a common Format dialog box, although many of the features and options are not available for every type of graphic you can add to an Office document. This section describes formatting and other modifications you can apply to graphics.

Resize and Rotate Graphics Precisely

You can change the size of graphics by setting exact dimensions and rotating them. (You can also drag handles to change them interactively. See "Use Handles and Borders to Position Graphics" later in this chapter for ways to resize and rotate graphics with a mouse.) The dialog boxes for Size differ slightly between Word, PowerPoint, and Excel.

1. Click the graphic you want to resize to select it. In the Picture (or other graphic type) Tools Format tab, click the **Size Dialog Box Launcher** in the Size group. (For some graphics, such as an organization chart, the Size Dialog Box Launcher will not exist.)

2. Click the **Size** tab, and, if it isn't already selected, click the **Lock Aspect Ratio** checkbox to size the graphic proportionally when entering either width or height values:

   Under **Size And Rotate** (depending on the graphic, the option may be Height And Width), enter either the height or the width dimension, or use the spinners to increase or decrease one of the dimensions from its original size.

   –Or–

   Under **Scale**, enter a percentage for either the height or the width to increase or decrease it, or use the spinners to increase or decrease the percentage of the original picture size.

3. To rotate the graphic, under **Size And Rotate** (or **Rotation**), enter a positive (rotate clockwise) or negative (rotate counterclockwise) number of degrees of rotation you want.

4. Click **OK**. The picture will resize and/or rotate according to your values.

Position Graphics

Graphics (including pictures that use absolute positioning) can be positioned
anywhere in the document by dragging or setting values. In either case, the
graphic retains its relative position within the document as text and other
objects are added or removed. You can override this behavior by anchoring
the graphic to a fixed location. You can also change how text and other objects
"wrap" around the graphic. Figure 14-19 shows several of these features.

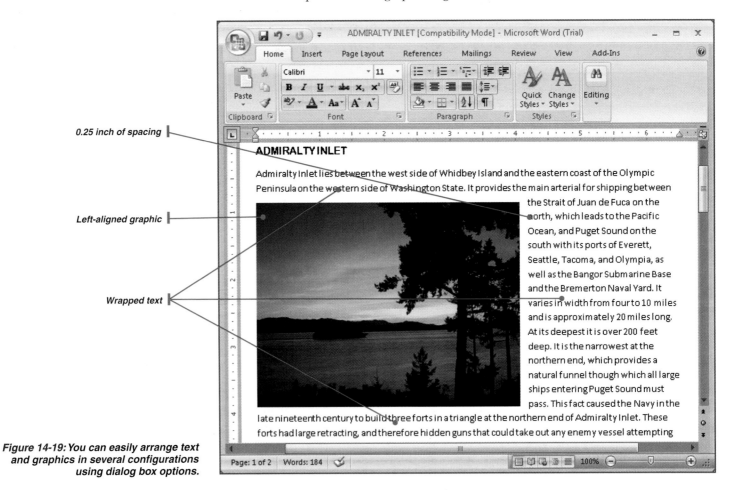

Figure 14-19: You can easily arrange text and graphics in several configurations using dialog box options.

QUICKFACTS

UNDERSTANDING GRAPHIC POSITIONING IN WORD

When you position a graphic (picture, clip art, drawing, or shape) on the page, the position can be *inline*, or *relative*, to the text and other objects on the page, where the graphic moves as the text moves, like a character in a word. The alternative is *absolute* positioning, where the graphic stays anchored in one place, regardless of what the text does. If the graphic uses absolute positioning, you can then specify how text will wrap around the graphic, which can be on either or both sides or along the top and bottom of the graphic. Also, for special effects, the text can be either on top of the graphic or underneath it. See "Position a Graphic Relative to Areas in a Document."

TIP

When a graphic uses absolute positioning, an anchor icon may be displayed. If the anchor is locked, a padlock icon may also be displayed. If you don't see the anchor icon and the graphic is using absolute positioning, click the **Office button**, click **Word Options**, and click **Display** in the left column. Under **Always Show These Formatting Marks**, click the **Object Anchors** checkbox. Click **OK** to display anchor icons in the document.

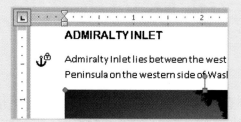

POSITION A GRAPHIC RELATIVE TO AREAS IN A DOCUMENT

Besides dragging a graphic into position, you can select or enter values that determine where the graphic is placed in relation to document areas.

1. Click the graphic that you want to position to select it. In the Drawing or Picture Tools Format tab, click **Text Wrapping** in the Arrange group. A menu is displayed.

2. Click **More Layout Options** to open the Advanced Layout dialog box.

3. Click the **Picture Position** tab. Select or enter the horizontal- and vertical-positioning entries by selecting them from the drop-down menus, entering the values, or using the spinners to increase or decrease distances, as shown in Figure 14-20.

4. To anchor a graphic in place, regardless of whether other content is added or removed—for example, a graphic you want in the upper-left corner of a specific page—click the **Lock Anchor** checkbox and clear all other options.

5. Click **OK** to close the Advanced Layout dialog box.

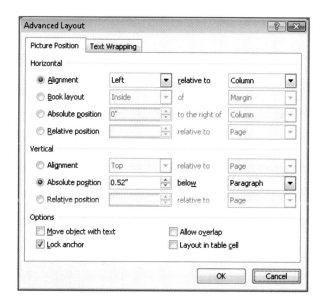

Figure 14-20: Using absolute positioning, you can choose where to place a graphic relative to other objects in the document.

Use Handles and Borders to Position Graphics

Graphics are easily manipulated using their sizing handles and borders.

- **Select a Graphic**   You select a graphic by clicking it. Handles appear around the graphic and allow you to perform interactive changes. Two exceptions include text boxes and text in text boxes:

  a. Click in a text box. A dotted border appears around the perimeter of the text box. (In Excel and PowerPoint the border itself becomes dotted.)

  b. Place the mouse pointer in the text in a text box; it will become an I-beam pointer. Click it to place an insertion point, or drag across the text to select it. The mini toolbar will dimly appear. Move the mouse pointer over the toolbar for it to fully appear, and then make a selection to change the formatting.

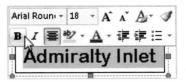

- **Resize a Graphic**   Drag one of the square or round (if using absolute positioning) sizing handles surrounding the graphic—or at either end of it, in the case of a line—in the direction you want to enlarge or reduce the graphic. Hold **SHIFT** when dragging a corner sizing handle to change the height and length proportionately. (In the Picture

WORKING WITH GRAPHICS

While graphics can be positioned absolutely by simply dragging them or choosing placement relative to other objects in a document, Office also provides a number of other techniques that help you adjust where a graphic is in relation to other graphics.

MOVE GRAPHICS INCREMENTALLY

Select the graphic or group of graphics (see "Combine Graphics by Grouping"), hold **CTRL**, and press one of the arrow keys in the direction you want to move the graphic by very small increments (approximately .01 inch).

REPOSITION THE ORDER OF STACKED GRAPHICS

You can stack graphics by simply dragging one on top of another. Figure 14-21 shows an example of a three-graphic stack. To reposition the order of the stack, in Word, Excel or PowerPoint, click **Bring to Front** or **Send to Back** (see below for description) in the Arrange group. In Word, you can also right-click the graphic you want to change and click **Order** on the context menu. (In Excel or PowerPoint, click **Bring To Front** or **Send to Back** in the context menu.) Then click one of the following:

- **Bring To Front** moves the graphic to the top of the stack.

- **Send To Back** moves the graphic to the bottom of the stack.

- **Bring Forward** moves the graphic up one level (same as Bring To Front if there are only two graphics in the stack).

- **Send Backward** moves the graphic down one level (same as Send To Back if there are only two graphics in the stack).

Continued . . .

or Drawing Tools Format tab, if you have Lock Aspect Ratio selected in the Size group Dialog Launcher dialog box, Size tab selected, the picture will remain proportionally sized without pressing **SHIFT**).

- **Rotate a Graphic**   Drag the green dot in the direction you want to rotate the graphic. Hold **SHIFT** when dragging to rotate in 15-degree increments.

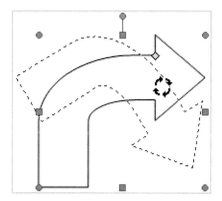

- **Change a Graphic's Perspective**   If the graphic supports interactive adjustment, a yellow diamond adjustment handle is displayed. Drag the yellow diamond toward or away from the graphic to get the look you want.

Figure 14-21: You can change the order of stacked graphics to achieve the look you want.

WORKING WITH GRAPHICS *(Continued)*

- **Bring In Front Of Text** moves the graphic on top of overlapping text.

- **Send Behind Text** moves the graphic behind overlapping text.

ALIGN GRAPHICS

To align two or more graphics relative to one another, select the graphics by holding down **SHIFT**.

EVENLY SPACE GRAPHICS

Select the graphics by holding down **SHIFT**. In the Picture Tools Format tab Arrange group, click **Align** and then click **Distribute Horizontally** or **Distribute Vertically**, depending on their orientation.

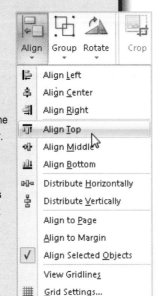

NOTE

If you don't see Order on the context menu when you right-click one of the graphics in a stack, click outside all the graphics, and then click one of the other graphics.

Combine Graphics by Grouping

You can combine graphics for any number of reasons, but you typically work with multiple graphics to build a more complex rendering. To prevent losing the positioning, sizing, and other characteristics of the individual components, you can group them so that they are treated as one object.

- To group graphics, select the graphics to be grouped by clicking the first graphic and then holding down **SHIFT** while selecting other drawings and pictures. In the Picture Tools Format tab Arrange group, click **Group | Group**; or right-click one of the selected graphics, click **Group | Group**. A single set of selection handles surrounds the perimeter of the graphics. Coloring, positioning, sizing, and other actions now affect the graphics as a group instead of individually.

- To separate a group into individual graphics, select the group. In the Picture Tools Format tab Arrange group, click **Group | Ungroup**; or right-click the group, and click **Group | Ungroup**.

- To recombine a group after ungrouping it, in the Picture Tools Format tab Arrange group, click **Group | Regroup**; or right-click a member graphic, and click **Group | Regroup**.

Index

A

About Microsoft Office dialog box, 18
absolute references, 156, 158
activating Microsoft Office, 17
alignment
 in Excel, 145–147
 of graphics, 354
 in PowerPoint, 232–233
 in Word, 56–57, 73
Apply Styles dialog box, 77
AutoComplete, 119, 277
AutoCorrect, 31, 98–99
 creating numbered lists using, 64–65
 in Excel, 126
 mathematical equations, 105
 in PowerPoint, 234–235, 236
AutoFill, disabling, 120
AutoFit, 235
AutoFormat, 99–100
AutoRecover, 46
AutoSum, 175

B

borders, 67–69
browse buttons, moving around a document
 with, 36, 37
building blocks, 101–102
bulleted lists
 creating before you type text, 65–66
 customizing, 66–67
 in PowerPoint, 231–233
 removing bulleting, 67

C

Calendar
 appointments, 315–316, 317, 318–320
 changing time scales, 300
 customizing views, 304–306
 entering dates and times, 316
 events, 315, 316, 318
 Field Chooser, 304
 font face and size, 301
 free/busy options, 308
 group schedules, 321–322
 Internet calendars, 315
 invitations, 324
 maintaining multiple calendars, 309–311
 meetings, 315, 322–323
 navigating, 300
 Other Settings dialog box, 301–302
 overview, 297–299
 printing calendars, 321–322
 publishing to Microsoft Office Online, 313–314
 recurring appointments, 318–319
 reminders, 320, 321
 Scheduling Assistant, 323–324
 sending a calendar in e-mail, 311–313
 setup, 306–307
 sharing an Exchange calendar, 314–315
 tasks, 315
 time zones, 309
 toolbars, 303
 View menu, 302–303
capitalization, 55
 drop caps, 55–56
cells
 cell addresses, 111
 changing cell names, 160
 changing references, 156
 changing to R1C1 references, 157
 deleting named cells, 160
 going to named cells, 158–159
 intersections, 159
 Name Manager, 160
 naming, 157–158
 ranges, 158
 reference operators, 158–159
 referencing, 155–159
 removing cell contents, 120–121
 selecting cells and ranges, 122–123
 sorting and filtering named cells, 160–161
 tracing precedent and dependent cells,
  176–177
 unions, 159
 viewing more data, 161
 watching, 177
 See also Excel; worksheets
centering text, 56–57
character count, 105
character spacing, 54–55, 219
clicking, 7

Clipboard, 33
 icon, 36
 Office Clipboard, 34–36
 options, 35–36
 Windows Clipboard, 33
closing Office programs, 4
color
 changing screen color, 12
 color schemes, 185–186
 custom colors, 204–206
 font color, 52
 theme colors, 137–138, 201–203
columns
 in Excel, 129–131
 in Word, 86–87
conditional formatting, in Excel, 168–172
copying text, 34
counting words and characters, 105
cutting text, 33

D

dates, entering, 114–117, 316
defaults, formatting, 53
deleting styles, 79–80
deleting text, 35
 recovering deleted text, 38
desktop, shortcuts, 3
diagnostics, 17
Dialog Box Launcher icon, 7
digital signatures, 286–287
direct formatting, in Excel, 135, 137
Display options, 13–14
Document Properties panel, 12
documents
 creating, 20–24
 entering text, 28
 importing, 27–28
 locating existing documents, 25
 moving around in, 35–38
 saving, 44–46
 searching for, 25–27
 special characters, 28–30
 templates, 21–24
double-clicking, 7
dragging, 7
drop caps, 55–56

E

e-mail
- addressing messages, 274–277
- archiving messages, 269
- arranging messages in folders, 265–266
- attachments, 269–271, 282–284, 334
- carbon and blind copies, 277–278
- changing the time for being read, 263
- checking for, 256
- creating messages, 274, 275
- delaying message delivery, 294–295
- deleting messages, 268–269
- digital signatures, 286–287
- distribution lists, 277
- downloading sender and subject information only, 258–260
- editing messages, 278–279
- embedding pictures into messages, 283–284
- filtering out spam, 259–262
- finding messages, 249–251
- flagging messages for follow-up, 263–264
- forwarding messages, 291–292
- getting online, 252
- headers, 258–260
- Hotmail accounts, 253–254
- including hyperlinks, 282
- installing accounts in, 254
- marking messages as read or unread, 262–263
- message priorities, 292
- pasting documents into messages, 334
- printing messages, 271
- reading, 257
- replying to messages, 289–291
- rules, 267–268, 294–295
- sending a calendar, 311–313
- sending messages, 293–294
- setup, 251–254
- signatures, 284–286
- spelling check, 287–288
- stationery, 279–281
- *See also* Outlook

endnotes, 91–93
entering numeric data, 113–114
entering text, 28
- in Excel, 111–113
- inserting vs. overtyping, 30
- line breaks and page breaks, 31

special characters, 28–30
- *See also* insertion point
equations, 103–105
Excel
- 3-D references, 157
- absolute references, 156, 158
- adding data quickly, 119–121
- alignment, 145–147
- arguments, 172
- AutoCorrect, 126
- AutoSum, 175
- background color and shading, 147–148
- canceling formulas, 163
- cell addresses, 111
- cell referencing, 155–159
- comments, 132–135
- conditional formatting, 168–172
- copying and pasting data, 122–123
- creating formulas, 159–161
- currency symbols, 116
- data types, 110
- deleting formulas, 163
- direct formatting, 137
- editing cell data, 119–120
- editing formulas, 161–162
- entering dates, 114–117
- entering numeric data, 113–114
- entering text, 111–113
- error checking, 175–176
- evaluating formulas, 177–178
- external references, 157, 164–168
- finding and replacing data, 123–125
- fonts, 144–145
- formatting, 135–137
- formula identifier, 172
- fractions, 116
- functions, 172–175
- intersections, 159
- KeyTips, 112
- mixed references, 157
- moving data, 121
- moving formulas, 162
- Name Manager, 160
- operators, 159
- overview, 110–111
- pasting data, 122–123
- percentages, 116
- ranges, 158

- recalculating formulas, 163–164
- relative references, 156
- removing cell contents, 120–121
- replacing formulas, 163
- scientific notation, 114
- selecting cells and ranges, 122–123
- spelling check, 125–126
- styles, 136, 140–144
- syntax, 155
- themes, 135, 136–140, 141–142
- times, 117, 118–119
- tracing precedent and dependent cells, 176–177
- transferring formatting, 149
- transitioning from Lotus 1-2-3, 159
- unions, 159
- views, 9
- watching cells, 177
- *See also* worksheets
external references, 157, 164–168

F

filters, searching with advanced filters, 26–27
finding text, 38–40
Font dialog box, 48–49, 51, 54
- in PowerPoint, 231–232
fonts
- applying bold or italic style, 51
- color, 52
- in Excel, 144–145
- in PowerPoint, 218–219
- selecting, 49–51
- size, 51
- theme font sets, 81–82
- theme fonts, 81, 139, 202–204
- underlining, 52
- *See also* formatting text
footers and headers, 88–91
- in notes, 215
- on slides, 207–209
footnotes, 91–93
Format Painter, 70, 149, 206–207, 234
formatting marks, showing and hiding, 69
formatting numbers, 115–116
formatting pages
- mirror margins, 71–72
- Page Layout dialog box, 71

moving or copying text, 235
notes, 212–217
outlining presentations, 186–191
text boxes, 226–230
text layouts, 225
themes, 180, 181–182, 183–184, 201–206, 221
views, 9
WordArt, 219
zooming, 200
See also presentations; slides
preferences
Display options, 13–14
Popular options, 13–14
presentations, 180
animation schemes, 186
art and graphics, 186
collapsing or expanding slides, 191
color schemes, 185–186
copying a design using Browse, 200
creating an outline, 187–188
creating from another presentation, 181
creating from scratch, 183–184
creating using a standard theme, 181–182
creating using a template, 182–183
displaying multiple presentations at once, 196–199
indenting text, 190
inserting outlines, 189–190
notes, 212
outlining commands, 191
passwords, 185–186
previewing the outline, 190
printing the outline, 191
showing formatting, 191
spelling check, 237–239
stripping file information from, 186
tables, 186
working with text, 185
See also PowerPoint; slides
printing documents
customizing a print job, 331
Print Preview, 327–330
printing envelopes in Word, 332
printing labels in Word, 333–334
Properties dialog box, 326–327
setting a default printer, 326
program windows, 4–6

Q

Quick Access toolbar
adding commands to, 10, 11
moving, 11
Quick Launch toolbar, 4
Quick Styles gallery, 76, 77

R

redoing, 35, 38
relative references, 156
replacing text, 40–41
Research task pane, 15
translating phrases, 16
resetting text, 53
resources, 17–18
ribbon, 6–7
accessing in PowerPoint, 194
right-clicking, 7
rows. *See* Excel; worksheets
ruler
setting tabs, 87–88
using for indents, 61–62

S

saving documents, 44–46
scientific notation, 114
screen display, changing background color, 12
ScreenTips, showing and hiding, 11
scroll bars, moving around a document with, 36, 37
searching
with advanced filters, 26–27
finding e-mail messages, 249–251
finding text, 38–40
and sorting, 26
for themes, 141–142
for Word documents, 25
section breaks, 31, 85–86
security
passwords, 185–186
Trust Center, 166
selecting text, 31–32
shading, 67–69
shortcuts
desktop, 3
shortcut keys for common characters, 29–30

slides
aligning text, 232–233
copying, 199
creating multiple slide and title masters, 221
editing a slide master or master layout, 218–220
font attributes, 218–219
inserting, 194–196
lists, 231–233
margins, 230
moving, 199
moving or copying text, 235
navigating, 194–195
placeholders, 194, 226, 233
slide masters, 217–222
spelling check, 236, 237–239
starting and ending slide shows, 195
text boxes, 226–230
themes, 201–206
title masters, 222
word wrap, 230
zooming in or out of, 200
See also PowerPoint; presentations
smart tags, Paste Options smart tag, 34
SmartArt, 232–233, 345–348
sorting, and searching, 26
spam, 259–262
special characters, 31
shortcut keys for common characters, 29–30
spelling check
in Excel, 125–126
in Outlook, 287–288
in PowerPoint, 236, 237–239
in Word, 41–44
Start menu
pinning a program to the top of the menu, 3
starting Office, 2
starting Office programs, 3
starting Office, 2
starting Office programs, 2–4
styles
in Excel, 135, 136, 140–144
in Word, 76–80
Symbol dialog box, 28–29, 30, 31